STUDIES IN MIGRATION

Studies in Migration

Internal and International Migration in India

Edited by

M.S.A. RAO

MANOHAR
2026

First published 1986
Reprinted 2026

ISBN 978-81-85054-08-7

Published by
Ajay Kumar Jain for
Manohar Publishers & Distributors
4753/23 Ansari Road, Daryaganj
New Delhi 110 002

Printed and bound in India

Preface

Migration is a multi-faceted phenomenon which is of vital importance in economic development, manpower planning, urbanization and social change. However, it has not received the attention that it deserves by the social scientists. The present volume is the first of its kind which fills in a major gap from a multi-disciplinary point of view. Theoretically, it covers the sociological, demographic, economic and historical perspectives, and empirically scans rural-urban, rural-rural, tribal and international migration situations.

The volume contains twelve chapters including Introduction and a general essay on some aspects of sociology of migration. The essays are equally divided into five sections. The section on demographic aspects concentrates on rural-urban migration dealing with the pattern of migration and socio-demographic features of migrants in different types of cities in general and in metropolitan cities in particular. The section on economic aspects deals with two major issues. One contribution examines the Indian evidence to show that it does not support the Todaro model of expected income differential as the basis for people to move from rural to urban areas. The other examines the dichotomy of formal-informal sector to show that it is not meaningful in the Indian urban context. Rural-rural migration forms the focus of section three in which the pattern and consequences of migration of peasants into tribal areas, and seasonal labourers from dry to wet villages are discussed. The section on tribal migration highlights the importance of colonial political economy framework in understanding the forces involved in the deprivations of the tribals, their violent resurgences and the consequent emigration to plantations. In the section on international migration, the historian examines the dynamics of migration of Indians to South Africa in the colonial period, from one colony to another within the British Empire. The second essay is concerned with the problems of adjustments, in the context of racial tensions, of the first and second generation Sikh migrants in England.

Many contributions point to the miseries and deprivations of the migrants and of the local tribals due to the immigration of the non-tribals as an ethnic problem, which have practical and policy implications. The volume, thus addresses itself not only to the academics but also to the administrators, politicians and social workers.

M.S.A. Rao

From the Publisher

A few weeks before going for his second operation, Professor M.S.A. Rao had handed me the manuscript of this volume for publication. We prepared the volume and hoped that we would secure his approval on his return for final printing of the book. Unfortunately, his sad and premature passing away left us, as indeed the academic world, stunned. We are publishing the manuscript as he had given us. We very much wish that Prof. Rao was still with us to see this work through the press.

Professor Rao's academic interests covered a wide range. In fact, he never felt happy working on the same theme. He always liked to explore and work on ever new themes, at the same time enriching and expanding the areas on which he had worked previously. Migration as a theme of sociological analysis had been engaging his attention for several years previously and, while on the UGC National Fellowship, he had carried out fieldwork in the tribal areas of Andhra Pradesh during 1978-79 to explore the sociological dimensions of migration. This book is a tribute to the range and expanse of his scholarship.

Whenever Professor Rao took up any theme for sociological investigation, he always liked to draw upon what other colleagues working on the subject might have to say. After his fieldwork in Andhra Pradesh, Professor Rao had organised a workshop on migration to which those working on the subject were invited to participate and contribute papers. This volume is comprised by the papers presented and discussed at the workshop. We are indeed happy at the opportunity of being able to publish the volume.

Professor Rao's genial and amiable personality and pleasing style earned him many friends who extended their very best for him. We are sure that in the organization of the workshop and in the preparation of the manuscript, Professor Rao would have incurred many debts. If he were with us today, we are sure that he would have liked to name and acknowledge the help of all such friends. We cannot mention them, but we are sure that all those who contributed to the workshop and the preparation of the volume for the press will identify their contribution.

Professor Rao was committed throughout his life to the enrichment of social life through sociological investigation and he moved from one problem to another because he felt that each relevant problem required to be sociologically investigated. We are confident that this volume too is a contribution towards the same goal and would be found to be a useful contribution to the study of a problem which is assuming ever greater importance. We offer this book as a tribute to a man who served sociology until the very end. We are confident that the book would have been greatly improved in quality if it had the benefit of Prof. Rao's benign supervision and advice and we wish to reserve to ourselves such deficiencies that may have still remained.

RAMESH JAIN
PUBLISHER

Contents

Part Five: International Migration

1. *Introduction*

Migration is an area of study which permits multidisciplinary approach in social sciences, including as it does, social demography, sociology, social and cultural anthropology, economics, history, geography and psychology. In some ways they are complementary although their assumptions, concepts and tools of analysis are different. An attempt is made in this volume to bring together essays on migration representing the sociological, demographic, economic and historical aspects, although the sociological viewpoint is the predominant one. The volume is divided into five parts consisting of eleven essays as well as a separate select bibliography compiled by N.E.C. Vidyasagar.

Parts one to five contain two essays each. Besides, there is a general essay on "Some Aspects of Sociology of Migration in India". In this essay M.S.A. Rao considers three major areas of migration studies. First, the nature of the process of migration—why people move and how migration occurs. He examines mainly the economic explanation and notes that economic factors provide only the necessary conditions of migration while the non-economic factors such as the information flow, resource networks, brokers and personality of the migrants provide the sufficient conditions for people's decision to migrate. The second area of study includes questions such as who migrates and what role factors of selectivity like age, sex, marital status and educational status play in migration; what happens to the migrants at the place of destination? How do they adjust themselves to the new social and physical environment? What changes have followed in their own life-styles and in their relations to other groups and situations? In this context Rao considers new social formations—caste, class and ethnicity, and cultural pluralism. There is also the possibility of ethnic conflict as evidenced by sons of the soil movements, and the conflict between the locals and the non-local migrants in the tribal areas.

The third area of investigation is the feed-back effects of migration, both internal and international, on the place of origin. A distinction is made between subsistence and development migration. In the latter the migrants send cash remittances home, and this money-order economy wherever it is substantial, as in the case of Punjab, has led to phenomena like the green revolution. In other cases, the standard of living of the members of the family left behind has improved. In the case of non-distress return migration, the migrants have been able to innovate in agriculture, trade and commerce. Rao suggests that migration should be studied from both the ends—place of origin and place of destination. He emphasizes the need to integrate the demographic, economic, historical and geographical *dimensions* of the problems in the sociological framework.

Part One comprises two essays on the Demographic Aspects, which are complementary. While M.K. Premi's eassy on "Migration to Cities in India" analyses the pattern of migration and characteristics of migrants in all the cities, K. Laxmi Narayan in his paper on "Growth of Metropolitan Cities and Their Migrants: A Historical and Demographic Profile" concentrates on the process of migration and migrants in the million plus cities.

M.K. Premi analysing the census data for all the cities with a population of 100,000+ notes that while there were only 25 cities in 1901, accounting for 25.8 per cent of urban population, in 1981, the number of cities rose to 216 accounting for 60.4 per cent of urban population. A single major factor in the growth of cities is migration. Premi discusses the pattern of migration, its trend and the social demographic features of migrants and non-migrants. Since the 1971 census had a detailed data base for migration for 140 cities, it is analysed extensively. He works out five types of classification of cities, one based on size of population; second, based on growth rate; third based on economic functions; fourth based on the decade year of their existence; fifth based on regional diversities. Similarly migrants are classified into lifetime migrants and current migrants based on their duration of stay.

In the second section of his paper Premi discusses the pattern of migration of lifetime and current migrants to different types of cities. He points out that lifetime migrants to class I cities (1,000,000+) constitute two-fifths of their population. Their proportion decreases as the size decreases. While the immigrants to the cities from rural areas constituted 53.3 per cent, those from urban areas constituted 40.8 per cent. A majority of the migrants came from the same district and other districts within the state in the case of non-million plus cities. The proportion of immigrants was highest in cities belonging to the Himalayan region. Service cities attracted more migrants than other types of cities based on economic function.

As regards the current migrants, Premi notes that they constitute only 7.2 per cent of the total migrants to the cities, the proportion being higher among males than among females. Their proportion was higher in cities with medium growth rates instead of cities with high growth rates and it was significantly higher in service cities, and in cities located in the Himalayan region, Punjab and upper Ganga plains.

Premi then goes on to discuss the characteristics of migrants and non-migrants. Contrary to the common impression that there is imbalance in sex ratio, it is noted that among the lifetime migrants this imbalance was lower than that of the total population. This may be due to associational migration of females. But along with age, in class I cities, the males in the age group 25-49 are more than females. The literacy rate of the total migrants to the million plus cities is higher than that of those to other cities. It is found that the work participation rates of migrant males are almost double than those of non-migrants. Similarly, the work participation of migrant females is higher than that of non-migrant females. While the non-migrant workers are proportionately more than the migrant workers in the manufacturing sector, the reverse is true in the trade, commerce, transport and service sectors.

Premi's study shows that there are rich internal variations in regard to the characteristics of migrants in terms of the different types of cities. He suggests that it is necessary to restructure the economic base of the intermediate cities so that they become the focal points for achieving balanced regional development.

K. Laxmi Narayan's treatment of million plus cities is both historical and demographic. He traces the growth of twelve metropolitan cities (in 1981) over three periods—pre-colonial, colonial and post-independence. He presents very rich data to show that the growth of cities during the colonial period has to be understood in the political economy framework. The primate cities (Calcutta, Bombay and Madras) formed part of the colonial mode of production. They were the centres of export of raw materials and of import of manufactured goods, especially under Company raj. But under the British raj their character changed in so far as the three port cities were also centres of industry, mainly jute, textiles and workshops. The development of transport and communication, industry, and location of military camps (cantonments) led to the growth of such inland cities as Ahmedabad, Kanpur, Lucknow, Poona, Hyderabad, Nagpur, Bangalore, Jaipur and Delhi. When the capital moved from Calcutta to Delhi in 1911, it started to grow in size, as the imperial capital.

Since independence, the metropolises have grown in size due to the influx of refugee migrants and location of industries and commerce. Many of them also became capitals of new linguistic states. All these economic and administrative activities attracted migrants of different kinds. In 1971 the migrant population in the twelve metropolitan cities constituted 42.67 per cent of their total population.

Laxmi Narayan analyses the census data in order to build up a demographic profile of the migrants. It is seen that the bigger metropolitan cities attracted more of inter-state migrants than the smaller ones. Between 40 to 68 per cent of migrants came from a rural background and a significant proportion of them have been staying in the cities for more than three years. There is also an element of selectivity in terms of age, sex, and marital status of migrants. They are young, masculine, and about one-third of them are unmarried. The educational background is diversified. A larger proportion of the migrants has primary and secondary education. As regards work participation, more males than females work. Secondly more migrants are to be found in the five important industrial categories of manufacturing, other services, trade and commerce, transport and construction. This is in contrast to Premi's observation, namely, non-migrant workers are proportionately more than the migrant workers in the manufacturing sector for all the cities put together.

The demographic features of the migrants reveal the nature of the process of migration, the elements of selectivity which determine who migrants to the cities. Although census data do not show why they move and how they move, and what kind of problems of adjustment they face and what consequences have followed, Laxmi Narayan makes a few general observations on all these aspects. He notes that while the main reason for migration is economic, there are also non-economic factors such as education and urban facilities. He points out that different streams of migrants such as unskilled and semiskilled, skilled and educated and men with capital and enterprise, enter into different strata of the job ladder. He shows that there are two major consequences of uncontrolled migration, namely, unemployment and poverty, which are reflected in the sprawling slums. In 1971, 14.21 males above the age of 14 in all metropolises were unemployed. Nearly half of the metropolitan population is poor. Growth of slums is a manifestation of urban poverty. Nearly 25 per cent of metropolitan population live in slums. The proportion is more in larger metropolises. Under these circumstances, Laxmi Narayan pleads for controlled migration and for a planned and balanced urban development.

It is evident that demographic analysis of migration from census data has certain limitations. It cannot answer such questions as to why people migrate, what are the resource networks through which they operate, whether the migrants get employed in the formal or informal sector, what are their problems of adjustment and how they relate themseves to the locals. In order to answer such questions, it is necessary to have micro studies or other survey data. In the second section on the Economic Aspects of Rural-Urban Migration there are two essays which seek to use NSS data and micro study to answer some of the important questions as why people migrate and what kind of work organization they will have.

K. Sundaram addresses himself to the most important theoretical issue in the economics of migration, namely, Todaro's model of rural-urban migration in less developed countries (LDCS). The Todaro's model highlights the part played by 'expected-income differential' in explaining rural-urban migration. This is an improvement on Lewis' model of rural-urban migration which presupposes unlimited supplies of labour being available to the modern urban sector at a fixed wage which is slightly higher than the average income in the traditional agricultural sector. The central variable in Todaro's model is 'expected' urban income. In relation to the income foregone in the rural area, the expected urban income provides incentive to the potential migrant. Holding other factors constant, the rate of rural-urban migration becomes a positive function of the proportion of high wage workers in the urban labour force.

Sundaram examines the relevance and applicability of Todaro's model to India, using two data sources—census and NSS-Survey 28th Round. He builds up his argument on the basis of a number of useful observations. First, rural-urban migration is not very significant when compared to rural-rural migration. Secondly, there is a bunching of migrants in larger metropolitan centres. Even here, the migrants comprise only 3.5 per cent of the labour force of the three metropolises—Bombay, Calcutta and Madras. Over a period of time between 1963-74, the immigration rate to urban areas drops from 241 per 10,000 of urban population to 194. Thirdly, the unemployment rate in urban areas is significantly high at 30 per cent, irrespective of their levels of education. Fourthly, migrants have 95 per cent chances of getting into the informal sector where the expected income is lower than that in the formal sectors.

All these pieces of evidence do not support the Todaro hypothesis that rural-urban migration occurs in response to expected income differentials. On the contrary, there is the absence of any significant rural-urban migration which needs to be explained with reference to imperfect market conditions and non-economic variations. Thus he concludes that the purely economic elements are less significant than the sociological and psychological issues.

U. Tataji in his paper on "Rural-Urban Migration and Work Organization in a Slum" takes up the question of the absorption of the migrant labour force in the formal and informal sectors of the urban economy and the pattern of work organization. The empirical situation is a slum in the city of Vijayawada in coastal Andhra. He questions the assumptions of the distinction between the formal and the informal sector and finds himself in agreement with other critics such as Sinclair, Breman and Papola. His major point of criticism stems from the way the migrants get themselves recruited to certain lower level jobs, and the nature of the work organization which does not permit an easy entry into them.

Vijayawada is a trade-transport centre. The low level jobs are only apparently open to all. But in reality they are not. There are not only preferences based on caste and kin links but the work organization is governed by norms relating to entry, exit and mode of payment which are agreed upon by the employers. The sand workers 'union' which mostly consists of Waderas (caste of earth workers) with a maistry (headman) is a case in point. Similarly entry into junk collection, cycle riksha or hand-cart pulling and other jobs are governed by kinship and political networks which manipulate the formal credit sources. Tataji shows that the work organization in the so called informal sector is highly diversified with regard to recruitment, scale of operation, level of skills and their collective action (union) to bargain with the employers for job security and benefits. Hence the dichotomy of formal and informal is simplistic and disaggregate analysis of the diversity of labour markets and work organizations is necessary for a proper understanding of the nature of employment of the rural migrants in the urban economy.

While Part Two considers the question of why people move from rural to urban and their work situation in the urban centres, Part Three looks at the migration process and consequences of people who move from rural to rural. Rural-rural migration is of great magnitude in India accounting for about 70 per cent of total migration. There are two papers which focus on this. While M.S.A. Rao's essay on "Peasant-Farmer Colonization, Development and Deprivation in Tribal Andhra" deals with the migration of farmers from rural to a tribal area in Andhra Pradesh, N.E.C. Vidyasagar's paper "Subsistence and Labour Mobility" considers the migration of labourers from dry to wet villages in northern Karnataka.

Rao discusses the process of colonization of non-tribal peasant-farmers in the Polavaram taluk of West Godavari District of Andhra Pradesh which is a tribal area inhabited by the Koyas. He discusses three phases of immigration of non-tribal peasants and farmers. The first phase of migration of the non-tribal peasants was between 1820 and 1950. The tribal zamindari of Gutala estate was auctioned for arrears of revenue in 1820. The Vaisya Zamindar from the delta area, who bought it encouraged the Kapu peasants to migrate. Other four streams of migrants were the agricultural labourers, cowherds, the toddy contractors and sellers, and merchants and traders. In the second phase which started in the 1950, migration of farmers was characterized by development. In the 1950s land in the Polavaram Agency came into the market in thousands of acres with the abolition of Zamindari and the anticipation of land ceiling Act. Those who bought land this time were the Kammas from the delta area who had knowledge of irrigation and who foresaw the possibilities of development of irrigation in the tribal area which had many rivulets and streams criss-crossing the region. They moved, in some cases, in a collectivity colonized the virgin land, lifted water from the streams and brought about significant agricultural development. The third phase of migration was characterized by tobacco rush. A new variety of tobacco (light soil flue cured virginia) was introduced in this region in 1962, as soil and water were found congenial, and it had a lucrative international market. Again the Kammas from the delta area moved to look for land in the Agency tract for cultivation of tobacco. Besides, Kamma and Kapu farmers who were already there started cultivating FCV tobacco. Since tobacco cultivation is labour intensive, a large contingent of harvesting gang labourers also moved in from Guntur and Kavoor areas. While many of them were seasonal, some of them settled down there. Rao describes the process of colonization in terms of the reasons for the migration of farmers and importance of kin networks with reference to one village, Kanakapalli, in detail.

What are the consequences of colonization of the non-tribal farmers who have brought about significant agricultural development? Deprivation of the tribals. One of the major forms of deprivation is land alienation. It has been found that although according to law it is not possible for a non-tribal to own or cultivate land in the tribal area, about one-third of the arable land which is irrigated is in the hands of the non-tribal farmers. Another form of deprivation is emigration of tribals in search of alternative employment out of their homeland. Thirdly, many tribals have become agricultural labourers—both casual and bonded—working for the non-tribal farmers. All these forms of deprivation have created tension between the tribals and the non-tribal farmers. The leaders of the Naxalite movement are trying to organize the tribals. Although the movement is not very strong here, in Sikakulam which is another tribal agency, the Naxalite movement did erupt. The government has initiated programmes of restoration of land to the tribals and many programmes under the intensive tribal development programmes. But unless these are meaningfully implemented, it would be difficult to control the conflict, some times actual and at other times potential, between tribals and the non-tribal farmers.

Vidyasagar discusses the problem of labour migration in the Bellary District of Karnataka where the canal irrigation was introduced in the late 1950s. He identifies factors that explain emigration of labourers of a dry village, Mahakhadaku, to the wet villages. He connects the migration of labour to the migration and colonization of entrepreneurial farmers who came from Andhra Pradesh, with their capital and skills of flow irrigation. They bought land from the local peasants who were skeptical of canal irrigation, even before canals were dug, and brought about dramatic agricultural development in the Tungabhadra canal region. Wet cultivation generated a demand for labour. In response agricultural labourers from the dry region migrated to the wet region mostly on a seasonal basis.

Vidyasagar disaggregates emigration from Mahakhadaku and identifies two streams. One consisting of those taking up service (such as teachers, drivers and contractors) in government and private undertakings. The second consists of agricultural labourers migrating to wet villages on a seasonal basis. The second category constitutes 74 per cent of the total emigrants in the sample. In order to explain migration, Vidyasagar statistically analyses several inter-related variables such as, size of landholding, production relationship, household size and type, family phase, number of children, dependency ratio and land-man ratio. He considers land-man ratio as the crucial variable only when it is seen in relation to others. He demonstrates how the poverty line shifts not only according to the land available to the household but also in relation to the number of workers, family phase and size, days of employment and the extent of indebtedness. He considers less than 2 acres per head as the threshold point. But the poverty line of the household varies in accordance with the combination of other variables.

Vidyasagar discusses the consequences of migration for the migrant labourers in the village. He shows that because of migration, the agricultural labourers can maintain themselves at the subsistence level and above the poverty line. Subsistence is the need, the stable resources lie outside the village in the wet area, and seasonal migration is the answer.

Part Four deals with tribal migration. It has two papers—"The Political Economy of Migration in Chota Nagpur and Santhal Parganas in the 19th Century" by S.D. Badgaiyan and "Migration of Tribes of Chotanagpur and Santhal Pargana to West Bengal: Some Sociological Aspects" by Niven C. Choudhury and Sharit K. Bhowmik. The two essays are complementary although they deal with the same region—Chotanagpur and Santhal Parganas. In the whole of tribal India, this region in Bihar has attracted the attention of many scholars since important tribes like Santhals, Mundas, Hos, Bhumij and Cheros rose in revolt against the non-tribal migrants and the British Administration in the nineteenth century.

S.D. Badgaiyan analyses the problems of the tribals in general and their migration in particular in the political economy framework. Many studies of labour migration in Africa show that colonial capitalism, including plantations, mines and factories, was the main force. Colonialism in India was not different. Colonial policy first made inroads into the tribal area through the Forest Act making it difficult for the tribals to have access to and use of forest resources. It also encouraged the non-tribal peasants to move into the tribal area to bring land under cultivation, as the Administration was interested in getting more and more revenue. The Administration also supported the merchants in the tribal areas, who appropriated the land of the tribals for petty loans. All these measures led to alienation of the tribals in many ways. Land alienation was the most significant one, as the non-tribal jagirdars indulged in intense subinfeudation, dispossession and ejectment of the native tribals.

The tribals reacted to the exploitation of the non-tribals and the British administration that supported the non-tribals against the tribals through violent insurrections. Many tribal uprisings marked the period between the last decade of the eighteenth century and the end of the nineteenth century. Some of the notable ones were the Kol insurrection in 1831, Santhal rebellion in 1857, and the Birsa Munda movement. The revolts were no doubt quelled by the superior military might of the British. Each time the revolt occurred the adminisiration made some concessions to the tribals by passing legislations which remained mainly in letter than in action.

Tribal emigration which was another significant consequence again has to be seen within the political economy framework as Badgaiyan argues. On the one hand the tribals were forced out of their homeland, by the colonial policy; on the other hand they were encouraged to join the labour force in plantations, mines and to some extent factories, as tribal labour was not only cheap but was committed. Hence migration was the result of the double-edged colonial policy of land alienation and labour recruitment. Colonial capitalists developed plantations in Assam and Bengal and the tribals were recruited through the *arkathi* and *sardari* systems. Thus in 1891, 10.5 per cent of the total population in the area emigrated to other regions. A majority of the tribal migrants settled in Assam. The decision to migrate was collective and there was also a strong tendency on their part to stay together and recreate their social and cultural milieu.

N.C. Choudhury and S.K. Bhowmik consider tribal migration, settlement and consequences instead of destination, thus complementing Badgaiyan's attempt to explain the process of out-migration of tribals in the political economy framework.

After tracing the causes of migration of the tribals from Chota Nagpur and Santhal Parganas to West Bengal in terms of land alienation, tribal unrest and natural calamities such as drought and famine, the authors show that the out-migration of the tribals is not a thing of the past but is a continuous process till today. While the earlier migrants were absorbed in the tea gardens of Bengal and Assam, the recent migrants have taken up agriculture in the three districts of South Bengal—Midnapur, Purutea and 24 Parganas. The magnitude of inmigration into West Bengal was phenomenal during 1951-61. For instance, while the percentage increase of the Santhals (in 1951-61) in West Bengal was 41.94, that of Malpaharia was 226.32.

The authors discuss in detail both the early and new settlement patterns of the tribals in their places of destination. The Chotanagpur tribals were mainly recruited to the tea gardens in Jalpaiguri district in 1874, through the *arkati* and *sardar* systems. Both *arkatis* and *sardars* (the recruiting agents) exploited the tribals to the hilt, making them destitutes. The unit of tribal migration was the family and not the individual, as employment was there for both males and females. But while the tribal migration to the tea gardens was a substantial stream, migration to rural areas after 1950 due to further land alienation, was in driblets, as there was no systematic recruitment. As there is a demand for labour in jute and paddy harvesting and transplantation many tribals migrate seasonally to West Bengal, and when they find more steady work, they settle down permanently in rural areas.

What are the social consequences of their movement and new settlement? The tribal migrants to the tea gardens had to adjust themselves to the new work situation. Initially when diverse tribes were forced to live together in the gardens, some tribes not only attempted to maintain their own identity but assert superiority by not accepting cooked food from other tribes whom they considered inferior. Thus although all the tribals work together in the work situation, they re-enter their stratified society in the non-work situations. But after 1947, the internal differentiation has become less significant. The tribals now are a part of the trade union movement.

The tribal migrants to the rural areas have a different kind of life-style from that of the plantation workers. The former are share-croppers and labourers to Hindu land owners. They interact with them closely. They speak a local Bengali dialect. They are clubbed together with scheduled castes in the villages. Although the Jharkhand movement is trying to organize the tribals in order to give them a new identity, it has not been successful. Thus the authors discuss the contrast between the two streams of migration—plantation and rural areas, in terms of the process of migration and its social, economic and political consequences.

Part Five is devoted to international migration. While Thomas R. Metcalf writes on 'Indian Migration to South Africa', Arthur W. Helweg discusses the problems of "Indians in England : A Study of the Interactional Relationship of Sending, Receiving and Migrant Societies". Although migration is a historical process, only a few historians have studied it from this perspective. Metcalf's paper fills up this gap. His interest is migration in the colonial era—from 1860 to 1911. He asks himself two questions. Why did certain Indian and not others migrate to South Africa and what was the character of Indian's integration in South Africa's socio-economic order? In order to answer these questions, he differentiates two kinds of streams: one which consisted of indentured labourers from northern Bihar, eastern U.P. and central and southern coastal districts of Madras; and the voluntary stream which comprised mostly the Gujaratis engaged in trade, commerce and other jobs.

The indentured labourers were recruited to work on the canefields. Although the migrants were pushed out of India due to poverty, certain regions sent more migrants than others which were equally poor. Secondly, certain regions sent migrants to Fiji and Ceylon, but others to South Africa. Metcalf very rightly explains this variation by bringing in the bias of the recruiting agents who came from a region and had social network relations. Similarly in explaining the variation in the quantum of supply of labourers over a period of time, he looks at the demand side rather than the usual factors of good and bad climatic conditions affecting the supply of labour. The sugar factory owners in Natal did not have a consistently steady demand for labour as the production of sugar varied with the world market demand of sugar. Ultimately in 1911, the

Government of India stopped overseas indentured labour system, as they needed labour for their own industries. By this time Natal also found that the Indian labourers were no longer as docile as they used to be. Hence gradually the indentured labourers shifted to urban areas and found jobs in the railways. Some of them also took up market gardening in villages near the plantations.

The story of the voluntary migrants was different. They were not destitute. They moved to South Africa through their kin networks. As regards the benefits of migration, Metcalf notes two kinds of benefits. While certain benefits accrued to the individual migrants, their family members back home also had benefits of remittances of money. But there was also the benefit for the larger British Empire. The Indian colony helped the South African colony by sending cheap labour. India laboured so that the British colonial empire might prosper. Evidently migration in colonial India, whether it is internal or international can be understood only when it is set in the political economy framework.

If Metcalf deals with overseas migration in the colonial period, Helweg considers the migration of Indians to England in the recent past—1950-1980. On the basis of his intensive fieldwork, he provides insights into the ongoing triangular interactional relationships among a Punjabi Sikh migrant group in England with their host society of Gravesend and Kent on the one hand, and the sending community, Jandiali in Punjab on the other.

A large number of Sikhs from rural Punjab started moving to England after the Second World War. They were absorbed in the factories as unskilled workers. The wave of migration continued until U.K. imposed immigration restrictions in the 1960s. Thus by 1978, Indians comprised 13 per cent of Gravesend's population. Of these a majority were Sikh Jats from rural Doaba region of Punjab. The sending community is the village of Jandiali located between the two cities of Jullundur and Ludhiana. While two-thirds of the working population of the village (1,608) have migrated to England, the rest are in other parts of India, Middle East, Australia and New Zealand.

Helweg describes four sequential phases of migration and interaction in terms of pre-migration, freedom, conflict and settlement. In the pre-migration period Sikhs of Jandiali were facing severe pressure on their village economy by the influx of refugees after partition. They were also attracted by the exaggerated reports of plenty and prosperity in England. The information flow and demonstration effect convinced them and gradually they could see how the families in the village with foreign residents enjoyed honour and prestige man. All these motivated the Jat Sikhs to move and the kin networks provided the instrumental resources to move.

In the freedom period, single men migrated leaving wives and children behind. The male migrants, sent money home, and occasionally returned home to demonstrate their affluence and new style of life. The external economy that had developed in Jandiali with foreign remittances played an exclusive part in the development of the village. In the host country they were helped by the Gravesend Gurudwara in finding jobs and lodging. The men were motivated to work hard to make more money. They were in between the British and Punjabi cultures. They had the peasant mentality which the British social order and culture could not accommodate.

The third phase is characterized by overt conflict. Racial tensions had started in British society by 1962. Before the immigration laws became rigid the male migrants brought their wives and children, although it meant loss of their freedom. The immigrant community was caught in the mesh of conflicting cultural demands. The females earned their freedom from their mothers-in-law. By 1970 the Gravesendians began to realize that their stay in England was permanent. The problem of the second generation migrants began to absorb their attention as they did not want the latter to become brown British. But the second generation migrants had their own wish. They diversified their educational and employment opportunities. The educated ones went into the professions and business. The influence of village community norms began to fade. The youth became aware of their rights as permanent citizens and began to fight racism. This was a new source of fear for the host country to cope with. However, for the sending community, the external economy became stronger, as it ushered in the green revolution.

Substantial sums of money were also spent on education, Gurudwaras and politics.

The *settlement* period was characterized by the realization on both the host and immigrant community that the notion of returning had little chance. Helweg notes that the Gravesendian community has not yet reached the phase of settlement, as much depends upon the response of the host country. He shows in the end that the triangular interactional model may be applicable in the case of other overseas migrant communities. The merit of this model is that it goes beyond the simple assimilation/alienation, melting pot/beyond the melting pot theories in so far as it emphasises the dynamics of the triangular interaction system, and lays bare the processual view rather than the structural (rigid either/or) notion of social reality. He also brings out the psychological dimensions of motivation and personality of the Jat migrants, the kind of dual socialization processes to which they are subjected and their consequences.

The Volume then covers important perspectives such as demographic, economic, historical (political economy) and psychological in migration studies. The contributions reveal how these are complementary in understanding the complex phenomenon of migration and the migrants as a social and cultural category.

Migration is one of the areas which has policy implications for population distribution, planned development and directed social change. Each one of the studies included in the Volume expresses these concerns and points to the humanistic considerations. Broadly four areas may be highlighted. That migration is an essential component of development is very well brought out in many of the contributions. Migration of certain streams and groups like some Gujeratis and Rajasthanis, with capital and entrepreneurial abilities to urban areas, especially metropolitan cities have brought about industrial and commercial development. Farmers (those who produce marketable surplus) have migrated to new areas of canal irrigation or to regions where they foresee possibilities of irrigation and have brought about agricultural development. There are also the feed effects of development migration mainly international, as in the case of Punjab. However, development in certain cases is accompanied by deprivation of different kinds for other sections of the local population which has a humanistic angle. For instance, in the tribal areas, there are the problems of land alienation, emigration and occurrence of violent revolts against the non-tribal migrants. Although the government has a policy of restoration of land and integrated tribal development, the measures are not meaningfully implemented. This is one of the areas which needs closer attention.

The second issue of practical concern that the contributions have laid stress on is labour mobility and the consequent miseries of migrant labourers in certain situations. That labour mobility is not just a question of demand and supply under perfect market conditions has been pointed out by some contributors. For instance, there is no significant rural-urban migration resulting from the assumption of expected income differential. Further, a large number of the rural migrants find employment in the so-called informal sector. There is also urban unemployment. It has been pointed out that the dual urban economy in terms of informal and formal is not meaningful. The 'informal' work organization has a great potentiality to check exploitative tendencies of the employers. All these pertinent observations are of immediate relevance to handle problems of urban employment and to give protection and benefits to the self-employed and the workers in the lowly paid jobs in the urban sector.

Uncontrolled migration of the unskilled and semi-skilled stream of workers into the large metropolitan cities is closely associated with the problem of slums and urban poverty. This points to the need for more welfare measures calculated to improve their conditions of living which is characterized by ill health, poor or no housing, insanitary environment, malnutrition illiteracy and high infant mortality.

The third area of policy consideration refers to the tribal migrants. As has been pointed out by some contributors, land alienation and emigration are not things of the past. In some cases where tribals move out as seasonal agricultural labourers to Punjab and other areas, they are exploited by the middlemen. Their conditions of misery are untold. It is not enough to pass migration laws. The government has to take appropriate steps first to check land alienation which leads to emigration, and secondly to ensure better working conditions for the seasonal and permanent migrants.

Lastly, the conditions of work and life of the overseas or overland migrants from India are as much a problem for the sending country as it is for the host country. In some cases there is also the question of repatriation of migrants. The government will have to have appropriate checks and agreements and enforce them properly, with a view to avoiding misery and hardship to the overseas migrants in the host countries. The two essays point to the problems of the overseas Indian migrants in South Africa and England in relation to racial discrimination, tensions and conflicts. Thus migration assumes humanistic importance not only within the country but also outside in the context of human rights and the just world order.

2. *Some Aspects of Sociology of Migration in India*[1]

M.S.A. RAO

The importance of migration for developing countries cannot be overestimated. Migration is a major factor in economic development and manpower planning. It has acquired special significance in the context of commercialization of agriculture because of labour mobility. It is a major factor in urbanization and social change. It has notable feed-back effects on the place of origin as the migrants from rural to urban areas maintain different kinds and degrees of contact. The importance that migration occupies in the social and cultural life of the people, however, has not been commensurate with the attention it has so far received from sociologists, anthropologists and demographers in our country. This paper points out briefly some of the important dimensions of sociology of migration. This is not intended to be a review of literature on migration[2] although some examples are given at relevant places.

It is necessary to consider migration and settlement as interrelated aspects of social and cultural life of the people. Migration is a shift in the place of residence for some length of time. While it excludes short visits and tours, it includes different types of both voluntary and involuntary movements.

1. An earlier version of the paper was presented in the sub-panel on Migration at the XV All India Sociological Conference, 2nd November, 1980, Meerut and was published in the *Sociological Bulletin*, Vol. 30, No. 1, March 1981. This has been reprinted in this volume, with only marginal alterations.
2. For a recent review article on migration, see J.P. Singh [1980 : see also Connell et. al. (1976)].

Examples of involuntary movements are migration under such crises as war, transfer of population, riots, floods, droughts and earthquakes. It also includes marriage migration, virilocal, uxorilocal or neolocal and transfer migration. There are other situations of migration where movement is part of people's earning a livelihood. These are nomads, shifting cultivators, itinerant traders and salesmen, artisans and labourers. Transhumance is a special type of migration between two sets of settlements in different seasons.

Historically, both internal and overseas migration have been associated with widespread military conquests, agricultural colonization and plantations, expeditions of merchant traders, and religious missionaries, slave trade and indentured labour. These instances of migration currents provided the basis for early diffusionist, culture contact and acculturation theories. Although in some cases this approach led to pseudo-historical reconstruction of the past, where authentic historical records were available, it has led to a meaningful study of the process of colonization, labour mobility, and the confrontation between the migrant colonizers on the one hand and the native peoples on the other.

Studies in migration stemmed from two theoretical sources: culture contact theories and the Marxian analysis of colonization and alienation. While the former approach is dated, the latter is still significant in studying the process of migration and its consequences in the context of the capitalist mode of production development and underdevelopment (Frank 1967). For instance, colonization of tribal areas in different parts of India (and in some other parts in the world) by peasants and merchants from the plains has led to conflicts between the migrants and the native tribes. Large-scale exploitation of the benefits of scarce resources by the non-tribal migrants has resulted in conditions of relatively acute deprivation of the tribals. The perception of such conditions by the local tribes has led to militant messianic and millenarian movements (See for instance, Singh K. Suresh 1966; Troisi, Joseph 1979; Raghaviah 1971). I have studied one such situation in the Polavaram taluk of West Godavari District where peasants from the plains have made steady inroads into the tribal area over a period of two hundred years. The peasant colonization has led to the alienation of the Koyas in terms of loss of land, emergence of wage labour and unequal distribution of the gains of the new tobacco economy (See Chapter 7). While in Polavaram, the situation has not led to a Naxalite outbreak, in a similar situation of ethnic conflict in Srikakulam the Naxalite movement was very intense during 1969-1970.

The problem of ethnicity has assumed an important place in migration studies especially in the urban context (Vatuk 1972; Punekar 1974; Mythili, K.I. 1974; Singh, Andrea M. 1976; D'Souza 1977; Nair, K.S. 1978; Caplan, L. 1976, 1977, 1980; Lewandowski, Susan 1980; Gore 1970). Migrants belonging to a particular region, language, religion, caste, and tribe tend to live together in separate neighbourhoods in cities and they form ethnic groups on the basis of shared elements of culture and ideology, merging lower levels of differences based on sub-caste or sub-region. The earlier migrants help the fresh ones in getting jobs and houses, and initiate them into urban ways of life. Some of the affluent ethnic groups establish their own housing cooperatives, schools, dispensaries, and census, marriage and employment bureaus. They also build their places of worship. The migrant groups try to recreate their cultures, of the place of origin at the place of destination, which results in cultural pluralism (Bose, N.K. 1968). It is in this context of inter-ethnic relations and developmental process of the first generation and second generation migrants, that we have to examine such concepts as integration, assimilation, isolation, simulation, fossilization, melting pot, beyond the melting pot, and ethno-class.

Urban ethnicity, however, is not just a case of cultural pluralism. Ethnic groups get politicized, act as vote-banks and pressure-groups articulating their interests, and compete for various benefits of urban life. This results in a situation of conflict between ethnic groups and between the migrant ethnic groups and the locals which goes by the name of sons-of-the-soil movements (Weiner 1978; Gupta 1977). The present situation in Assam presents one such case which needs to be analysed in all its dimensions. It should be noted that the situation of conflict cannot be entirely explained in the straightjacket Marxian approach. The situational contexts of class and ethnicity and their varying interactions have to be checked against empirical evidence.

One of the chief reasons for conflicting relations of migrants and locals is in the sphere of employment. Some economists have proposed a dual-market hypothesis in the context of international migration. While the locals seek employment in the primary sector, the migrants are found in the secondary sector. Further while the locals are found in the higher levels of the job hierarchy the migrants occupy job in the lower levels. These two features minimize the spirit of competition. The limitation of such a hypothesis has been pointed out by Piore (1979), namely the second generation migrants who are local at any rate acquire the necessary skills and compete for the same jobs which were once monopolized by the locals.

The dual-market hypothesis, however, is not applicable to internal migration in the Indian context, where migrants having diverse skills and resources enter the job market at various levels. For instance, there are affluent migrants from Marwar and other regions of Rajasthan who have shown a high propensity to migrate to different parts of India and who have established industries and have engaged themselves in trade and commerce. The educated people from Kerala, Tamil Nadu, Karnatak and Bengal have moved to different places in search of white-collar and professional jobs. The unskilled and semi-skilled workers from Rajasthan, Andhra Pradesh, Tamil Nadu, Eastern U.P., Bihar and Orissa have moved to distant places in search of jobs in plantations, factories and in the informal sector. Hence although the competition from the migrants is endemic at every level, the question is whether the migrants belong to the same linguistic group or not. If they are not, then there are more chances for conflicting relations.

It may be argued that at least in certain sectors the competition is eliminated as the locals themselves would not like to work as plantation labourers or domestic workers, or to take up work which is considered less prestigious. This may be true only at a particular point of time, but over a period of time when jobs in the preferred sectors are taken, the locals might look for jobs in the self-employed and other categories in the informal sectors which were earlier left to the migrants. Such a situation is also productive of conflict between the locals and migrants. It is necessary to investigate the social, economic and political conditions due to which conflicts between the locals and migrants arise and crystallize into sons-of-the-soil movements.

Another consequence of large scale migration of unskilled and semi-skilled workers to the cities, especially in metropolitan cities is the development of slums (Rao 1974). This category of migrants, having little resources to pay for the urban facilities such as housing, sewerage, drainage, water and electricity, tend to squat on public land and pavements which results in the formation of slums. Sociologists and anthropologists have shown considerable interest in the problems of slums which mainly consist of migrants (Desai and Pillai 1970; Wiebe 1975; Ranga Rao, et al. 1977; Ranga Rao and M.S.A. Rao 1984; Lynch 1974; Singh, Andrea M. and A. de Souza 1980).

Three problems are of relevance to the study of migration in the context of slums. First, most unskilled and semi-skilled rural migrants to metropolitan cities seek jobs in the informal sector of the urban economy, i.e., as construction workers, domestic servants, vendors, peddlers and hawkers, paperboys, cycle and auto mechanics, junk collectors, loaders and unloaders, basket weavers, barbers, cycle riksha drivers and shack shop and tea-stall keepers. All these jobs are an essential part of the urban economy catering to the needs of people belonging to different socio-economic strata. Often small workshops and industries manufacture machine parts to feed into bigger organised industries in the formal sector. Similarly, persons employed in the formal sector might follow certain occupations in the informal sector. The two sectors are complementary and provide a continuum in some respects depending upon the nature and levels of demands. Hence I agree with Breman (1976, 1980) and Papola (1980, 1981) who rightly question the dualism of the formal and informal sector. Further, the jobs in the informal sector should not be considered as unorganised and open. For instance, it is difficult for a migrant to get a job as loader and unloader of goods. There are norms governing recruitment and conditions of work and wages by the unions, which may not be the formal trade unions.

Another aspect of the informal sector is that the job structure here is governed more by primordial ties of caste, region, religion, language, village, kinship and friendship. These network relations are important in getting urban jobs for the migrants (Klass 1979). In fact the resource network is also an important factor in motivating people to move out of their places of origin, which will be considered later.

Thirdly, there are two ways of looking at the economic and social aspects of the migrant slum dwellers. One, that a slum is a community, a village writ large and it holds possibilities of occupational and social mobility. The other is that it is a den of vices and a home for the urban poor with a distinct subculture of their own, often called by the term culture of poverty. Some studies of slums show that they exhibit features of organised community life, and the migrants have achieved a level of occupational and social mobility when compared to their occupation and social standing in the place of origin, as shown by Tataji (See Chapter 6). However, we cannot rule out that there are certain slums where the social life is characterized by organized crime, delinquency, prostitution and beggary, and migrants are easily recruited into these situations. The notion of the culture of poverty (Lewis 1966) characterizing the social and economic conditions of slum dwellers in the United States, needs to be examined carefully in order to see whether it is applicable to the Indian slums. Wiebe (1975), Ranga Rao and the author (1984) in any case think that it does not.

Of the different sections of rural-urban migrants, women constitute an important section. Usually women's migration is mostly considered marriage migration. This is not entirely correct. Since many women belonging to the working class work in various capacities, even when they migrate after marriage to the places where their husbands live, they are potential workers in the place of destination. In many cases the whole family consisting of husband, wife and children moves from rural to urban areas either for a season or on a semi-permanent basis. There are also situations where some women move all by themselves, others move along with their husbands and brothers for work. All this suggests that female migration cannot be treated as wholly marriage migration. Marriage is incidental whereas their work status is stable.

Internal migration is related to the international migration either overseas or overland. The latter creates imbalances in certain regions in labour supply and internal migration comes as an answer. For instance, in Punjab continuous waves of overseas migration to England, United States, Canada, and now to the Gulf countries have created a shortage of labour and this gap is filled by the migrants, including the tribals, from Bihar, and U.P. (Gupta and Bhakoo 1980). However, international migration—both immigration and emigration needs to be studied in its own right. There are immigrants from Tibet who have been rehabilitated in different parts of India. There are also migrants from Nepal and Bangladesh—both legal and illegal, and they need to be studied from the point of view of adjustments. Another aspect of international migration is the question of return migration and repatriation of Indian overseas migrants. For instance, there are about 80,000 Tamil repatriates in Tamil Nadu (Cole and Wiebe 1981).

Overseas Indian migrants in different parts of the world, South and South-East Asia, Africa, England, United States, Canada and Gulf countries form a distinct category and there have been studies of these migrant Indian communities in their places of destination (see for instance the recent works by Jain 1970; Jayaraman 1975; Kannah 1978; Helweg 1979). There are significant problems of cultural adjustments, inter-ethnic relations and relations between the Indians and the locals in the host countries. The new developments of tension and riots in this regard need to be studied and analysed for promoting harmonious ethnic relations.

From the point of view of the place of origin (India) the feed-back effects of overseas migration are significant. The overseas Indians maintain contact with their places of origin and send large sums of money home for the maintenance of the family. The foreign remittances are used in buying machinery, equipment, automobiles, houses and land. Thus, it has contributed both to developmental activities and high consumerism. This money-order economy has been partly responsible for the green revolution in Punjab and the white revolution in Gujarat. However, in Kerala, gulf money is converted into status through conspicuous consumption, large houses and automobiles. But there are some investments in land, picture houses, restaurants and trade and commerce (Prakash 1978; Mathew and Nair 1978).

Feed-back effects of internal migration have different implications. Migrants here maintain more close and frequent contacts with their places of origin, through sending money home, visits and property and political relations. A distinction may be made between subsistence and development migration, with reference to the nature of consequences. Many of the unskilled and semi-skilled migrants' families at the place of origin have been able to rise above the line of poverty but still at the subsistence level. There are other families who have been able to clear all their debts, build houses and improve their standard of living. Besides these feed-back effect on the standard of living of members of the family at the place of origin, there is the problem of demographic imbalance, economic and political consequences. Way back in 1964 I.P. Desai (1964) described the patterns of emigration in a South Gujarat village, over a period of about 50 years. He showed that, as a result of cut-migration of both the upper and lower castes traditional power structure underwent significant changes. The Anavils who were once economically and politically dominant had lost that position. Valunjkar (1966) has also described the changes in a village due to migration.

Of all the different streams of migration in India (and other developing countries) rural-rural occupies a central place as it accounts for about 70 per cent of total migration. A few demographers consider this as unimportant, because they consider much of it as marriage migration of females. As we have noted, this is a simplistic explanation because among the working class, women also work for a living. Husband and wife either together or separately migrate to places where employment opportunities are available. Rural migration consists of movement of landowning peasants and farmers, labourers, artisans and service castes and tribes. Under programmes of rehabilitation, such sections of population as nomads, criminal tribes, Harijans, and refugees, are settled into various types of colonies. In this context the matter for investigation is the way a new community organization emerges involving diverse migrant social groups which are thrown together. Another area of investigation is the process of sedentarization of groups which were hitherto nomads and its social and cultural consequences.

Migration of tribals to plantations, other rural areas, industrial complexes and urban areas poses several specific questions for sociological investigation. Their problems of adjustment are different from those of non-tribal labourers and peasants. There are both the problems of inter-tribal relations and the tribal and non-tribal relations, in such cities as Shillong and Imphal which need to be investigated besides their changing economic and property relations and family and religious life. N.C. Choudhuri (1963) shows that tribes move in groups maintaining their ethnic identity at the place of destination (See also Chapter 10).

Peasant and farmer migration in the rural context has several variations. Peasants have moved to large river valley project areas either on their own or under the sponsorship by the government. It is seen that peasants who have had experience of flow irrigation voluntarily move to the new river valley project areas. They legally buy land from the locals and establish their settlements called 'camps'. The labourers also move as it becomes a labour demand area. These processes of colonization and labour mobility are discussed by N.E C. Vidyasagar in his thesis (1982).

Migration of agricultural labourers, both seasonal and permanent, in other rural areas gives rise to a different set of problems related to their conditions of work, nature of their exploitation by the middle men and the relationship between the migrant farmers and locals, and the impact of migration on their places of origin. Labourers move in units of household and also singly. The situation of single female migrants provides an interesting area of sociological investigation. I have examined (study in progress) the reasons and social consequences of migration of single females who grade tobacco with the farmers and factories in Andhra Pradesh and Karnataka. Their movements involve a distance of 200 to 800 miles.

Seasonal migration occupies a very important place in

migration studies, but unfortunately it is the most neglected area. Since the census data are not useful in this regard, primary studies are needed to unravel the different dimensions of the problem, including working conditions, the role of middle men, nature of exploitation and an assessment of relevant legislations. Seasonal migration has acquired a singular importance in the context of commercial crops, such as cotton, sugarcane, tobacco, potato, groundnut and mulberry. There are other operations which need seasonal labour such as bamboo cutting, felling of trees for timber and cutting wood for fuel, construction of roads in forest and other areas and desilting of tanks and canals and building tanks, bridges and dams. I have pointed out elsewhere (Rao, M.S.A., 1981a, 1981b) that contrary to the popular impression, seasonal migration is work specific and a certain group specializes in a particular job. For instance, Muslims of Nambur, a village near Guntur, are expert tobacco curers; agricultural labourers, mostly Malas and Madigas in Guntur and Krishna districts are known for their skills in harvesting and grading flue cured virginia tobacco; labourers from Palamuri (Andhra Pradesh) and Orissa are known for earth work; labourers from Rajasthan are good construction workers; labourers from Khandesh are good cane cutters; labourers from Rajamundri District are good bamboo cutters. Such specialized skills are built over two or three generations.

Seasonality of migration is relative to economic and social conditions of migrants at the place of origin and of destination. Migrants who, in the first instance, intend to stay only for the duration of the task, tend to stay on if economic conditions are favourable. After all, they say that they live on the strength of their shoulders and it does not matter where they work. But by and large seasonal migrants have a place of origin where they might have some land and a hut and they might move out for two different seasons in a year after spending some time, in between, in their village.

Seasonal migrants tend to be exploited by the middle men, and hence the process of recruitment and different patterns of organization of work needs to be studied in detail. Breman (1978) has discussed the jobber type of organization of migrant cane cutters from Khandesh in the sugar factories in South

Gujarat. This pattern of organization is an agreement between the cooperative sugar factories and the jobbers. However, there are other types of organization. The one which is popular in Andhra Pradesh is the *banta* type (Rao 1978) in which a *maistry* builds up a team of twenty workers and enters into contract with the farmers directly to execute particular operations, such as harvesting of tobacco, rice, cane or cotton. In this type the degree of exploitation by the middle men is reduced to the minimum. In fact, the *maistry* is himself a worker and gets only one day's wages of each worker in his team as his commission. Hence there is a need to investigate all the different types of work situations and their social consequences.

So far we have discussed two aspects of migration and migrants, first, what happens to the migrants in the place of destination, how do they adjust themselves, what kind of relations they would establish with the locals, and what kind of social consequences would follow. Secondly, what are the feed-back effects of migration on the place of origin of the migrants. There is the third aspect of migration studies which is very significant, namely why people move and under what conditions migration materializes. This problem has been the subject of much theorizing. Of all the social scientists, interested in migration, economists have been the foremost in advancing theories to explain migration flows. Migration is considered to be a function of labour reallocation in response to market demands, so that the demand and supply of labour are always in equilibrium. Labour mobility occurs in direct response to expected wage differential between rural and urban areas (Harris and Todaro 1970). It is also argued that if the wage differential between the rural and urban sectors is in excess of the equilibrium, the intersectoral transfers will continue until there is equality. Further, given higher wages in urban areas, people would be attracted from low income underdeveloped regions in numbers much larger than the available employment opportunities on the chance of their getting into a job. One way out of this puzzle is to say that migrants may enter into informal sector. Migration is also considered as an investment in human capital involving cost-benefit analysis at different levels. At the individual level, it is argued that migration is based on careful calculations involving money and non-money (psychological) costs. While some economists do consider the importance of non-economic factors in explaining migration (for instance Piore 1979), others assume that the individual is a rational economic man interested in maximization of profit or utility, and it is the poor who move out attracted by higher wages. The limitation of this theory is that it does not explain why, among people placed in the same economic circumstances, some move and others do not. Secondly, why people who are well off also move to cities. Hence it is safer to assume that economic considerations do not wholly explain why people move. Further where they are important, they provide only the necessary conditions for people to migrate, the sufficient conditions are provided by non-economic factors which explain how migration occurs.

Some economists and demographers have tried to explain migration in terms of push and pull on the basis of higher land-man ratio, underemployment at the place of origin and the pull of higher wages, the bright lights of the city, opportunities for education and training. The push and pull approach like the economic one assumes that it is only the poor and low paid that move out, and there are no pulls in the rural areas and no pushes in the urban areas (Bose 1965). Further, these approaches are concerned with the rural-urban migration and not rural-rural which accounts for about 70 per cent of migration.

The demographic approach to migration is mainly based on census data which takes place of birth as the criterion for determining the migratory status although recently place of last residence and duration of stay have been added. I have pointed out the inadequacy of place of birth criterion (Rao 1976) elsewhere. Further, some demographers equate intra-district migration with short distance migration and inter-district and inter-state with long distance migration as Premi (1980 : 716) does. One can see the absurdity of this statement. In the case of inter-district or inter-state migration, place of origin and place of destination may be adjacent lying on the two sides of the district boundary line. In such a case it is a case of short distance migration. However, I consider good demographic studies of migration are important in knowing the magnitudes of the different aspects of migration.

Sociological approach to migration has been built up over a period of years in bits and pieces since Marxian culture-contact, and Revenstien's (1885) theories. For instance, with reference to step migration of Revenstien, it is observed that it is only one of the analogies of the way in which migration occurs. There are others: radial, circular and zig-zag migration patterns. Similarly, the notion that people initially move to places which are nearer is contradicted by the evidence that people also migrate first to far-off places because they have prior kin, caste, regional and other links with that place. Hence, selectivity is based on social factors and not on the factor of propinquity of the place of destination.

In my studies of migration, I have found that social network (including ties of kin, caste, village language) is the most effective channel of communication (information system) which favours decision making in migration. Very rarely people move without prior information and a linkage of some kind or the other.

It is not my intention here to expand and add to the insights provided by several sociological studies regarding different dimensions of migration. I believe that any adequate sociological analysis should recognize the complexity and the multi-dimensional aspects of the problem and seek not only to isolate variables but work out their interconnections. Thus, any study of migration should consider the historical development of the region, the wider economic and political conditions which regulate and condition the nature of employment opportunities. Secondly, economic and social conditions at the place of origin need to be examined in order to understand why people move or do not move. At the individual level we have to consider not only the level of skills and family circumstances but the whole process of socialization and personality factors. It is important to realize that economic factors provide only the necessary conditions of migration, the sufficient conditions are the motivations to move, presence of resource networks and access to information flows. The latter make migration selective in terms of age, sex marital status and the phase of development of the domestic group.

What happens to the migrants at the place of destination, their problems and process of settlement, employment, success and failure and their social organization are not entirely unrelated to their contacts with the place of origin. Hence the continuing interaction process between the place of origin and of destination is an essential aspect of migration studies. The best methodology to study migration is to make double ended studies, i.e. studies of migrants both at the place of destination and of origin. The distinct advantage of studying the process of migration at the place of origin is to place the migrants in the wider contexts of their family, caste, village and region, and to explain why out of persons who are similarly situated, some migrate and others do not. It helps investigation of the return migration. Under what circumstances, people return to their place of origin. Broadly, there are three circumstances: one where people return because of frustration and secondly people return for a short period in order to go again. Thirdly, people return for good. In some case they will have both capital and skills and are capable of innovation in agriculture, trade, commerce and industry.

In the end I will argue that a cultural interpretation is important in gaining a deeper understanding of the process of migration.[3] In this context we have to treat migration and settlement of mobile and stationary states (*jangama* and *sthavira*) as a binary opposition. Staying out and moving about are related to people's conceptions of space and time. People invest meaning to a place or territory in which they live and they also attach meaning to their movements. In this process they develop a set of symbols of both rootedness and mobility. In the context of Kamma peasants, who are known for their migratory propensity, the following oppositions are observed. Place of birth is considered to be sacred as the body first touched the ground there. Blood ties (agnatic ties) make people stick to the place of origin as they form the base of descent, succession and inheritance. Ancestral land is also sacred as it is symbolic of ancestor worship. There is the custom of burying

3. This brief exposition is based on my fieldwork on migration of peasants and labourers in Andhra Pradesh and Karnataka during my UGC National Fellowship (1977-79). See also Chapter 7 in this volume

the aged grandparents after death in the ancestral land and erect tombs for them. Kamma peasants also develop attachment to the village in which they grew up with specific associations to ancestral home, play-ground and school; to events of quarrel and love, and to sounds of hooting flour mill, and smells of cooking, flowers and crops. Thus, territoriality becomes an ethno-phenomenon. The question is how do they overcome the limitations of these cultural symbols of rootedness?

Kammas argue that they value the set of symbols associated with mobility more than that associated with rootedness. They say that while a tree strikes roots and gets fixed, the seeds are free to fly. The blood sticks but semen spreads. That is, while agnatic ties encourage rootedness to property through inheritance, the affinal relations sponsor mobility. Future is more attractive than the past. Acquired land is more prestigious than the ancestral. Territoriality is bondage but migration is freedom. Spirit of adventure and risk are more desirable than conservatism. This set of symbols promotes spatial mobility. Therefore, migration is a structural transformation of symbols of rootedness into symbols of mobility.

It may be argued that when Kammas move from their ancestral village to another place and establish a settlement, they will be striking roots again. While this is true for the time being, after some time the same process of dispersal (of seeds) starts. Staying put and moving about are relative. Both territoriality and movement need to be explained, and the symbolic interpretation emphasizing the native categories of thought regarding space and time, stationary and mobile states enables us to gain deeper insights in understanding the process of migration.

Cultural symbols far from being fixed are dynamic and undergo significant changes in the context of cumulative experience of people, changing interests and demonstration effects. They enter into the socialization process and influence peoples' interests, and attitudes towards migration and their consequent behaviour. Hence, there is no hiatus between cultural and sociological interpretations in analysing and understanding migration.

REFERENCES

Bose, Ashish, "Why Do People Migrate to Cities", *Yojana* 25-26, 37, 1965.

Bose, N.K., *Calcutta : A Social Survey*, Lalvani, Bombay, 1968.

Breman, Jan C., "A Dualistic Labour System? A Critique of the Informal Sector", *Economic and Political Weekly*, 11 (48), 1870-1876; and (49 and 50) 1976.

—— : "Seasonal Migration and Cooperative Capitalism : Crushing of Cane and of Labour by Sugar Factories of Bardoli", *Economic and Political Weekly*, 13 (31, 32 and 33), 1317-1360, 1970.

—— : "*The informal Sector in Research : Theory and Practice*, Erasmus University, Rotterdam, 1980.

Caplan, L., "Class and Urban Migration in South India : Christian Elites in Madras City", *Sociological Bulletin*, 25 (2), 207-24, 1976.

—— : "Social Mobility in Metropolitan Centres—Christians in Madras" *Contributions to Indian Sociology*, New Series, 11 (1), 1977.

—— : "Mortality and Polyethnic Identity in Urban South India". In Mayer A.C. (ed.) *Morality and Culture*, Oxford University Press, New Delhi, 1980.

Connell, John et al., *Migration From Rural Areas : The Evidence From Village Studies*, Oxford University Press, New Delhi, 1976.

Choudhury, N.C., "Munda Settlement in Lower Bengal—A Study in Tribal Migration", *Bulletin of the Cultural Resarch Institute* 2 (2), 23-32, 1963.

Cole, P.D. and Wiebe, P.D., "Tamil Repatriates in Madurai : Problems and Prospects", *Economic and Political Weekly*, 16 (15), 159-162, 1981.

Desai, A.R. and Pillai, S.D. (eds.) *A Profile of an Indian Slum*, University of Bombay, Bombay, 1970.

Desai, I.P., *The Patterns of Migration and Oceupation in a South Gujarat Village*, Poona Deccan College, 1964

D'Souza, Victor S., *Inequality and Integration in an Industrial Community*, Indian Institute of Advanced Study, Simla, 1977.

Gore, M.S., *Immigrants and Neighbourhoods*, Tata Institute of Social Sciences, Bombay, 1970.

Gupta, Dipankar, "The Causes and Constraints of an Urban Social Movement", *Contributions to Indian Sociology* (NS), 11 (1), 69-90, 1977.

Gupta, A.K. and A.K. Bhakoo, "Rural to Rural Migration and Characteristics of Migrants in Punjab", *Social Change*, 10 (3 and 4) 18-22, 1980.

Harris, J.R. and Todaro, M.P., "Migration, Unemployment and Development : A Two Section Analysis", *American Economic Review*, 60, 126-142, 1970.

Helweg, Arthur, *Sikhs in England. The Development of Migrant Community*, Oxford Universty Press, Delhi, 1979.

Jain, R.K., *South Indians on the Plantation Frontier in Malaya*, Yale University Press, New Haven, 1970.

Jayaraman, R., *Caste Continuities in Ceylon*, Popular Prakashan, Bombay, 1975.

Kannan, C.T., *Cultural Adaptation of Asian Immigrants : First Generation and Second Generation*, C.T. Kannan, Green Ford, 1978.

Klass, Van-Der Veen, "Migration and Primordial Attachments". In S. Devadas Pillai and C. Baks (eds.), *Winners and Losers*, Popular Prakashan, Bombay, 1979.

Lewandowski, Sussan, *Migration and Ethnicity in Urban India*, Manohar, New Delhi, 1980.

Lewis, Oscar, *La Vida*, Random House, New York, 1966.

Lynch, O.M., "Political Mobilization and Ethnicity among Adi Dravidas in a Bombay Slum", *Economic and Political Weekly*, 9 (39), 1974.

Mathew, E.T. and P.R.C. Nair, "Socio Economic Characteristics of Emigrants and Emigrants' Households: A Case Study of Two Villages in Kerala", *Economic and Political Weekly*, 13 (28), 1141-1153, 1978.

Mythili, K.L., "Little Madras in Bombay City". In M.S.A. Rao (ed.), *Urban Sociology in India*, Orient Longman, New Delhi, (241-50) 1974.

Nair, K.S., *Ethuicity and Urbanization. A Case Study of the Ethnic Identity of South Indian Migrants in Poona*, Ajanta, Delhi, 1978.

Papola, T.S., "Informal Sector : Concept and Policy", *Economic and Political Weekly*, (May 3), 1980.

—— : "Urban Informal Sector in a Developing Economy", Vikas, Delhi, 1981.

Piore, Michael J., *Birds of Passage*, Cambridge University Press, New York, 1979.

Prakash, B.A., "Impact of Foreign Remittances : A Case Study of Chavakkad Village in Kerala", *Economic and Political Weekly*, 13 (27), 1107-1111, 1978.

Premi, M.K., "Aspects of Female Migration in India", *Economic and Political Weekly*, 15 (15), 714-720, 1980.

Punekar, V.B., *Assimilation : A Study of North Indians in Bangalore*, Popular Prakashan, Bombay, 1974.

Raghaviah, V., *Tribal Revolts*, Andhra Rashtra Adimjati Sevak Sangh, Nellor, 1971.

Rao, K. Ranga, et al., "Migration Experience of Urban-Dwellers", *The Indian Journal of Social Work*, 38(1), 1977.

Rao, K.R. and M.S.A. Rao, *Cities and Slums*, Concept, New Delhi, 1984.

Rao, M.S.A., "The Migrant to the City", *Yojana* 18(20), 7-13, 1974.

—— : "Migration and Urban Area Development", *Social Change* 6(3 and 4) 3-7, (1976).

Rao, M.S.A., "Tobacco Development and Labour Migration", *Economic and Political Weekly*, 13 (29), 1183-1186, 1978.

——: "Migration and Poverty among the Agricultural Labourers" Paper presented at the National Conference on Social Science Research and the Problem of Poverty, Indian Association of Social Science Institution, January 12-15, (MSS), 1981a.

——: "Seasonal Migrant Labour". Paper presented at the National Seminar on Migrant Labour in India. National Labour Institute, February 16-18, MSS. 1981b.

Singh, Andrea M., *Neighbourhood and Social Networks in Urban India*, Marwah, New Delhi, 1976.

Singh, Andrea M. and A. de Souza, *The Urban Poor Slum and Pavement Dwellers in Major Cities of India*, Manohar, New Delhi, 1980.

Singh, J.P., "Population Mobility in India : Studies and Prospects", *Sociological Bulletin* : 29 (1), 33-62, 1980.

Singh, K. Suresh, *Dust Storm and Hanging Mist* : *Store of Birsa Munda and His Movement*, Firma K.L. Mukhopadhyay, Calcutta, 1966.

Troisi, Joseph, "Social Movements Among the Santals" in M.S.A. Rao (ed.), *Social Movements in India*, Vol. 2, Manohar, New Delhi, 123-148, 1979.

Valunjkar, T.N., *Social Organization, Migration and Change in a Village Community*, Deccan College, Poona, 1966.

Vatuk, Sylvia, *Kinship and Urbanization* : *White Collar Migrants in North India*, University of California Press, Berkeley, 1972.

Vidyasagar, N.E.C., A Study of Migration and Social Structure in a District of Rayalaseema, Unpublished Ph.D. Thesis submitted to the Department of Sociology, University of Delhi, 1980.

Weiner, Myron, *Sons of the Soil* : *Migration and Ethnic Conflict in India* Oxford University Press, Delhi, 1978.

Wiebe, Paul D., *Social Life in an Indian Slum*, Vikas, New Delhi, 1975.

PART ONE

Demographic Aspects

3. *Migration to Cities in India*

MAHENDRA K. PREMI*

After the Second World War, an increasing number of nations gained independence from colonial rule and launched their programmes of economic and social development to improve the levels of living of their people. This led to exploitation of natural resources, growth of industries, and development of infrastructural facilities on the one hand, and rapid urbanization on the other. As the major investments for setting up of industries in many less-developed countries were made in the already existing dominant urban centres—generally put in place by the colonial rulers as centres of trade and commerce, and the seat of the government—they developed further and very fast due to unprecedented rates of inmigration. This, in turn, led to the accentuation of primacy of one city in the urban hierarchy in many countries. The most striking example is of Bangkok (Thailand) which is about forty-five times larger than Chiang Mai, the next largest city in that country. This phenomenon is found to a somewhat lesser degree in Afghanistan, Burma, Iran, the Philippines and the Republic of Korea (United Nations, ESCAP, 1977 : 3).

In comparison, the Indian urbanisation scene has been quite different. At the turn of the century 25.9 million persons, or 10.8 per cent of the country's population lived in urban areas. The proportion of urban population to the total did not change in any appreciable manner until the 1921 census, after which it increased gradually. By 1971, one-fifth of India's population

*Professor, Centre for the Study of Regional Development, Jawaharlal Nehru University, New Delhi.

had become urban and, in 1981, the urban population constituted 23.7 per cent of the total population of the country (excluding Assam, and Jammu and Kashmir) (Table 3.1). The gain in the proportion of urban population to the total over the past four censuses may seem modest, especially in relation to the gains achieved by many other less developed countries since the Second World War; but between 1951 and 1981, India's urban population became two-and-a-half times from 62.4 million to 156.2 million. This was the third largest urban population in the World and was much higher than the total population of any country except China, the Soviet Union, and the United States in 1980/81.

In 1901 there were 25 cities, each with a population of 100,000 and above, accounting for a quarter (25.8 per cent) of the urban population. The biggest city was not even twice as large in size as the next city. In contrast, in 1981 the number of urban agglomerations and cities with a population of 100,000 and above increased to 216 (excluding Assam and Jammu and Kashmir) accounting for 94.3 million persons that is 60 4 per cent of the urban population or 14.3 per cent of the total population (Table 3.1). The largest metropolis, Calcutta, with a population of 9.17 million was closely followed by Greater Bombay with 8.23 million persons. In fact, there were 12 metropolises with a population of one million or over.

It is generally believed that cities in India have been growing very fast, basically due to migration from rural areas and smaller urban settlements. Further migration to cities is male selective which turns the sex ratio in the cities more in favour of males. For example, Zachariah (1968) showed that migrants in Greater Bombay formed a selected group with respect to age, sex, marital status and family status. There was an excess of adolescents and young adults among migrants as compared to non-migrants in Bombay as well as the general population at the places of origin. The high sex ratio (males per 100 females) among migrants was due not only to high rates of inmigration of single males as compared to single females, but also to migration of married males unaccompanied by wives and children. Mitra (1967a) observed that the sex ratio, although above 100, became somewhat favourable to females with longer duration of residence. Analysing the 1971

TABLE 3.1

Population of India by Rural-Urban Residence and Number and Population of Urban Agglomerations and Cities of 100,000 and above Persons, 1901-1981

Year	Population (in millions)			Per cent distribution		Cities with Population 100,000+		
	Total	Rural	Urban	Rural	Urban	No.	Population (in million)	Per cent of total urban population
1901	238.4	212.5	25.9	89.2	10.8	25	6.7	25.8
1911	252.1	226.1	25.9	89.7	10.3	24	7.1	27.2
1921	251.3	223.2	28.1	88.8	11.2	29	8.3	28.9
1931	279.0	245.4	33.5	88.0	12.0	34	10.3	30.0
1941	318.7	274.4	44.2	86.1	13.9	48	16.7	36.8
1951	361.1	298.7	62.4	82.7	17.3	75	25.6	43.4
1961	439.2	360.2	17.9[a]	82.0	18.0	105	40.0	50.2
1971	548.2	439 0	109.1[a]	80.1	19.9	148	60.9	55.8
1981[b]	658.1	501.9	156.2	76.3	23.7	216	94.3	60.4

Note : The number of cities is affected by changes in the concept of town, town group, and urban agglomeration besides demographic changes between one census and another.

(a) The figures prior to 1961 and from 1961 onward are not strictly comparable because of change in definition of urban areas on the eve of the 1961 census when the same became stringent. For the two definitions, see Srivastava, 1972 : (95-98).

(b) Figures exclude Assam, and Jammu and Kashmir where the 1981 census could not be conducted synchronously. Census in Assam has not been conducted to date.

Sources : Census of India 1971 (1975 : 201-05) ; Census of India 1981 (1981 : 59).

census data on migrants to urban agglomerations and cities with population 100,000 and over (called class I cities in the Indian census), Mitra et al. (1980) have concluded that the bulk of the migrants to cities came from the rural areas. Inter-state migration of adult males exceeded intra-state migration in the bigger class I cities, that is, rural migrants to these cities also came from far-off rural areas. Intra-district migration was, nevertheless, prominent in smaller class I cities.

The Government of India has been making serious efforts to bring down its growth of population to the replacement level. Assuming that the same would be achieved by the end of the present century, the major factors in future urban growth will be the emergence of new towns or cities and migration to the existing cities and towns. A study of cityward migration in India, therefore, becomes very relevant. It gains further importance because, so far, the trend of migration, its causes and implications on demographic, social and economic development have not been well understood.

With these aspects in view, utilizing the 1971 census data[1] on migration, this paper provides an improved documentation of the pattern of migration to 100,000+ cities in India and examines some of the demographic, economic and social characteristics of the migrants in comparison to the non-migrants. The paper also envisages to bring out certain desirable policies and programmes of population distribution for the next two decades or so.

Data Base and Derived Tables

Data Base

Information on migrants was collected in the 1971 census by canvassing the following three questions :

1. Birth place a) Place of birth

1. It will still be quite a few years before the migration tables of the 1981 census become available. Moreover, looking at the 1981 Census Tabulation Plan (Census of India 1981, 1980), it will not be possible to make as detailed an analysis of the pattern of migration and characteristics of migration as one could make from the 1961 or 1971 censuses, hence the work in this paper is based on the analysis of 1971 census data.

b) Rural/Urban[2]
c) District
d) State/Country

2. Last residence
a) Place of last residence
b) Rural/Urban[2]
c) District
d) State/Country

3. Duration of residence at the village or town of enumeration.

These questions along with certain other items of information obtained in the "individual slip"[3] made it possible to generate several tables regarding the migrants in the country, and for the inmigrants to all urban agglomerations and cities with population 100,000 and above. Specifically, information contained in the following three tables has been utilized in the present analysis:

(1) Migrants to cities classified by sex, broad age groups, educational level, and, in case of workers, by occupational divisions.

This table is prepared only for cities and urban agglomerations of 100,000+ population and relates to migrants on the basis of "place of last residence" This provides an indication of occupations that attract migrants to cities. The educational standards give an insight into the skilled and unskilled labour.

(2) Workers and non-workers according to main activity classified by place of last residence.

2. For those born outside the village or town of enumeration, the rural or urban status was taken as at the time of birth of the migrant. In the case of last residence, rural and urban status was determined with reference to the time of migration from the place of last previous residence (Census of India 1971, 1975 : 18-19).
3. The form in which information is collected about each person in the Indian Population Census is known as "individual slip". For the "individual slip" used in the 1971 census and instructions to enumerators to fill the same, see Census of India 1971 (1975: 12, 16-24).

This table provides information on the quantum of migrants to class I cities by their place of last residence—rural or urban, intra-district, interdistrict, or interstate, and from countries outside India. Workers in this table are classified into nine industrial categories.

(3) Migrants classified by place of last residence, sex, age groups, marital status, and duration of residence.

Data on certain characteristics of the total population of each city—its sex and age composition and that of the workers, number of literates and educated persons, and industrial classification of workers—are also available from the census. These data, in conjunction with data on migrants, help in making comparisons of the particular characteristics of the migrants and non-migrants.

Some limitations of the migration data emanating from the census may be mentioned here before discussing the analytical framework. First, some of the urban agglomerations are composed of a number of cities and towns. For example, in 1971, Calcutta agglomeration comprised 73 settlements of which 10 had a population 100,000 and above besides Calcutta. In treating urban agglomeration as one unit separate information is lost for such cities. Second, at the time of processing of data, migration tables were not available for Shillong, a city with 122,752 population in 1971. Data on sex, age and marital status of the migrants pertaining to Calcutta, Trivandrum, Calicut, Cochin, Alleppy, Quilon and Farrukhabad-cum-Fatehgarh were defective and these cities had to be deleted from analysis relating to these characteristics. Third, since Calcutta, Greater Bombay, and Madras, each formed a separate district, the question of migrants from within the district of enumeration did not arise. Similarly, in case of the Union Territories of Chandigarh and Delhi, there were no migrants from other districts of the same state/union territory as these union territories are not divided further into districts. Fourth, the published data has several typographical errors. Although every effort was made to correct those errors, some could not be corrected and this has limited the scope of the analysis. Finally, migration tables for each city were generated from a 20 per cent sample selected systematically from the "individual slips". Because of large sampling error in the cell values of detailed cross-tables, many of these figures are not reliable. Analysis of migrant's and non-migrants characteristics involving detailed cross-tabulations has been consistently avoided.

Classification of Cities

As the cities in India differ from one another in several respects, a better understanding of the migration phenomenon can be obtained when they are grouped into categories on different axes. For example, it has been generally argued that the metropolises are the major magnets for the migrants, particularly long-distance migrants, and have been growing much faster than other cities. In order to determine the differentials in migration pattern and in the characteristics of the migrants by city size, they have been classified into the following four categories :

(a) 1,000,000+
(b) 500,000—999,999
(c) 200,000—499,999
(d) 100,000—199,999

An analysis of the growth of cities during 1951-71—comprising two decades of development planning—has shown that some cities had grown very fast while some others did not experience a growth rate even commensurate with their natural increase.[4] Since this is largely a result of the extent of net migration, I have classified the cities into three categories based on their growth rates:

4. In the absence of reliable statistics on birth and death rates of each city, I have assumed that the national exponential growth rate represented the natural growth rate of each city. Hence growth rates of all those cities wherein the same was lower than the national growth rate have been considered as non-commensurate with the natural increase rate.

(a) High growth rate, that is, higher than the growth rate of the nation's urban population during 1951-71.
(b) Medium growth rate, that is, growth rate falling between that of urban population and that of total population during 1951-71.
(c) Low growth rate, that is, growth rate below the national growth rate during 1951-71.

Although cities generally perform diversified functions, yet it is possible to determine their functional specialization. Moreover, the pattern of migration to the cities, particularly the characteristics of the migrants, are likely to differ according to their main functions. Several methods have been developed in the past to determine functional specialization of the settlements (Harris 1943; Pownall 1953; Duncan and Reiss 1956; Lal 1957; Ahmad 1965; Mitra 1967b). Different methods, however, yield almost similar results when the classification is sufficiently broad. As the purpose of this study is to understand the pattern of migration according to the functional specialization of the cities, I have borrowed Mitra's functional classification of Indian cities on the basis of 1971 census data since this was readily available to me.[5] Instead of using his detailed classification based on the extent of accentuation of particular functions, I have, however, regrouped the cities into the following three categories:

(a) Manufacturing.
(b) Trade, Commerce, and Transport, etc.
(c) Other Services.

Some of the cities in India have been in existence as important centres of economic activity for a very long time while some others graduated to the class I category much later. Some of the cities came into existence only after Independence and

5. The functional classification of the 1971 cities (applying the methodology adopted for the classification of the 1961 cities) has not been published. I am grateful to Prof. Asok Mitra who readily lended it to me.

have grown very fast, mostly through net inmigration, to fulfil the functions for which they were established. I have, therefore, classified the cities in the following categories according to the length of their existence:

(a) Cities having population of 100,000+ prior to 1901.
(b) Cities in existence prior to 1901 but graduated to class I between 1901 and 1951.
(c) Cities in existence prior to 1901 but graduated to class I since 1951.
(d) New cities that came into existence after the turn of the century and attained class I status any time during 1901 and 1971.

Finally, India displays peculiar regional diversities in economic and socio-cultural characteristics, which has influenced the migration pattern to the cities and is partly influenced by it. The cities have, therefore, been classified into the following categories:

(a) North and north-eastern Himalayan mountain ranges including Assam plains.
(b) Punjab and upper Ganga plains including Rajasthan desert region.
(c) Middle and lower Ganga plains.
(d) Central India plateau, north of Satpura range.
(e) Deccan plateau.
(f) Coastal plains of the Eastern and Western Ghats.

The cross-classification of cities on two axes indicated certain relationships. For example, an association was found between size of cities and their growth rates (Chi-square=15.6 with 6 d.f., significant at 2 per cent level). Similarly, there was association between functional specialization and regional type (Chi-square= 28.3 with 10 d.f., significant at 1 per cent level). There was also significant association between regional type and growth rate. Because of these interaction effects it would have been more useful to classify the cities into further sub-categories considering these relationships for a better understanding of the migration process but this would have reduced the number of cities in each category very substantially and many of the categories would have gone without a single city. Hence, the cities were not classified beyond what is stated above.

Keeping the above aspects in view, in what follows, the pattern of migration and the characteristics of the migrants and, in some cases, non-migrants, have been analysed on the basis of 1971 census data on about 140 cities. The averages for each category of cities are unweighted averages. This helps in testing the statistical significance of the differences between the means wherever necessary.

Pattern of Migration to Cities in India

Lifetime Migrants to Class I cities in India constitute about two-fifths of their population, the proportion being somewhat higher among females than males (Table 3.2). The proportion of migrants was significantly lower in cities in 500,000—999,999 population size category in comparison to other cities although half of them had fast growth rates and the other half medium growth rates during 1951-71. Besides natural increase, accretion of peripheral areas through expansion of municipal boundaries seems to be a major cause of high growth rates of these cities rather than inmigration.

As one would expect, cities with high growth rates had a higher proportion of migrant population than other cities (Figure 1). Service cities as well as the comparatively new cities, had a much higher proportion of inmigrants than other cities. The proportion of migrants to cities of middle and lower Ganga plains was just 30.2 per cent compared to cities of central plateau (44.3 per cent) or cities in the coastal plains (Figure 1).

The sex ratio among the lifetime migrants was favourable to females for most categories of cities; however, it was in favour of males in the million plus cities, in cities which had come into existence comparatively more recently, and in those belonging to north and north-eastern Himalayan region (Figure 1). The problem of living space in the metropolises probably acts as a deterrent to female migration which keeps their proportion low in them. In the new cities, the initial job opportunities were largely for males which made the sex ratio high but the reasons for a high sex ratio among migrants to cities in the north and north-eastern-Himalayan region are not very clear and need some probing.

TABLE 3.2

Proportion of Total Male and Female Migrants by Characteristics of the Cities, 1971

Characteristics of the cities	N	Total	Males	Females
All cities	140	39.13	37.64	40.75
A. *City size*				
1. Million plus cities	8	39.77	41.13	38.05
2. 500,000—999,999	10	32.13	31.31	33.09
3. 200,000—499,999	51	40.98	40.20	41.77
4. 100,000—199,999	71	38.72	36.30	41.41
B. *Growth rates*				
1. High	64	45.27	44.76	45.75
2. Medium	50	34.15	32.03	36.54
3. Low	24	33.21	30.32	36 42
C. *Functional specialization*				
1. Manufacturing	65	38.80	37.16	40.62
2. Trade & Transport	55	38.46	36.83	40.19
3. Service	20	42.05	41.41	42.77
D. *Length of existence as class I cities*				
1. Before 1901	24	33.34	33.30	33.36
2. Between 1901 and 1951	21	33. 6	31.08	35.31
3. Since 1951	84	39.83	37.84	42.01
4. New Cities	10	60.61	61.10	59.92
E. *Regional type*				
1. Himalayan	6	36.87	38.29	34.96
2. Upper Ganga plains	24	38.00	35.96	40.41
3. Mid & lower Ganga plains	19	30.20	28.22	32.54
4. Central plateau	27	44.29	42.95	45.77
5. Deccan plateau	35	38.88	37.58	40 30
6. Coastal plains	29	41.88	40.20	43.51

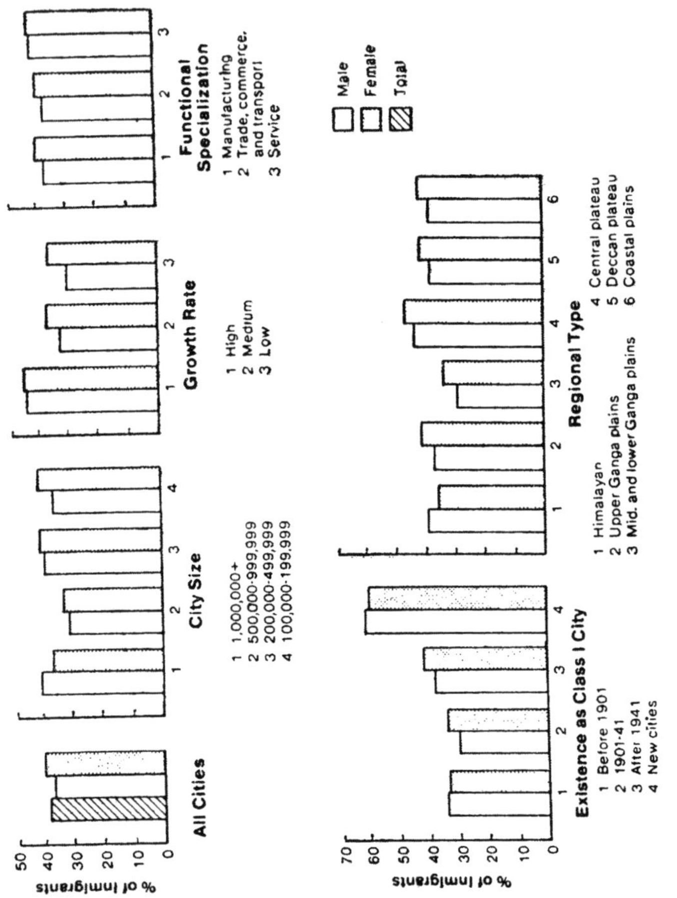

FIGURE 3·1 Percentages of inmigrants by city characteristics: India, 1971

Table 3.3 gives the distribution of migrants by their place of origin. As the table is based on "place of last residence", many of those persons who were born outside India but, after coming to India, subsequently changed their place of residence were counted as migrants within the country; in contrast, persons born in India but who returned from abroad before the 1971 census were enumerated with last residence "outside India". Hence, this Table may not provide an exact quantum of immigrants to the cities.

Inmigrants to the cities from rural and urban areas constituted 53.3 per cent and 40.8 per cent respectively, the rest coming from other countries. In relation to the population of sending areas, however, the proportion of urban migrants to the cities was much higher than rural migrants. A significant share of urban migration seems to be turn-round migration among class I cities but its quantum could not be estimated in the absence of city-by-city flows.

Intra-district migration (rural and urban) accounted for one-third of the lifetime migrants whereas inter-district (intra-state) and inter-state migrants constituted 38.3 per cent and 21.9 per cent respectively (Table 3.3).

The proportion of intra-district migration was lowest in the million plus cities (Figure 3.2) owing to the fact that Bombay, Calcutta and Madras form districts in themselves and, hence, they did not have intra-district migrants. Intra-district migration was more than 50 per cent in 29 cities all of which (except four which belong to Bihar) are situated in the Deccan plateau or in the coastal plains, and some of them have been important manufacturing or trading centres. Large scale intra-district migration to the cities in a particular region, however, requires detailed investigation.

Million plus cities have a comparatively higher proportion of interstate migrants. It is also higher in cities with high growth rates, in those that are comparatively new or the ones located in the Central India plateau. There is a certain amount of interaction among these variables as a number of new cities lie in the Central India plateau and had very high growth rates during 1951-71.

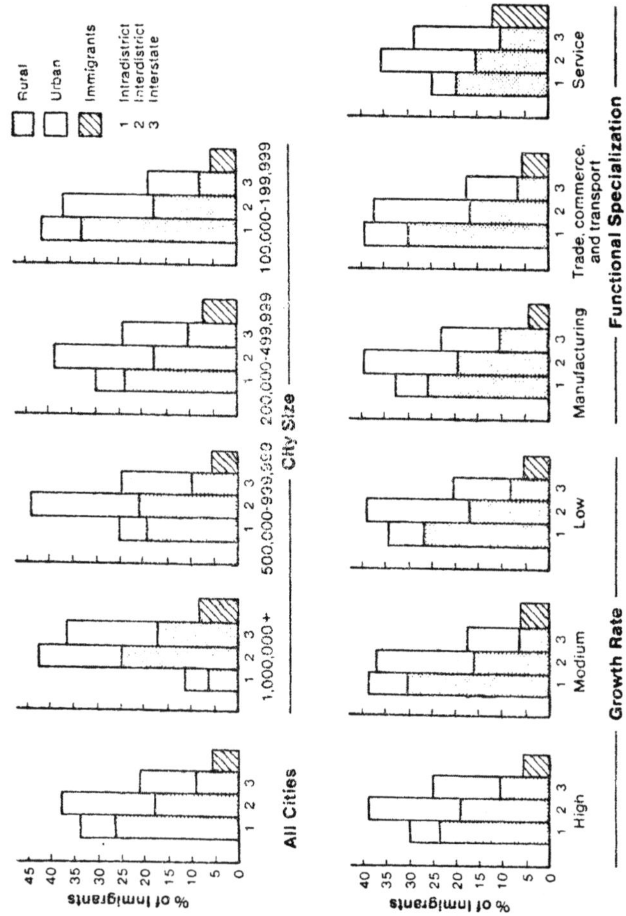

FIGURE 3.2a Distribution of immigrants in different migration streams by city size, growth rate, and functional specialization: India, 1971

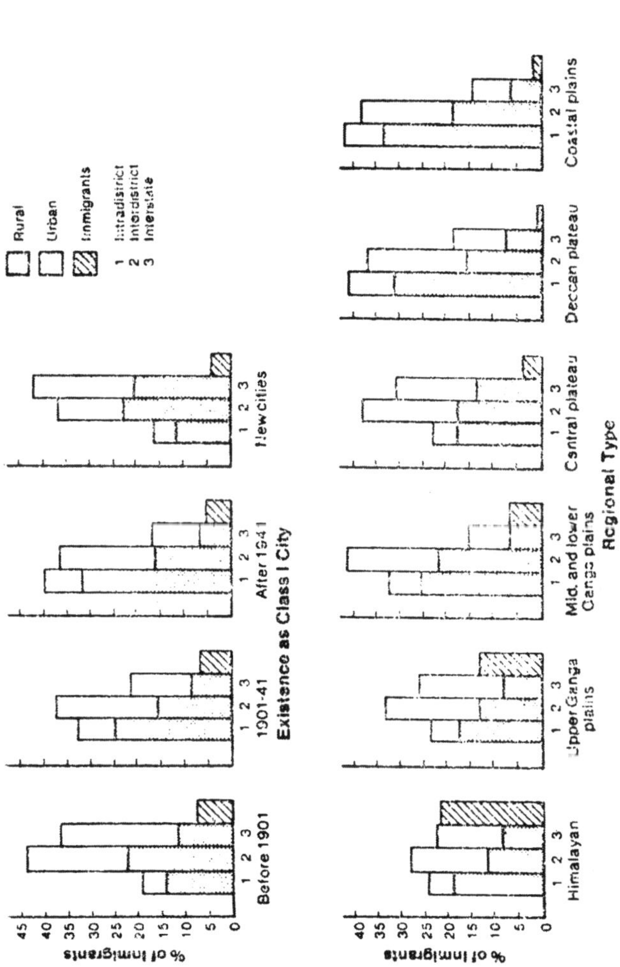

FIGURE 3.2b Distribution of inmigrants in different migration streams by city's existence as a class I city and regional type: India, 1971

TABLE 3.3
Distribution of Immigrants to Cities in Different Migration Streams, 1971

Characteristics of the cities		N	Intra-district		Inter-district		Interstate		Resided in India		Immigrants	Total
			Rural	Urban	Rural	Urban	Rural	Urban	Rural	Urban		
All cities	Total	146	26.48	7.48	17.84	20.45	8.99	12.88	53.31	40.81	5.87	99.99
	Male	146	25.41	7.02	18.57	20.03	9.91	12.95	53.89	40.00	6.11	100.00
	Female	146	27.59	7.95	17.09	20.98	7.88	12.81	52.56	41.74	5.70	100.00
A. *City Size*												
1. 1,000,000+		9	6.36	5.08	25.41	17.75	17.15	19.96	48.92	42.79	8.22	99.93
2. 500,000—999,999		10	19.65	5.51	21.04	23.67	9.42	15.38	50.11	44.56	5.32	99.99
3. 200,000—499,999		54	23.41	6.74	17.44	21.28	10.01	14.02	50.86	42.04	7.11	100.01
4. 100,000—199,999		73	32.17	8.58	16.78	19.73	7.16	10.83	56.11	39.14	4.75	100.00
B. *Growth rates*												
1. High		68	23.63	6.67	19.04	19.85	10.76	14.48	53.43	41.00	5.56	99.99
2. Medium		50	30.16	8.30	16.31	21.11	6.49	11.16	52.96	40.57	6.46	99.99
3. Low		26	26.75	7.98	17.17	21.88	8.80	11.85	52.72	41.71	5.58	100.01
C. *Functional specialization*												
1. Manufacturing		68	25.96	6.87	19.46	20.34	10.41	12.69	55.83	39.90	4.26	99.99
2. Trade & Transport		57	29.63	9.13	16.86	20.67	6.98	10.91	53.47	40.71	5.81	99.99
3. Services		21	19.62	4.94	15.29	20.23	9.80	18.86	44.71	44.03	11.26	100.00

D. *Length of existence as a class I city*											
1. Before 1901	25	14.71	5.04	23.07	21.81	11.50	16.10	49.28	42.95	7.75	99.98
2. Between 1901 & 1951	24	25.31	7.89	15.79	22.22	8.49	13.38	49.62	43.49	6.88	99.99
3. Since 1951	86	31.99	8.49	16.49	20.53	6.78	10.47	55.26	39.49	5.25	100.00
4. New City	10	12.06	4.53	23.08	13.91	20.64	21.57	55.78	40.01	4.20	99.99
E. *Regional type*											
1. Himalayan	6	19.92	5.14	12.34	16.81	8.57	14.76	40.83	36.71	22.45	99.99
2. Upper Ganga plains	24	18.53	6.07	13.90	20.46	8.75	18.15	41.18	44.68	14.15	100.01
3. Mid & lower Ganga plains	20	25.12	6.81	22.69	20.44	7.95	9.08	55.76	36.33	7.92	100.01
4. Central plateau	27	18.98	5.09	18.95	20.26	14.49	17.67	52.42	43.02	4.54	99.98
5. Deccan plateau	35	32.02	9.77	16.22	21.74	8.22	11.18	56.46	42.69	0.85	100.00
6. Coastal plains	34	34.30	8.80	19.54	19.93	6.26	9.03	60.10	37.76	2.13	99.99

The proportion of interstate migrants, particularly from urban areas, is highest in "service" cities, and lowest in "trade and transport" cities, pointing to a greater pull of service cities on long-distance migrants. The reasons associated with the quantum of intra-district, inter-district, and interstate migration to the various cities in India, however, have to be examined in detail.

The proportion of immigrants was highest in cities belonging to the Himalayan region followed by Punjab and upper Ganga plains. The proportion was almost three-fourths (72.2 per cent) in Agartala (capital of Tripura which borders Bangladesh). It was 35.0 per cent in Jullundur; 33.3 per cent in Burdwan; 32.4 per cent in Amritsar; 32.3 per cent in Rohtak; and 32.2 per cent in Calcutta. Most of these immigrants came from Pakistan and present Bangladesh after the partition of the country in 1947.

Current migrants[6] constitute 7.2 per cent of the total migrants to the cities, the proportion being higher among males than females (Table 3.4). There were large variations in this proportion from city to city from a low of only 0.84 per cent in Shahjahanpur (Uttar Pradesh) to a high of 19.5 per cent in Jammu (Jammu & Kashmir) for varying reasons. For instance the high proportion of current migrants (16.4 per cent) in Meerut (Uttar Pradesh) was probably due to the counting of those people as migrants who had come to an annual fair which attracts thousands of shopkeepers and others for three to four weeks from different parts of the country as this fair was being held at the time of 1971 census enumeration.

Proportion of current migrants among the total migrants from other urban areas of the same district was significantly higher than those from rural areas of the district. In contrast, the proportion of current migrants among total migrants from rural areas in the combined inter-district and interstate stream was higher than current migrants from urban areas in this stream implying that the pull of the cities on medium and long

6. Current migrants are those who moved to the city within one year of census enumeration in contrast to lifetime migrants who came to the city at some point during their life and have been living there since then.

TABLE 3.4

Percentage of Current Migrants among all Migrants by Place of Last Residence, 1971

1	2	3	4	5	6	7	8	9	10	11	12	13
Characteristics of the city			Total migrants	Resided in India			Intra-district			Inter-district and interstate		
		N		Total	Rural	Urban	Total	Rural	Urban	Total	Rural	Urban
All Cities :	Total	140	7.24	7.61	7.22	8.29	6.62	6.01	8.34	8.58	9.96	8.39
	Males	140	8.33	8.78	8.40	9.50	7.82	7.22	9.68	9.69	10.06	9.54
	Females	140	6.11	6.41	5.97	7.11	5.54	4.90	7.22	7.37	7.72	7.24
A. *City size*												
1. 1,000,000+		8	5.86	6.06	5.78	6.38	6.44	5.31	8.97	6.66	6.79	6.67
2. 500,000—999,999		10	6.31	6.57	6.11	7.11	4.58	4.24	5.52	7.30	7.74	7.16
3. 200,000—499,999		51	7.61	8.07	7.81	8.59	6.76	6.30	8.12	9.03	9.63	8.76
4. 100,000—199,999		71	7.25	7.59	7.12	8.46	6.83	6.10	8.83	8.60	9.03	8.45
B. *Growth rate*												
1. High		64	7.10	7.45	6.93	8.16	6.88	6.23	8.68	8.16	8.42	8.12
2. Medium		50	7.70	8.08	7.67	8.90	6.38	5.98	7.82	9.65	10.26	9.40
3. Low		24	6.59	7.02	6.96	7.51	6.53	5.52	8.72	7.37	8.10	7.10
C. *Functional specialization*												
1. Manufacturing		65	6.64	6.88	6.49	7.54	5.96	5.34	7.64	7.86	8.39	7.60
2. Trade & Transport		55	7.06	7.34	6.90	8.16	6.98	6.22	9.19	8.19	8.47	8.16
3. Services		20	9.66	10.68	10.50	11.11	7.79	7.56	8.27	11.96	12.82	11.56

1	2	3	4	5	6	7	8	9	10	11	12	13
D.	*Length of existence as class I city*											
	1. Before 1901	24	6.91	7.30	7.10	7.54	5.85	5.35	7.39	8.27	9.03	7.84
	2. Between 1901 & 1951	2ι	7.29	7.89	7.44	8.59	7.19	6.01	9.40	8.47	8.96	8.35
	3. Since 1951	84	7.43	7.78	7.31	8.65	6.61	6.11	8.16	9.01	9.46	8.83
	4. New Cities	10	6.34	6.42	6.46	6.65	7.13	6.40	9.00	6.20	6.34	6.26
E.	*Regional type*											
	1. Himalayan	6	10.72	12.63	11.89	12.63	9.24	9.51	8.59	14.31	14.94	13.48
	2. Upper Ganga plains	24	8.75	9.91	10.42	9.72	7.59	7.33	8.34	10.88	12.67	9.94
	3. Mid & lower Ganga plains	19	3.57	3.73	3.45	4.29	2.87	2.85	3.10	4.32	4.04	4.64
	4. Central plateau	27	7.05	7.22	6.92	7.71	6.12	5.81	7.26	7.76	7.98	7.77
	5. Deccan plateau	35	7.06	7.10	6.34	8.15	7.08	5.41	10.99	7.81	8.68	7.40
	6. Coastal plains	29	8.05	8.17	7.43	9.55	7.73	7.24	9.61	10.10	9.66	10.44

distance migrants from rural areas was greater than on similar urban migrants during 1970-71.

The proportion of current migrants in the million plus cities was somewhat lower than other size categories although the differences are not statistically significant. The proportion of current migrants was higher in cities with medium growth rates instead of cities with high growth rates; it was significantly higher in service cities, and in cities located in the Himalayan region or in Punjab and upper Ganga plains. The cities of the middle and lower Ganga plains had significantly low proportion (3.6 per cent) of current migrants (Figure 3.3 and Table 3.4). These cities had a much smaller proportion of lifetime migrants (Figure 1), and most of them had medium to low growth rates. These facts point toward the stagnation of the cities of this region.

It is noteworthy that whereas the comparatively new cities had the highest proportion of lifetime migrants, the proportion of current migrants among them was the lowest although the difference was not statistically significant. This may probably be because one phase of development of these new cities was over and unless they get new investments, their attractive power would be limited.

Characteristics of the Migrants

After discussing the pattern of immigration to the cities in terms of total lifetime migrants and in different migration streams, and current migrants among total migrants, I shall now analyse some of the important characteristics of the inmigrants. A comparison of the characteristics of the migrants and non-migrants will also be made to the extent data are amenable. The characteristics that will be covered in this paper are sex and age composition of the migrants and the non-migrants, educational attainment, and pattern of employment.

Sex Composition

It is generally believed that urbanward migration in India, particularly to cities and metropolises, is male selective and

TABLE 3.5

Sex Ratio in the Total Population among all Migrants and Current Migrants by Different Characteristics of the Cities, 1971

Characteristics of the cities	N	Total population	All migrants	current migrants
All cities	140	115.6	107.0	145.6
A. City size				
1. 1,000,000+	8	120.8	131.2	148.3
2. 500,000—999,999	10	117.1	110.8	159.9
3. 200,000—499,999	51	117.8	113.6	150.6
4. 100,000—199,999	71	113.2	99.0	139.8
B. Growth rate				
1. High	64	117.5	115.1	142.9
2. Medium	50	114.0	101.6	144.3
3. Low	24	112.9	94.4	151.0
C. Functional specialization				
1. Manufacturing	65	115.4	105.9	147.8
2. Trade & Transport	55	114.0	105.0	138.2
3. Service	20	120.7	116.0	159.1
D. Length of existence as class I city				
1. Prior to 1901	24	118.7	119.7	158.8
2. Between 1901 and 1951	21	113.9	99.8	148.4
3. Since 1951	84	113.4	102.3	141.2
4. New Cities	10	131.3	133.7	150.0
E. Regional type				
1. Himalayan	6	119.7	135.1	180.5
2. Upper Ganga plains	24	119.2	107.2	148.9
3. Mid & lower Ganga plains	19	123.4	106.3	166.0
4. Central plateau	27	119.2	111.4	150.5
5. Deccan plateau	35	111.1	104.0	140.7
6. Coastal plains	29	108.8	101.0	123.8

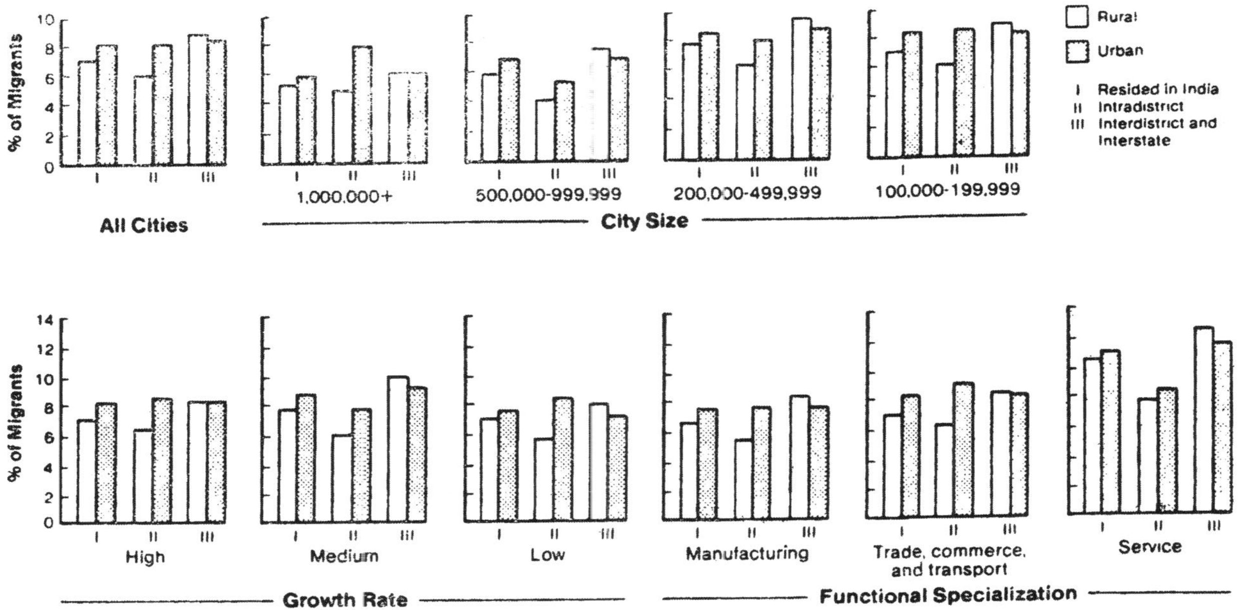

FIGURE 3.3a Percentages of current migrants among all migrants by last residence and by city size, growth rate, and functional specialization: India, 1971

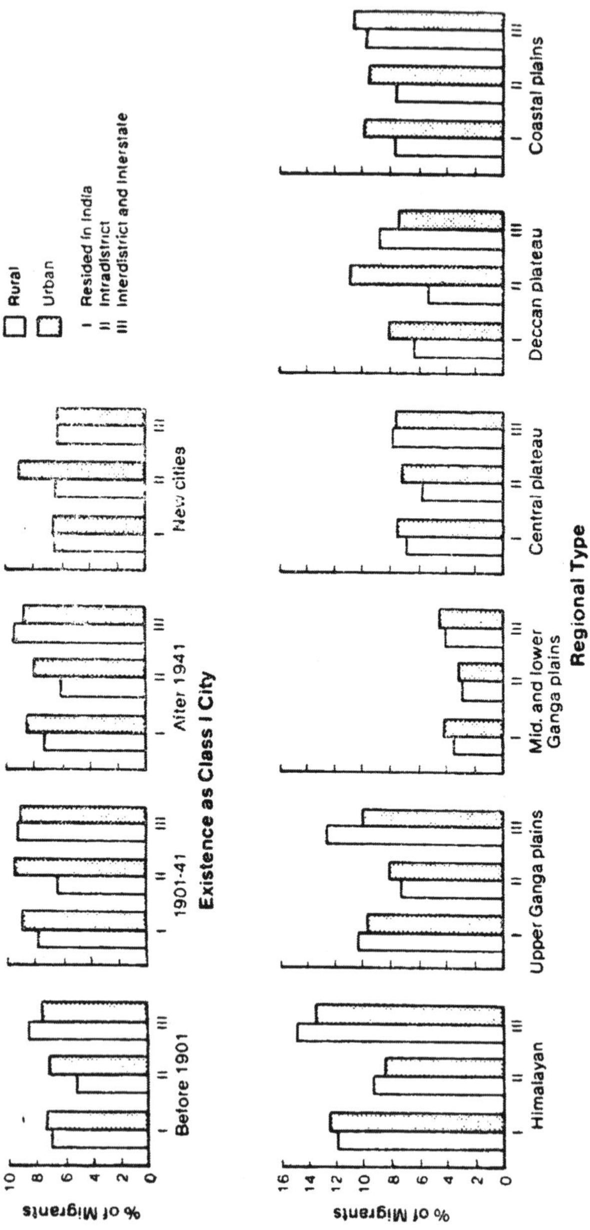

FIGURE 3.3b Percentages of current migrants among all migrants by last residence and by city's existence as a class I city and regional type: India, 1971

leads to an imbalance in the sex ratio (a higher male to female ratio in urban population than in the total). But, the 1971 census data for the 140 cities show that the sex ratio among the lifetime migrants to these was lower than that of the total population, and so lower still as compared to non-migrants (Table 3.5). The sex ratio of the current migrants, however, was higher (145.7) as against 106.9 for all migrants and 121.1 for the non-migrants.

Mitra (1967) had observed that the sex ratio, although above 100, became somewhat favourable to females with increasing duration of residence. Two factors seem to explain the above pattern: (1) the sex ratio of the non-migrant population increases with increasing age up to age group 25-49 indicating marriage related migration of females to the cities, and (2) the sex ratio of the migrants aged 20 and above falls precisely for the same reason the "associational movement of females" (Table 3.5 and Figure 3.4). The opposite trend, which is unfavourable towards the proportion of females, in the sex ratio in young lifetime migrants and all current migrants, is not clear and needs examination.

It is noteworthy that the sex ratios for different age groups were higher for the rural migrants than urban migrants. There was an excess of females over males in all duration intra-district migration but inter-district and interstate migration streams had the excess of males over females. Detailed data including those on causes of migration are, however, required to determine the exact quantum of male and female selectivity in different migration streams and in different age groups.

The sex ratio of the migrants to cities with population 100,000 to 199,999 was 99.0. It was only 94.4 in cities with population growth rate below the national average, pointing to a weak pull of these cities.

Sex ratio in the million plus cities, new cities, or those situated in the Himalayan region was higher than that of their total population but the reverse was true for cities falling in other categories. The high sex ratio in the total and migrant populations of the cities in the Himalayan region is most probably because three out of six have military cantonments. In the new cities, the high sex ratio, seems to have resulted from migration mainly for economic reasons.

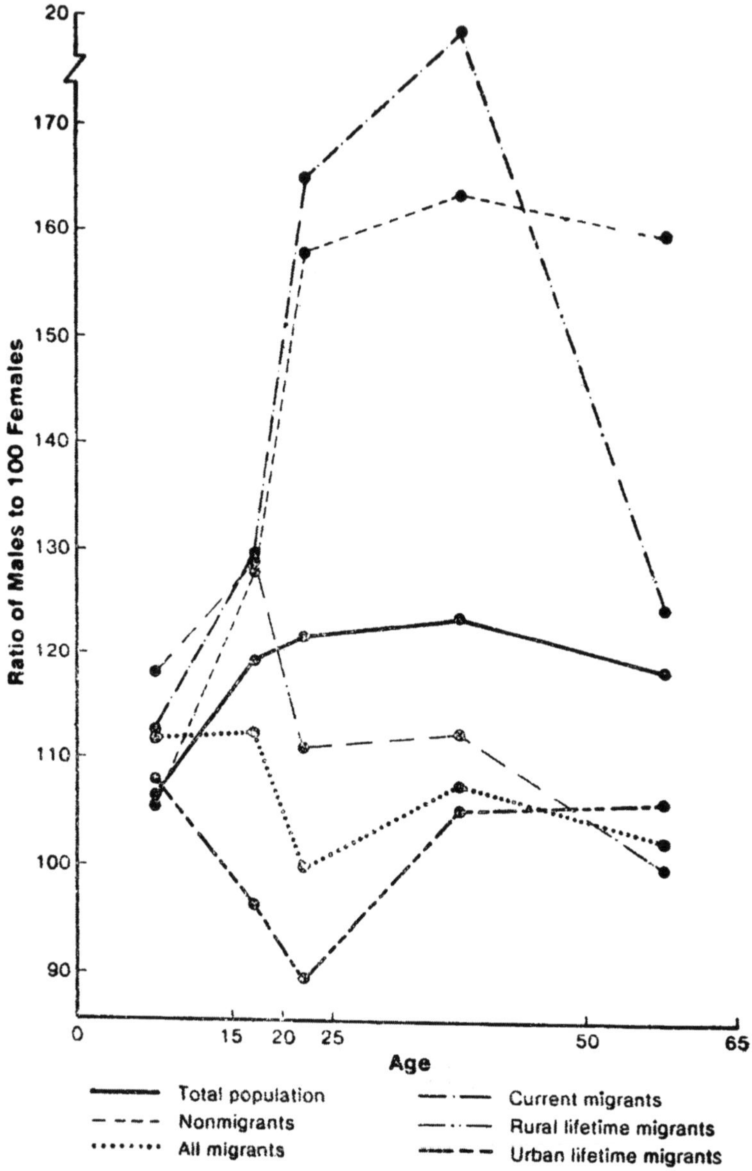

FIGURE 3.4 Sex ratios by age among the total population, nonmigrants, and migrants to cities: India, 1971

TABLE 3.6

Age Distribution of the Total Population, Non-Migrants, and Migrants to the Cities, Migrants being Further Classified by Their Place of Last Residence and by Duration

Sex	Age group	Total population	Non-migrant population	Total migrants		Migrants with last residence in India				Migrants with last residence within the district of enumeration			
						Rural		Urban		Rural		Urban	
				All duration	Current	All duration	Current	All duration	Current	All duration	Current	All duration	Current
Total	0—14	39.47	54.78	17.49	29.61	15.88	27.89	21.50	32.17	16.09	29.84	21.76	35.27
	15—19	10.19	10.52	9.56	14.08	10.07	16.59	9.75	11.29	10.37	15.31	10.34	12.49
	20—24	9.77	7.63	12.79	16.80	13.35	17.53	12.89	16.09	12.45	15.27	12.45	14.67
	25—49	30.28	19.82	45.36	31.86	45.52	30.22	43.35	33.33	44.77	30.55	42.51	30.60
	50+	10.29	7.26	14.80	7.65	15.17	7.78	12.50	7.11	16.33	9.03	12.93	6.97
	Total	100.00	100.01	100.00	100.00	99.99	100.01	99.99	99.99	100.01	100.00	99.99	100.00
Males	0—14	38.11	51.50	18.12	26.64	16.54	25.05	22.41	29.40	17.61	26.78	23.62	32.74
	15—19	10.34	10.68	9.75	12.84	10.69	15.61	9.42	9.59	11.04	14.15	9.74	10.27
	20—24	9.99	8.38	12.31	16.98	13.16	18.18	11.87	15.55	12.05	16.27	11.38	13.79
	25—49	31.17	21.71	45.24	36.42	45.13	34.27	43.52	38.63	43.73	34.56	41.99	36.12
	50+	10.38	7.73	14.58	7.12	14.48	6.88	12.79	6.84	15.57	8.24	13.27	7.07
	Total	99.99	100.00	100.00	100.00	100.00	99.99	100.01	100.01	100.00	100.00	100.00	99.99

Females 0—14	41.14	58.89	17.09	34.58	15.47	33.26	20.94	36.56	14.88	35.50	20.27	37.19
15—19	10.00	10.31	9.36	15.34	9.42	17.29	10.09	13.42	9.70	16.86	10.86	16.02
20—24	9.51	6.70	13.25	16.28	13.49	15.94	13.84	16.68	12.74	13.46	13.34	15.58
25—49	29.18	17.47	45.24	25.49	45.68	24.58	42.89	25.79	45.64	24.33	42.84	24.23
50+	10.17	6.63	15.05	8.31	15.94	8.92	12.24	7.54	17.04	9.84	12.69	6.98
Total	100.00	100.00	99.99	100.00	100.00	99.99	100.00	99.99	100.00	99.99	100.00	100.00

Age Distribution of the Migrants

Table 3.6 gives the mean proportions of the total population, non-migrants, and migrants in different age groups. The age distribution of the total population of class I cities seems to conform largely with the age distribution of country's total population. The proportion of male children (below 15) is somewhat lower than that of females; consequently males are proportionately more in the age group 25-49 than females. Among the non-migrants, children below the age of 15 form more than half the total population; it being almost three-fifths in the case of females. There can be three separate reasons for the above pattern: (1) After marriage, females shift to their husbands' home which, for a large majority, is located at a different place. Thus, a very substantial proportion of women above the age of 20 become out-migrants. (2) Although cities attract migrants from far and wide, they also send their people to other cities (turn-round migration), small urban areas, and even to rural areas; this reduces the proportion of young workers in the non-migrant population. (3) New cities having a comparatively high proportion of migrant population have very little of original residents above the age of 20, but children born to the migrants over the years are non-migrants and this raises the proportion of 0-14 years old among the non-migrants population. In contrast, there being limited family migration, the proportion of children below 15 among the migrants remains quite small (col. 5 of Table 3.6). Moreover, in case of family migration, children who were below 15 at the time of migration, many of them would have crossed the age of 15 by the time of the census. This aspect becomes clear from col. 6 which gives the age distribution of the current migrants, the figure for 0-14 age group being much higher for them than "all duration" migrants.

Young migrants (below the age of 15) to cities from urban areas constitute a significantly higher proportion than those from rural areas probably owing to higher family, migration from them. This tendency seems to be more prevalent among intra-district (or short distance) migrants.

Literacy and Educational Attainment

Various surveys conducted in India and in other countries have established that the migrants possess higher educational qualifications than others staying back in the places of origin, but somewhat lower qualifications than the non-migrants at destinations. This section presents a comparison of (1) literacy rate[7] of non-migrants and migrants by migration streams and by characteristics of the cities, and (2) educational attainment of the migrants, migrant workers, and of non-migrant workers.

(1) *Literacy Rates*

Table 3.7 gives the literacy rates of non-migrants and migrants by characteristics of the cities, migrants being further classified by various migration streams. The rates of the migrants are much higher than those of others remaining behind probably because of the variations in the age composition of the two sub-populations. The difference is much greater in the case of males than that of females. Literacy rates of intra-district migrants are consistently lower than of inter-district or interstate migrants in all categories of cities. This probably implies that illiterate migrants travel short distances because (a) they are generally poor and do not possess enough resources to go to far-off places, and (b) they do not get as much reliable information about job opportunities at distant places as those whose are literate.

Further, the literacy rates of migrant workers to million plus cities are higher than the average for migrants to all categories of cities, which is quite understandable. It is, however, noteworthy that the literacy rates of female migrant workers to large cities are lower than the average for all female migrants. This means that most literate or educated females

7. The definition of literacy in the Indian Census is "ability to read and write simple letters in any language with understanding". The literacy rate is computed by taking the total population in the denominator as the detailed age composition of the literates and total population of each city is not available.

migrate due to marriage or associational reasons, and not to take up jobs as such.

Although the literacy rate of the total migrants to the million plus cities is higher than migrants to other cities, the difference becomes statistically significant only between the highest and the lowest city-size classes. Similarly, the literacy rate of migrants to "service" cities is significantly higher than migrants to "manufacturing" ones but not from "trade and transport" cities. Further, migrants to the cities of the Indo-Gangetic plains have significantly lower literacy rates than migrants to the cities in the coastal plains.

(2) *Educational Attainment of the Sexes*

Table 3.8 gives the distribution of migrants of each sex in different migration streams by level of educational attainment. As one would expect, the proportion of females with matriculation and higher levels of educational attainment is significantly lower than males in all the migration streams. Further, the proportion of intra-district migrants is consistently lower than inter-district and interstate migrants for all educational levels; the differences, however, become significant only at middle level (VIII grade) education. No differences are observed in the educational attainment of the inter-district and interstate migrants.

Educational Attainment of the Non-Migrant and Migrant Workers

On the basis of certain studies conducted earlier, it was stated that the educational attainment of the migrant workers is generally lower than that of non-migrant workers. I wanted to test this hypothesis on the basis of data for all the 147 cities. However, whereas census data on educational attainment of migrant workers in each city are available even by occupational divisions, no such data are available for the total population of each urban agglomeration/city or for the non-migrant population. Fortunately, these data are available from census publications for the urban population of each district. I therefore selected 17 such districts where the population of the main city constituted more than 85 per cent of the total urban population of the district. I assumed that the urban population of these districts represented the characteristics of the total

TABLE 3.7

Literacy Rates of the Non-Migrants, Migrants—Migrants being Further Classified by Migration Streams—and Migrant Workers by Characteristics of the Cities, 1971

Characteristics of the cities		N	Non-migrants	Total migrants	Migrants with last residence in India: Total	Elsewhere in the district	In other districts of the same state	In other states	Migrant workers
1	2	3	4	5	6	7	8	9	10
All Cities	Total	147	48.23	61.57	61.27	54.25	66.24	66.13	71.81
	Males	147	55.35	74.34	73.89	71.28	76.72	74.35	75.73
	Females	147	39.63	48.46	48.40	38.57	55.22	56.45	41.71
A. *City size*									
1. 1,000,000+		9	54.76	64.31	62.82	57.45	64.83	65.71	72.29
2. 500,000—999,999		10	48.25	62.51	62.06	46.70	66.36	71.52	73.54
3. 200,000—499,999		54	48.75	62.88	62.64	54.22	67.47	67.66	72.50
4. 100,000—199,999		74	47.05	60.15	59.98	55.03	65.50	64.33	71.02
B. *Growth rate*									
1. High		68	49.00	62.68	62.42	56.61	66.75	64.71	71.77
2. Medium		51	47.65	61.14	60.73	51.86	66.24	68.06	71.68
3. Low		26	48.11	60.13	59,95	54.06	65.13	66.42	72.87

1	2	3	4	5	6	7	8	9	10
C.	*Functional specialization*								
	1. Manufacturing	68	48.09	6C.10	59.81	52.97	64.31	65.08	70.58
	2. Trade & Transport	58	48.48	62.31	61.93	56.33	67.36	65.78	72.09
	3. Services	21	48.02	64.28	64.22	52.78	69.74	70.45	75.03
D.	*Length of existence as class I city*								
	1. Before 1901	25	49.91	62.74	61.93	50.28	64.92	68.57	72.74
	2. Between 1901 & 1951	24	49.21	62.57	62.46	53.64	69.13	69.13	73.30
	3. Since 1951	87	48.63	60.90	60.74	56.06	65.73	65.21	71.16
	4. New Cities	10	37.73	61.83	61.33	49.03	65.23	60.94	71.06
E.	*Regional type*								
	1. Himalayan	6	51.30	63.51	63.80	55.52	70.42	69.01	70.37
	2. Upper Ganga plains	24	44.45	58.14	57.70	48.60	60.91	65.09	70.86
	3. Middle & lower Ganga plains	21	43.30	59.07	58.10	47.94	66.59	67.15	71.36
	4. Central plateau	27	46.27	61.01	60.64	49.68	63.84	64.75	71.28
	5. Deccan plateau	35	49.25	61.02	60.97	56.89	66.72	63.44	70.61
	6. Coastal plains	34	53.90	66.20	66.13	63.15	70.16	69.57	74.66

TABLE 3.8

Distribution of Migrants of each Sex by Educational Attainment in Different Migration Streams and of Migrant Workers, 1971

(Percentages)

Migration stream	N	Sex	Level of educational attainment: Illiterate	Literate without formal education	Up to primary level	Above primary but up to middle	Matriculate & diploma holders	Graduate and above	Total
1	2	3	4	5	6	7	8	9	10
Total migrants	147	T	38.43	12.59	15.27	13.03	16.09	4.59	100.00
	147	M	25.66	13.17	15.89	15.28	22.95	7.05	100.00
	147	F	51.54	12.06	14.70	10.75	8.95	2.00	100.00
With last residence	147	T	38.73	12.60	15.13	12.93	15.99	4.62	100.00
in India	147	M	26.11	13.18	15.72	15.11	22.77	7.12	100.01
	147	F	51.60	12.06	14.59	10.74	9.00	2.02	100.01
Last residence else-	144	T	45.75	12.34	14.63	11.66	12.75	2 87	100.00
where in the district	144	M	28.72	13.73	16.20	15.45	20.77	5.12	99.99
of enumeration	144	F	61.43	11.16	13.24	8.19	5.22	0.77	100.01
Last residence in	145	T	33.76	12.78	15.18	13.92	18.38	5.99	100.01
other districts of the	145	M	23.28	12.75	14.71	14.82	25.25	9.22	100.03

1	2	3	4	5	6	7	8	9	10
state	145	F	44.78	12.90	15.71	13.01	11.06	2.54	100.00
Last residence in other	147	T	33.87	13.03	15.75	13.99	18.06	5.30	100.00
states/U.Ts.	147	M	25.65	13.42	16.20	15.02	22.59	7.12	100.00
	147	F	43.55	12.62	15.22	12.59	12.79	3.23	100.00
Migrant workers	147	T	28.19	10.48	15.52	14.42	22.75	8.64	100.00
	147	M	24.27	11.19	16.89	15.52	23.41	8.72	100.00
	147	F	58.29	4.41	4.90	5.44	17.55	9.42	100.01

urban population of the cities which belonged to them and, hence, the difference between the urban population of the district and the migrant population of the city reflected the characteristics of the non-migrants. Among these 17 cities, some are in the million plus category, some fall in the half-a-million to one million range and some are below half-million population in size. They represent different functional specializations and are located in different regions. Table 3.9 gives the distribution of male and female migrant and non-migrant workers by their educational attainment for the 17 cities put together. The data clearly reflect that the proportion of illiterates is significantly higher among the non-migrant male workers than migrant male workers. In contrast the proportions of (1) matriculates and diploma holders, and (2) graduates and above are much higher among the migrant male workers than non-migrants. A similar pattern is observed in the case of female workers. These data clearly establish the superiority in educational attainment of the migrant workers over the non-migrant workers. They also imply that migrants to the cities in India largely come because of better job opportunities and the pull of the cities rather than push from rural areas. It is noteworthy

TABLE 3.9

Educational Attainment of the Migrant and Non-Migrant Workers by Sex (average for 17 cities), 1971

Level of educational attainment	Migrant workers		Non-migrant workers	
	Males	Females	Males	Females
Illiterate	25.03	50.59	33.67	56.59
Literature without formal education	11.29	3.73	12.90	5.09
Up to primary level	14.76	3.95	16.99	4.82
Above primary but upto middle	13.31	5.25	13.85	5.30
Matriculates and diploma holders	25.23	22.21	17.60	17.95
Graduate and above	10.38	14.27	4.99	10.25
Total	100.00	100.00	100.00	100.00

here that the male non-migrant workers in Greater Bombay, Poona, Nagpur, Ahmedabad, and Indore, have somewhat higher levels of educational attainment than their migrant counterparts.

Work Participation Rates of Migrants and Non-Migrants

As male migration to cities is largely for economic reasons, one expects a higher work participation rates from male migrants of all age groups than non-migrants. In contrast, female migration is largely due to marriage or for accompanying the principal bread-winner, their work participation rates are expected to be lower than those of non-migrants. Table 3.10 persents the work participation rates of migrant and non-migrant males and females for the total and for 15-29 and 30-59 age groups respectively. The work participation rates of migrant males are almost double those of non-migrants. Similarly, work participation rates of migrant females are about one-and-a-half times those of non-migrant females. Further, there are variations in the work participation rates according to the characteristics of the cities as well. For example, work participation significantly higher in million plus cities as compared to that of cities in other size categories. It is significantly higher in cities with high growth rates, or in the cities with very long standing (established prior to 1901) or in new cities, and higher in cities of Himalayan region or of Punjab and Upper Ganga plains. In contrast, the work participation rates of non-migrant males do not differ significantly by city size-class, but are significantly lower for cities with high growth rates. They are also low in the "service" cities, or in those which are comparatively new, or in the cities that are situated in the Himalayan region.

Work participation rates of migrant males aged 15-29 are significantly higher than those of non-migrants in this age group but the rates for the age group 30-59 are almost the same since every able-bodied man in this age group is expected to be engaged in some economic activity. It is noteworthy that the participation rate of migrant males aged 15-29 is highest in million plus cities but it is lowest for the non-migrant males, the difference being highly significant. The higher participation of migrants males in this age group is probably due to the fact that (1) most migration is for jobs and very little for educational purposes, and (2) non-migrants continue to pursue higher education and, quite often, wait for jobs commensurate with their educational qualification or fam ily status.

It is interesting to note that whereas the work participation rate of all migrant females is significantly higher than non-migrant females, in contrast, it is significantly higher for non-migrant females in the age-group 30-59, and almost same in the age group 15-29. This anomaly arises probably due to higher participation rate of female migrants below the age of 15 as well as above the age of 60. The reasons for this seem to be both economic and sociological and need careful examination according to different categories of cities.

Industrial Classification of Workers in Total Population, Non-Migrants and Migrants

Industrial classification of the workers reflects the economic structure of the working population. The differences in the placement of non-migrant and migrant workers, particularly when migrants are classified by rural and urban migration streams, indicate the nature of the pulls of city economy, and reflects the extent to which the mix of the two modifies the overall pattern of economic activities. The industrial classification of all workers in class I cities, non-migrant workers, and migrant workers by sex[8] (Table 3.11) indicates that 7.6 per cent of all workers in class I cities are engaged in agricultural and related primary activities. The proportion is significantly higher for non-migrants than migrants and, similarly, for females than males. There is, however, no significant difference in the employment of male and female non-migrant workers in primary activities. The difference between the non-migrant and migrant female is also small and insignificant.

8. Information regarding female migrants is limited to total and with last residence in India by its rural and urban status. Further breakdown by migration streams is not given in Table 3.11 since the number of workers in different industrial categories became too small for a large number of cities and did not provide reliable estimates.

TABLE 3.10

Work Participation Rates of the Migrants and the Non-Migrants of each Sex and in Selected Age Groups by Characteristics of the Cities, 1971

Characteristics of the cities	N	Migrants						Non-migrants					
		Males			Females			Males			Females		
		Total	15-29	30-59	Total	15-29	30-59	Total	15-29	30-59	Total	15-29	30-59
All cities	147	64.17	61.91	93.52	7.88	7.72	11.36	36.13	56.53	92.86	4.81	7.95	14.92
A. *City size*													
1. 1,000,000+	6	72.07	72.39	94.63	7.77	88.0	10.64	34 41	52.93	92.00	4.29	7.22	12.63
2. 500,000—999,999	10	65.99	62.05	92.09	7.20	6.10	10.61	37.75	57.10	93.23	4.41	6.35	13.62
3. 200,000—499,999	54	65.11	63.92	93.88	7.80	8.06	11.12	34.64	56.00	92.59	4.59	8.18	14.12
4. 100,000—199,999	74	62.28	59.15	93.32	8.03	7.64	11.72	37.21	57.27	93.11	5.09	8.09	15.97
B. *Growth rates*													
1. High	68	65.80	65.60	94.27	8.93	8.93	13.01	33.29	56.52	93.04	4.98	8.86	16.58
2. Medium	51	62.78	58.62	93.26	6.71	6.44	9.68	38,27	57.24	93.22	4 56	7.12	13.23
3. Low	26	62.31	57.82	92.40	6.63	6.22	9.30	39.11	55.35	92.33	4.45	6.66	13.01
C. *Functional specialization*													
1. Manufacturing	68	64.95	64.55	93 23	8.48	8.24	12.22	36.10	57.92	92.54	5.27	8.86	16 38
2. Trade and Transport	58	63.45	59.23	93.90	7.55	7 28	11.02	37.41	56.08	93.16	4.80	7.37	14.60
3. Services	21	63.67	60,76	93.44	6,83	7.25	9.49	32.71	53.26	93.05	3.36	6.61	11.09

D. *Length of existence as class I city*													
1. Prior to 1901	25	68.64	67.16	93.38	6.44	6.19	9.13	37.64	56.45	92.62	3.79	6.05	10.88
2. Between 1901 and 1951	24	64.28	60.57	93.14	7.68	7.72	10.43	36.95	55.57	92.67	5.09	7.74	14.06
3. Since 1951	87	62.37	60.00	93.43	8.37	8.12	12.24	36.78	56.95	92.91	5.27	8.49	16.37
4. New Cities	10	68.69	68.08	96.16	7.44	7.85	11.21	24.54	55.42	93.98	2.54	8.54	14.49
E. *Regional type*													
1. Himalayan	6	67.58	64.32	92.26	8.20	7.94	11.47	29.08	43.96	89.11	4.76	7.98	14.97
2. Upper Ganga plains	24	67.09	66.79	93.27	4.47	4.60	6.02	33.88	57.34	92.86	1.88	4.36	7.65
3. Middle & lower Ganga plains	21	63.46	53.05	92.59	4.79	4.24	6.51	38.48	52.86	91.68	2.72	3.88	8.33
4. Central plateau	27	65.38	65 05	94.73	8.05	7.81	11.99	32.77	56.56	93.65	4.16	7.40	16.72
5. Deccan plateau	35	61.22	59.15	93.72	9.35	8.89	14.22	37.93	59.32	93.85	6.42	10.30	18.87
6. Coastal plains	34	64.04	63.86	93.34	10.48	10.75	14.64	38.32	57.54	92.60	7.03	11.02	18.64

There are proportionately more non-migrant workers in the manufacturing sector than migrant workers but the reverse is true with respect to the services sector. "Trade and Commerce" and "Transport, communication and storage" sectors have almost the same proportions of migrant and non-migrant workers. Even in manufacturing cities which are supposed to attract industrial labour from different places, the proportion of non-migrant workers in the "manufacturing" sector is higher (38.7 per cent) than of migrant workers (32.7 per cent). This might mean that the industrial pull to these cities is no longer as great as it is generally believed to be.

As the services sector is a mixed sector involving all professional, technical and related workers on the one hand, and those providing personal services or working as maid servants on the other, it is difficult to say much about the nature of employment of the migrant workers vis-a-vis the non-migrant ones. Mitra et al. (1980: 151) think that the migrants to the cities have little skill education and training and, as such, most of them are absorbed in either low-grade services or in low-grade production processes and indigenous means of transport. This aspect will be analysed here with the help of data on occupational classification of migrant and non-migrant workers.

The industrial classification of migrant workers by rural and urban residence shows a higher proportion of rural migrants in the primary and secondary sector activities, and urban migrants in tertiary activities. The differences, however, are not very large. Further, intra-district migrants were engaged in primary sector activities to a somewhat greater extent than inter-district or interstate migrants. No significant difference is observed in the pattern of employment in the secondary sector activities but the employment of inter-district migrants particularly from urban areas in services is significantly higher than of migrants in other streams; similarly employment of interstate migrants is significantly higher in trade, commerce, transport, communication and the storage sector. This observed pattern, however, needs further probing for possible reasons.

TABLE 3.11

Industrial Classification of Workers of each Sex in the Total Population, among Non-Migrants, and Migrants—Migrants being Further Classified by Different Migration Streams

Sex	Total population or type of migration system	Rural or Urban	Industrial categories of the workers: Agriculture	Mining & quarrying	Manufacturing	Construction	Trade and commerce	Transport & communication	Other services	Total	Broad Industrial categories: Primary	Secondary	Trade and transport	Services
Both	Total population		7.58	0.90	28.56	3.79	19.99	11.75	27.43	100.00	8.48	32.35	31.74	27.43
	Non-migrants		10.61	0.82	31.03	3.91	20.23	10.78	22.62	99.99	11.42	34.94	31.01	22.62
	Migrants	Total	5.29	0.92	24 53	3.36	19.75	12.61	33.55	100.01	6.21	27.90	32.35	33.55
	Residence in India	R	7.35	1.09	25.59	3.89	17.92	12.28	31.87	99.99	8.44	29.48	30.20	31.87
		U	2.42	0.62	23.52	2.91	18.95	13.63	37.96	100.01	3.03	26.43	32.58	37.96
	Elsewhere in the	R	10.86	0.97	24.08	3.64	17.49	11.49	31.47	100.00	11.82	27.72	28.98	31.47
	distt. of enumeration	U	3.94	0.66	23.62	3.16	18.49	12.64	37.48	99.99	4.60	26.78	31.13	37.48
	In other distts. of	R	5.25	0.76	24.87	3.59	17.98	13.04	34.50	99.99	6.01	28.47	31.02	34.50
	the same state	U	2.24	0.48	21.74	2.83	17.33	13.98	41.40	100.00	2.72	24.57	31.32	41.40
	In other states	R	3.04	1 12	25.88	3.39	23.81	12.24	30.52	100.00	4.16	29.27	36.05	30.52
		U	1 88	0.70	25.92	2.66	23.43	13.40	32.01	100.00	2.57	28.59	36.83	32.01

Males	Total population		7.15	0.90	28.74	3.84	21.23	12.62	25.51	100.00	8.05	32.58	33.85	25.51
	Non-migrants		10.42	0.82	31.14	4.04	21.36	11.56	20.65	99.99	11.24	35.18	32.92	20.65
	Migrants	Total	4.55	0.90	24.78	3.35	21.18	13.63	31.63	100.02	5.44	28.13	34.81	31.63
	Resided in India	R	6.27	1.06	25.76	3.80	19.22	13.31	30.59	100.01	7.34	29.55	32.53	30.59
		U	2.18	0.60	23.96	2.98	20.35	14.72	35.21	100.00	2.78	26.94	35.07	35.21
	Elsewhere in the	R	9.23	0.93	24.33	3.65	18.84	12.65	30.36	99.99	10.16	27.98	31.50	30.36
	distt. of enumeration	U	3.30	0.64	23.57	3.21	19.91	13.91	35.46	100.00	3.94	26.78	33.82	35.46
	In other distts. of	R	4.69	0.74	25.14	3.49	19.22	14.05	32.67	100.00	5.43	28.63	33.27	32.67
	the same state	U	2.13	0.46	22.35	2.95	18.64	15.25	38.22	100.00	2.59	25.30	33.89	38.22
	In other states	R	2.73	1.12	26.25	3.31	25.06	12.81	28.72	100.00	3.85	29.56	37.87	28.72
		U	1.69	0.70	26.64	2.70	24.99	14.23	29.05	100.00	2.39	29.34	39.22	29.05
Females	Total population		11.07	0.93	22.16	3.38	8.55	4.02	49.89	100.00	12.00	25.54	12.57	49.89
	Non-migrants		12.45	0.84	24.87	2.69	9.17	3.67	46.31	99.99	13.29	27.56	12.85	46.31
	Migrants	Total	10.67	1.08	18.83	3.58	8.09	4.10	53.65	100.00	11.75	22.41	12.19	53.65
	Resided in India	R	15.07	1.21	20.19	4.90	8.54	4.22	45.86	99.99	16.29	25.09	12.76	45.86
		U	4.30	0.72	16.67	2.33	7.39	3.94	64.66	100.01	5.02	18.99	11.33	64.66

Occupational Classification of Migrant and Non-Migrant Workers.

As the occupational pattern of workers is not available for each city, consideration of the occupational pattern of the urban population of the district has been resorted to as it is taken to represent that of the city in cases where the city's population is more than 85 per cent of district's urban population. Thus the occupational pattern for 17 cities becomes available and, after subtracting the information for migrant workers, the pattern for non-migrant workers has been obtained. These data presented in Table 3.12 by sex clearly indicate that a significantly higher proportion of male and female migrants were engaged in the professions, technical, administrative, executive and managerial types of jobs than non-migrants. The proportion of male migrants was significantly higher than non-migrants in clerical and related occupations also. In contrast, the proportion

TABLE 3.12

Occupational Distribution of Migrant and Non-Migrant Workers of Selected Cities

Occupational division	Migrants		Non-migrants	
	Males	Females	Males	Females
0-2. Professional, technical, administrative, executive managerial and related workers	15.67	37.34	8.53	27.24
3. Clerical related workers	18.44	8.36	13.42	7.50
4. Sales workers	12.23	6.00	15.97	8.25
5. Service workers	12.69	19.47	8.76	23.28
6. Farmers, fishermen, hunters, lumber jacks and related workers	1.05	0.99	1.68	1.31
7-9. Craftsmen, production process workers and labourers not elsewhere classified	36.79	26.88	49.88	31.40
X Workers not classifiable by occupation	3.01	0.98	1.76	1.01

of non-migrants (both males and females) was much higher than migrants in production process activities. A higher proportion of migrant males were found engaged in service activities than non-migrant males but the reverse held good for females.

The data for the 17 cities relating to the educational attainment of migrant and non-migrant workers (Table 3.9) and their occupational placement (Table 3.12) thus contradict the findings of Mitra et al. who say that migrants to the cities have little skill, education and training and, as such, most of them are absorbed in either low grade services or in low grade production process activities and in indigenous means of transport (1980: 151). These data also establish that the migrants to cities come because of their pull and not so much due to the push from rural areas. It is also quite likely that a large proportion of workers in white collar jobs have come to the cities from other cities or non-city urban areas as two-fifths of the migrants to class I cities came from urban areas (Table 3.3) but this can be established only after an analysis of the occupational placement of workers by different migration streams.

CONCLUSION

Analysing the 1971 census data relating to the migrants to cities with a population of 100,000 and over this paper has brought out certain patterns of cityward migration as well as the differentials in the characteristics of the migrants according to the migration streams, the characteristics of the cities, and in comparison to the non-migrants.

Lifetime migrants to class I cities comprised two-fifths of their 1971 population, the proportion of females being slightly higher than males, which negated the view that migration to cities is male selective. The proportion of migrants was comparatively higher in cities with high growth rates, in cities with administrative and service functions, in new cities, or in those which belong to the central plateau or the coastal plains.

Among the inmigrants, rural migrants exceeded the urban

migrants by 12.5 per cent (Table 3.3). In comparison to the population of sending areas, however, urban migration to class I cities seems to be much greater than rural migration.

Rural migrants prefer to go to the nearest city in greater proportion than urban migrants probably because a large proportion of rural migrants are illiterate and the available intervening opportunities hold them as soon as they get them.

Although the male/female sex ratio of the lifetime migrants was lower than that of the total population of the cities, the sex ratio of the current migrants (with duration of residence less than one year) was much higher pointing to male selectivity. Mitra had also observed that "female migration improves over time and is generally at its worst for shorter durations, particularly less than one year and less than five years" (Mitra 1967: 608). To understand the processes more clearly, it is necessary to have an analysis of both in- and out-migration of women.

The literacy rate of the migrants was much higher than non-migrants but this required standardization for differentials in sex and age composition of the two sub-populations which could be done if data on literates and educated persons were available by sex and age.

Illiterate migrants generally travelled short distances as compared with literate and educated migrants. Similarly, the educational attainment of short-distance migrants was comparatively lower than other migrants.

The educational qualifications of migrant workers were found to be much higher than of the non-migrant workers. They were significantly more than those of non-migrants, with matriculation and higher qualifications.

Work participation rates of male migrants were significantly higher than those of non-migrants for all categories of cities. The rates were higher for migrant males aged 15-29 but there was no difference in 30-59 age group. While the work participation rate of migrant females was higher than non-migrant females, the opposite was true for 30-59 age group, while there was no significant difference in the work participation rate of women aged 15-29. It is, therefore, necessary to make a detailed analysis of the socio-economic factors associated with work participation of non-migrant and migrant females.

Occupational classification of the migrant and non-migrant workers for certain selected cities has indicated that the proportions of migrant workers in white-collar jobs—particularly professional, technical, administrative, executive and managerial—is significantly higher than of non-migrant workers. In contrast, non-migrant workers are to be found more in production process activities.

The data for the Indian cities analysed in this paper established that there is a high proportion of urban to urban migration part of which seems to be turn-round migration among the class I cities themselves, the sex-ratio among the lifetime migrants is not higher than the total population of the cities, in fact, it is significantly lower. The educational attainment of the migrants is higher than non-migrants and they are better placed occupation-wise than non-migrants.

The analysis in this paper indicated that migration to cities of the middle and lower Ganga plains was the lowest, the current migration was almost half in comparison to other cities. The level of education of the migrants to the cities of this region was comparatively low and, in many of the cities, the work participation rates of the migrants were also very low.

Some of the cities, particularly those belonging to the Deccan plateau and coastal plains region had high proportions of intra-district (or short distance) migrants. It would be useful to analyse the reasons for this selectivity and relate it with the economy of these cities.

What will be the structure 25 or 50 years hence of the population of those cities which are comparatively new and have a high proportion of migrants now? This question becomes important from the planning point of view to answer the related question: Is it economically more advantageous to construct more and more cities or should efforts be made to improve the economy of the stagnating cities or of the already existing medium and small towns? To my mind, it may be more useful to restructure the economic base of the intermediate cities and medium sized towns so that they become the focal points for achieving balanced regional development.

REFERENCES

Ahmad, Qazi, "Indian Cities : Characteristics and Correlates." Department of Geography, Research Paper No. 102, University of Chicago, Chicago, 1965.

Census of India 1971, Series 1, India, Part II-A (i), *General Population Tables*, Controller of Publications, Delhi, 1975.

Ceneus of India 1981, *Tabulation Plan*, New Delhi : Registrar General and Census Commissioner, India, 1980.

——Series 1, India, Paper 2 of 1981, *Provisional Population Totals : Rural-Urban Distribution*. Registrar General and Census Commissioner, India, New Delhi, 1981.

Duncan, Otis D. and Albert J. Reiss, *Social Characteristics of Urban and Rural Communities 1950*, John Wiley and Sons, New York, 1956.

Harris, C.D., "A functional classification of cities in the U.S.A.", *Geographical Review*, XXXIII, January, 1943.

Lal, Amrit, "Some Characteristics of Indian Cities of Over 100,000 Inhabitants in 1951 with Special Reference to Their Occupational Structure and Functional Specialization". Unpublished Ph.D. dissertation, Department of Geography, Indiana University, 1957.

Mitra, Asok, "Internal migration and urbanisation in India, 1961". In *International Union for The Scientific Study of Population : Contributed Papers*. Sydney Conference, 1967a.

——Internal Migration and Urbanisation, Paper for the meeting of the ECAFE's Expert Working Group on "Problems of Internal Migration and Urbanization", Bangkok, Office of the Registrar General, India (mimeographed), New Delhi, 1967b.

Mitra, Asok, Shekhar Mukherji, and Ranendra Nath Bose, *Indian Cities*. The r Industrial Structure, In-migration and Capital Investment, 1961-71. An ICSSR/JNU Publication (mimeographed), New Delhi, 1980.

Pownall, L.L., "The functions of New Zealand towns". *Annals of The Association of American Geographers*, XLVII, December, 1953.

Srivastava, S.C., *Indian Census in Perspective*. Census of India 1971. Census Centenary Monograph No. 1, Office of the Registrar General India, New Delhi, 1972.

United Nations, Economic and Social Commission for Asia and the Pacific (ESCAP)

——*Report of the Expert Group Meeting on Migration and Human Settlements*. Asian Population Studies Series, No. 38. Bangkok, 1977.

Zachariah K.C., *Migration in Greater Bombay*. Asia Publishing House, Bombay, 1968.

4. *Growth of Metropolitan Cities and their Migrants: A Historical and Demographic Profile*

K. LAXMI NARAYAN

This paper attempts to consider the nature of growth of metropolitan centres in India with special reference to streams of migration (Section I) and analyse the social demographic features of migrants (Section II). An attempt is also made in the concluding section to indicate the social and economic consequences of metropolitan bias in urban development. After describing briefly, the problem of the sheer size of the metropolitan component in urbanization and the contribution that migration has made to its development and change, I consider metropolitan development in its historical context of colonial capitalism—commercial and industrial, and the notion of centre-periphery relations. This political economy framework helps us to understand the nature of metropolitan development and that of the migration streams which contributed to its development. The post-independence phase in the development of metropolitan centres is seen as presenting both contrast and continuity with the colonial phase. With the growing emphasis on industrialization, commerce and administrative functions, the migration streams also underwent a modification. Colonial capitalistic development and centre-periphery relations came to be less significant in this period. However, metropolitan development includes deprivation in the form of unemployment, urban poverty and growth of slums which presents a challenge to the planners.

I

Growth of Metropolises

Phenomenal growth of metropolises (cities having more than a million inhabitants) is a recent phenomenon in the history of India's industrial urbanization. While Calcutta and Bombay emerged as metropolises only in 1901 and 1911 respectively, in 1951 there were five such cities with a population of 11,662,860. In 1981, 26.91 per cent of the urban population of India (156,188,507) lived in the twelve million-plus cities, namely, Calcutta, Bombay, Delhi, Madras, Bangalore, Hyderabad, Ahmedabad, Kanpur, Pune, Nagpur, Lucknow and Jaipur. The total population of these metropolises was 42,022,854. The country is witnessing an unprecedented flow of migrants from the rural to the urban areas, especially to the bigger cities, mainly due to the job opportunities created there in such sectors of the economy as industry, commerce, administration, services, and construction. The total population of all the metropolises in 1971 was 29,558,582 of which the migrants' share was 11,757,395 (39.77 per cent). Let us consider the growth of these twelve metropolitan cities during three periods: pre-colonial, colonial and post-independence.

Even before the establishment of the East India Company some of these cities were flourishing trade and industrial centres, besides being the capitals of princely states. Mention may be made of Delhi, Hyderabad, Ahmedabad, Poona, Lucknow and Jaipur. All these places had attracted a large number of businessmen, bankers, artisans and labourers from various places. Delhi and Ahmedabad, at the peak of their glory, had a population of a quarter to half-a-million.

Delhi, the oldest of all the metropolises, which prospered under the Khiljis and Tughlaqs had a population of about 250,000 during the third quarter of the fourteenth century according to Cunningham (Delhi Administration 1976 : 52). Under the Mughuls Delhi was at the peak of her glory. Abdul Fazl who visited Delhi during Akbar's reign described Delhi as one of the greatest cities of antiquity. During the Mughul period Delhi was well-known for her indigenous crafts like ivory carving, carpet weaving, gold and silver embroidery works, gold and silver ware, copper and brassware and muslin manufacture. It attracted skilful artisans from the countryside (Bopegamage 1957: 53).

Hyderabad, founded in 1589 by Muhammad Kuli, the Kutb Shahi King, outside the city of Golkonda, the capital of Kutb Shahi dynasty, had a military population of more than 40,000 in 1591. It grew into a commercial centre within a short period. Abbe Carre observed in 1672 that this town was full of strangers and merchants and trade was carried on by foreigners and others without any restrictions as to their nationality or particular business. There was such a concourse of every kind of people, merchandise and riches that the place seemed to be the centre of all trade in the East (Fawcett 1947). Till 1687, Hyderabad was the administrative, cultural, commercial and intellectual centre of the kingdom supplanting Golkonda both in size and wealth. The population of the city in the seventeenth century was between 150,000 and 200,C00 according to an estimate of Guenther Haberland. The city's growth was suddenly halted by the annexation of the kingdom by the mughuls in whose possession it remained until the first Nizam proclaimed his independence and made it his capital (Alam 1965 : 5). Again the city grew in power and wealth. There was an increase in commerce, land revenue and building activity. A number of indigenous industries such as handloom weaving, dyeing and printing of clothes, diamond cutting and polishing and the manufacture of steel weapons prospered during the Kutb Shahi period. These goods had an international market (Alam 1965 : 54).

Ahmedabad was founded in 1411 A.D. by Sultan Ahmad Shah of Gujarat to replace the old Hindu capital of Anhilvad. The Sultan invited merchants, weavers and skilled craftsmen to Ahmedabad for making it a flourishing commercial and industrial city. Due to the encouragement given by the king the city grew in wealth and splendour for a hundred years. During the next sixty years, however, Ahmedabad lost its importance with the decline of the Gujarat dynasty as well as Portuguese interference with its trades (Gillion 1968 : 13-14). Ahmedabad has been a textile centre since its foundation. The cloth manufactured in Ahmedabad was sent not only to other parts of India but exported through Cambay the main port, to the Persian Gulf and the Arabian ports, south-east Asia. Fine velvet, silk and gold and silver brocades were exported to the Middle East and Europe and coarse and brightly dyed Ahmedabad cottons were exported to Africa, and South-east Asia. The merchants of Ahmedabad had correspondents in places as far as Constantinople (Commissariat 1931: 28). During the second quarter of the seventeenth century the city started declining and the population of the city which was quarter to half-a-million once decreased to 80,000 in 1817 when the East India Company annexed it. During Maratha rule many financiers and merchants, textile workers, jewellers, painters, inlayers emigrated from Ahmedabad to Surat, Poona, Patna, Banaras, and other flourishing cities in the western districts of Hindostan (Forbes 1913 : 257-8). This led to a contraction in Ahmedabad trade and industry and financial transactions, though they still survived (Gillion 1968 : 33).

Lucknow became an important town during the reign of Akbar mainly due to the emperor's liking for the place (Wright 1907 : 54-55). Its development continued unimpaired during the reign of Jehangir when it was an important and thriving trade centre, a magnum emporium (De-Laet n.d. : 64).

Poona became the official seat of the Maratha empire in 1749 (Grant-Duff 1921). By 1760 Poona had a population of around 40,000 (Gadgil 1952: 11). In 1780 the population of the city was estimated at 1,50,000 (Poona Gazetteer, III : 287) and in 1808 at 1,00,000 (Mckintosh 1836 : 459).

Jaipur was founded by Maharaja Jai Singh, the ruler of Amer, in 1727 and within six or seven years the main portions of the city were completed. Jaipur's growth was rapid due to its administrative and commercial functions. Giridhari's *Bhojanasara* (1739) said that Jaipur with thousands of shops on chopars had become a place of extensive business for traders from many different places (Gode 1946). "Elephants, Arab horses, camels from Kutch, bullocks and buffaloes are being bought and sold. In this beautiful town built by the Rajadhiraj, embroidered cloth from many countries, plain cloth and jewellery are being transacted. Hundies of lakhs and crores of rupees are current here. Thirty-two kinds of weights are all used correctly here" (Gode 1946 : 197-201). Since Jaipur was a Hindu kingdom, it attracted a large number of Hindu and Jain merchants from the neighbouring Muslim kingdoms. There were about six to ten thousand Jain merchants in the city (Roy 1978 : 57). The city was not merely a flourishing market place but also had many industries and handicrafts. The city had thirty-six industries many of which were government owned, meeting the demand for arms, weapons, jewellery, stables for elephants, camels, horses, cows etc. Some of the industries were for the supply of food, pan, medicines, perfumes, etc. (Saha 1967).

The foregoing account of the growth of cities in pre-colonial period shows that they were the political and administrative centres with enormous scope for commercial and non-power based industry to expand on indigenous lines. All these economic activities attracted a lot of labourers and skilled workers. With political stability, these cities would have grown into large centres of trade, commerce and industry. But urban development assumed a completely different character under the colonial rule.

Colonial Period

The British, the Portuguese, the French, the Dutch and the Danish opened several trade centres in various parts of the country. Most of these trade stations were situated on the coastal belt. Spencer (1954) has divided the trade stations into five categories : (i) Portuguese ports (1560 A.D)—Diu, Daman, Bassein, Chaul and Goa; (ii) British trade stations (1700 A.D.)—Bombay, Surat, Madras and Calcutta; (iii) French trade stations (1700 A.D.)—Mahe, Calicut, Karikal, Santhame (Madras), Calcutta and Pondicherry; (iv) Dutch trade stations (1700 A.D.)—Cochin, Pulicat, Madras and Calcutta; (v) Danish trade stations (1700 A.D.)—Tranquebar and Calcutta.

Of these, the three British trade stations namely Calcutta, Bombay and Madras have grown into metropolises due to British initiative. Calcutta was a small village in 1690 when the East India Company bought it for making it a base to trade with the rest of India. A settlement, with a fort around it, was constructed by the British. Due to the encouragement given by the Company, a large number of traders from different parts of the world and India settled in Calcutta (Ghosh et al. 1972: 11). In 1707 the East India Company declared it a separate presidency accountable only to the Directors in London. In 1710, according to Hamilton, the estimated population of Calcutta was 12,000. Calcutta grew very fast afterwards. In the third decade of the eighteenth century its population was about two lakhs (Census of India 1921, City of Calcutta, I). In 1727 the total tonnage of ships which entered and cleared Calcutta port was estimated at 10,000. By the middle of the eighteenth century the settlement around the fort had taken the form of a commercial, administrative, residential and military complex within an area of roughly two hundred and fifty acres (Sinha 1978: 5). Later the Company bought another thirty-eight villages including Howrah across the river which facilitated the suburban development of Calcutta (Lahiri 1978 : 44).

The British acquired the Bombay island from the Portuguese in 1661 and built a township, a castle for housing the factory and the harbour on the island and with the help of mercantile communities who were induced to migrate to Bombay, established trade (Anderson 1856). The population of an ethnically diverse city of Bombay in 1698 was 10,000 according to John Fryer (Fryer 1698 : 68). By mid-eighteenth century Surat was outrivalled by Bombay as an important western seaport (Furber 1965: 46-65). The East India Company's monopoly on Indian trade ended in 1813 and several British and other mercantile companies made connections with Bombay (Spear 1961 : 224).

The East India Company bought Madras, a fishing village, in 1639, established a trading post there and built a fort and named it St. George. Madras became the company's headquarters on the Coromandel coast in 1641. During the period 1693-1749 the Company acquired the surrounding villages and expanded the city around the fort (Imperial Gazetteer XVI : 368). Later it became the headquarters of the newly formed Madras Presidency.

India came under the rule of the East India Company after the Battle of Plassey (1757). During the next hundred years, 1757-1857, the East India Company's political expansion and economic development was tremendous. Growth of cities under the Company's rule was different from that under British rule after 1857. There were three main factors in the development of cities under East India Company. First there were the three port cities of Calcutta, Bombay and Madras. Secondly, there were the inland trade emporia like Ahmedabad and Lucknow. Thirdly, the Company established military camps called cantonments in order to carry out their programme of expansion by annexation of more and more territory as well as to control the princely states. Under the latter may be included Hyderabad, Poona, Kanpur and Bangalore.

The first set of three port cities became important centres. The goods collected from various parts of the country were exported to Europe and the imported European goods were distributed in the hinterland. The places having East India Company's trading stations grew very fast. Calcutta emerged as a great imperial city, only second to London, in the British Empire. In 1807 Lord Valentia hailed it as a 'Second Florence' (Valentia 1971 : 59). Its rise was phenomenal since 1850. Bombay became the administrative capital of the newly formed Bombay Presidency in 1818 after the annexation of the Peshwa territory. Bombay's population in 1846 was 5,66,119. Madras became the headquarters of the newly formed Madras Presidency and emerged as a major port in 1791.

While the port cities were centres of export and import, the Company encouraged inland trading centres as well established some industries. Of these Ahmedabad, Lucknow and Nagpur were important. Ahmedabad came under the rule of the British after the Maratha war in 1817. A number of steps taken by the British government like reduction in duties on imports and exports and abolition of private rights to collect dues on the trade of the city paved the way for the recovery of trade and industries as a result of which Ahmedabad was "in a most flourishing condition and progressing rapidly" in 1839 (Revenue Dept. 1840). Opium trade became its most important activity in which more than 5,000,000 rupees capital was invested as compared to the export trade in cotton which had employed 5,00,000 to 6,00,000 rupees (Fewcett 1854 : 82-88). Improved conditions in Ahmedabad led to extensive immigration of merchants and artisans from the neighbouring districts of Gaikwad dominion into Ahmedabad.

Kanpur became an important trade centre due to natural advantages and stable government during this period. Traders from the neighbouring areas such as Etawa, Farrukhabad, Kanauj, Bilgram, Mirzapur, Kalpi, Hamipur, Fatehpur, Unnao, Lucknow etc. settled in Kanpur to do business in clothes, oil and general provisions. In 1801 Kanpur was made the head-quarters of the district (Nevill 1909 : 268).

Lucknow grew into an important trading centre of the East India Company. English factories were doing a brisk business in sugar, indigo and calico (Foster 1914 and 1915). There was a ready market for Avadh's calico in London, and in 1640 the English East India Company started a factory at Lucknow for the manufacture of calico pieces (Moreland : 127-28). The clothes bleached at Lucknow were exported to other places (Sarwar 1874 : 482-84). Lucknow became the capital of the Oudh dynasty after the decay of the Mughul empire and emerged as a great commercial centre known for lacework, gold and silver embroidery, *chikan*, *kamdani*, zardozi, shoes, haber-dashery, cotton bleaching and dyeing, ivory work, *gota* work, panni, gold and silver warq (leaves) etc. (Lucknow District Gazetteer 1959 : 135). The British annexed territories belonging to the Avadh dynasty on 4th February 1856, and in March 1858, after defeating the Oudh forces the British captured the city.

Nagpur became the capital of the Gond Kingdom in 1702. It attained importance during 1746-1816 under the rule of the Bhonsales. Trade flourished and the weaving industry was promoted.

The third important factor in the growth of cities under the Company was the establishment of cantonment. Kanpur became an important town after 1773 when the British army, which was stationed at Faizabad, was moved to Kanpur for the protection of Oudh dynasty as per the Faizabad Treaty of 1773. After Kanpur became an army camp several leather, textile and food industries were started to meet the demands of the large army. Kanpur, under the East India Company's rule, grew at a faster pace due to the expansion of commercial activities, establishment of administrative offices, law courts, jail etc. Montogomery's Statistical Report of Kanpur published in 1844 had recorded the population of the city and cantonment respectively at 58,821 and 49,975 (Montogomery 1849). During the Mutiny Kanpur was destroyed by the British since it was the centre of Nana Saheb's activities against the British.

Poona, after its occupation by the British in 1817, became the headquarters of a British district as well as the principal cantonment in the Deccan. (Poona Gazetteer III : 421-22). The earliest figures pertaining to the ethnic composition of the population are available for the year 1822. Then the population was composed largely of indigenous Hindus (Marathi speaking) constituting about 85% of the total with 9% immigrant Hindus, and 6% Muslims, other religious communities being very small (Kosambi 1980: 158). Poona was not a large trade industrial centre even though it had sizeable trade. During the eighteenth and early nineteenth centuries it had large and flourishing markets selling local and imported goods from Europe and China (Gadgil 1952, Vol. II : 15-17). Textiles and metalware were the major industrial produce. The production of silver and gold ornaments increased considerably at the beginning of the nineteenth century (Joshi 1971: 57). Poona's prosperity was affected after its occupation by the British for it lost a considerable amount of its population due to emigration after the fall of the Peshwa empire. "Poona may be reckoned to contain about 1,10,000 inhabitants, having lost from a tenth to a fifteenth since the removal of Bajee Row with his Court and Army" (Elphinstone 1838 : 5). It lost its former political, military and economic functions with the conquest of the British and about 10,000 persons of Peshwa's army lost their jobs (Choksey 1948 : 227-28). Trade.and industries suffered due to lack of demand for goods and this state of decline continued for several years (Thornton, IV: 162). In 1851 Poona's population was 73,209 (Census of Poona 1851). About nine per cent of the city's population in 1851 consisted of the immigrants who were largely traders or labourers. The notable immigrant communities were Lingayats from Karnataka, Pardeshis from North India, Gujeratis, Marwaris and Telugu speaking Kamathis. Except the Kamathis and Pardeshis who were skilled labourers, all other communities were traders (Kosambi 1980 : 164-65).

As for Hyderabad, 5,000 British troops came and settled outside the town which came to be known as the Cantonment (Secunderabad) as a result of the Subsidiary Alliance between the Nizam and the East India Company in 1798 which permitted the British East India Company to permanently keep its troops inside the territory of the Nizam. The Cantonment's population rose to 50,000 within seven years. The duty-free market of the cantonment expanded its commerce rapidly which led to a farther rise in population and extension of the Cantonment towards Hyderabad. Another important step taken by the Nizam was to allow the British to construct their Residency which was completed in 1806.

Bangalore became the capital of the Gowda dynasty in 1537 A.D. During Mempe Gowda II's time, Bangalore attracted many outsiders for trade (Venkatarayappa 1957 : 101-2). Hyder Ali and his son Tipu Sultan developed the town. It was occupied by the British army in 1799 after the fall of Tippu Sultan. Bangalore cantonment came to be developed after that.

Post 1857 Period : The British Raj

Great changes started taking place in different fields after the British Crown took over the administration of the country in 1857. During the post 1857 period the administration was consolidated, land settlement acts were passed and new sources of revenue introduced. There was a tremendous growth in the field of communications. The country got the first railway line in the year 1854 and by the end of the nineteenth century all the important places except Jammu and Srinagar were connected by railways. The railways which were started mainly for military reasons helped in economic development. New roads were constructed connecting various parts of the country and postal and telegraph facilities became available. The country was gradually "drawn within the orbit of the capitalistic system" (Roy 1971 : 10).

Due to the above factors drastic changes took place in the urbanization pattern under the colonial economy. Distortions were introduced in the spatial structure of the economy during the colonial period in response to the exploitative requirements of imperialist rule (Raza et al. 1978a). The centrifugal pulls generated by the metropolitan economy through the establishment of the new port towns replaced the centripetal pulls exerted by inter-settlement linkages. The new port towns namely Calcutta, Bombay, Madras and Karachi replaced the old port towns which had evolved over the centuries. Several cities important for their commerce and manufactures which could not compete with the cheap European manufactured goods dumped in India by the British government, decayed. The import of manufactured articles hindered the economic development of the country. The colonial exploitative economy did not allow technological advances in the field of agriculture and the growth of a self-sustaining industrial sector. The decay of indigenous industries and a stagnant agricultural sector forced millions of rural unemployed or underemployed people to go to the big cities which did not have the capacity to absorb them.

Gunder Frank (1967) developed the concept of centre and periphery in the context of analysing economic development of the imperial powers and underdevelopment of the colonial countries. The colonial mode of production was characterized by exploitation of natural and human resources from the colonies and on using the latter as the market for the goods manufactured in their countries. The metropolises of India were part of the imperial political economy.

Moonis Raza and Atiya Habeeb (1976) have given the important characteristics of primate cities that functioned as satellites of the colonial economy which were fundamentally different from the primate cities of the western countries: "While the emergence of the latter reflected the consolidation and integration of the national market, the emergence of the former reflected its fragmentations; while the latter emerged as poles in the national field of centripetal forces, the former became effective instruments for operationalising the centrifugality of the colonial economy; while the latter were autonomous nodes for the diffusion of development impulses, the former were the foci of the exploitative mechanism. They were primates, no doubt, but they were satellitic primates" (Raza and Habeeb 1976 : 185-90).

The satellitic primate, according to Moonis Raza and A. Habeeb (1976) is generally a seaport located outside the system of indigenous urban centres, which grows much faster than the indigenous urban centres mainly due to heavy immigration from the rural hinterland which is continuously denuded of its active working population. The age-sex structures, sex ratios and participation rates in the satellitic primate reflect the bipolar relationship of dysfunctional development in the enclave on the one hand and of the hinterland on the other. The economic base of the satellitic primate is characterised by a weak secondary sector with a strong bias towards ancillary and processing industries and by a marked development of the tertiary sector, having a high incidence of non-productive elements.

Several urban places in India, especially the bigger ones, experienced rapid growth in trade, commerce, transport and industries during the post-1857 period. The three port cities namely Calcutta, Bombay and Madras benefited more than other urban centres due to these factors. In Calcutta the import and export trade grew very fast after 1857. In 1853 the total value of import and export trade for the whole of Bengal had been less than £29 million. But by 1901, in Calcutta alone, it was about £111 million. From 1860 coal mines to the north-west of Calcutta began production; the first modern wet dock in Calcutta went into action in 1884; and the first iron and steel factory in Burnapur-Kulti in West Bengal started producing pig-iron in 1875. After the opening of the Suez Canal in 1870 the manufacturing industries started growing rapidly in Hooghly resulting in the establishment of the first cotton mills in 1817, the first jute mills in 1874, the workshop of Calcutta, a number of engineering industries besides the rope, sugar, flour and indigo factories and distillaries and dockyards. Between 1874 and 1900 a number of jute mills came into being. Calcutta became an important distribution centre of India by the middle of the 19th century and articles carried were mainly cotton, sugar, indigo, salt, grains and pulses (Chatterjee 1976 : 505). It was due to these developments that the population of Calcutta grew from 2,00,000 in 1822 to 4,13,000 in 1850 and 14,88,323 (U.A.) in 1901.

In 1876, 32.50 per cent of Calcutta's population consisted

of permanent residents and the remaining 67.50 per cent consisted of migrants. In 1901 while 45.25 per cent population of Calcutta had been born there, 54.75 per cent had been born elsewhere. (Census of Calcutta 1872-1901). Among the immigrants there were only 279 females to 1,000 males. The majority of the immigrants were temporary settlers who had left their families at home. As a consequence of male migration 44 per cent of the entire population consisted of male adults, which was double the proportion for the whole of Bengal (Imperial Gazetteer of India, IX: 268). The decay of the ancient irrigation system, frequent attacks of malaria in the countryside from which the majority of the population suffered chronically were the two important factors which prompted people from the countryside and towns of Bengal to migrate to Calcutta (Bose 1973 : 257). The second dock at Kidderpore was opened in 1902. In 1903-4, 1,563 vessels (3,174,946 tons) entered and 1,569 vessels (3,175,263 tons) cleared the port (Imp. Gaz. Vol. IX : 271).

In Bombay the first spinning and weaving mill commenced work in 1857 and by 1860 six more mills were added and Bombay was established as the great cotton market of western and central India. In 1882 about 32,000 persons were working in the cotton mills (Imp. Gaz. III: 408). Bombay benefited greatly during the cotton boom which lasted from 1861 to 1865. The profits of the cotton trade were utilized for diverse purposes like building of textile mills, railway construction, construction of public buildings development of the city, establishment of banks, and financial institutions, insurance and joint-stock companies etc. In 1854-55 the whole trade of Bombay was valued at 16 crores and twelve years later (1866-77) it rose to 47 crores. During the period 1876-77 and 1895-96 the total value of imports and exports increased from 61 crores to 105 crores. The total value of the sea-borne trade passing through Bombay in 1903-4 was 123 crores (Imp. Gaz., VIII : 414). The number of vessels which entered and cleared with cargoes from and to foreign countries at the port of Bombay in 1903-4 was 1607 with a tonnage of 2,764,303 (Imp. Gaz. VIII : 45).

There was a phenomenal growth of industries in the second half of the nineteenth century and by 1901 the city had 138 factories employing fifty or more workers and a railway workshop. About one lakh persons were employed in these industries, mainly from Konkan and Satara districts (Bombay City Gazetteer, I : 485). The unprecedented population growth was the result of "swarms of adventurers from all parts of India and abroad" who came to Bombay to do business, and by the "vast numbers of labourers and artisans (who) had flocked from the moffusil in consequence of the demand for and the high prices of labour" (Edwardes 1902 : 297). Several international passenger steamer lines extended their operations to Bombay after the opening of the Suez Canal in 1869 by which the overseas communications of Bombay improved considerably (Edwardes 1902 : 272-73).

In the nineteenth century the major Indian mercantile communities in Bombay were Parsis, Hindus, Jain Banias from Gujerat, Muslim Bohras, Bhatias, Khojas and Mamons from Sind, Sonars and Kasars from Maharashtra. The Brahmins who migrated from different parts of Maharashtra were working as clerks. The two other important communities were Bene Israels and Konkani Muslims (Dobbin 1972 : 2-8). In 1896 an epidemic of bubonic plague broke out in Bombay which took a toll of 1,14,000 between 1896 and 1900 and about 43,000 persons left the city during this period (Census of India 1901, XI, Part 5 : 5-8). In 1901 the city's population had come down to 7,76,006 from 8,21,764 in 1891 mainly due to the plague epidemic and the general economic decline. In 1881 a majority of the city's population consisted of migrants. Only 28% of the city's population were born in Bombay island, 59% in the rest of Bombay presidency, 9% in the rest of India, and 2% outside India (Census of 1881 : 104). The immigrant population was male dominated. There were 143 males per 100 females.

Madras was connected by railway with Arkonam in 1873 and later with other important places of the presidency and with Calcutta, Bombay and West Coast. The British India Company's steamers started sailing periodically from Madras to Calcutta, Bombay, Rangoon and the straits (Shivaramakrishnan 1978 : 12). The construction of a screw-pile pier was completed in 1862 and in 1881 the construction of the harbour was completed. The harbour could hold nearly 3,000 to 7,000 tons. An annual average of 1,200 vessels with a tonnage of 23,91,000 entered and cleared the port in cargo or in ballast (Imp. Gaz. XVI : 376-77). During the period 1874-1883 Buckingham and Carnatic and two other mills were established. Together they employed 7,000 persons. At the beginning of the twentieth century Madras ranked fifth among the ports of India in the value of trade and fourth in the tonnage of vessels. In 1900, the city had 97 tanning industries, nine iron foundries and four cigarette factories. The city's population in 1901 was 5,94,396 (Imp. Gaz., XVI : 375-76).

Delhi was one of the worst affected places during the Great Revolt of 1857. In that 3,837 British soldiers lost their lives and about 26,000 persons were killed by soldiers (Delhi Gazetteer : 91). A considerable number of inhabitants were expelled from the city and the population of the city which was about 1,60,000 in 1847 diminished by over 20,000 (Bopegamage 1957: 12). Soon after the events of 1857 the British Government took over the reins of the country and the capital was shifted from Delhi to Calcutta and Delhi was relegated to a secondary position until 1912 when it again became the imperial capital. During the period 1870 to 1890 three engineering works and two cotton spinning and weaving mills were installed and Delhi soon became one of the biggest and most flourishing commercial centres in northern India. Modern industries made great progress in Delhi during the last quarter of the nineteenth century and in 1904 Delhi had 22 industries in which 3,460 persons were working.

In Bangalore, the Bangalore Woollen, Cotton and Silk Mills was the first large scale industry to be started in 1884 and in 1901 Bangalore had a spinning mill, textile mill, a locomotive workshop and a few other industries (Imp. Gaz. VI : 369).

In Hyderabad, political stability as a result of the emergence of the British East India Company in the early nineteenth century led to the growth of commerce and encouraged immigration during the last quarter of the nineteenth century. Hyderabad was connected with Bombay, Madras and many places of Hyderabad state which helped the growth of trade and industries. The population of Hyderabad in 1881 was 3,67,417. During this period a railway workshop and four factories sprang up.

Ahmedabad was connected with Bombay by railway in 1864, and soon, with other places in the north and west as well, as a result of which it became the largest trade centre in Gujarat and a major entrepot for the distribution of imported goods. The introduction of railways severely affected the handloom production due to competition from the mills of Bombay. Likewise, the paper and calico industries suffered due to competition from the European countries and China and so did the opium trade (Gillion 1968 : 70-71). In 1861, the first textile mill came into being and eight more textile mills were started during the next thirty years. By 1920, the city had 51 cotton mills employing 43,515 workers. The population of the city which was 1,16,873 in 1872 rose to 1,81,774 in 1901.

Kanpur, in 1863, was connected by railway with Calcutta and soon rail links with Lucknow and Bombay were established. When the demand for cotton arose during the American Civil War, it was found easiest to send it from Bundelkhand to the railway at 'Cawnpore' (Imp. Gaz. IX : 1908). By the end of the 19th century most of the important places in India were connected with Kanpur by railway network and in the first quarter of the present century several branch lines were added and the rail tentacles spread. The Grand Trunk Road connecting Calcutta with Delhi passed through Kanpur. Trade and commerce prospered. A number of large leather and cotton industries were started to meet the needs of the British army. The first cotton mills, the Elgin Cotton Spinning and Weaving Co., came into existence in 1869. During the next twenty years three other mills namely the Muir Mills (1875), The Cotton Mills Ltd. (1882) and the Victoria Mills (1887) were opened. In 1903-4, 6,395 persons were working in these mills. Soon after the Elgin Mills commenced its operations, a Government Harness and Saddlery Factory (leather tanning) was opened which, in 1901, employed 2,500 hands. The Army Boot and Equipment Factory employed 3,000 persons. In 1903 the three large tanneries employed 4,915 persons. A woollen mill, started in 1876, employed 1,500 hands. Kanpur also had a sugar mill, a jute mill, seven cotton ginning and pressing mills, a tent factory, two flour mills, a brush and cabinet making factory, two iron foundries, a tape factory and chemical works. The total capital invested in the manufacturing industries was about one million sterling (Imp. Gaz., IX). In 1901 Kanpur had forty registered industries employing 22,857 workers (Singh Harihar 1972 : 86). The Unnao Sugar Works, the Ganges Flour Mills, the Kanpur Electric Supply and Traction Company were established in 1906. The Swadeshi Cotton Mills was started in 1911 followed by several oil, flour, spinning and ginning mills (Singh Harihar 1972: 87). The population of Kanpur, however, declined from 2,02,797 in 1901 to 1,78,557 in 1911 due to the outbreak of plague and cholera resulting in the exodus of a large number of people from the city.

The resurgence and expansion of Poona started after mid-nineteenth century due to the revival of trade now that it was connected by rail and road with Bombay, growth of the British sections of the city, and of educational institutions. In the 1880s the city had about five hundred cotton handlooms and 800 silk handlooms due to a greater demand for silks. The majority of cotton weavers were Hindus, Koshtis and Salis, immigrants from the famous cotton centres in the region. The rest were Muslims, also immigrants. A large majority of the looms were owned by immigrant Muslims (Kosambi 1980 : 211). The brass and copper industry which grew mainly after 1860, supported 70 dealers and, 2,320 workers in 1883 and the gold and silver ornaments industry engaged over 600 craftsmen (Gadgil 1952 : 124-96). During the years 1885 to 1920 the development of Poona received a setback however, due to epidemics such as plague and influenza. The population of the city in 1901 was 1,11,381. About 87% of the city's population consisted of Hindus, 10% of Muslims, 2% of Jews, Parsis and Christians. During the first decade of this century several important factories had come up in the city and its vicinity, chief among them being the gun-carriage factory and arsenal in the cantonment and the small arms and ammunition factories at Kirkee. In addition, there were two cotton mills, some iron and brass foundries and a paper mill (Imp. Gaz. XX : 185).

Nagpur became the capital of the Central Provinces in 1861. The opening of a series of railway such as Great Indian Peninsular Railway (1867) and the Chanda line (1913) connected the city with Bombay, Calcutta, Chanda, Hyderabad, Madras, etc. which facilitated reestablishment of several entrepots

(Kashyap 1961). The first large-scale industry, The Empress Mills, was opened in 1877. In 1901, the cotton market was established near the mills. In 1892 the Swadeshi Spinning and Weaving Mills was opened. In addition to these mills twelve cotton ginning and pressing mills were working during the first decade of this century. About 5,000 persons were employed in the cotton weaving industry. Nagpur's population grew from 82,000 in 1864 to 1.27 lakhs in 1901 and like Poona, it decreased to one lakh in 1911 due to epidemics.

Lucknow was captured by the British in 1858 after the defeat of the Oudh forces and was made the capital of Avadh Province. In January 1877 the Province of Avadh was amalgamated with the neighbouring province of Agra and the capital of the combined province was shifted to Allahabad. Even after the British conquest, Lucknow continued as a prosperous commercial city, as it was before. The wealthiest bankers in India had either their headquarters or a branch of their firms in Lucknow and their business had extended throughout the country and in Europe (Lucknow Gazetteer 1959 : 134). The Lucknow's industries, however, found it impossible to compete with the cheaper British and foreign commodities that started pouring into the market and started decaying (Lucknow Gazetteer 1959 : 147). But it continued as the distributing centre for the goods imported into Avadh due to its location on the main trade routes. The city, in 1869, had 797 moneylenders (Lucknow Gazetteer 1959 : 154). After the reoccupation of Lucknow it was connected with many places by road. Between 1867 and 1893 it was connected by railway with Kanpur, Faizabad, Bareilly, Saharanpur, Moghul Sarai, Bombay, Calcutta, etc. The second half of the nineteenth century witnessed the establishment of large-scale industries on European lines. The city had a number of large-scale industries, namely, Lucknow Distillery (1855), The Upper India Couper Paper Mills Ltd. (1879), two railway workshops, four large printing presses, an iron foundry, a rice mill and a flour mill, etc., employing about 5,296 persons in 1903. The population of Lucknow which was 2,84,779, decreased to 2,64,049 in 1901. The decrease was mainly due to the transfer of the capital from Lucknow to Allahabad and a lessening of the commercial activities of the city.

Jaipur which had been affected by the plundering of the countryside by the large bands of Marathas and Pindaris, prospered during the period 1835-80. Its ruler, Ram Singh II modernized the city considerably and made it a cultural centre. Jaipur not only got modern water works, a gas plant for lighting, proper city roads and hospitals, but also schools and colleges, a public library, museums and gardens, during the latter half of the nineteenth century. Its remarkable economic prosperity showed in an increase in population. In 1871 the population of the city was 1,37,887 (Report 1871: 84-85). Banking and jewellery and cutting of precious stones were the important trades of this period (Roy 1978).

The reign of Madho Singh III, Ram Singh's successor (1880-1922) was a period of stagnation and decay for the city. The famine of 1899-1900 together with the plague which was prevalent during 1901-21 and the great influenza epidemic of 1918 took several thousands of lives. The outbreak of cholera in 1900 took a toll of 13,874 lives (Imp. Gaz. XIII : 401). The population of Jaipur which was 1,42,578 in 1881 came down to 1,20,207 in 1921.

The earliest figures pertaining to the urban population of India are available for the year 1881. In that year the total population of the country was 20,34,15,000 and the percentage of population of the country living in urban areas was 9.3 rising to 10.00 in 1901. The famine of 1900 in several parts of India drove many persons from rural areas to the towns and cities, while the ravages of plague around 1911 brought about an exodus of urban population to the rural areas. This contributed largely to the slow growth of urbanization during 1901-11.

The First World War came as a boon to Indian industries. The demand for Indian manufactured goods outside and non-availability of imported industrial goods were of great help for the rapid growth of Indian industries. Not merely did those cities, which came into being during the British period, grow rapidly, but also many new towns and cities were affected by the new wave of industrialization and new means of transportation. Present-day industrial metropolises were the greatest beneficiaries.

With the decade 1921-31 urbanization became a noticeable

phenomenon in India, and the rate of urban growth has accelerated with each decade since then. The percentage of urban population which was 11.38 in 1921 in India (boundaries of 1948) rose to 12.13 in 1931, 13.91 in 1941 and 17.34 in 1951 (Hoselitz 1962 : 158). During the period there was no addition of metropolises.

The Second World War further accentuated industrialization and urbanization. Many industries did brisk business during the war period due to unprecedented demand for goods from the inland and foreign markets. The rapid industrialization lead to mass migration of people from the rural areas to the cities to work in the secondary and tertiary sectors.

The decade 1941-51 witnessed the highest increase of urban population, i.e., 41.1% which was faster than that experienced by Japan and about two-thirds as fast as that in the U.S.A. with roughly the same level of economic development. The partition of India in 1947 brought the mass migration of displaced persons which had a phenomenal impact on India's urban growth. The migrants from Pakistan settled mostly in urban areas and were far more in number than the urban migrants from India to Pakistan (Bogue 1962). In the first fifty years of this century the population of India in the cities of one lakh, and more, population increased almost fivefold, and that in the sixty-five years from 1890 to 1955 this population in the territory of the former British India increased more than sixfold (Hoselitz 1962 : 163). Delhi, Madras and Hyderabad became metropolises in the Census of 1951.

Calcutta felt the impact of the demand created by the First World War for jute and steel goods besides machinery for bigger industries which was further accentuated during the Second World War. The growth of industries in Bombay was phenomenal between the two world wars and in 1941 Greater Bombay had 1,078 registered factories employing 3,14,045 workers (Bombay Metropolitan Regional Planning Board 1974 : 40). In Delhi, a new township known as New Delhi, the new capital of India, was completed in 1930 to house the administrative offices and accommodate about half-a-lakh persons. In 1923, the city had 56 registered industries in which 9,945 persons were working (Delhi Gazetteer 1976 : 312). World War II accelerated the growth of industries. During the three years period from 1939 to 1942 the number of industries increased from 111 in 1939 to 222 in 1942 with a corresponding increase in the number of persons employed from 17,400 to 36,870. Among the industries which developed during this period the leather goods industry leads, followed by metal industries, rubber goods, food and drinks and machinery (Sundaram 1978 : 123).

Bangalore, in the mid-twenties, had 46 large industrial establishments employing 8,348 workers. Of them 4,792 were working in three textile mills (Rao Hayavadana 1930 : 57-60). In 1931 the city's population was 3,06,470, of which, 1,05,212 were immigrants. Due to the encouragement given by the princely state of Mysore the city attracted many industries, and by 1951, the city had 283 industrial units employing 45,878 workers (Mahadev 1978 : 26). The noteworthy industries started during this period were Hindustan Aircraft Ltd. (1940), now known as Hindustan Aeronautics Ltd., the Minerva Mills (1919) and the Govt. Electric Factory (1934).

In Hyderabad a number of large and medium industries came up during this period to meet wartime needs. There was a spurt in the growth of medium and small-scale industries making items such as cigarettes, humepipes, edible oil, buttons as well as a distillery and an iron foundry. During the forties Praga Tools Corporation, the Bren-Gun factory (now the Allwyn Metal Works) and the Hyderabad Asbestos Cement Products were set up. The Second World War came as a boon for industrial growth. The growth of industries, however, adversely affected the handicraft sector. The number of cottage industries decreased from 8,137 in 1931 to 1,083 in 1941. The population of the city decreased from 5,02,106 in 1911 to 4,05,630 in 1921 due to the outbreak of cholera and plague epidemics which took a heavy toll of life and caused large-scale out-migration. The population of the city rose to 4,66,894 in 1931.

Ahmedabad in 1920 had 51 cotton mills employing 43,515 workers. In 1930, the city had 64 mills (Jain 1978 : 21). The growth of textile mills in Ahmedabad and Bombay ruined the market for handloom products and led to rural impoverishment and migration of the unemployed handloom weavers and landless labourers to Ahmedabad to work in the newly started textile mills. Most of the mill workers brought their families to the city (Ahmedabad Mill Owners' Association's Report 1929-30). The city's higher sex ratio of 765 as compared to Bombay's 525 in 1921 supports this statement. Of the cotton mill workers in 1926 only 20 per cent were born in the city, 25 per cent elsewhere in Ahmedabad district, 20 per cent in Baroda, 10 per cent in Rajputana, 5 per cent in Kathiawar, 10 per cent elsewhere in Gujarat, 5 per cent in the Deccan and Konkan, and 5 per cent elsewhere (Govt. of Bombay 1929 : 1-7). Large-scale industrialization and mass migration of people to Ahmedabad resulted in the growth of the city's population. The population of the city in 1921 was 2,74,007. The First World War was a boon to Ahmedabad's textile industry and city emerged economically stronger after the war (Gillion 1968 : 154). The growth of trade and industries continued even after the First World War.

In Kanpur the period, 1915-47, is characterized by the development of medium and small scale industries. The two world wars provided great impetus for the growth of these industries (Singh Harihar 1972 : 87). During the period 1911-21 there was an appreciable increase in the number of industries and industrial workers. There was a slow growth of industries during the post-war period. Depression came to an end in the early thirties and a number of factories mostly belonging to the J.K. group were started. J.K. Jute Mills (1931), M.P. Sugar Mills (1932), J.K. Cotton Manufacturing (1933), J.K. Iron and Steel Co. Ltd. (1934), and M.D. Jute Mills (1936) were set up. The decade 1931-41 witnessed unprecedented growth of industries and population and migration of people from the rural areas to Kanpur in search of employment due to a fall in agricultural prices. The declaration of the Second World War in 1939 and the consequent demand for industrial products led to fast growth of industries. In 1943 Kanpur had 165 industries employing 1,02,726 workers (Singh Harihar 1972 : 86). The population of the city which was 2,43,755 in 1931 rose to 4,87,324 in 1941. During the Second World War there was a huge influx of people from the rural areas. The post-war period brought in its wake retrenchment, unemployment and chronic labour problems.

Poona's population rose due to the intallation of the defence industries near Poona during the Second World War while Nagpur and its surrounding areas had twelve registered industries in 1925 and by 1947 there were 53 registered factories. These were mainly forest-based and engineering industries. Meanwhile Nagpur became famous for its orange trade. The population of the city rose from 1,01,415 in 1911 to 3,01,957 in 1941. Nagpur University was started in 1943.

Lucknow became the capital of the United Provinces in 1922 (Mukerjee and Singh 1961 : 1). Lucknow University was established in 1920. Its population was 2,74,659 in 1931. In Jaipur, after the Second World War, three engineering units and one textile mill came into existence.

The foregoing account of the process of urbanization under the British raj shows that the metropolises of colonial India served to export raw materials to Britain and to import manufactured goods. Development of transport and communication connected different centres of trade and commerce and made exploitation of resources easier for the British administration. Thirdly, when the World Wars broke and movement of goods became difficult, incipient industries (mainly textiles) were encouraged to develop, which consequently attracted more and more immigrants. There was the need to train English educated youth to fill up various ranks of administrative cadre, and this resulted in the development of schools, colleges and universities. Thus the development of metropolitan centres in India was closely linked with British political economy.

The character of Indian cities, however, underwent a significant change with the attainment of Independence when they started serving national interests. Tne following section describes the development of metropolitan cities in the post-Independence period.

Post-Independence Period

The post-Independence period was marked by a huge influx of refugees from Pakistan into the metropolises and other large cities, rapid industrialization, growth of trade and commerce, educational research and medical facilities and administrative machinery, the green revolution in certain pockets, growth of industrial, educational, administrative and recreational townships in various parts of the country. All these factors led to rapid urbanization. The successive Five Year Plans aided the development of industries in the country. Industries started concentrating mainly in big cities and rarely in the towns and rural areas because of the presence of infrastructural facilities. The class I cities attracted large number of industrial establishments and their growth during the post-Independence period was unprecedented. "It is an established fact that outside the natural resources development areas most of the industrial development in the country has taken place in and around large cities of India such as Bombay, Calcutta, Delhi, Madras, Hyderabad, Bangalore, Ahmedabad, Poona, Lucknow, Kanpur and Jaipur. These eleven cities have more than 40 per cent of the urban industrial workers in the country and have over 50 per cent of the workers in the tertiary sectors. This is further substantiated by the fact that the four national metropolises (Bombay, Calcutta, Delhi and Madras) receive over 60 per cent of the bank credits while their contribution to bank deposits hardly exceed 40 per cent. It is in these cities that the national educational and research centres and over 90 per cent of the highly paid jobs are concentrated" (Alam 1982 : 3).

India had 12 million-plus cities in 1981 namely Calcutta (9,165,650), Greater Bombay (8,227,332), Delhi Urban Area (U.A.) (5,713,581), Madras U.A. (4,276,635), Bangalore U.A. (2,913,537), Hyderabad U.A. (2,528,198), Ahmedabad U.A. (2,515,195), Kanpur U.A. (1,688,242), Poona U.A. (1,685,300), Nagpur U.A. (1,297,977), Lucknow U.A. (1,006,538) and Jaipur U.A. (1,004,669). Except Kanpur, Poona and Nagpur most of the other metropolises are also the administrative capitals of different states.

After partition, till 1970, about eleven million refugees migrated from East Pakistan to India. Of them, at least one million settled in the Calcutta Metropolitan District (Shivaramakrishnan 1978 : 40). In 1973, the refugee population in the Calcutta conurbation was 18,37,965 (Chatterjee 1976 : 506). The population of the Calcutta Urban Agglomeration in 1981 was 91,65,650. In 1966 Calcutta had 2,231 registered factories employing 1,76,545 persons (Lahiri 1978 : 58-59). The major industries located at Calcutta are jute and engineering. The registered factory employment in engineering, jute and other industries in Calcutta in 1970 was respectively

29,400, 22,500 and 29,000 (approximately). In 1961 about 4,00,000 persons were directly or indirectly employed in port affairs. About 1.8 million persons, including the families of the total force employed in port affairs, as well as banking trade and outside industrial activities were dependent on port traffic (Bose and Banerjee n.d. : 21). During 1971-72 Calcutta port handled 6,800 thousand tonnes of cargo.

Bombay became the capital of the newly formed Maharashtra state a little after the linguistic states were formed. During the post-Independence period numerous small, light and medium engineering, chemical and drug industries, refineries and associated petro-chemicals including fertilizers came up. According to an economic census conducted in 1977, Greater Bombay had 89,730 industrial units (registered and unregistered). More than 42 per cent of the industrial units of Maharashtra were concentrated in Greater Bombay. These industrial establishments had employed 5,72,460 workers (National Institute). With the expansion of industrial activities during the post-Independence period the commercial and port activities also increased. Bombay today is the biggest financial centre of the country with the head offices of the Reserve Bank and a number of Indian banks, Life Insurance Corporation, the Stock Exchange, the bullion and cotton markets located there. The total weight of cargo handled at Bombay docks rose from 5.5 lakh tonnes in 1937-38 to 61.1 lakh tonnes in 1971-72 which was 43 per cent of the maritime trade of the country. The city, in 1971, had 99,009 trade and business establishments employing 4,69,571 persons. In 1981 the population of Greater Bombay was 82,27,332.

In Delhi, following partition, there was a huge influx of about 4,00,000 of displaced persons from West Pakistan and about 1,50,000 left the city for West Pakistan (Bopegamage 1957 : 17). The growth of industries in Delhi after Independence was very fast and by 1971 Delhi had 2,266 registered industries and 28,343 unregistered industries employing 242,733 workers. Majority of the industries started during the post-partition period are engineering industries followed by metal goods, rubber goods, glass and ceramics, textiles, printing presses and food and drinks (Sundaram 1978 : 123). Delhi being the biggest commercial metropolis of northern India had in 1971, 66,500 commercial establishments employing 2,39,719 persons. During the first half of the fifties there was a vast increase in the size of the government employment. By 1958 there were 500 offices of the Government of India and Delhi Administration with a staff of nearly 2.3 lakhs (Shivaramakrishnan 1978 : 25). During this Period Delhi became a focal point for educational facilities in the country. The Jawaharlal Nehru University, Jamia Millia University and several educational and research institutions including the All India Institute of Medical Sciences, Indian Agricultural Research Institute, Council of Agricultural Research National Council of Educational Research and Training, Indian Institute of Technology etc. were established.

In Madras, during the post-Independence period a number of public and private sector undertakings namely T.V.S. group of industries, Ashok Leylands Ltd. (1948), T.I. Cycles of India (1951), Standard Motors (1952), Integral Coach Factory (1955), Enfield India Ltd. (1955), Hindustan Teleprinters (1960), Heavy Vehicles Factory (1961), Dunlop Rubber Co. (1961), Madras Refineries Ltd. (1969), Madras Fertilizers Ltd. (1971), Ennore Thermal Plant etc. came into existence. Two large industrial estates were started in Guindy and Ambattur. Madras had 586 industrial units in 1973 (Directorate of Town Planning, Tamilnadu 1973 : 26). In 1971, 249,860 persons were working in the manufacturing industries in Madras U.A. Madras is also a commercial centre having the head offices of most of the joint stock companies and financial institutions of the state. In 1971 Madras urban area had 196,335 persons working in trade and commerce. Madras Urban area population rose from 930,356 in 1941 to 4,276,635 in 1981.

In Bangalore a number of public sector undertakings like Hindustan Aeronautical Laboratory, Indian Telephone Industries, Hindustan Machine Tools, Bharat Electronics Ltd., Government Electric Factory, New Government Electric Factory, etc. and a number of large-scale undertakings in the private sector besides large number of medium and small-scale industries came into existence. In 1971, the city had 3,709 industrial units employing 1,06,008 persons (Mahadev 1978 : 269). There were 20,266 trade and business establishments employing 43,887 persons. Bangalore University and a number of research institutions, namely, Indian Institute of Science,

Indian Space Research Organisation, Indian Institute of Astrophysics, National Institute of Mental Health and Neuro Sciences, National T.B. Institute, Raman Research Institute, Indian Institute of Management etc. came into being. The population of Bangalore rose from 406,760 in 1941 to 2,913,537 in 1981.

Soon after partition a large number of Muslims from north India migrated to Hyderabad city. In 1948 the Government of India launched police action and integrated the state of Hyderabad with the Indian Union. This action resulted in the mass migration of Muslims from different states to Hyderabad and emigration of wealthy Muslims to Pakistan. The population of the city grew very fast from 466,894 in 1931 to 1,127,581 in 1951. Terrorism in Telangana resulted in the migration of landlords from Telangana to Hyderabad and Secunderabad where they invested their money in commerce and industries and buildings. The reorganisation of states in 1956 resulted in the formation of Telugu-speaking Andhra Pradesh of which Hyderabad became the capital. The growth of the twin cities was very fast since that date. The two cities grew into a vast community. Even though they remained separate administratively until 1964 (Alam 1965 : 1-16). The post-1955 period opened up opportunities for rapid industrial progress in the city. During the period 1931-65 the number of industrial units of all sizes rose from 130 (Master Plan for Hyderabad 1960) to 626 and the total employment in all these industries was 33,101. During the period 1960-68, in the public sector alone, six large-scale units with a combined investment of Rs. 650 million were set up (Alam 1972 : 208). In 1971, Hyderabad urban area had 559 registered and 7,388 unregistered industries in which 69,998 persons were working. The city had 24,666 commercial establishments in which 70,829 persons were working. Hyderabad being an important educational centre has two universities namely Osmania University and the University of Hyderabad and a number of research institutions and institutions of higher learning including the National Institute of Nutrition, National Institute of Rural Development, International Crop Research Institute for Semi-Arid Tropics, Regional Research Laboratories, Electronics Corporation of India, Administrative Staff College of India etc. The population of Hyderabad grew from 1,248,969 in 1961 to 2,528,198 in 1981.

In Ahmedabad the growth of trade and commerce and industries was very rapid during the post-Independence years. In 1960 Ahmedabad became the capital of the newly formed Gujarat state. Besides textile mills other types of industries came up in the city. In 1971, Ahmedabad had 21,936 trade or business establishments in which 98,264 persons were working. There were 627 registered factories and 8,156 unregistered workshops in which 221,938 persons were employed. The population of Admedabad urban area grew eightfold during 1931-81 from 313,789 to 2,515,195.

In Kanpur the partition of the country in 1947 created scarcity of raw cotton and raw jute resulting in lay-offs, so that the number of workers in 1953 was only 68,832 (Singh Harihar 1972:86). Soon, however, especially during the sixties and seventies a number of large and medium scale industries and hundreds of small-scale industries were started in Kanpur. Important among them were woollen and cotton textiles, leather, chemical and various types of light industries. In addition to the above there are now several establishments catering to the defence needs. In 1971, Kanpur had 589 registered factories and 8,628 unregistered workshops in which 107,383 persons were working. 48,405 persons were working in 21,001 trade establishments. There were 116,993 persons employed in other services. Kanpur became a metropolis in 1971 when its population was 1,275,242, and in 1981 its population rose to 1,688,242.

The population of Poona suddenly increased from 324,286 in 1941 to 605,504 in 1951. Due to its proximity to Bombay and infrastructural facilities provided by the Maharashtra Industrial Development Corporation, Poona and its neighbouring areas attracted a large number of industries after Independence. The development of an industrial area at Hadapsar in 1956 by the Poona Municipal Corporation and the octroi concessions helped in industrial and ancillary development. After the establishment of Hindustan Antibiotics Ltd. at Pimpri there was considerable industrial progress. The establishment of the National Defence Academy, the National Chemical Laboratory, Poona University and expansion of the Central Water and Power Research Station etc. in and around Poona city during the fifties and sixties contributed a great deal towards the growth and expansion of Poona. The development of a large industrial area by the Maharashtra Industrial Development Corporation in the Pimpri-Chinchwad industrial complex near Poona since 1960 attracted more industries and Poona became an important city, next to Bombay. According to a survey of industries in the region carried out by the Regional Plan Office in 1966-67 there were 668 registered factories in the region (excluding defence factories employing about 54,000 workers. The defence factories had employed about 22,000 workers. (Poona Metropolitan Regional Planning Board 1970 : 2-4). Although manufacturing is the new dynamic addition to the economic activity of the city, the other functions have by no means lost their importance in absolute terms. The city and its metropolitan area continue to draw new administrative offices of the central as well as state governments. They also continue to attract research and technological institutions, defence establishments and a growing number of educational institutions (Deshpande 1978 : 309).

Nagpur continued as the capital of Madhya Pradesh till the reorganisation of states in 1956 when it was included in the newly formed Maharashtra state. It became the divisional headquarters and the second capital of Maharashtra. Nagpur University was started in 1943. By 1947, there were 53 registered factories in the region and the population of Nagpur in 1951 was 449,099. The industrial development in the region was accelerated during the three plan periods when as many as 210 registered factories were established. The establishment of a defence project at Ambazari, the M.I.D.C. Estate also resulted in increasing industrial activities in and around Nagpur. By the end of March 1967 there were 374 registered factories in the Nagpur Metropolitan Region (Nagpur Metropolitan Region Planning Board 1970: 59-64). In 1971, the household and other industries had employed 22,910 and 50,656 persons respectively in the Nagpur municipal limits. In commerce, transport, storage and communications and other services respectively another 43,525, 30,232 and 62,740 persons were working. Nagpur area is noted for its orange cultivation and for the cotton and silk fabrics woven by the *Kosti* (handloom weavers). Nagpur is by far the biggest orange market in India. Nagpur district is as also known for its manganese mines and the office of the Indian Bureau of Mines is situated in Nagpur (Nagpur Gazetteer).

Lucknow became the capital of Uttar Pradesh after the reorganisation of states. Due to the opening of several central and state government offices, growth of industries and commerce, educational and health services the city's population which was stagnant till 1931 (274,659) started growing with each successive decade and in 1981 it became a metropolis with a population of 1,006,538. Lucknow, in 1971, had 13 registered factories and 2311 unregistered ones in which 11,598 persons were working. 21,684 persons were working in 10,418 trade establishments. 93,914 persons were working in other services.

Jaipur, in 1949, became the capital of the newly formed state of Rajasthan. Consequently several government departments and agencies were shifted to the city. During 1951-61 some major industries were set up as a result of which a large number of migrants who came to Jaipur in search of employment ultimately settled with their families in the city. In 1977 Jaipur had a number of large industries, namely, the National Engineering Industry, Man Industrial Corporation, Loco Workshop, Jaipur Metals and Electricals, Jaipur Spinning and Weaving Mills, etc. The growth of population in Jaipur after Independence has been considerable as it rose from 180,940 in 1941 to 304,380 in 1951. This high growth rate was mainly due to the influx of refugees from Pakistan. There was large-scale migration of people to Jaipur during the post-Independence period. The immigrants included Marwari businessmen who came to Jaipur following the industrial unrest in West Bengal in the late sixties. Many other migrant Rajasthanis who returned to their state for various reasons also preferred to settle down in Jaipur in preference to their own towns in Rajasthan (Arora 1977:10). In 1981 the population in Jaipur was 1,004,669. The fast growth of population during the post-Independence period was mainly due to the growth of employment opportunities in services other than household industry or trade and commerce in which respectively 60,957, 33,063 and 32,581 persons were working in 1971.

The pace of urbanization in India became quite sharp during the forties and has remained at a high level during the fifties and the sixties. There has again been a sudden spurt in

TABLE 4.1

Population of Million Plus Urban Agglomerations and Cities 1901-81

Rank in 1981 U.A./City	1901	1911	1921	1931	1941	1951	1961	1971	1981
1. Calcutta U.A.	1,488,323	1,718,426	1,850,650	2,105,708	3,577,789	4,588,910	5,736,697	7,031,382	9,194,018
2. Greater Bombay M.C.	812,912	1,018,388	1,244,934	1,268,306	1,686,127	2,966,902	4,152,056	5,970,575	8,243,405
3. Delhi U.A.	214,115	237,944	304,420	447,442	695,686	1,437,134	2,359,403	3,647,023	5,729,283
4. Madras U.A.	594,396	604,034	627,824	774,513	930,356	1,542,333	1,944,502	3,169,930	4,289,347
5. Bangalore U.A.	159,046	189,485	237,496	306,470	406,760	778,977	1,199,931	1,653,779	2,921,751
6. Hyderabad U.A.	448,466	502,104	405,630	466 894	739,159	1,127,581	1,248,969	1,796,339	2,545,836
7. Ahmedabad U.A.	185,889	216,777	274,007	313,789	595,210	877,329	1,206,001	1,741,522	2,548,057
8. Kanpur U.A.	202,797	178,557	216,436	243,755	487,324	705,383	971,062	1,275,242	1,639,064
9. Poona U.A.	164,117	172,884	198,543	250,187	324,286	605,504	790,798	1,135,034	1,686,109
10. Nagpur U.A.	127,734	101,415	145,193	215,165	301,957	449,099	643,659	917,244	1,302,066
11. Lucknow U.A.	264,049	252,114	240,566	274,659	387,177	496,861	655,678	818,992	1,007,604
12. Jaipur U.A.	160,167	137,098	123,896	148,755	180,940	304,380	410,376	636,768	1,015,160

Note : The population for the previous Census years have been adjusted only up to 1971 area jurisdiction. The population for each of the Census years 1901 to 1971 has, in other words, nor been adjusted to the current jurisdiction of these million plus cities. The data for 1981, therefore includes a component of population attributable to addition of new areas or expansion of jurisdiction after 1971.

Source : **Census of India, 1981,** Provisional Population Totals Rural Urban Distribution, Series 1, India, Paper-2 of 1981.

the growth of urban population during the seventies. For example, during 1961-71 the rural growth rate was 21.8 per cent and the urban growth rate was 37.8 per cent. During 1971-81 the rural growth rate declined to 19.0 per cent but the urban growth increased to 46.0 per cent although the overall growth rate was almost the same during these two decades. In 1981, India had 3,245 urban areas of all sizes having a population of 156,188,507. Rapid urbanization has led to unprecedented migration of people from the rural areas to the urban areas. According to the 1971 census there were about 43,634,000 migrants staying in the urban areas constituting about 27.9 per cent of India's urban population. As one would expect, cities with high growth rate had higher proportion of migrant population than the other cities. In 1971 ten million-plus cities had migrants' population ranging between 56.86 and 19.05 per cent. Let us examine in the section that follows, some of the chief demographic features of migrants in metropolitan cities.

II

Demographic Features of Migrant Population

The only source of data used here for analyzing the demographic features of migrants is the census reports. Since the 1981 census reports on migration are not yet available, 1971 census data have been made use of. The mean percentage of migrants living in the twelve metropolitan cities (42.67) is far higher than the percentage of all India migrants (30.42) and higher than the percentage of migrants living in urban India (39.26) as per 1971 census figures. The metropolis having the highest migrants' population is Greater Bombay. As per 1971 census it has 3,395,095 migrants constituting 56.86 per cent of its population. Calcutta Urban Area (U.A.) the biggest metropolis of the country, stands next to Bombay having 2,619,940 migrants constituting 37.26 per cent of its population. The percentage of migrants to the total population in the remaining ten metropolises various between 51.72 and 22.82 (see Table 4.2 showing the migrants' population and their

TABLE 4.2

Migrants' Population in the Metropolises and their Percentage to Total Population, 1971

Rank	Urban City	Agglomeration/Population of the City			Migrants' Population			Migrants' Population in Per cent of the City's/ Agglomeration's Population		
		Total	Males	Females	Total	Males	Females	Total	Males	Females
1.	Calcutta U.A.	7,031,382	4,140,011	2,891,371	2,619,940	1,652,925	967,015	37.26	39.93	33.41
2.	Greater Bombay M.C.	5,970,575	3,478,378	2,492,197	3,395,095	2,126,285	1,268,810	56.86	61.13	50.91
3.	Delhi U.A.	3,647,023	2,028,091	1,618,932	1,886,285	1,073,563	812,722	51.72	52.93	50.20
4.	Madras U.A	3,169,230	1,665,376	1,504,554	1,163,810	622,930	540,880	36.71	37.40	35.95
5.	Bangalore U.A.	1,653,779	882,304	771,475	624,215	347,460	276,755	37.74	39.38	35.87
6.	Hyderabad U.A.	1,796,339	937,200	859,139	409,980	226,385	183,595	22.82	24.16	21.37
7.	Ahmedabad U.A.	1,741,522	951,669	789,853	769,780	427,995	341,785	44.20	44.97	43.27
8.	Kanpur U.A.	1,275,242	723,641	551,601	471,360	273,260	198,100	36.96	37.76	35.91
9.	Poona U.A.	1,135,034	609,920	525,114	553,735	297,325	256,410	48.79	48.75	48.83
10.	Nagpur U.A.	930,459	490,712	439,747	342,030	176,745	165,285	36.76	36.02	37.59
11.	Lucknow U.A.	813,982	445,277	368,705	272,360	151,250	121,110	33.46	33.97	32.85
12.	Jaipur U.A.	636,768	342,836	293,932	206,975	104,460	102,515	32.50	30.47	34.88
	Total	29,802,035	16,695,415	13,106,620	12,715,565	7,480,583	5,234,982	42.67	44.81	39.94

Source : Census of India, 1971, Geographic Distribution of Internal Migration in India, pp. 68-79.

percentage of total population). The percentage of migrants is least in Hyderabad U.A. (22.82). It ranges between 30.00 to 40.00 in Jaipur U.A. (32.50), Lucknow U.A. (33.46), Madras U.A. (36.71), Nagpur U.A. (36.76), Kanpur U.A. (36.96), Calcutta U.A. (37.26), and Bangalore U.A. (37.74); between 40.00—50.00 in Ahmedabad U.A. (44.20) and Poona U.A. (48.79); and between 50.00—60.00 in Delhi U.A. (51.72) and Greater Bombay (56.86).

We shall describe the social demographic features of the migrant population in the twelve metropolises in terms of their place of last residence, rural-urban background, duration of residence, sex and age composition, marital status, educational level and employment patterns.

Place of Last Residence

In the twelve metropolises 5.55 per cent of the migrants have migrated from the same district in which the city is situated as per 1971 Census. (See Table 4.3 showing place of last residence of migrants in the metropolises). The percentage of migrants from the same district varies between 0 and 29.32 in different cities/agglomerations. It is nil in Greater Bombay and Calcutta U.A. and insignificant in Madras U.A. where city/agglomeration boundaries coincide with the district boundaries. The percentage of migrants from the same district is only 4.76 (89,725) in Delhi U.A. the reason being the urban agglomeration of Delhi covers a large part of the union territory of Delhi. The percentage of migrants varies between 7.54 and 9.83 in Lucknow U.A., Hyderabad U.A. and Ahmedabad U.A.; between 10.00 and 20.00 in Kanpur U.A. and Bangalore U.A.; and between 20.00 and 30.00 in Poona U.A., Nagpur U.A. and Jaipur U.A.

The mean population of migrants from other districts of the same state in the twelve metropolises is 36.42. The cities having the highest and lowest percentage of migrants from other districts of the same state are respectively Madras U.A. (70.11) and Calcutta U.A. (22.75). The percentage of migrants from other districts of the state varies between 30.00 to 40.00 in Jaipur U.A. (37.63), Bangalore U.A. (37.75) and Nagpur U.A. (39.81); between 40.00 to 50.00 in Greater Bombay

TABLE 4.3

Place of Last Residence of Migrants in the Metropolises

Sl. No.	Name of the City/ Agglomeration	Total Migrants	In India			Outside India
			With the State of Enumeration		Beyond the State of Enumeration	
			With the District of Enumeration	Beyond the District of Enumeration		
1.	Greater Bombay	3,395,095	. .	1,424,000	1,850,250	120,845
		(100.00)	. .	(41.94)	(54.50)	(3.56)
2.	Calcutta U.A.	2,276,985	. .	518,025	1,012,135	746,825
		(100.00)		(22.75)	(44.45)	(32.80)
3.	Delhi U.A.	1,886,285	89,725	. .	1,410,560	386,000
		(100.00)	(4.76)		(74.78)	(20.46)
4.	Ahmedabad U.A.	769,780	75,670	421,190	242,120	30,800
		(100,00)	(9.83)	(54.72)	(31.45)	(4.00)
5.	Bangalore U.A.	624,215	115,285	235,645	266,930	6,355
		(100.00)	(18.47)	(37.75)	(42.76)	(1.02)
6.	Madras U.A.	786,545	145	551,430	205,380	29.590
		(100.00)	(0.02)	(70.11)	(26.11)	(3.76)

7.	Poona U.A.	553,735	129,030	257,290	153,535	13,880
		(100.00)	(23.30)	(46.46)	(27.73)	(2.51)
8.	Kanpur U.A.	471,360	49,735	326,785	65,645	29,195
		(100.00)	(10.55)	(69.33)	(13.93)	(6.19)
9.	Hyderabad U.A.	409,980	31,655	234,035	140,040	4,250
		(100 00)	(7.72)	(57.08)	(34.16)	(1.04)
10.	Nagpur U.A.	342,030	92,835	136,175	102,865	10,155
		(100.00)	(27.14)	(39.81)	(30.08)	(2.97)
11.	Lucknow U.A.	272,360	20,535	185,765	49,885	16,175
		(100.00)	(7.54)	(68.20)	(18.32)	(5.94)
12.	Jaipur U.A.	206,975	60,690	77,885	47,420	20,980
		(100 00)	(29.32)	(37.63)	(22.91)	(10.14)
	Total	11,995,345	665,305	4,368,225	5,546,765	1,415,050
		(100.00)	(5.55)	(36.42)	(46.24)	(11.79)

Source : Census of India, B K. Roy, Geographic Distribution of Internal Migration in India.

(41.91) and Poona U.A. (46.46); between 50.00 to 60.00 in Ahmedabad U.A. (54.72) and Hyderabad U.A. (57.08); and between 60.00 to 71.00 in Lucknow U.A. (68.20), Kanpur U.A. (69.33) and Madras U.A. (70.11). Delhi U.A. does not have migrants from other districts of the state since the entire union territory is treated as a single district.

The average percentage of migrants from other states of India in the twelve metropolises, as in 1971, is 46.24. The highest percentage of migrants from other states is found in Delhi U.A. (74.78) followed by Greater Bombay (54.50), Calcutta U.A. (44.45), Bangalore U.A. (42.76), Hyderabad U.A. (34.16), Ahmedabad U.A. (31.45), Nagpur U.A. (33.08), Poona U.A. (27.73), Madras U.A. (26.11), Jaipur U.A. (22.91), Lucknow U.A. (18.32) and Kanpur U.A. (13.93). The above figures indicate that generally the bigger metropolises have attracted more interstate migrants than the smaller ones. Interestingly, Madras U.A., the fourth biggest metropolis has only 26.11 per cent of its migrants from other states. The separatist and anti-Hindi movement led by the Dravida Mannetra Kazagam Party during the sixties and its ascendency to power in 1967 must have acted as hindering factors for migrants from other states, especially, from the northern states. Another interesting observation is that the metropolises located in high density states have attracted less number of migrants from other states than those situated in other states.

The average percentage of migrants from outside India settled in all the metropolises as per 1971 Census, is 11.79. This figures is far higher than the percentage of migrants from outside India settled in India (4.50) and in urban India (7.65). Migrants from outside India, most of whom are refugees, have always preferred to settle down in the urban areas, that too in large cities mainly due to the rapidly increasing avenues of employment that they offer. The city having the highest per cent of migrants from outside India is Calcutta (32.80) followed by Delhi U.A. (20.46), Jaipur U.A. (10.14), Kanpur U.A. (6.19), Lucknow U.A. (5.94), Ahmedabad U.A. (4.00), Madras U.A. (3.76), Greater Bombay (3.56), Nagpur U.A. (2.97), Poona, U.A. (2.51), Hyderabad U.A. (1.04) and Bangalore U.A. (1.02). The cities situated close to the Pakistan and Bangladesh border like Calcutta, Delhi and Jaipur received a major share of refugees from Pakistan at the time of partition as compared to the other cities. The refugees from Pakistan and Bangladesh have mainly settled in the north Indian cities. Besides refugees from Pakistan and Bangladesh, refugees and others from different countries, as for instance, Nepal, Burma, Ceylon, Malaysia and African countries have settled in the metropolitan cities.

The average sex ratio of the migrants in the twelve metropolitan cities according to the 1971 Census is 699.39 which is far below than the average sex ratio of non-migrants (854.07) and the sex ratio of urban India (858) and India (930) in 1971 (See Table 4.5) The lowest sex ratio is found in the two biggest metropolises namely Calcutta U.A. (584.94) and Greater Bombay (596.72). The sex ratio ranges between 700-800 in Kanpur U.A. (724.95), Delhi U.A. (756.97), Bangalore U.A. (796.50) and Ahmedabad U.A. (798.55); between 800-900 in Lucknow U.A. (800-71), Hyderabad U.A. (810-98), Pune U.A. (862.38), Madras U.A. (868.27) ; and between 900-1000 in Nagpur U.A. (935.15) and Jaipur U.A. (981.37). The sex ratio of Pune, Madras, Nagpur and Jaipur is higher than the mean sex ratio of all the metropolises and also the sex ratio of urban India. The sex ratio of Jaipur is far higher than the sex ratio of even rural India (939). These figures disclose that the larger metropolises have a lower sex ratio and smaller metropolises have a higher sex ratio. The product movement correlation between the size of the metropolis and sex ratio is strong (0.66 approx.). The industrial-cum-commercial cities have a lower sex ratio than the service and multi-functional cities. In the larger cities acute housing problem and lack of living space have come in the way of migrants settling down with their families. "A large proportion of the adult male migrants to the cities are married and they leave their families behind in the rural areas. The enforced separation from the family persists for long spells in the working life of the migrant" (Bose 1965: 26).

Rural/Urban Background of the Migrants

The migrants have been classified into rural or urban on the basis of the place of last residence. In the metropolises the percentage of rural migrants varies between 41.68—67.07. The percentage of rural migrants to total migrants varies between 40.00—50.00 in Bangalore U.A. (41.68), Madras U.A. (43.51), Jaipur U.A. (45.4), Delhi U.A. (45.54), and Hyderabad U.A. (46.66); between 50.00—60.00 in Lucknow U.A. (51.15), Poona U.A. (52.24), Nagpur U.A. (55.79) and Calcutta U.A. (56.74); and between 60.00—70.00 in Kanpur U.A. (63.03), Ahmedabad U.A. (63.96) and Greater Bombay (67.07). Industrial and commercial cities namely Bombay, Ahmedabad, Kanpur, Calcutta, Nagpur and Poona have attracted more rural migrants than the service and multi-functional cities, the exception being Bangalore. The cities having maximum rural population are textile, jute and leather industrial centres which attract large number of unskilled workers from rural areas. Bangalore is an exception since the majority of its industrial labourers are working in electric, electronic and engineering industries which need skilled workers, who are drawn mainly from the urban areas.

The city which has the highest percentage of urban migrants is Bangalore U.A. (58.33) followed by Madras U.A. (56.49), Jaipur U.A. (54.58), Delhi U.A. (54.44), Hyderabad U.A. (53.23), Lucknow U.A. (48.84), Poona U.A. (47.76), Nagpur U.A. (44.21), Calcutta U.A. (43.26), Kanpur U.A. (36.97), Ahmedabad U.A. (35.99) and Greater Bombay (32.93). The cities having high percentage of urban migrants are mainly service-cum-industrial and multi-functional which have attracted a large number of educated and skilled urban migrants to work in various services and industries which required skilled labourers.

Duration of Residence

The migrants have been divided into two broad categories in the Census, namely those whose duration of residence is less than three years and those whose duration of residence is more than three years, in order to distinguish the temporary and permanent migrants. The percentage of migrants from rural areas with less than three years' duration of residence to total population of migrants ranges between 10.46 and 18.35 in different metropolises (See Table 4.4 showing the migrants in

TABLE 4.4

Migrants in Metropolises According to Last Residence and Duration, 1971

Sl. No.	City/Urban Agglomeration	Total Population	Total Migrants	Resided in Rural Areas				Resided in Urban Areas			
				Less than 3 years		More than 3 years		Less than 3 years		More than 3 years	
				Males	Females	Males	Females	Males	Females	Males	Females
1	2	3	4	5	6	7	8	9	10	11	12
1.	Greater Bombay	5,823,770	3,248,290	265,685	173,655	1,161,805	577,410	123,320	95,935	491,845	358,595
			(100,00)	(8.18)	(5.35)	(35.77)	(17.77)	(3.80)	(2.95)	(15.14)	(11.04)
2.	Calcutta U.A.	5,985,295	1,573,885	137,820	66,090	510,965	178,115	96,015	83,810	278,220	222,710
			(100.00)	(8.76)	(4.20)	(32.46)	(11.32)	(6.10)	(5.33)	(17.68)	(14.15)
3.	Delhi U.A.	3,237,454	1,476,716	107,566	64,756	304,570	195,616	121,584	97,178	315,966	269,194
			(100.00)	(7.28)	(4.39)	(20.62)	(13.25)	(8.23)	(6.58)	(21.40)	(18.23)
4.	Ahmedabad U.A.	1,704,880	733,150	77,055	57,470	191,840	142,585	47,325	40,245	91,180	85,125
			(100.00)	(10.51)	(7.84)	(26.16)	(19.45)	(6.45)	(5.49)	(12.44)	(11.61)
5.	Bangalore U.A.	1,640,184	610,620	44,175	34,840	96,295	79,170	67,610	51,940	131,485	104,970
			(100.00)	(7.23)	(5.71)	(15.77)	(12.97)	(11.07)	(8.51)	(21.53)	(17.19)
6.	Madras U.A.	3,169,930	1,126,315	64,200	53,650	203,950	168,285	96,940	86,465	237,300	215,520
			(100.00)	(5.70)	(4.76)	(18.11)	(14.94)	(8.61)	(7.68)	(21.07)	(19.13)
7.	P. ona U.A.	1,113,619	532,320	42,415	32,685	105,480	97,480	44,905	32,495	92,530	84,290
			(100.00)	(7.97)	(6.14)	(19.82)	(18.31)	(8.44)	(6.10)	(17.38)	(15.84)
8.	Kanpur U.A.	1,240,435	436,525	38,145	26,620	126,125	84,225	25,295	19,020	63,570	53,525

1	2	3	4	5	6	7	8	9	10	11	12
			(100.00)	(8.74)	(6.10)	(28.89)	(19.30)	(5.79)	(4.36)	(14.56)	(12.26)
9.	Hyderabad U.A.	1,790,910	404,600	136,795	26,025	67,545	58,440	43,605	30,685	74,900	66,190
			(100.00)	(9.09)	(6.43)	(16.70)	(14.44)	(10.78)	(7.58)	(18.51)	(16.36)
10.	Nagpur U.A.	917,244	323,815	21,980	17,885	74,165	69,445	20,440	17,785	52,835	54,280
			(100.00)	(6.68)	(5.44)	(22.55)	(21.22)	(6.22)	(5.41)	(16.07)	(16.51)
11.	Lucknow U.A.	791,270	254,755	26,700	13,540	49,460	40,620	24,510	17,215	40,725	41,960
			(100.00)	(10.48)	(5.31)	(19.42)	(15.94)	(9.62)	(6.76)	(15.99)	(16.47)
12.	Jaipur U.A.	612,305	182,445	12,475	9,700	30,535	30,135	15,270	14,730	32,850	36,730
			(100.00)	(6.84)	(5.31)	(16.74)	(16.51)	(8.37)	(8.07)	(18.01)	(20.13)

Note : The population and migrants of U.A.'s given in this table are less then those given in other table, due to the following reasons :—

(i) Returns in which place of last residence Rural/Urban classification is not reported have been excluded.
(ii) Returns with 'Unclassifiable" place of last residence have been Encluded.
(iii) Persons last resided outside India are excluded.

Source : Census of India, 1971, *Geographic Distribution of Internal Migration in India*, pp. 61-67.

metropolises according to last residence and duration in 1971). The city having the highest percentage of migrants belonging to this category is Ahmedabad U.A. (18.35) followed by Lucknow U.A. (15.79), Hyderabad U.A. (15.52), Kanpur U.A. (14.84), Poona U.A. (14.11), Greater Bombay (13.53), Calcutta U.A. (12.96), Bangalore U.A. (12.94), Jaipur U.A. (12.15), Nagpur U.A. (12.12), Delhi U.A. (11.67) and Madras U.A. (10.46). The industrial and commercial cities have a higher percentage of migrants belonging to this category than the multi-functional and service centres with the exception of Lucknow which is a service centre.

The percentage of migrants from the rural areas with more than three years' residence, to total population varies between 53.54 and 28.74 in different metropolises. The city having the highest percentage of rural migrants with more than three years' stay is Greater Bombay (53.54) followed by Kanpur U.A. (48.19), Ahmedabad U.A. (45.61), Calcutta U.A. (43.78), Nagpur U.A. (43.67), Poona U.A. (38.13), Lucknow U.A. (35.36), Delhi U.A. (33.87), Jaipur U.A. (33.25), Madras U.A. (33.05), Hyderabad U.A. (31.14) and Bangalore U.A. (28.74). The industrial-cum-commercial cities namely Greater Bombay, Kanpur, Ahmedabad, Calcutta and Nagpur have normally a higher share of population belonging to this category than the service, service-cum-industrial and multi-functional cities.

Among the twelve cities Bangalore U.A. has the highest percentage (19.58) of urban migrants with less than three years' residence followed by Hyderabad U.A. (18.36), Jaipur U.A. (16.44), Lucknow U.A. (16.38) Madras U.A. (16.29), Delhi U.A. (14.81), Poona U.A. (14.54), Ahmedabad U.A. (11.94), Nagpur U.A. (11.63), Calcutta U.A. (11.43), Kanpur U.A. (10.15) and Greater Bombay (6.75). The highest percentage of urban migrants with less than three years' residence is found in the service, service-cum-industrial and multi-functional cities namely Hyderabad, Jaipur, Lucknow, Madras, Delhi and Poona, Bangalore being an exception for it is an industrial-cum-service-cum-commercial centre.

The percentage of urban migrants with more than three years' residence varies between 24.05 and 40.02 with Madras having the highest percentage (40.2) followed by Delhi U.A. (39.63), Bangalore U.A. (38.72), Jaipur U.A. (38.14), Hyderabad

TABLE 4.5

Sex Ratio of Migrants and Non-Migrants in Indian Metropolises, 1971

Rank	City/Urban Agglomeration	Sex Ratio	Sex Ratio of Migrants	Sex Ratio of Non-Migrants
1.	Calcutta U.A.	698.27	584.84	773.59
2.	Greater Bombay	716.26	596.72	904.69
3.	Delhi U.A.	798.13	756.97	844.59
4.	Madras U.A.	903.33	868.27	924.36
5.	Bangalore U.A.	874.31	796.50	924.98
6.	Hyderabad U.A.	916.70	810.98	950.36
7.	Ahmedabad U.A.	829.90	798.55	855.59
8.	Kanpur U.A.	762.26	724.95	784.88
9.	Poona U.A.	860.92	862.38	859.58
10.	Nagpur U.A.	896.12	935.15	874.16
11.	Lucknow U.A.	828.01	800.71	848.07
12.	Jaipur U.A.	857.34	981.37	802.99
	Total	783.78	699.39	854.07

U.A. (34.87), Poona U.A. (33.22), Nagpur U.A. (32.58), Lucknow U.A. (32.46), Calcutta U.A. (31.83), Kanpur U.A. (26.82), Greater Bombay (26.18) and Ahmedabad U.A. (24.05). Here also the service, service-cum-industrial and multi-functional cities namely Madras, Delhi, Jaipur, Hyderabad, Poona and Lucknow have a higher percentage of urban migrants than the industrial and commercial cities.

Sex Composition

In India, as in many other countries of Asia, migrants to large cities have been predominantly males (Zacharia 1964 : 72). Kingsley Davis gives reasons for predominance of male outmigration from the rural areas. He says (Davis 1977: 160).

> In Asian and African countries out-migration from rural areas tends to be more masculine than feminine. The reasons for this are complex and differ somewhat from

one region to another. In Asia and North Africa the customary seclusion of women involves prejudice against their migrating to the city on an individual basis, but in Africa and Asia in general, and in Central Africa in particular, there is, or has been, great reliance on hoe and hand culture, both of which tend to be performed by women. Also high agricultural density in these continents gives rise to surplus labour in off-seasons, thus facilitating migration to cities on a seasonal basis, the men being by tradition more mobile. Finally, the extremely high fertility and early marriage prevailing in Asia and Africa burden young women with children to a greater extent than was ever true in the west.

Age Composition

Migration is age and sex selective. The figures pertaining to the age composition of the migrants of all the twelve metropolises show the predominance of migrants in the 20+ age group (See Table 4.6 showing the age composition of the migrants). As per 1971 Census the percentage of population in the age group 0-14 is 41.86 in India; 23.88 among the migrants in India; and 12.41 among the migrants living in the metropolises. (Table 4.7 shows the age composition of the migrants of metropolises, all-India migrants and India (total) in 1971). The percentage of males of this age group varies between 9.08 (Calcutta U.A.) and 17.04 (Poona U.A.) in the metropolises. The bigger cities namely Calcutta U.A. (9.08), Greater Bombay (11.46) and Delhi U.A. (12.08) have lesser percentage of males in this age group than the smaller metropolises. Similarly the percentage of girls in this age group is 42.10 in India; 14.56 among the migrants in India; and 15.34 among the migrants living in the twelve metropolises. The percentage of females of this age group ranges between 12.72 (Calcutta U.A.) and 11.54 (Poona U.A.). In the age group 15-19, the percentage of males in the country is 8.87; among the migrants in India is 8.96; and among the metropolitan migrants is 8.04. The percentage of females of the same age group in India, among the migrants in India and metropolitan migrants is respectively 9.86, 9.04 and 8.32.

In the age group 20-24 the percentage of males is higher (12.93) in the metropolises than among the migrants in India (10.47) and the general population of India (8.28). Same is the case with females. In the Indian metropolises the percentage of females in this age group is 13.25 whereas it is 12.83 among the migrants in India and 8.55 among the general population of India. It is evident that the migration of males and females is considerable in this age group. Men migrate to cities for work and education and women, usually, migrate after marriage to settle down with their husband. A negligible percentage of women of this age group migrate for obtaining higher education and to work. Most females migrants move to join a settled and successful husband that Heisler finds them less likely to return to the village, rather than because they find town life more attractive as he suggests (Heisler 1973: 196). Patterns of female migration may well follow patterns of family or household migration (Wyon and Gordon 1971: 214). A small proportion of women migrate to work in the city. According to N.S.S. estimates (18th round) it is evident that among female migrants more than 60 per cent are those who have migrated either due to marriage or to join the earning member (Srivastava 1979:58).

Approximately half the population of the migrants in the metropolises is found in the age group 25-49. 52.29 per cent males in the metropolises are in this age group, whereas 41.30 per cent and 29.36 per cent males are found in the same age group respectively among the migrants in India and in India (total). Similarly 47.96 per cent female migrants are in this age group in the metropolises as compared to 45.53 per cent among the migrants in India and 29.45 per cent in India (total). The magnitude of the volume of migration of people of this age group could be guessed from these figures. Migration of people to the metropolises is highest in this age group. Majority of men and a small number of women migrate to work and majority of women migrate to their husbands' house. Dorothy S. Thomas, after an exhaustive study of the existing knowledge about migration, came to the conclusion that persons in their late teens, twenties and early thirties were more migratory than other groups (Thomas 1938). The figures pertaining to the percentage of migrants in the age group 50+make

TABLE 4.6

Age Composition of the Migrants in the Metropolises, 1971

Sl. No.	City/Urban Agglomeration	(a) No. (b) %	Persons	Total			0-14		
				Males	Females	Persons	Males	Females	Persons
1.	Calcutta U.A.	(a)	2,619,940	1,651,925	967,015	273,045	150,015	123,030	192,755
		(b)	(100.00)	(100.00)	(100.00)	(10.42)	(9.08)	(12.72)	(7.36)
2.	Greater Bombay	(a)	3,395,095	2,126,285	1,268,810	454,910	243,710	211,200	273,215
		(b)	(100.00)	(100.00)	(100 00)	(13.40)	(11.46)	(16.64)	(8.05)
3.	Delhi U.A.	(a)	1,886,285	1,073,563	812,722	237,521	129,654	107,867	146,303
		(b)	(100.00)	(100.00)	(100.00)	(12.59)	(12.08)	(13.27)	(7.76)
4.	Madras U.A.	(a)	1,163,810	622,930	540,880	194,595	99,980	94,615	98,100
		(b)	(100.00)	(100.00)	(100.00)	(16.72)	(16.05)	(17.49)	(8.43)
5.	Bangalore U.A.	(a)	624,215	347,460	276,755	101,745	54,455	47,290	62,680
		(b)	(100.00)	(100.00)	(100.00)	(16.30)	(15.67)	(17.09)	(10.04)
6.	Hyderabad U.A.	(a)	409.980	226,385	183,595	69,580	36,955	32,625	39,605
		(b)	(100.00)	(100.00)	(100.00)	(16.97)	(16.32)	(17.77)	(9 66)
7.	Ahmedabad U.A.	(a)	769,780	427,995	341,785	122,340	65,630	56,710	63,335
		(b)	(100.00)	(100.00)	(100.00)	(15.89)	(15.33)	(16.59)	(8.23)
8.	Kanpur U.A.	(a)	471,360	273,260	198,100	58,490	32,135	26,355	36,985
		(b)	(100.00)	(100.00)	(100.00)	(12.41)	(11.76)	(13.30)	(7.85)
9.	Poona U.A.	(a)	553,735	297,325	256,410	98.210	50,675	47,535	50,835
		(b)	(100.00)	(100.00)	(100.00)	(17.73)	(17.04)	(18.54)	(9.18)
10.	Nagpur U.A.	(a)	342,030	176,745	165,285	47,620	24,815	22,805	28,725
		(b)	(100.00)	(100.00)	(100.00)	(13.92)	(14.04)	(13.80)	(8.40)
11.	Lucknow U.A.	(a)	272,360	151,250	121,110	42,045	24,005	18,040	24,245
		(b)	(100.00)	(100.00)	(100.00)	(15.43)	(15.87)	(14.89)	(8.90)
12.	Jaipur U.A.	(a)	206,975	104,460	102,515	31,645	16,615	15,030	20,935
		(b)	(100.00)	(100.00)	(100.00)	(15.29)	(15.90)	(14.66)	(10.11)
	Total	(a)	12,715,565	7,480,583	5,234,982	1,731,746	928,644	803,102	1,037,718
		(b)			(100 00)	(13.62)	(12.41)	(15.34)	(8.16)

Sl. No.	City/Urban Agglomeration	(a) No. (b) %	15-19			20-24			25-49	
			Males	Females	Persons	Males	Females	Persons	Males	Females
1.	Calcutta U.A.	(a)	115,325	77,430	292,120	176.615	115,505	1,425,735	949,335	476,400
		(b)	(6.98)	(8.01)	(11.15)	(10.68)	(11.94)	(54.42)	(57.43)	(49.26)
2.	Greater Bombay	(a)	172,445	100,770	482,490	313,275	169,215	1,755,935	1,137,520	618,415
		(b)	(8.11)	(7.94)	(14.21)	(14.73)	(13.34)	(51.72)	(53.50)	(48.24)
3.	Delhi U.A.	(a)	85,052	61,251	238,021	131,936	106,085	978,113	562,861	415,252
		(b)	(7.92)	(7.54)	(12.62)	(12.29)	(13 05)	(51.85)	(52.43)	(51.10)
4.	Madras U.A.	(a)	49,740	48,360	160,305	83,785	76,520	540,990	301,140	239,850
		(b)	(7.99)	(8.94)	(13.77)	(13.45)	(14.15)	(46.49)	(48.34)	(44.35)
5.	Bangalore U.A.	(a)	34,305	28,375	90,605	49,645	40,960	283,415	162,295	121,120
		(b)	(9.87)	(10.25)	(14.52)	(14.29)	(14.80)	(45.40)	(46.71)	(43.76)
6.	Haderabad U.A.	(a)	19,965	19,640	60,995	32,690	28,305	188,270	110,655	77,615
		(b)	(8.82)	(10.70)	(13.88)	(14.44)	(15.42)	(45.92)	(48.88)	(42.27)
7.	Ahmedabad U.A.	(a)	36,095	27,240	100,955	54,680	46,275	370,765	207,590	163,175
		(b)	(8.43)	(7.97)	(13.11)	(12.78)	(13.54)	(48.17)	(48.50)	(47.74)
8.	Kanpur U.A.	(a)	21,220	15,765	59,420	32,320	27,100	242,155	141,090	101,065
		(b)	(7.77)	(7.96)	(12.61)	(11.83)	(13.68)	(51.37)	(51.63)	(51.02)
9.	Poona U.A.	(a)	27,325	23,150	74,585	40,070	34,515	248,340	135,890	112,450
		(b)	(9.19)	(9.17)	(13.47)	(13.48)	(13.46)	(44.85)	(45.71)	(53.85)
10.	Nagpur U.A.	(a)	15,200	13,525	42,045	21,630	20,415	160,785	82,515	78,270
		(b)	(8.60)	(8.18)	(12.29)	(12.24)	(12.35)	(47.01)	(46.68)	(47.35)
11.	Lucknow U.A	(a)	14,795	9,450	31,350	16,770	14,580	134 045	73,415	60,630
		(b)	(9.78)	(7.80)	(11.51)	(11.09)	(12.04)	(49.22)	(48.54)	(50.06)
12.	Jaipur U.A.	(a)	10,410	10,525	28,420	14.315	14.105	94,665	47,690	46,975
		(b)	(9.96)	(10.27)	(13.73)	(13.70)	(13.76)	(45.73)	(45.65)	(45.82)
	Total	(a)	601,877	435,841	1,661,311	967,731	693,580	6,423,213	3,911,996	2,511,217
		(b)	(8.04)	(8.32)	(13.06)	(12.93)	(13.25)	(50.51)	(52.29)	(47.96)

Sl. No.	City/Urban Agglomeration	(a) No. (b) %	50+ Persons	50+ Males	50+ Females	Age not Specified Persons	Age not Specified Males	Age not Specified Females
1.	Calcutta U.A.	(a)	435,935	261,435	174,500	350	200	150
		(b)	(16.64)	(15.82)	(18.05)	(0.01)	(0.01)	(0.02)
2.	Greater Bombay	(a)	428,340	259,215	169,125	205	120	85
		(b)	(12.62)	(12.19)	(13.33)	N.	(0.01)	(0.01)
3.	Delhi U.A.	(a)	286,129	163,952	122,177	198	108	90
		(b)	(15.17)	(15.27)	(15.03)	(0 01)	(0.01)	(0.01)
4.	Madras U.A.	(a)	169,730	88,215	81.515	90	70	20
		(b)	(14.58)	(14.16)	(15.07)	(0.01)	(0.01)	N.
5.	Bangalore U.A.	(a)	85,750	46,740	39.010	20	20	..
		(b)	(13.74)	(13.45)	(14.10)	N.	(0.01)	..
6.	Hyderabad U.A.	(a)	51,445	26,050	25,395	85	70	15
		(b)	(12.55)	(11.51)	(13.83)	(0.02)	(0.03)	(0.00)
7.	Ahmedabad U.A.	(a)	112,345	63,970	48,375	40	30	10
		(b)	(14.59)	(14.95)	(14.16)	(0.01)	(0.01)	N.
8.	Kanpur U.A.	(a)	74,310	46,495	27,815	..	..	..
		(b)	(15.76)	(17.01)	(14.04)	..	..	..
9.	Poona U.A.	(a)	81.655	43,300	38,355	110	65	45
		(b)	(14.75)	(14.56)	(14.96)	(0.02)	(0.02)	(0.02)
10.	Nagpur U.A.	(a)	62,835	32,575	30,260	20	10	10
		(b)	(18.37)	(18.43)	(18.31)	N.	N.	N.
11.	Lucknow U.A.	(a)	40,665	22,255	18,410	10	10	..
		(b)	(14.93)	(14.71)	(15.20)	N.	N.	..
12.	Jaipur U.A.	(a)	31,305	15,430	15,875	5	..	5
		(b)	(15.12)	(14.77)	(15.48)	N.	..	N.
	Total	(a)	1,860,444	1,069,632	790 812	1,133	703	420
		(b)	(14.63)	(14.30)	(15.11)	(0.01)	(0.01)	(0.01)

us to presume that the majority of migrants of metropolises go back to their places after retirement and a small portion of them prefer to stay back in the city. Zachariah says "as suggested by the age composition of net migration, return migration seems to be quite widespread in India. Workers moved out from their place of birth when they were young but a large proportion of them returned at older ages. . . . The gaining areas on the whole tended to lose at older ages and loosing areas to gain at these ages" (Jain 1964). In the age group 50+ only 14.30 per cent male migrants are found in the metropolitan cities. The respective figures pertaining to migrants in India and India (total) are 15.36 and 12.27. Likewise the percentage of females of this age group in the metropolises is 15.11 whereas it is 18.02 among the migrants in India and 11.83 in India (total).

TABLE 4.7

Age Composition of the Migrants of Metropolises, All-India Migrants and Indian Population, 1971

Age Group	Males/ Females	Migrants in the Metropolitan Cities	Migrants (All-India)	India (Total)
0—14	M	12.41	23.88	41.86
	F	15.34	14.56	42.10
15—19	M	8.04	8.96	8.87
	F	8.32	9.04	8.44
20—24	M	12.93	10.47	7.59
	F	13.25	12.83	8.16
25—49	M	52.29	41.30	29.36
	F	47.96	45.53	29.45
50+	M	14.30	15.36	12.27
	F	15.11	18.02	11.83

Marital Status

In the twelve metropolises 30.21 per cent migrants are not married. The percentage of never-married population is considerably higher in the metropolises than the all-India migrants

TABLE 4.8

Migrants By Martial Status, 1971

Sl. No.	City/Urban Agglomeration	(a) No. (b) %	Persons	Never Married Males	Never Married Females	Persons
1	2	3	4	5	6	7
1.	Calcutta U.A.	(a)	707,200	502,170	205,030	1,716,965
		(b)	(26.99)	(30.38)	(21.20)	(65.54)
2.	Greater Bombay	(a)	1,081,460	752,710	328,750	2,137,475
		(b)	(31.85)	(35.40)	(25.91)	(62.96)
3.	Delhi U.A.	(a)	508,867	336,194	172,673	1,272,781
		(b)	(26.98)	(31.32)	(21.25)	(67.48)
4.	Madras U.A.	(a)	419,040	275,070	143,970	662,120
		(b)	(36.01)	(44.16)	(26.62)	(56.89)
5.	Bangalore U.A.	(a)	236,250	159,985	76,265	353,310
		(b)	(37.85)	(46.04)	(27.56)	(56.60)
6.	Hyderabad U.A.	(a)	137,555	91,345	46,210	247,765
		(b)	(33.55)	(40.35)	(25.17)	(60.43)
7.	Ahmedabad U.A.	(a)	218,650	141,550	77,100	507,165
		(b)	(28.40)	(33.07)	(22.56)	(65.89)
8	Kanpur U.A.	(a)	108,155	74,060	34,095	335,165
		(b)	(22.94)	(27.10)	(17.21)	(71.11)

1	2	3	4	5	6	7
9.	Poona U.A.	(a)	189,955	123,605	66,350	325,255
		(b)	(34.30)	(41.57)	(25.88)	(58.74)
10.	Nagpur U.A.	(a)	98,370	64,865	33,505	214,015
		(b)	(28.76)	(36.70)	(20.27)	(62.57)
11.	Lucknow U.A.	(a)	79,400	52,860	26,540	176,795
		(b)	(29.15)	(34.95)	(21.91)	(64.91)
12.	Jaipur U.A.	(a)	56,480	36,495	19,985	136,550
		(b)	(27.29)	(34.94)	(19.49)	(65.97)
	Total	(a)	3,841,382	2,610,909	1,230,473	8,085,361
		(b)	(30.21)	(34.90)	(23.50)	(63.59)

	Married		Widowed-Divorced			Unspecified		
	Males	Females	Persons	Males	Females	Persons	Males	Females
	8	9	10	11	12	13	14	15
1.	1,091,400	625,565	157,815	29,370	128,445	37,960	29,985	7,975
	(66.03)	(64.69)	(6.02)	(1.78)	(13.28)	(1.45)	(1.81)	(0.83)
2.	1,335,345	802,130	173,230	35,710	137,520	2,930	2,520	410
	(62.80)	(63.22)	(5.10)	(1.08)	(10.84)	(0.09)	(0.12)	(0.03)
3.	704,526	568,255	104,211	32,485	71,726	426	358	68
	(65.62)	(69.92)	(5.52)	(3.03)	(8.82)	(0.02)	(0.03)	(0.01)
4.	334,380	327,740	82,620	13,450	69,170	30	30	—
	(53.68)	(60.59)	(7.10)	(2.16)	(12.79)	N	N	—
5.	181,370	171,940	34,335	5,800	28,535	320	305	15
	(52.20)	(62.13)	(5.50)	(1.67)	(10.31)	(0.05)	(0.09)	N
6.	131,210	116,555	24,470	3,660	20,810	190	170	20
	(57.96)	(63.49)	(5.97)	(1.62)	(11.33)	(0.05)	(0.07)	(0.01)
7.	275,900	231,265	43,965	10,545	33,420	—	—	—
	(64.46)	(67.66)	(5.71)	(2.47)	(9.78)	—	—	—
8.	186,615	148,550	28,040	12,585	15,455	—	—	—
	(68.29)	(74.99)	(5.95)	(4.61)	(7.80)	—	—	—
9.	166,195	159,060	37,820	7,040	30,780	705	485	220
	(55.90)	(62.03)	(6.83)	(2.37)	(12.00)	(0.13)	(0.16)	(0.09)

	8	9	10	11	12	13	14	15
10.	105,475	108,540	29,560	6,335	23,225	85	70	15
	(59.68)	(65.67)	(8.64)	(3.58)	(14.05)	(0.02)	(0.04)	(0.01)
11.	93,125	83,670	16,060	5,160	10,900	105	105	—
	(61.57)	(69.09)	(5.90)	(3.41)	(9.00)	(0.04)	(0.07)	—
12.	64,700	71,850	13,720	3,140	10,580	225	125	100
	(61.94)	(70.09)	(6.63)	(3.01)	(10.32)	(0.11)	(0.12)	(0.10)
Total	4,670,241	3,415,120	745,876	165,280	580,596	42,976	34,153	8,823
	(62.43)	(65.24)	(5.86)	(2.21)	(11.09)	(0.34)	(0.45	(0.17)

(24.32) (See Table 4.8 showing the marital status of migrants). The higher percentage of never-married population in the metropolises may be due to the large student population since a large number of higher educational institutions are located in the metropolises and the practice of late marraige in the urban areas as compared to the villages. This category contains more males (34.90 per cent) than females (23.50). The percentage of female migrants of this category is higher in the metropolises (23.50) as compared to all-India migrants (16.42). This shows that considerable number of women postpone their marriage in order to complete higher education. Some postpone their marriage until they get a decent job since the educated men prefer to marry an employed woman.

The mean percentage of male and female married migrants is respectively 62.43 and 65.24 in the twelve metropolises. The corresponding figures pertaining to the migrants of India are 55.11 and 70.79 respectively.

The percentages of males and females who are widowed and divorced are respectively 2.21 and 11.09 and the corresponding figures pertaining to the all-India migrants are 3.68 and 12.72 respectively.

Educational Levels

In order to know the educational levels of the working and non-working migrants, they have been grouped under five broad categories as follows: 1. Primary and Middle; 2. Matric, higher secondary and diploma below degree level; 3. Graduate, post-graduate and other technical degrees; 4. Literate (without educational level); 5. Illiterate.

(Table 4.9 gives the educational levels of the working and non-working migrants).

The percentage of illiterates among migrants in the metropolises, according to the 1971 Census, is 36.12 whereas it is 47.6 in urban India. The highest percentage of illiterates among working migrants is found in Calcutta U.A. (39.90) followed by Kanpur U.A. (34.22), Ahmedabad U.A. (28.48), Nagpur U.A. (28.43), Greater Bombay U.A. (27.66), Lucknow U.A. (27.66), Delhi U.A. (27.33), Hyderabad U.A. (27.20), Jaipur

TABLE 4.9

Educational Levels of Working and Non-working Migrants in the Metropolitan Cities, 1971

Sl. No.	City/Urban Agglomeration	Total Population	Migrants' Population	(a) Total Workers (b) Total Non-Workers	Educational Levels				
					Primary and Middle	Matric or Hr. Sec. and Diploma below Degree Level	Graduate, Post-Graduate and other Technical Degree	Literate (without educational level)	Illiterate
1	2	3	4	5	6	7	8	9	10
1.	Great Bombay	5,970,575	3,395,095	(a) 1,747,755 (51.48)	704,145 (40.29)	304,625 (17.43)	102,675 (5.87)	152,930 (8.75)	483,380 (27.66)
				(b) 1,647,340 (48.52)	586,880 (35.63)	165,390 (10.04)	31,315 (1.90)	193,935 (11.77)	669,820 (40.66)
2.	Calcutta U.A.	7,031,382	2,276,985	(a) 1,216,630 (53.43)	335,165 (27.55)	207,505 (17.05)	90,715 (7.46)	97,790 (8.04)	485,455 (39.90)
				(b) 1,060,355 (46.57)	317,205 (29.91)	144,485 (13.63)	40,140 (3.79)	99,805 (9.42)	458,640 (43.25)
3.	Delhi U.A.	3,647,023	1,886,285	(a) 881,851 (45.75)	221,134 (25.08)	234,051 (26.54)	119,074 (13.50)	66,585 (7.55)	241,007 (27.33)
				(b) 1,004,434 (53.25)	260,421 (25.93)	153,059 (15.24)	41,953 (4.18)	123,079 (11.25)	425,922 (42.40)

1	2	3	4	5	6	7	8	9	10
4.	Ahmedabad U.A.	1,741,522	769,780	(a) 321,770	80,720	63,950	22,920	62,550	91,630
				(41.80)	(25.09)	(19,87)	(7.12)	(19.44)	(28.48)
				(b) 448,010	97,320	55,575	8,075	89,820	197,220
				(58.20)	(21.72)	(12.41)	(1.80)	(20.05)	(44.02)
5.	Bangalore U.A.	1,653,779	624,215	(a) 259,865	75,130	82,530	25,650	13,695	62,860
				(41.63)	(28.91)	(31.76)	(9.87)	(5.27)	(24.19)
				(b) 364,350	109,965	64,665	10,750	37,330	141,640
				(58.37)	(30.18)	(17.75)	(2.95)	(10.25)	(38.87)
6.	Madras U.A.	3,169,930	603,945	(a) 252,900	96,325	71,145	19,530	21,195	44,705
				(41.87)	(38.09)	(28.13)	(7.72)	(8.38)	(17.68)
				(b) 351,045	114,280	50,345	8,055	44,445	133,920
				(58.13)	(32.55)	(14.34)	(2.30)	(12.66)	(38.15)
7.	Poona U.A.	1,135,034	553,735	(a) 221,190	83,805	52,535	18,945	15,680	50,225
				(39.95)	(37.89)	(23.75)	(8.56)	(7.09)	(22.71)
				(b) 332,545	112,010	39,830	8,570	36,450	135,685
				(60.05)	(33.68)	(11.98)	(2.58)	(10.96)	(40.80)
8.	Kanpur U.A.	1,275,242	471,360	(a) 209,640	48,530	45,695	15,885	27,790	71,740
				(44.48)	(23.15)	(21.80)	(7.58)	(13.25)	(34.22)
				(b) 261,720	57,890	31,925	8,810	36,185	126,910
				(55 52)	(22.12)	(12.20)	(3.37)	(13.82)	(48.49)
9.	Hyderabad U.A.	1,796,339	409,980	(a) 175,895	38,250	48,200	26.295	15.300	47,850
				(42.90)	(21.75)	(27,40)	(14.95)	(8.70)	(27.20)

1	2	3	4	5	6	7	8	9	10
				(b) 234,085	61,725	36,315	6,545	34,300	95,200
				(57.10)	(26.37)	(15.51)	(2.80)	(14.65)	(40.67)
10.	Nagpur U.A.	930,459	342,030	(a) 135,935	50,490	26,335	11,420	9,040	38,650
				(39.74)	(37.14)	(19.38)	(8.40)	(6.65)	(28.43)
				(b) 236,095	66,220	27115	5,255	19,995	87,510
				(60.25)	(32.13)	(13 16)	(2.55)	(9.70)	(42.46)
11.	Lucknow U.A.	813,982	272,360	(a) 107,490	22,720	30,330	15,020	9,690	29,730
				(39.47)	(21.14)	(28 22)	(13.97)	(9.01)	(27.66)
				(b) 164,870	39,295	27,385	9,370	23,475	65,345
				(50.53)	(23.83)	(16.61)	(9.68)	(14.24)	(39.64)
12.	Jaipur U.A.	636,768	206,975	(a) 74,545	17,515	20,530	9,420	8,555	18,525
				(36.02)	(23.49)	(27.54)	(12.64)	(11.48)	(24.85)
				(b) 132,430	29,460	18,305	4,610	17,235	62,820
				(63.98)	(22.25)	(13.82)	(3.48)	(13.01)	(47.44)

Source : Census of India, B.K. Roy, Geographic Distribution of Internal Migration in India.

U.A. (24.85), Bangalore U.A. (24.19), Poona U.A. (22.71) and Madras U.A. (17.68). The percentage of illiterates is high in those cities where the industries have employed large number of unskilled labourers.

The percentage of illiterates among non-working migrants is considerably higher than the percentage of illiterates among the workers. It varies between 48.49 and 38.15 in different cities. Kanpur U.A. has the highest percentage of illiterates among the non-working migrants (48.49) followed by Jaipur U.A. (47.44), Ahmedabad U.A. (44.02), Calcutta U.A. (43.25), Nagpur U.A. (42.46), Delhi U.A. (42.40), Poona U.A. (40.80), Hyderabad U.A. (40.67), Greater Bombay (40.66), Lucknow U.A. (39.64), Bangalore U.A. (38.87) and Madras U.A. (38.15). Normally, the cities having high percentage of working illiterates also have high percentage of non-working illiterates with a few exceptions. Jaipur U.A. which has 24.85 per cent working illiterate migrants has 47.44 per cent illiterate non-working migrants. Poona U.A. which has 22.71 per cent illiterate working migrants has 40.80 per cent non-working illiterate migrants. Greater Bombay which has 27.66 per cent illiterate working migrants has 40.66 per cent illiterate non-working migrants. Lucknow U.A. having 27.66 per cent working illiterate migrants has 39.64 per cent non-working illiterate migrants.

The percentage of literates (without educational levels) is 10.64 in the metropolitan cities whereas it is 14.6 in urban India. The percentage of literates (without educational levels) among workers varies between 6.65 and 19.44 in different metropolises. Ahmedabad U.A. has the highest percentage of literates (19.44) followed by Kanpur U.A. (13.25), Jaipur U.A. (11.48), Lucknow U.A. (9.01), Greater Bombay (8.75), Hyderabad U.A. (8.70), Madras U.A. (8.38), Calcutta U.A. (8.04), Delhi U.A. (7.55), Poona U.A. (7.09), Bangalore U.A. (5.27) and Nagpur U.A. (6.65). Ahmedabad has the highest percentage of non-working literates (20.05) followed by Hyderabad U.A. (14.65) Lucknow U.A. (14.24), Kanpur U.A. (13.82), Jaipur U.A. (13.01), Madras U.A. (12.66), Delhi U.A. (12.25), Greater Bombay (11.77), Poona U.A. (10.96), Bangalore U.A. (10.25),

Nagpur U.A. (9.70) and Calcutta U.A. (9.47). All the metropolises have higher percentage of literates among the non-workers than among the workers.

The percentage of migrants with primary and secondary education is 30.70 in the twelve metropolises, whereas it is 25.4 in urban India. The percentage of working migrants having primary and middle education varies between 40.29 and 21.14 in the twelve cities. The city having the highest percentage of working migrants is Greater Bombay (40.29) followed by Madras U.A. (38.09), Poona U.A. (37.89), Nagpur U.A. (37.14), Bangalore U.A. (28.91), Calcutta U.A. (27.55), Ahmedabad U.A. (25.09), Delhi U.A. (25.08), Jaipur U.A. (23.49), Kanpur U.A. (23.15), Hyderabad U.A. (21.75) and Lucknow U.A. (21.14). The percentage of non-working migrants having primary and middle education varies between 35.63 and 21.72 in the twelve metropolises, and Greater Bombay has the highest percentage (35.63) followed by Poona U.A. (33.68), Madras U.A. (32.55), Nagpur U.A. (32.13), Bangalore U.A. (30.18), Calcutta U.A. (29.91), Hyderabad U.A. (26.37), Delhi U.A. (25.93), Lucknow U.A. (23.83), Jaipur U.A. (22.25), Kanpur U.A. (22.12), and Ahmedabad U.A. (21.72). Normally the cities having high percentage of working migrants with primary or middle education also have high percentage of non-working migrants with primary or middle education and vice-versa with a few exceptions like Ahmedabad, Hyderabad U.A. and Lucknow U.A. In Ahmedabad U.A. the percentage of working and non-working migrants with primary and middle education is respectively 25.09 and 21.72. In Hyderabad U.A. it is 21.75 and 26.37 and in Lucknow it is 21.14 and 23.83 respectively.

In the twelve metropolises 16.95 per cent migrants have studied up to matric or higher secondary and diploma below degree level whereas in urban India only 10.1 per cent of the total population have studied up to that level. In the category of matric or higher secondary and diploma below degree level Bangalore U.A. ranks first with 31.76 per cent working migrants belonging to this category followed bo Lucknow U.A. (28.22), Madras U.A. (28.13), Jaipur U.A. (27.54), Hyderabad U.A. (27.44), Delhi U.A. (26.54), Poona U.A. (23.75), Kanpur U.A. (21.80), Ahmedabad U.A. (19.87), Nagpur U.A. (19.38), Greater Bombay (17.43) and Calcutta U.A. (17.05). Bangalore also has the highest percentage of non-working migrants belonging to this category (17.75) followed by Lucknow U.A. (16.61), Hyderabad U.A. (15.51), Delhi U.A. (15.24), Madras U.A. (14.34), Jaipur U.A. (13.82), Calcutta U.A. (13.63), Nagpur U.A. (13.16), Ahmedabad U.A. (12.41), Kanpur U.A. (12.20), Poona U.A. (11.98) and Greater Bombay (10.04). The cities having high or low percentage of working migrants in this category also have high or low percentage of non-working migrants with exceptions like Calcutta U.A. and Poona U.A.

Graduates, post-graduates and other technical degree holders account for 5.59 per cent of the migrants in the twelve metropolises whereas they account for 2.3 per cent of the total migrant population in urban India. Hyderabad U.A. ranks first in the percentage of graduates, post-graduates and other technical degree holders among working migrants (14.95) followed by Lucknow U.A. (13.97), Delhi U.A. (13.50), Jaipur U.A. (12.64), Bangalore U.A. (9.87), Poona U.A. (8.56), Nagpur U.A. (8.40), Madras U.A. (7.72), Kanpur U.A. (7.58), Calcutta U.A. (7.46), Ahmedabad U.A. (7.12) and Greater Bombay (5.87), Lucknow U.A. tops in the non-working migrants belonging to this category (9.68) followed by Delhi U.A. (4.18), Calcutta U.A. (3.79), Jaipur U.A. (3.48), Kanpur U.A. (3.37), Bangalore U.A. (2.95), Hyderabad U.A. (2.80), Poona U.A. (2.58), Madras U.A. (2.30), Bombay U.A. (1.90) and Ahmedabad U.A. (1.80).

The above figures reveal that the migrants in the metropolises are relatively more educated than the people in other parts of the country. "In India the propensity to migrate does indeed increase with increased education" (Greenwood 1971 : 137-151). Large cities have attracted the best brains of the country.

Employment Pattern

The mean work participation rate of Indian metropolises as per 1971 Census is 46.37 which is far higher than that of urban India (29.3) and India (total) (32.92). The male work participation rate is 73.38 which is far higher than the male work participation rate of urban India (48.82) and India (total) (52.50). Bombay has the highest male work participation rate (76.66) and Poona (66.25) has the lowest. The cities having manufacturing and trade and commerce as chief functions, normally,

TABLE 4.10

Occupational Structure of Migrants in the Metropolises, 1971

Sl. No. City/Urban Agglomeration	(a) No. (b) %	Persons	Total Migrants		Total Workers		Workers: I Cultivators		Workers: II Agricultural Labourers	
			Males	Females	Males	Females	Males	Females	Males	Females
(1)	(2)	(3)	(4)	(5)	(6)	(7)	(8)	(9)	(10)	(11)
1. Calcutta U.A.	(a)	2,619,940	1,652,925	967,015	1,240,595	63,115	1,355	60	7,185	510
	(b)	(100.00)	(100.00)	(100.00)	(75.05)	(6.52)	(0.08)	(0.01)	(0.43)	(0.05)
2. Greater Bombay	(a)	3,395,095	2,126,285	1,268,810	1,630,095	117,660	1,240	190	1,230	240
	(b)	(100.00)	(100.00)	(100.00)	(76.66)	(9.27)	(0.06)	(0 01)	(0.06)	(0.02)
3. Delhi U.A.	(a)	1,886,285	1,073,563	812,722	819,340	62,511	1,036	68	1,492	214
	(b)	(100.00)	(100.00)	(100.00)	(76.31)	(7.69)	(0.10)	(0.01)	(0.14)	(0.03)
4. Madras U.A.	(a)	1,163,810	622,930	540,880	417,945	38,705	1,605	175	3,175	1,990
	(b)	(100.00)	(100.00)	(100.00)	(67.08)	(7.15)	(0.26)	(0.03)	(0.51)	(0.37)
5. Bangalore U.A.	(a)	624,215	347,460	276,755	234,605	25,260	1,090	70	850	140
	(b)	(100.00)	(100.00)	(100.00)	(67.52)	(9.13)	(0.31)	(0.03)	(0.25)	(0.05)
6. Hyderabad U.A.	(a)	409,980	226,385	183,595	156,545	19,350	1,180	215	1,490	1,675
	(b)	(100.00)	(100.00)	(100.00)	(69.15)	(10.54)	(0.52)	(0.12)	(0.66)	(0.91)
7. Ahmedabad U.A.	(a)	769,780	427,995	341,785	300,850	20,920	455	65	555	230
	(b)	(100.00)	(100.00)	(100.00)	(70.29)	(6.12)	(0.11)	(0.02)	(0.13)	(0.07)
8. Kanpur U.A.	(a)	471,360	272,260	198,100	202,855	6,785	1,085	70	·915	165
	(b)	(100.00)	(100.00)	(100 00)	(74.24)	(3.43)	(0.40)	(0.04)	(0.34)	(0 08)
9. Poona U.A.	(a)	553,735	297,325	256,410	196,980	24,210	800	295	1,195	945
	(b)	(100.00)	(100.00)	(100.00)	(66.25)	(9.44)	(0.27)	(0.11)	(0.40)	(0.37)
10. Nagpur U.A.	(a)	342,030	176,745	165,285	118,200	17,735	1,270	180	1,090	865
	(b)	(100.00)	(100.00)	(100.00)	(66.86)	(10.73)	(0.71)	(0.11)	(0.62)	(0.52)
11. Lucknow U.A.	(a)	272,360	151,250	121,110	101,715	5,775	745	75	515	165
	(b)	(100.00)	(100.00)	(100.00)	(67.25)	(4.77)	(0.49)	(0.06)	(0.34)	(0.14)
12. Jaipur U.A.	(a)	206,975	104,460	102,515	69,535	5,010	550	205	435	150
	(b)	(100.00)	(100.00)	(100.00)	(66.57)	(4.89)	(0.53)	(0.20)	(0.42)	(0.15)
Total	(a)	12,715,565	7,480,583	5,234,982	5,489,260	407,036	12,411	1,668	20,127	7,289
	(b)	(100.00)	(100.00)	(100.00)	(73.38)	(7.77)	(0.16)	(0.03)	(0.27)	(0.14)

Sl. No. City/Urban Agglomeration	Workers: III Livestock, Forestry, Fishing, Hunting Plantations, Orchard and Allied Activities		IV Mining and Quarrying		V(a) Household Industry		V(b) Other than Household Industry		VI Construction	
	Males	Females	Males	Females	Males	Females	Males	Females	Male	Females
	(12)	(13)	(14)	(15)	(16)	(17)	(18)	(19)	(20)	(21)
1. Calcutta U.A.	8,405	210	770	30	12,640	945	473,050	11,840	28,205	400
	(0.51)	(0.02)	(0.05)	N	(0.76)	(0.10)	(28.62)	(1.23)	(1.71)	(0.04)
2. Greater Bombay	13,160	610	1,270	310	19,975	2,685	699,210	24,495	50,995	4,780
	(0.62)	(0.05)	(0.06)	(0.02)	(0.94)	(0.21)	(32.88)	(1.93)	(2.40)	(0.38)
3. Delhi U.A.	6,567	162	79	7	13,957	929	176,023	4,116	46,268	5,083
	(0.61)	(0.02)	(0.01)	N	(1.30)	(0.11)	(16.39)	(0.51)	(4.31)	(0.62)
4. Madras U.A.	3,545	125	145	10	5,380	800	114,385	4,975	17,885	1,315
	(0.57)	(0.02)	(0.02)	N	(0.86)	(0.15)	(18.36)	(0.92)	(2.87)	(0.24)
5. Bangalore U.A.	1,485	210	115	10	4,040	1,130	74,980	5,090	9,795	1,385
	(0.43)	(0.08)	(0.03)	N	(1.16)	(0.41)	(21.58)	(1.84)	(2.82)	(0.50)
6. Hyderabad U A.	1,000	170	450	230	1,825	765	27,855	1,780	5,635	1,100
	(0.44)	(0.09)	(0.20)	(0.12)	(0.81)	(0.42)	(12.30)	(0.97)	(2.49)	(0.60)
7. Ahmedabad U.A.	1,835	135	2,085	90	3,635	660	142,280	4,090	8,675	1,815
	(0.43)	(0.04)	(0.49)	(0.02)	(0.85)	(0.19)	(33.24)	(1.20)	(2 03)	(0.53)
8. Kanpur U.A.	990	40	70	..	5,965	275	65,255	470	2,250	65
	(0.36)	(0.02)	(0.03)	..	(2.18)	(0.14)	(23.88)	(0.24)	(0.82)	(0.03)
9. Poona U.A.	2,220	210	555	305	2,260	760	60,610	4,140	8,370	1,385
	(0.75)	(0.08)	(0.19)	(0.12)	(0.76)	(0.30)	(20.38)	(1.61)	(2.81)	(0.54)
10. Nagpur U.A.	2,110	175	1,620	630	6,110	1,660	26,180	2,645	4,520	730
	(1.19)	(0.11)	(0.92)	(0.38)	(3.46)	(1.00)	(14.81)	(1.60)	(2 56)	(0.44)
11. Lucknow U.A.	595	35	..	10	2,285	145	11.395	290	1,190	30
	(0.39)	(0.02)	..	N	(1.51)	(0.02)	(7.53)	(0.24)	(0.79)	(0.02)
12. Jaipur U.A.	220	55	80	..	2,340	555	12,510	420	1,710	170
	(0.21)	(0.05)	(0 08)	..	(2.24)	(0.54)	(11.98)	(0.41)	(1.64)	(0.17)
Total	42,132	2,137	7,239	1,632	80,412	11,309	1,883,733	64,351	185,498	18,258
	(0.56)	(0.04)	(0.14)	(0.03)	(1.07)	(0.22)	(25.18)	(1.23)	(2.48)	(0.35)

Sl. No. City/Urban Agglomeration	Workers							
	VII Trade and Commerce		VIII Transport, Storage and Communications		IX Other Services		X Non-Workers	
	Males	Females	Males	Females	Males	Females	Males	Females
	(22)	(23)	(24)	(25)	(26)	(27)	(28)	(29)
1. Calcutta U.A.	267,525 (16.18)	3,750 (0.38)	163,955 (9.92)	2,745 (0.29)	277,505 (16.79)	42,670 (4.41)	412,330 (24.95)	903,900 (93.47)
2. Greater Bombay	372,900 (17.54)	14,155 (1.12)	184,965 (8.70)	6,075 (0.48)	285,150 (13.41)	64,120 (5.05)	496,190 (23.33)	1,151,150 (90.73)
3. Delhi U.A.	179,927 (16.76)	4,543 (0.56)	86,706 (8.08)	2,050 (0.25)	307,285 (28.62)	45,339 (5.58)	254,223 (23.68)	750,211 (92.31)
4. Madras U.A.	114,840 (18.44)	4,275 (0.79)	66,255 (10.64)	3,090 (0.57)	90,730 (14.56)	21,950 (4.06)	204,985 (32.91)	502,175 (92.85)
5. Bangalore U.A.	47,200 (13.59)	2,450 (0.88)	25,755 (7.41)	2,785 (1.01)	69,295 (19.94)	11,990 (4.33)	112,855 (32.48)	251,495 (90.87)
6. Hyderabad U.A.	29,850 (13.19)	1,730 (0.94)	20,510 (9.06)	1,425 (0.78)	66,750 (29.48)	10,260 (5.59)	69,840 (30.85)	164,245 (89.46)
7. Ahmedabad U.A.	56,905 (13.29)	1,645 (0.48)	23,735 (5.54)	1,055 (0.31)	60,690 (14.18)	11,135 (3.26)	127,145 (29.71)	320,865 (93.88)
8. Kanpur U.A.	37,485 (13.72)	595 (0.30)	21,545 (7.88)	90 (0.05)	67,295 (24.63)	5,015 (2.53)	70,405 (25.76)	191,315 (96.57)
9. Poona U.A.	30,920 (10.40)	2,310 (0.90)	16,825 (5.66)	1,635 (0.64)	73,225 (24.63)	12,225 (4.77)	100,345 (33.75)	232,200 (90.56)
10. Nagpur U.A.	22,740 (12.87)	1,900 (1.15)	17,130 (9.69)	965 (0.58)	35,430 (20.05)	7,985 (4.83)	58,545 (33.12)	147,550 (89.27)
11. Lucknow U.A.	17,655 (11.67)	345 (0.29)	18,010 (11.91)	240 (0.20)	49,325 (32.61)	4,440 (3.67)	49,535 (32.75)	115,335 (95.23)
12. Jaipur U.A.	16,275 (15.58)	315 (0.31)	7,925 (7.59)	130 (0.13)	27,490 (26.32)	3,010 (2.94)	34,925 (33.43)	97,505 (95.11)
Total	1,194,222 (15.96)	37,968 (0.76)	653,316 (8.73)	22,285 (0.42)	1,410,170 (18.85)	240,139 (4.59)	1,991,323 (26.62)	4,827,946 (92.22)

TABLE 4.11

Five Important Industrial Categories in which Migrants are Employed in the Metropolises

Sl. No.	City/Urban Agglomeration	1	2	3	4	5
1.	Calcutta U.A.	Manufacturing	Other Services	Trade & Commerce	Transport	Construction
2.	Greater Bombay	Manufacturing	Trade & Commerce	Other Services	Transport	Construction
3.	Delhi U.A.	Other Services	Trade & Commerce	Manufacturing	Transport	Construction
4.	Madras U.A.	Manufacturing	Trade & Commerce	Other Services	Transport	Construction
5.	Bangalore U.A.	Other Services	Manufacturing	Trade & Commerce	Transport	Construction
6.	Hyderabad U.A.	Other Services	Trade & Commerce	Manufacturing	Transport	Construction
7.	Ahmedabad U.A.	Manufacturing	Other Services	Trade & Commerce	Transport	Construction
8.	Kanpur U.A.	Other Services	Manufacturing	Trade & Commerce	Transport	Household Industry
9.	Poona U.A.	Other Services	Manufacturing	Trade & Commerce	Transport	Construction
10.	Nagpur U.A.	Other Services	Manufacturing	Trade & Commerce	Transport	Construction
11.	Lucknow U.A.	Other Services	Transport	Trade & Commerce	Manufacturing	Household Industry
12.	Jaipur U.A.	Other Services	Trade & Commerce	Manufacturing	Transport	Household Industry

have a higher male work participation rate than the cities having other functions. The mean female work participation rate of the metropolises is 7.77 which is slightly higher than the female work participation rate of urban India (6.62) and lower than that of India (total) (11.85). The female work participation rate varies between 10.73 and 3.43 in different metropolises.

The sex ratio of migrant workers in the metropolises (74.15) is far lower than the sex ratio migrant of workers in urban (116) and rural India (232). It means fewer women are employed in the metropolises than in urban and rural India. There is need to throw more light on this aspect which has not received much attention so far. The five important industrial categories in which migrants are employed in the metropolises are manufacturing, other services, trade and commerce, transport and construction (See Table 4.11). In the other than household industry 25.18 per cent male migrants and 1.23 per cent female migrants are working in the twelve metropolises. In the other services 18.85 per cent male migrants and 4.59 per cent female migrants are employed. The participation of male and female migrants in trade and commerce is 15.96 and 0.76 per cent respectively. In transport, storage and communications 8.73 per cent male and 0.42 per cent female migrants are employed, and in construction 2.48 per cent male migrants and 0.35 per cent female migrants are working (See Tables 4.10 & 4.11).

The foregoing account of the different social characteristics of the migrants in metropolitan cities throws light on the process of migration. People tend to move from rural areas to larger cities in search of jobs when they are young. Men migrate more than women, and they migrate from different states to larger metropolises. A large proportion of them are unmarried, and have lower educational skills. This reveals the elements of selectivity such as age, sex, economic, educational and marital status in the process of migration.

Many studies of urbanization (See Bulsara 1964) have shown that people migrate from rural areas to metropolises mainly for economic and educational reasons. Economic reasons provide only the necessary conditions of rural-urban migration. If economic reason was the only factor one would expect that only the poor from the rural areas would move. But it is seen that the well-to-do also move to larger cities for different reasons.

Hence the social and cultural factors provide the sufficient conditions for people to move.

Conclusion

In the previous sections we have shown the nature of development of the metropolitan cities in the colonial and independence periods. It was seen that the main factor in the urban growth has been migration of different streams into the cities which provided economic opportunities and social and cultural attractions to the people. Colonial economy thwarted the development of indigenous trade, commerce and industry and the scientific and cultural advancements made in several directions. The character of traditional urbanization changed under the Company and British raj insofar as the traditional political and administrative features of the capital cities were relegated to the background. New port cities emerged which became centre of trade and commerce. However they served, as the periphery of the urban centres in England.

Under British raj, the character of urbanization changed further with the development of rail and road transport, mining textiles and other industries. The migration streams to urban centres became steady and large. In the post-independence period, the limitations of the colonial economy were overcome. The metropolitan cities became the nerve centres of industries trade, commerce and administration. In addition to the old, new metropolitan centres emerged and we have seen that in 1981, there were twelve of them and they have grown in size mainly due to migration from rural areas. The magnitude of migration was highest in Bombay with 56.86 per cent of migrants constituting its population in 1971.

What are the main characteristic features of migrants (42.67 per cent in 1971) in the twelve metropolitan cities? By analysing the features we gain an insight into the nature of the process of migration and the social and economic consequences of migration in the urban centres. It is found that the bulk of the migrants (46.24 per cent on an average) into twelve metropolitan cities came from other states (in 1971). Bigger metropolises attracted more interstate migrants than the smaller ones. The migration stream has been from rural to urban. Between 41.68 and 67.07 per cent migrants were from rural background. A significant proportion of them have been staying in the cities fore more than three years. There are more male migrants than female ones as is revealed by the sex ratio. Lowest sex ratio of 584.94 females per thousand male migrants was found in Calcutta Urban Area in 1971. Besides sex, age selectivity is also shown among the migrants. Approximately half the population of the migrants in the metropolises is found in the age group 25-49. Less than one-third of the migrants are not married. In terms of education, larger proportion of migrants in metropolises has primary and secondary education. Larger metropolises also have more migrants who are highly educated. As regards work participation, male are preponderant over females. Secondly, more migrants are to be found in the five important industrial categories of manufacturing, other services, trade and commerce, transport and construction The metropolitan centres provide more economic opportunities in those secondary and tertiary sectors, and consequently the major stream of migrants consists of unskilled, semi-skilled and skilled workers who find their ways in construction, factories, petty trade and self-employed categories. The second large stream of migrants consists of educated persons who get observed in blue-collar and white-collar jobs. The other streams of professionals, industrialists and high trade and commerce are numerically not significant.

The character of these streams of migrants has a bearing on the social and economic consequences of urbanization in terms of unemployment and underemployment and the growth of slum population.

Concentration of industries, commercial establishments, government and semi-government offices, universities and research institutions, specialised medical services etc. in the metropolises has led to unprecedented immigration to them so that the number of migrants living in these metropolises is far higher than what the cities actually require. The inadequacy or absence of land for cultivation, low fertility, absence of irrigational facilities, frequent droughts, lack of employment opportunities, in the non-agricultural industrial categories, unemployment and underemployment, low wages, caste/class feuds, untouchability, lack of basic civic amenities including clean potable water supply, educational, medical and recreational facilities, etc. are some of the factors motivating people of the rural areas and small towns to migrate to the bigger cities in search of jobs in the rapidly expanding industrial, commercial, construction, transport and service sectors. The bigger cities are unable to prevent the increasing inflow of migrants and provide employment and minimum civic services to all of them due to a number of constraints, including financial. As a result all these metropolises are facing three most disturbing problems, namely, unemployment/underemployment, poverty and housing about which a brief mention has been made below.

As per the 1971 Census, the percentage of male and female migrant non-workers in all the metropolises is respectively 26.62 (1,991,323) and 92.22 (4,827,946). If we exclude from the above figures the percentage of males (928,644) and females (803,102) in the age group 0-14, the percentage of unemployed males and females is 14.21 (1,062,679) and 76.88 (4,024,844). The magnitude of the problem of unemployment in the metropolises is alarming. In the organised as well as the unorganised sectors it is the men who are preferred. This has resulted in higher unemployment rate among women. Providing more employment opportunities to women in all the employment categories is one of the possible ways to curb the growing menace of urban poverty. Regarding underemployment no data is available for us to know the gravity of the problem since census does not collect data pertaining to underemployment. The percentage of underemployed persons must be higher among the migrants than among the permanent residents since the migrants are predominant in the unorganised sector. There is a need for studies to throw light upon the problem of underemployment in the cities and especially the metropolises.

With the rise in the urban population due to uncontrolled immigration, the number of urban poor has also risen. As per the statement made by the then Minister for Planning in Rajya Sabha in August 1973, the actual population below the poverty line in the urban areas (defined on the basis of per capita monthly expenditure of Rs. 30 or less at the 1964-65 prices) is 54.5 million or over half the total urban population in the country (Town and Country Planning Organisation 1975: 9). As per a survey conducted during the early seventies nearly a fourth of the urban population is severely destitute, a seventh destitute while a sixth just poor (Monthly Commentary 1975). "The larger the city, the greater is the spread of poverty and sharper its contrast to the ostensible symbols of urbanisation" (Shivaramakrishnan 1978:7). Poverty severely hampers the provision of basic civic services to all the urban residents thereby allowing the cities to decay gradually. The large cities of India have ceased to be places congenial for living.

Growth of slums in the metropolises is a manifestation of urban poverty. The poor who can't afford to pay for houses live in slums. According to a Planning Commission Working Group's estimation, around 22 million out of the total 108 million urban population of India were living in slums in the early seventies (Planning Commission 1972). In Calcutta approximately 35% of the city's population was living in recognised or unrecognised slums in 1974 (C.M.D.A., n.d. : 10). In Madras 33.49% of city's population lived in slums in 1971 (Arangannal 1975:11-12). In Bombay according to recent estimates one-third of the city's population is living in slums (Singh Andrea Menefee & Alfred De Souza 1980 : 8). In Delhi an estimated four million constituting 17% of the city's population were living in unauthorised squatter settlements alone. According to another study which utilised the broader definition of a slum, it was estimated that approximately 73.7% of the city's population of 4.5 million lived in slums or near-slum conditions (Sengupta 1975 : 3). Besides the slum population mentioned above the total number of pavement dwellers in the four largest cities of India in 1971 was 130,156 which works out at 0.7% of the total population of the four cities, which in 1971, was 19,074,038.

As a result of uncontrolled immigration the biggest cities namely Calcutta, Bombay and Madras have started dying gradually, unable to cope with the enormous problems they are facing like air, water and sound pollution, inadequacy of water and electric supply, disposal of rubbish and sewage, transport, educational, medical and recreational facilities, mushroom growth of slums due to inadequate housing and lack of sites for constructing houses, high rate of unemployment and under-employment, rise in the population of the urban poor etc. Other metropolises have started decaying. There is an immediate need to curb the growth of the metropolises and other bigger cities by not issuing licenses for starting new industries, decentralising the existing industries, starting industries in the industrially backward districts, encouraging the establishment of cottage and small-scale industries in the villages and small towns, improving agriculture, horticulture, dairying and animal husbandry, bringing more land under irrigation, implementing land reforms, providing drinking water, schools and higher educational institutions, primary health units and primary health centres and hospitals, constructing homes for the lower middle and lower classes, removing untouchability and bringing about communal harmony in the villages. All these measures will help arrest the migration inflow to metropolitan cities and bring about balanced urban development.

REFERENCES

Ahmedabad Mill Owners' Association, Ahmedabad Mill Owners Association's Report, 1929-30, 1930.

Alam S. Manzoor, *Hyderabad-Secunderabad : A Study in Urban Geography*, Allied Publishers Pvt. Ltd., Bombay, 1965.

——, *Metropolitan Hyderabad and its Region—A Strategy for Develop ment*, Asia Publishing House, Bombay, 1972.

——, "Issues in Planning and Development of Metropolitan Cities of India". Paper presented in the Seminar on 'Urbanization and Planned Economic Development—Present Scenario and Future Perspectives' held at Jawaharlal Nehru University, New Delhi in September 1982.

Anderson, P., *The English in Western India*, 1856.

Arangannal, Rama, *Socio-Economic Survey of Madras Slums* (1971 Survey), Tamilnadu Slum Clearance Board, Madras, 1976.

Arora, Ramesh K., Rakesh Hooja and Shashi Mathur, *Jaipur : Profile of a Changing City*, Indian Institute of Public Administration, Rajasthan Branch, Jaipur, 1977.

Bogue D.J. et al., "Urbanization and Migration in India", in Roy Turner (ed.), *India's Urban Future*.

Bombay, City Gazetteer, Vol. I., 1962.

Bombay Metropolitan Regional Planning Board, Regional Plan for Bombay Metropolitan Region, 1970-71, 1974.

Bopegamage, *Delhi : A Study in Urban Sociology*, University of Bombay, Bombay, 1957.

Bose, Ashish, "Why do People Migrate to Cities", *Yojana*, Vol. IX, No. 1, 1965.

Bose, D.K. and Banerjee S.K., (n.d.), "Economic Activities related to the Bhagirathi-Hooghly River System", (mimeo), Indian Statistical Institute, Calcutta.

Bose, Nirmal Kumar, "Calcutta : A Premature Metropolis", in Kingsley Davis (ed.), *Cities : Their Origin, Growth and Human Impact*, W.H. Freeman & Co., San Francisco, 1973.

Bulsara, J.F., (1964) : *Problem of Rapid Urbanisation in India*, Popular Prakashan, Bombay, 1964.

Calcutta Metropolitan Development Authority (n.d.) : Some Facts and Figures, Calcutta Metropolitan Development Authority.

Cambridge History of India, IV.

Census of Poona, 1851.

Census of India, 1881.

Census of 1881 : *Operations and Results in the Presidency of Bombay including Sind*, Vol. I, Bombay.

Census of India, 1901, XI, Part 5.

Census Report of Jaipur, 1901, *Occupations or Means of Livelihood.*

Census of India (1921) : City of Calcutta, Vol. I.

Census of India (1921) : City of Calcutta, 1872-1921.

Chandrasekharan, T., (ed.), *Poona Pet Kaifiyat*, Madras Government Oriental Manuscript, Series No. 54, Madras, 1956.

Chatterjee, A.B., "The Evolution, Land-Use and Social Characteristics of Calcutta and its Conurbation", in S. Manzoor Alam and V.V. Pokshishevsky (ed.), *Urbanization in Developing Countries*, Osmania University Press, Hyderabad, 1976.

Choksey, R.D., *The Last Phase : Selections from the Deccan Commissioners' Files* (Peshwa Daftar), 1815-1818, Bombay, 1948.

Commissariat, M.S., *Mandelslo's Travels*, London, 1931.

Davis, Kingsley, "The Effects of Outmigration on Regions of Origin", in Alan A. Brown and Egon Neuberger (eds.), *Internal Migration*, Academic Press, New York, 1977.

De-Laet, (n d.), The Empire of the Great Mogol.

Delhi Administration : Delhi Gazetteer, Delhi Administration, Delhi, 1976.

Deshpande, C.D., "Pune : A Metropolis in Transition", in R.P. Misra (ed.), *Million Cities of India*, Vikas Publishing House Pvt. Ltd., New Delhi, 1978.

Directorate of Town Planning, Hyderabad, *Draft Master Plan for Hyderabad*, Hyderabad, 1960.

Directorate of Town Planning, Tamilnadu, Madras-Chengleput Region—A Draft Regional Plan, 1973-74.

Dobbin, C., *Urban Leadership in Western India*, London, 1972.

Edwardes, S.M., *The Rise of Bombay*, Bombay, 1902.

Elphinstone, M., *Report of the Territories Conquered from the Peshwa*, Second Edition, Bombay, 1838.

Fawcett, *The Abbe Carre : Travels of the Abbe Carre in India and the Near East*, 1672-74, Haklayt Society, Series No. XVC—1947.

Fawcett, E.G., "Report on the Collectorate of Ahmedabad, 1849", in *Selections from the Records of the Bombay Government*, Vol. V, New Series, Bombay, 1854.

Forbes, *Oriental Memoirs*, Vol. I, London, 1913.

Foster, William, *The English Factories in India, 1646-50*, Oxford, 1914.

Foster, William, *The English Factories in India, 1650-1654*, Oxford, 1915.

Frank, Andre Gunder, *Capitalism and Underdevelopment in Latin America*, Monthly Review Press, New York, 1967.

Fryer, John, A., *A New Account of East-India and Persia . . . begun 1672 and finished 1681*, London, 1698.

Furber, H., *Bombay Presidency in the Mid-eighteenth Century*, Bombay, 1965.

Gadgil, D.R., *Poona : A Socio-Economic Survey*, Vols. I & II, 1952.

Ghosh, Murari, Alok K. Dutta and Biswanath Ray, *Calcutta : A Study in Urban Dynamics*, Calcutta : Firma K.L.M., 1972.

Gillion, Kenneth, L., *Ahmedabad : A Study in India Urban History*, University of California Press, Berkeley, 1968.

Gode, P.K., "Two Contemporary Tributes to Minister Vidyadhara the Bengali Architect at the Court of Sawai Jai Singh of Amber (1699-1744 A.D.)", in *Dr. C.K. Raja Presentation Volume*, Madras, 1946.

Government of Bombay: Memorandum from the Government of Bombay to Royal Commission on Labour, II, 1939.

Grant-Duff, J., *A History of the Mahrattas*, Oxford, 1921.

Greenwood, Michael, J., "An Analysis of the Determinants of Internal Labour Mobility in India", *Annals of Regional Science*, 5, 1971.

Heber, R., *Narrative of a Journey through the Upper Provinces of India in 1824-25*, Vol. II, London.

Heisler, H., "The Pattern of Migration in Zambia", *Cahiers d'Etudes Africaines*, Vol. XIII, No. 2, 1973.

Hoselitz, Bert, F., "A Survey of the Literature on Urbanization in India", in Roy Turner (ed.), *India's Urban Future*, Oxford University Press, Bombay, 1962.

Imperial Gazetteer of India, Vols. III, VI, VIII, IX, XIII, XVI, XX.

Indian Institute of Public Opinion, Bombay : "Third World and Destitution", *Monthly Commentary*, Annual Number, 1975.

Jain, K.C., "Ahmedabad : An Expanding Metropolis", in R.P. Misra (ed.), *Million Cities of India*, Vikas Publishing House Pvt. Ltd., Delhi, 1978.

Jain, S.P., "Indian Fertility—Our Knowledge and Gaps". Paper Presented at the Population Conferenbe at Delhi, 1964.

Joshi, N.V., *Pune Sahaharache Vernan* (Marathi), (Poona : Ancient and Modern), Bombay, 1971.

Kashyap, Annapurna, "Nagpur : A Study in Urban Morphology", Ph.D. Dissertation, University of Nagpur, 1961.

Kosambi, Meera, *Bombay and Poona : A Socio-Ecological Study of Two Indian Cities—1650-1900*, University of Stockholm, Stockholm, 1980.

Lahiri, T.B., "Calcutta : A Million City with a Million Problems", in R.P. Misra, (ed.), *Million Cities of India*, Vikas Publishing House Pvt. Ltd., New Delhi, 1978.

Lucknow District Gazetteer, (1959).

Mahadev, P.D., "Bangalore : A Garden City of Metropolitan Dimensions", in R.P. Misra (ed.), *Milllon Cities of India*, Vikas Publishing House Pvt. Ltd., New Delhi, 1978.

Majumdar, D.N., *Social Contours of an Industrial City—Social Survey of Kanpur, 1954-56*, Asia Publishing House, Delhi, 1960.

McKintosh, J., *Memoirs*, Vol. I, Second Edition, London, 1836.

Montgomery, Robert, *Statistical Report of the District of Cawnpore*, Calcutta, 1849.

Moreland, *From Akbar to Aurangzeb.*

Mukerjee, Radhakamal and Baljit Singh, *Social Profiles of a Metropolis : Social and Economic Structure of Lucknow—Capital of Uttar Pradesh*, Asia Publishing House, Bombay, 1961.

Nagpur Metropolitan Regional Planning Board : *Regional Plan for Nagpur Metropolitan Region, 1971-91*, Part I, Surveys and Studies, Nagpur : Nagpur Metropolitan Regional Planning Board, 1970.

National Institute of Urban Studies, New Delhi (N.D.) : The Development Plan of Greater Bombay—A Case Study of Urban Planning and Development (mimeo).

Nevill. H.R., *District Gazetteer of Cawnpore*, 1909.

Planning Commission "Report of the Working Group on Slums", Planning Commission, New Delhi, 1972.

Poona Gazetteer, III.

Poona Metropolitan Regional Planning Board : *Regional Plan for Poona Metropolitan Region, 1970-1991*, Part-I, Surveys, 1970.

Rao, Hayavadana, *Modern Mysore*, Vol. II, Higginbothams, Bangalore, 1936.

Raza, Moonis and Atiya Habeeb, "Characteristics of Colonial Urbanization—A Case Study of the Satellite "Primacy" of Calcutta (1850-1921)", in S. Manzoor Alam and V.V. Pokshishevsky (eds.), *Urbanization in Developing Countries*, Osmania University Press, Hyderabad, 1976.

Raza, Moonis etc., "Valley of Kashmir : A Geographical Interpretation, VI", *The Land*, Vikas, New Delhi, 1978a.

Raja, Moonis etc., ed., Sources of Economic and Social Statistics of India, Emeka Pub., New Delhi, 1978b.

Razi, Amin and Ahmed, (n.d.), *Haft-Iqlim*, Aligarh Muslim University, Manuscript.

Report on the Political Administration of the Rajputana States for the Year 1870-71.

Revenue Development, Government of Bombay (1840) : 13/1217/1840 (Minute), 1.

Roy, Ashim Kumar, *History of the Jaipur City*, Manohar, New Delhi, 1978.

Roy, M.N., *India in Transition*, Nichiketa Publications Ltd., Bombay, 1971.

Saha, Bakht Ram, *Buddhivilasa*, Rajasthan Oriental Research Institute, Jodhpur, 1964.

Sarwar, Ghulam, *Khazinat-ul-Asafiya*, Vol. I, Lucknow, 1874.

Sengupta, Sunanda, "Squatter Settlements in Delhi", Unpublished Paper, 1975.

Shivaramakrishnan, K.C , *Indian Urban Scene*, Indian Institute of Advanced Study, Simla, 1978.

Singh, Harihar, *Kanpur : A Study in Urban Geography*, Indrasani Devi, Banaras, 1972.

Sinha, Pradip, *Calcutta in Urban History*, Firma K.L.M. Pvt. Ltd, Calcutta, 1978.

Spear, P., *India : A Modern History*, Ann Arbor, 1961.

Spencer, J.E., *Asia, East by South : A Cultural Geography*, London, 1954.

Srivastava, S.C., *Migration in India*, Paper No. 2 of Census of India, 1971, 1979.

Sundaram, K.V., "Delhi : The National Capital", in R.P. Misra (ed.), *Million Cities of India*", Vikas Publishing House Pvt. Ltd., New Delhi, 1978.

Thomas, D.S., "Research Memorandum on Migration Differentials", *Social Science Research Council Bulletin*, New York, 43, 1938.

Thornton, E., *A Gazetteer of the Territories under the Government of the East India Company and of the Native States on the Continent of India*, Vol. IV.

Town and Country Planning Organisation, Government of India: "Urbanization in India—A Statistical Abstract and National Urbanization Policy", (Draft Paper), 1975.

Valentia, Lord, *Voyages and Travels to India (1809)*, London : Quoted in Geoffrey Moorhouse, *Calcutta*, Weidenfeld and Nicholson, London, 1971.

Venkatarayappa, K.N., *Bangalore—A Socio-Ecological Study*, University of Bombay, Bombay, 1957.

White Paper on Indian States, New Delhi, 1950.

Wright, H.N., *Catalogue of the Coins in the Indian Museum*, Vol. III, Calcutta, 1907.

Wyon, J.B. and Cordon, J.E., *The Khanna Study : Population Problems in the Rural Punjab*, Harvard, Cambridge, Universty Press, 1971.

Zachariah, K.C., "A Note on Internal Migration in India", in *Urban-Rural Differences in Southern Asia*, UNESCO Research Centre on Social and Economic Development in Southern Asia, Delhi, 1964.

PART TWO

Economic Aspects of Rural-Urban Migration

5. *Rural-Urban Migration: An Economic Model and the Indian Evidence**

K. SUNDARAM

In this paper we shall consider the applicability and relevance in the Indian context of Todaro's model of rural-urban migration in less developed countries (LDCs). The model is focused on migration in search of (better) employment. While formally allowing for the play of non-economic factors, the model accords primacy to economic factors. In particular it highlights the role of the 'expected-income differentials'.

In considering the relevance and applicability in the Indian context of the Todaro model we do not attempt an econometric test of the migration function because of data limitations. Our approach would be to show that the extent of rural-urban migration in search of employment is so small as to border on the negligible even though there exists a sizeable defferential between income-foregone on in the rural areas and the expected income (adjusted for the probability of unemployment) in urban areas. This evidence for one time point in the early 1970s will be supplemented by evidence of a decline in the rate of rural-urban migration over the period 1963-64—1973-74 with no concurrent decline in the expected-income differentials.

*A revised version of a paper presented to the Workshop on "Social, Economic and Demographic Aspects of Migration" held on February 12-13, 1982 at the Department of Sociology, Delhi School of Economics, Delhi-110007. I am grateful to M.S.A. Rao, Suresh Tendulkar, J. Krishnamurty and Kaushik Basu for extremely useful discussions. The usual disclaimers apply.

The overall thrust of the Indian evidence would thus be to cast serious doubts on the significance of 'expected income differentials' as a major determinant of rural-urban migration (or rather, in this case, the absence of such migration).

In Section I we discuss the background to, and present our outline of, the model of migration considered in this paper. The evidence on the extent of rural-urban migration in search of employment is presented in Section II which shows that such migration is extremely limited in the early 1970s. For the same time point it is shown in Section III that the near absence of rural-urban migration in search of employment is despite the presence of fairly significant 'expected-income differentials'. Supplementary evidence for early 1960s is presented and the conclusions drawn in Section IV.

I

The Background of the Model

One of the 'stylized facts' to emerge from the past experience of the now developed countries is the shift of the working population from the low-productivity agricultural sector in rural areas to the high productivity modern industrial and services sectors in urban areas. This gave rise to a characterization of the process of economic development itself as a process of labour transfer from low to the high productivity sectors, as for instance, in the celebrated paper by Sir Arthur Lewis. In fact, one can interpret the central assumption of Lewis' Model of unlimited supplies of labour being available to the modern sector at a fixed wage that is slightly higher than the average income in the traditional agricultural sector, as a theory of migration of rural workers to urban centres. Here the wage (income) differential serves as a signal powerful enough to ensure a supply of as much labour as is necessary for the expanding modern sector.

The development experience of the present-day LDCs in the two decades and more since World War II has thrown up a set of 'stylized facts' which necessitated a review of the Lewis-type migration function. Thus, in this period, the urban population of these countries grew at rates significantly in excess of the rate of growth of the total population and in several instances, urban growth was concentrated in one or two large cities. Rural-urban migration has been viewed as a significant contributory factor in the rather rapid growth of urban population in general, and the emergence of primate cities in particular. Secondly, such rural-urban migration occurred in an urban environment of high (and possibly rising) rates of open unemployment. So that the view of migration as a response to opportunities for (certain) employment at a higher wage needed to be modified. Todaro's migration model with its focus on 'expected' as opposed to 'observed' wage (income) differentials is essentially a response to the new stylized facts from the LDCs.

Todaro's model of migration is an avowedly 'economic' model. As he himself puts it : "while the factor (affecting the decision to migrate) include both economic and non-economic variables, the economic ones are assumed to predominate" (7, p. 29). His focus is on migration in search of (better) employment.

The central variable in the model is the *expected* income in the urban centre [$E(Y_u)$]. Judged in relation to the income foregone in the rural area (Y_r), the *expected* urban income provides the signals to the potential migrant. In a simplified framework, the potential migrant faces (by assumption) only two mutually exclusive and exhaustive alternatives : (i) being employed in the high wage modern sector, and (ii) remaining unemployed. In this case, with P defining the probability of finding employment in the high wage sector and Y_u the income in the high wage sector in the urban area

$$E(Y_u)=P.\ Y_u+(1\text{-}P).\ O\ ,\ \text{with}\ O<P\leqslant 1$$

In his aggregative model of labour demand and labour supply in urban areas, Todaro relates the probability P of the migrant finding a job in the high wage sector to the proportion of high wage workers in the urban labour force. That is,

$$P = \frac{\text{Number of workers in the urban high wage sector}}{\text{Total urban labour force}} = \frac{E_u}{L_u}$$

Defining $\frac{Y_u}{Y_r} = W$ and denoting the *flow* of rural migrants (in search of work) as a proportion of the rural labour force as $m = \frac{M}{L_r}$, the migration function can be written as

$$m = F(\frac{E_u}{L_r}, W, Z).$$

Here Z, denotes "*other factors*" such as distance, personal contacts, urban amenities, etc., which also exert some influence on the migrant's perception of the relative 'costs' and 'benefits' of origin and destination opportunities" (Todaro, (7), p. 34, italics in the original).

Holding W and Z constant, the rate of rural-urban migration—m— becomes a positive function of the proportion of high wage workers in the urban labour force. It is obvious that with unemployment as the only alternative, the migration rate would be a negative function of the urban unemployment rate.

The migration function briefly sketched above has already become a part of the tool-kit of many a development economist. There is a fairly sizeable body of literature incorporating this migration function in the analysis of development problems and the derivation of policy-oriented results [see for example the papers by Harris-Todaro (4), Srinivasan and Bhagwati (6) and Kaushik Basu (1)]. Attempts have also been made, with varying degree of success, to empirically validate the Todaro model of migration, or variants thereof, by reference to migration data for several countries (see, Todaro (7) for a review of these studies).

In considering the relevance and applicability of the Todaro model of migration to India, the first question to be answered is whether at all there is significant rural-urban migration of people in search of (better) employment. It will be shown that in India the rate of rural-urban migration is extremely small, even as a proportion of the urban labour force, so that, at one level, such migration does not appear to matter for analysis of urban labour markets. If this low level of rural-urban migration is viewed as an 'equilibrium' situation, a second question arises; is the situation reflective of the absence of 'expected-income differentials'. But as is shown, considerable differentials exist between the income foregone in rural areas and the expected income in urban areas; accordingly, migration as a force competing away the income differential does not seem to be important.

II

Extent of Rural-Urban Migration in India

Before considering questions of measurement and data base, it is useful to remember that we are looking for an estimate of the flow over, say, a one year period of rural migration into urban areas in search of employment. The stock of migrants in urban areas undifferentiated by length of residence in the place of enumeration is thus not a relevant measure. (However, the stock of migrants whose duration of stay is less than a year can be a useful proxy for the annual flow of migrants). Equally relevant in defining a migrant is not the place of birth of the resident but the place of last residence.

Given our requirements, two data sources provide the information on rural-urban migration in India. These are, respectively, (i) the Census of India, 1971 and (ii) the National Sample Survey, 28th Round (NSS Survey) on Internal Migration in India, 1973-74. In both cases, a migrant is defined by reference to his last place of residence. In the case of the NSS-Survey, a migrant was defined as a person whose residence a year earlier was different from the place of enumeration. Thus the definition of a migrant in the NSS-Survey provides an estimate of the annual migration. The 1971 Census definition (rather one of the definitions adopted) was based simply on the place of last residence being different from the place of enumeration. Also, in the Census, the migrants so defined were further classified by duration of stay in the place of enumeration; 'duration less than 1 year' as one of these classes thus can also be a proxy for the desired estimate of the annual flow of migrants. However, only the NSS-Survey provides a break-up of annual migrants by "Reason for Migration". The 1971 Census, while providing motivational data for all migrants (i.e. irrespective of duration), does not contain similar information about migrants in the less than 1 year duration category. It is why we will be relying primarily on the NSS 28th Round Survey on Internal Migration in India.

A number of steps (and assumptions) are required in obtaining an estimate of the proportion of 'rural-migrants in search of work in urban areas' in the urban labour force from the results of the NSS Survey. These details are presented in the Appendix.

Under the extreme assumption that all the interstate and intra-state migrants in search of work into the urban areas of the state emanate from the rural areas, the (maximal) estimate of 'rural migrants in search of work in urban areas' is a little less than 45 per 10,000 of urban population at the all-India level. Even in the three major industrialized and urbanised states, Maharashtra, Tamil Nadu and West Bengal, this proportion is only marginally higher at 50, 63 and 49 per 10,000 respectively. As a proportion of the urban labour force, these numbers would be roughly thrice as large (since only a little over one-third of the population is in the labour force), but would still be insignificant at 1.28 per cent at the all-India level, 1.37 per cent in urban Maharashtra, 1.69 per cent in urban Tamil Nadu and 1.30 per cent in urban West Bengal. Under more plausible assumptions, these proportions would be only half as much or even less (see Appendix for details).

It may be suggested that the rural migrants in search of work in urban areas are not spread all over the urban areas of a State but are concentrated in one or two of its big metropolitan cities. Clearly, with such bunching of rural migrants estimates presented above relating to urban areas of the State as whole would understate the proportion of migrant workers in its cities. How significant is this correction? NSS does not provide this tabulation, and therefore some further assumptions are involved. Let us make the assumption that the rural migrants in search of work in urban areas of a State are *all* located in *one* big metropolitan city of the State, viz., Greater Bombay (Maharashtra), Madras city (Tamil Nadu) and Calcutta.

Let us further assume that the labour force participation rates in the cities are the same as those in the urban areas of the States where they are located.[1]

Even under the extreme assumptions that (i) *all* the in-migrants in search of work in urban areas come from rural areas, *and* that (ii) *all* 'rural migrants in search of work' in urban areas so estimated are located in *one* metropolitan city each in the three States, they would comprise no more than 3.5 per cent of the labour force of the three major metropolitan cities (Bombay, Madras, Calcutta) taken together. In the case of Madras city the proportion at 6.5 per cent[2] is higher, but is only 2 per cent in that of Calcutta.

Even if we retain assumption (ii), more plausible assumptions to replace (i) would lower these proportions further. The alternative estimates would then be : 1.83 per cent for Greater Bombay, 2.32 for the Madras city and 0.97 per cent for Calcutta.

It may be argued, with some justification, that NSS Surveys cannot adequately capture the migration phenomenon since they are based on a 'household' frame. In particular, the NSS Surveys may fail to capture the houseless population in cities which includes a sizeable number of migrants. To meet this objection, we turn to the 1971 Census estimates of rural in-migrants into the two big cities : Greater Bombay and Calcutta

1. In the absence of Labour Force Participation Rates (LFPRs) specific to the metropolitan cities in question, we are forced to assume that the LFPRs for a city will be the same as that for the urban area of the State in which the city is located. It is possible that city specific LFPRs are lower (and, correspondingly, the proportion of rural migrants in search of work to the city labour force higher). Note, however, that the range of variations in LFPRs in general is fairly small. Further, given the sizeable share of the city in the urban population of the State, the city-specific LFPR would have a considerable weight in determining the Urban-LFPR in the State.
2. The relatively high ratio for Madras city has to be seen against the fact that 64 per cent of the migrants into urban Tamil Nadu come from other urban centres located within, and outside, the State. Accordingly, the assumption that *all* migrants seeking work come only from the rural areas becomes particularly untenable. Further, unlike Greater Bombay and Calcutta, Madras city is not yet a megalopolis, and there are 15 other cities with a population of 1 lakh and above in Tamil Nadu.

Urban Agglomeration.[3] Consistent with our requirements of *flow* estimates of migrants, one may consider the number of rural in-migrants (by place of last residence) with a duration of stay of less than 1 year. According to the 1971 Census, such migrants numbered about 72,000 (42,000 males and 30,000 females) in Greater Bombay city and a little over 21,000 in Calcutta (14,000 males and 7,000 females). Even if we make, once again, the extreme assumption that *all* such migrants, irrespective of sex and age (30 per cent of them were children in the age group 0-14 in Greater Bombay and 25 per cent in Calcutta Urban Agglomeration) are in the labour force, they would form only a little over 3 per cent of the labour force of the city of Greater Bombay and under 1 per cent of the labour force of Calcutta.

It thus seems quite clear that 'rural migrants in search of work in urban areas' form a very small proportion (well-below 4 per cent) of the *urban* labour force, whether we consider the flows at the all-India level, or flows into the urban areas of the three major industrialised or urbanised States, Maharashtra, Tamil Nadu and West Bengal, or into the three major metropolitan cities, Greater Bombay, Madras and Calcutta.

Let us now recall that the migration variable in the model is the number of rural migrants in search of work in urban areas as a proportion of the *rural labour force*. Given the fact that the rural labour force is 4 to 5 times as large as the urban labour force, the annual flow of rural migrants in search of work in urban areas would, as a proportion of the *rural labour force*, be extremely small, bordering on the negligible.[4]

If the evidence concerning the very low levels of rural migration relative to the *urban* labour force, and even more so relative to the *rural* labour force, is accepted, it raises the

3. In this context, it is worth noting that Census authorities conduct a special mid-night enumeration of the pavement dwellers.

4. It would perhaps be more appropriate to consider the flow of rural migrants in search of work as a proportion of the rural work force 'potentially at risk' as far as migration is concerned. Thus, if we take only the workers in non-cultivator households who also have very little else by way of assets, they would be a little over 1/4th of the rural work force, or roughly as much as the total urban labour force. So that the ratios to urban labour force may also be interpreted as proportion to the rural labour force 'at risk of migration'.

fundamental question whether one needs at all to model such flows.

More pertinently, in the context of the Todaro model of migration outlined in the first section, the following question needs to be raised: does the relative insignificance of work seeking migration reflect the absence of significant expected rural-urban income differentials in India. We examine this question in the next section.

III

In considering the evidence on expected-income differentials, the following points need to be kept in view : (i) rural-urban differentials will relate to the country as a whole, and so could be smaller than those derived for the metropolitan cities and (ii) ideally, we should estimate the discounted present values of the income-foregone in the rural areas and of the expected incomes in the urban areas over the (working) life of the potential migrant.[5] We shall, however, be setting up a one-point comparison. In our judgment this should not seriously distort the estimates of expected-income differentials, considering that the time-horizons covering these decisions are not very long. Also, unlike in the modern organised sector, where one can postulate both a secular rise in productivity and a share in the productivity gains for the workers, the real wage incomes in the agricultural sector—a proxy for Y_r—is likely to be kept down by the pressure of growing population and labour having to be residually absorbed in that sector. With these two caveats outlined, we may consider the evidence on expected-income differentials.

As a first step in the analysis, let us consider Y_r, the estimate of income foregone in the rural areas. A problem one encounters immediately is that, contrary to the model specification, the rural sector is not homogeneous but differentiated in terms of ownership of land and other assets as well as access to inputs and new technology. In this situation the

5. See Todaro (7, p. 32).

income foregone by a potential migrant is not independent of his economic and social status and it is no longer meaningful to postulate a single Y_r as the measure of income foregone.

In view of the foregoing, we set up the expected-income comparisons for the class of rural workers in the assetless 'pure' (i.e. landless) agricultural labour households which predominate among the rural poor. In terms of numbers, there were about 26 million workers in the 'pure' agricultural labour households in 1971.[6]

The *Rural Labour Enquiry, 1974-75* provides information about the average daily earnings and the number of days of wage employment[7] of male, female and child workers in agricultural labour households. For a male worker from a 'pure' agricultural labour household the annual earnings[8] work out to Rs. 684 at 1974-75 rural prices. Adjusting for factors such as (i) valuation of the 'kind-component' of rural wages at on farm prices rather than rural retail prices, (ii) urban prices are higher than rural prices, and (iii) there may be tangible or psychological costs of working and living in an urban environment, raises this estimate of annual earnings by 50 per cent. Thus earnings, comparable to expected income in urban areas, for this class of workers would be Rs. 1,025.

In computing the 'expected income' in urban areas, we shall expand the set of options to include 'employment' in the urban informal sector, in addition to those of finding a job in the high wage modern sector and of remaining unemployed.

That is, we shall define the expected income $E(Y_u)$

$$= P_1 . Wc + P_2 . YuI + (1 - P_1 - P_2) \times O.$$

Where YuI stands for annual earnings in the urban informal sector, and $(1 - P_1 - P_2)$ defines the probability of remaining unemployed.

6. This may be contrasted with a total urban work force of 36 millions in 1976. See footnote 3 above.
7. For a worker drawn from assetless households only days in wage-employment are relevant as they have no base for self-employment in agricultural or non-agricultural occupations.
8. Since the number of days in employment is variable and uncertain, it is more meaningful to set up the comparison in terms of annual earnings. It may also be noted that the annual earnings of a female or a child worker from such a household would be lower even as the average daily earnings are lower.

Let us begin by considering YuI. The National Sample Survey (NSS) 29th Round Survey on *Self-employment in non-agricultural enterprises* provides information on the value-added per worker (males and females together) in a variety of urban informal sector activities, which, given the extremely meagre levels of capital employed, could be treated as the returns to labour services. The value-added per worker would, naturally, differ from one activity to another. Confining ourselves to the lower end of the range, it was Rs. 2,315 in construction, Rs. 2,110 in restaurants and hotels and Rs. 1,500 in personal services. Only retailing *pan*, *supari* and similar activities yields a value-added per worker lower than in personal activities. An estimate of YuI equal to Rs. 1,500 is thus quite plausible, the more so if we allow for some upward mobility even within the urban informal sector.

Let us next examine the probability of remaining unemployed with zero income. According to the NSS 27th Round Survey on Employment and Unemployment, 1972-73, the 'usual status' unemployment rate for males in the urban labour force was about 5 per cent. Two points may be noted. First, though the usual status rate is generally identified with 'chronic' unemployment, *less than half* of the usual status unemployment among urban males was for one year or more. In fact, about 30 per cent of them had been unemployed for less than six months. Second, this is the unemployment rate for *all* male workers in urban areas irrespective of their levels of education. Given the fact that the unemployment rate among educated workers is significantly higher, the unemployment rate applicable to the illiterate male worker (the relevant group in considering the probability of a potential-migrant drawn from 'pure' agricultural labour households) would be much lower—nearer 3 per cent rather than 5 per cent. Thus, if we equate the probability of remaining unemployed to the usual status urban unemployment rates for males, that is 5 per cent, we would only be *overstating* it (and so *understating* the expected income).

Since we do not have any direct measure of the probability of finding a job in the urban informal sector, we will estimate it residually. Now at any point of time, there are only three mutually exclusive and exhaustive possibilities; and the probability of remaining unemployed has been taken to be 5 per cent. Accordingly, if we make the extreme assumption that the potential-migrant has a zero probability of finding a job in the high wage modern sector, he would have 95 per cent probability of finding a place in the urban informal sector. In this case, his expected income would be 0.95 times, Rs. 1,500 or Rs. 1,425, which is about 40 per cent higher than the income foregone.

The data relating to the factory sector for 1974-75, place the earnings of a production process worker at about Rs. 4,800. However, this level has to be adjusted downwards for possible lesser skill and experience of migrants, although, with rising productivity in the sector and given that workers do share productivity gains to some extent, it is quite attainable over time. For our calculations, we may accept a significantly lower figure of Rs. 3,000 as a measure of annual earnings in the modern sector if the potential migrant finds a job within it.

Following Todaro, one may equate the probability (P_1) of finding a job in the modern sector in the urban area with the ratio:[9]

$$\frac{\text{Work force in the organised sector in urban India}}{\text{Urban Labour Force}}$$

With about 14 million workers in the urban organised sector and about 38 million in the urban labour force in 1971, P_1 would be roughly 37 per cent. We have already taken $(1-P_1-P_2)$ to be 5 per cent, so that P_2 equals 58 per cent. In this case, the expected income $E\,(Yu) = 0.37 \times 3{,}000 + 0.58 \times 1{,}500 + .05 \times 0 = \text{Rs. } 1{,}980$.

A more realistic estimate of P_1 would be in terms of the ratio:

$$\frac{\text{Number of jobs filled annually in the organised sector}}{\text{Number of workers competing for the same}}$$

Now, the number of jobs filled annually is the sum of new jobs and the turnover of the existing stock. According to the Labour

9. It is worth noting that most economists modelling rural-urban migration cited earlier, use this version of the probability variable.

Bureau Statistics for 1974-75, the turnover rate is about 30 per cent in the organised factory sector. Thus, with a stock of 14 million workers in the urban organised sector, turnover would account for a little over 4 million jobs. In addition, annual additions to organised sector employment have averaged about 1/2 million since the 1950s, having risen to about 3/4 million during the 1970s. Since those who are stably employed in the organised sector can be excluded from the set of those competing for the new jobs and others seeking a job change, the total number competing would be a little over 28 million. As such, an alternative estimate of P_1 would be about 16 per cent.

The corresponding expected income, would then be $E(Yu) = 0.16 \times 3{,}000 + 0.79 \times 1{,}500 + 0.05 \times 0 =$ Rs. 1,665. Thus, the expected income of a potential migrant male from a 'pure' agricultural labourer household, at least Rs. 1,425 on the extreme assumption of zero probability of high wage employment and any non-zero job probability in the urban organised sector, would increase, possibly, to only as much as Rs. 1,665.

We thus have a juxtaposition of two facts : (i) the presence of an expected income differential of between 40 and 60 per cent, and (ii) an extremely small flow of rural work seeking migrants relative to the size of the urban labour force becoming even smaller as a proportion of the rural labour force. *Prima facie* this casts doubt on the link between the rural and urban labour markets operating via migration in response to expected income differentials. Equally obvious is the fact that the observed flow of migrants is too small a fraction even of the urban labour force to 'compete away' or iron out, the differentials.

IV

It may be argued that the evidence relating to a single point of time is not conclusive. Unfortunately, due to lack of data one cannot construct time-series of the annual flow of internal migration and of the variations over time in the constant price expected-income differentials. However, a comparison of the migration flows as between the 18th and 28th Rounds of the NSS does suggest a drop in the rate of rural-urban migration (see (5)). Thus at the all-India level, the in-migration rate into urban areas drops from 241 per 10,000 of urban population in the 18th Round (1963-64) to 194 per 10,000 in the 28th Round 1973-74. Also, the proportion of the in-migrants into urban areas coming from rural areas drops from 58.45 per cent to 45.43 per cent over the same period.

It is not possible to directly estimate the expected-income differentials in 1963-64 at constant prices. However, the following evidence may be regarded as suggestive. Productivity per worker at constant 1960-61 prices (NDP Originating/WF) increased by over 25 per cent from Rs. 3,201 to Rs. 4,019 in the organised manufacturing sector compared to an unchanged Rs. 500 in the agricultural sector. In the rest of the non-agricultural sector too there was some increase in productivity per worker, so that for all-sectors taken together it went up from Rs. 734 to Rs. 859. We also have move direct evidence (3) of an increase in the Index of Real Wages of Workers in the Factory Sector from 112.67 in 1963 to 119.32 in 1973. It is also worth noting that the proportion of organised work force to total work force increased from 7.7 per cent in 1961 to 8.9 per cent in 1971 (see (2)). Also, in urban area itself, the proportion of workers in the organised manufacturing industry remained roughly constant between 1961 and 1971. Considering these developments one can reasonably take the view that there was no clear reduction in the expected-income differentials between 1963-64 and 1973-74. Thus, a comparison at two points of time, 1963-64 and 1973-74 shows that the flow of annual migrants from rural India into urban areas of the country fell significantly without a concurrent decline in expected income differentials.

In sum, the hypothesis that rural-urban migration takes place primarily in response to expected income differentials is not supported by the available Indian evidence relating to the early 1960s and early 1970s. In our view, an understanding of the presence, or absence, of rural-urban migration in India would require a closer analysis of other factors, such as imperfections in the capital market, access to information and the 'distance' separating the two populations. Thus, a migrant with a low level of income from the rural areas has to wait for some period in the urban area without any means of support before he finds sustenance in the urban informal sector, or a job in the organised sector. He would need to borrow to finance his consumption during this waiting period. In theory he should be able to borrow against his future earnings, but in practice he is not able to do so Since he does not have much collateral to offer, he is out of the organised credit market. And, while in the informal credit market personal loans are possible, such loans require some prior contact between the borrower and the lender. These would be the operative aspects of imperfections in the capital market as they affect the migration decision. Similarly, access to information about factors like job opportunities and living conditions of potential rural migrants is still largely a matter of links forged by ties of caste, of religion or even of the village. Finally, the relevant measure of 'distance' between the village and the city is not simply the geographical distance separating the two locations, which can readily be converted into the equivalent economic cost of transportation. There is, instead, a whole range of non-economic factors introducing, what may be called a 'social' or 'cultural' distance which possibly weighs more significantly in migration decisions of the rural population in India.[10] Thus, in understanding rural-urban migration in India not only do factors other than expected-income-differentials appear significant, but the purely 'economic' elements of these 'other factors' are, perhaps, less significant than the sociological and psychological ones incorporated in them.

10. Of relevance in this context is the absence of a rural-urban continuum of population densities in terms of the population size of villages/towns/cities in India. Thus, as per the 1971 Census, 64 per cent of rural population lives in villages each with a population of 2000 or less. In contrast, only 6½ per cent of the urban population lives in towns of 10,000 or less. At the other end, 49 per cent of urban population lives in cities of 1 lakh or more. This fact that the bulk of the rural population lives in units with 1/50th size of urban centres in which the majority of the urban population lives, introduces a major 'distance factor' that could possibly be more important than the geographical distance separating any particular village from an urban city centre.

REFERENCES

Basu, Kaushik C., "Optimal Policies in Dual Economies", *Quarterly Journal of Economics*, Vol. 95, No. 1, August 1980.

Government of India, Planning Commission, *Draft Five Year Plan 1978-83*, New Delhi, 1978.

Government of India, CSO., *Wages are Productivity in Organised Manufacturing Sector 1960-61—1976-77*, New Delhi, August 1979.

Harris, J.R. and M.P. Todaro, "Migration, Unemployment and Development : A Two-Sector Analysis", *American Economic Review*, Vol. 60, 1970.

Mukherjee, S.R. and S.K. Banerjee, "Some Aspects of Internal Annual Migration in India", *Sarvekshana*, Vol. 2, No. 2, October 1978.

Srinivasan, T.N. and J.N. Bhagwati, "Shadow Prices for Project Solution in the Presence of Distortions", *Journal of Political Economy*, Vol. 86, No. 1, February 1978.

Todaro, M.P., *Internal Migration in Developing Countries*, ILO, Geneva, 1976.

APPENDIX

'Rural Migrants in Search of Work' in Urban Labour Force: All-India and 3 Major States

The estimates presented here are based on the results of the National Sample Survey 28th Round (NSS Survey) on Internal Migration (Survey period : October 1, 1973 to June 30, 1974) as reported in a paper by S.R. Mukherjee and S.K. Banerjee (5). In this survey, a migrant is defined as one whose place of residence *one-year* preceding the enumeration was different from his place of enumeration. Thus, our estimates relate to the flow of *annual migrants*. Now in an urban area of any State, migrants can be and are drawn from : (a) rural areas of that State, (b) Other urban areas of that State, (c) rural areas of other States, and (d) urban areas of other States. Categories (a) and (b) together constitute the intra-state migrants, categories (c) and (d) making up inter-state migrants. Clearly, categories (a) and (c) together constitute the *rural migrants* into the urban areas of the State; and all-India estimates would be a weighted average of State level estimates.

In the paper referred to (the only published source which goes beyond the presentation of the migration rates), Mukherjee and Banerjee have provided, for the different States and at the all-India level, the relative importance of 'migrants in search of work' separately for inter-state migrants and intra-state migrants into urban areas of the State.

The proportions of such migrants, per 10,000 of the corresponding population, into urban areas of the three Indian States, Maharashtra, Tamil Nadu and West Bengal, where the three major metropolitan cities are located, as well as for the country as a whole are resumed in Table A.1.

TABLE A.1

Estimates of Inter-and Intra-state Migrants in Search of Work : All India and Selected States (1973-74)

	Inter-state in-migrants in urban areas (per 10,000 persons)	Intra-state in-migrants in urban areas (per 10,000 persons)
All-India	12.31	32.40
Maharashtra	12.10	38.15
Tamil Nadu	9.24	53.32
West Bengal	22.13	27.12

As noted previously, inter-state migrants in search of work, as indeed all inter-state migrants, can and do come from both rural and urban areas of other States. Similarly, intra-state migrants, whether in search of work or for other reasons, can and do come from rural areas and other urban locations (other than the place of enumeration) within the State. Since we do not have a breakdown of the inter-state (and intra-state) migrants in search of work in terms of their rural or urban location prior to migration, we have to resort to an allocation procedure. An extreme assumption one can make is that *all* intra-state (and inter-state) migrants in search of work into urban areas of a State come only from the rural areas. This would be the upper bound on 'rural migrants in search of work' in urban areas, and will be our Estimate 1.

Fortunately, we do have the distribution of all in-migrants into urban areas by the four locations (though not by purpose of migration) (Table A.2).

TABLE A.2

Percentage Distribution of In-migrants in Urban Areas by Place of Residence One Year Ago

Place of Previous Residence	Within the State		From other States		All Areas
Place of Enumeration	Rural	Urban	Rural	Urban	
All-India Urban	36.70	44.80	8.73	9.77	100.00
Maharashtra Urban	42.22	45.22	7.10	5.46	100.00
Tamil Nadu Urban	32.37	56.32	3.35	7.96	100.00
West Bengal Urban	26.13	47.26	16.47	10.14	100.00

If we use this distribution to pro-rate the intra-state (and inter-state) 'migrants in search of work' into urban areas, we can obtain an alternative, and more plausible, estimate of the 'rural migrants in search of work' in urban areas. This will be our Estimate 2. The two estimates of rural migrants in search of work in urban areas (per 10,000 of the urban population) is set out in Table A.3. below.

TABLE A.3

Estimates of Rural Migrants-in-Search of Work in Urban Areas : All-India and Selected States : 1973-74

(Rate per 10,000 of urban population

State	Estimate 1	Estimate 2
All-India	44.71	20.40
Maharashtra	50.25	25.26
Tamil Nadu	62.56	22.20
West Bengal	49.25	23.36

In order to express the 'rural migrants in search of work' as a proportion of the urban labour force, we need the labour force participation rates (LFPRs) of persons in urban areas, expressed as a proportion of population of all-ages. The NSS 27th Round Survey on Employment and Unemployment provides us the LFPRs (by usual status) for the population aged 5 and over as well as the estimated proportion of the population in the age-group 0-4 (which is assumed, by definition, to be outside the labour force). Combining the two, we can obtain the LFPRs relative to population of all ages, and, in turn, the two estimates of the 'rural migrants in search of work' in urban areas as a proportion of the urban labour force (Table A.4).

Thus, it is seen that, at the all-India level and in the three major States, even the upper bound estimate of rural migrants in search of work in urban areas relative to the urban labour force is close to 1 per cent, the plausible estimate being about one-half of one per cent.

TABLE A.4

Labour Force Participation Rates (LFPRs) and Rural Migrants in Urban Areas: All-India and Selected States : 1973-74

States	(Per cent) LFPRs (to populated OP)	Rural Migrants in search of work in urban areas as a proportion of urban labour force	
		Estimate 1	Estimate 2
All-India	34.93	1.28	0.58
Maharashtra	36.57	1.37	0.69
Tamil Nadu	37.06	1.69	0 60
West Bengal	37.85	1.30	0.62

6. *Rural-Urban Migration and Work Organization in a Slum*

U. TATAJI

In 1978, according to the Government of India, 48 per cent of the rural population and 41 per cent of the urban population in India lived below the poverty line. Jolly *et al*. noted that "... almost everywhere in the developing world rural poverty is greater than the urban poverty" (1973:115) due to lack of employment in the villages, dearth of land, uneconomic landholdings, etc. In India, the rural poor consist largely of landless labourers, small farmers, tenants, share-croppers and artisans (ILO 1975) who do not have sufficient employment and earnings in the villages (Dandekar and Rath 1971). One of the means of overcoming unemployment and poverty is migration—seasonal, semi-permanent, permanent—to other rural and urban areas (Connel *et al.* 1976; Rao 1976).

Massive rural poverty and unemployment as against investment in and concentration of various economic activities in the cities which resulted in relative urban prosperity—perceived or real, has generated large streams of rural-urban migration in India. Several village and urban studies conducted in India show that small cultivators and landless labourers migrate to cities (Prabhu 1956; Deshmukh 1956; Rowe 1973; Connel *et al.* 1975, etc.) but those with prior contacts and acquaintances (in the cities) have greater propensity to migrate (Epstein 1973; Connel *et al.* 1976). The presence of acquaintances also influences destination of migration and hiring practices in the

* The author expresses his deep sense of gratitude to his research director Prof. K. Ranga Rao of the Department of Sociology, Andhra University and Prof. M.S.A. Rao of the Department of Sociology, Delhi University for their valuable comments and suggestions on the earlier version of this paper.

cities (Eames 1954; Connel *et al.* 1976; De Souza 1978). Further, caste and/or class background of the migrants influence the nature of migration in terms of single or associational (Woodruff 1960; Rowe 1973), the reasons for and consequences of migration in terms of subsistence or development (Rao 1976).

It is opined that most of the poor migrants in cities all over the third world are predominantly employed in the informal sector of the urban economy which includes transport, construction, services, etc. (Sethuraman 1978; Joshi and Joshi 1976; Safa and Du Toit 1975; Radhakrishna *et al.* 1977). Joshi and Joshi (1976 : 7) state that those who fail to secure employment in the organized sector are forced into the unorganized sector which has capacity to absorb them as casual labourers and low wage employees. The studies of Deshmukh (1956), Woodruff (1960), Lynch (1977), Desai and Pillai (1972) and Rao *et al.* (1977) of Indian slums show that poor migrants are employed both in the organized and unorganized sectors of the urban economy.

Different schemes of classification such as organized and unorganized, modern and traditional, capitalist and peasant or subsistence, large and small and formal and informal have been used in the analyses of urban economic structures and labour markets in the third world countries (Sinclair 1978; Joshi 1980; Papola 1980:818). Among these, the formal-informal dichotomy is the latest and is currently in vogue. The formal sector is a term used to refer to large-scale units in industry, services and administration, which are characterized by use of accounting methods, the payment of regular wages and salaries, the use of a fixed place of business and some fixed capital (Sinclair 1978 : 7), official recognition, regulation and support, access to formal credit systems, restricted competition and protection in the market, better wages and working conditions for the personnel (Weeks 1975), unionization among the employees (Joshi 1980), etc. Several writers (Sinclair 1978; Joshi 1980:142; Papola 1980) point out that the informal sector is treated as a residual category consisting of enterprises which are not covered under the formal sector and self-employed individuals. According to the ILO-UNDP Employment Mission to Kenya which used the term 'informal sector' for the first time the characteristics are : easy entry for the new enterprises or individuals, reliance on indigenous resources, family ownership of the enterprises, small scale operations, unregulated and competitive markets, labour intensive technology, and informally acquired skills of the workers, informal work situation, etc. (ILO 1972). Other characteristics like service to the low-income groups (Joshi and Joshi 1976) non-unionization of the workers (Papola 1980), etc., came to be associated with the informal sector.

The concept of informal sector was subjected to serious criticism by Bienfeld and Godfrey (1975), Elkan (1976), Breman (1976), Gerry (1977), Sinclair (1978), Joshi (1980), Papola (1980) among others. The criticisms of Sinclair (1978) could be summarized under three headings: aggregation, linkages and dynamics. First, the concept is too aggregative to permit useful analysis and it implies greater degree of homogeneity within the sector which is empirically untenable. Secondly, its phrasing "obscures and does not allow examination of the linkages which exist between different parts of the 'informal' sector's components and other parts of the economy"; and thirdly, it "does not facilitate analysis of the dynamic forces at work in changing the 'informal' sector's parts through time" (Sinclair 1978 : 96). The validity of certain other characteristics of the informal sector like easy entry (Sinclair 1970; Joshi 1980), unregulated markets (Joshi 1980), small size (Papola 1980) have also been challenged.

In the light of the above discussion an attempt is made in this paper to examine the extent to which the labour market of urban poor fits into the framework of the informal sector as defined in recent writings and to what extent and in what respects it differs from the conceptual scheme that is in vogue. This is proposed to be enquired into with reference to the economic activities of the slum dwellers in the Vijayawada city in the State of Andhra Pradesh.

City Growth and Migration

The city of Vijayawada is situated in the District of Krishna in the State of Andhra Pradesh. It occupies the third rank among the thirteen cities of the State with a population of 344,607 in 1971 and around half-million in 1981. Located on the northern bank of River Krishna it is one of the ancient cities of the State. It connects the Northern Circar districts, Telangana, Southern Circar and the Rayalaseema regions of Andhra Pradesh, and the northern, western and eastern States with the southern States of the country through roads and railways. The city is one of the biggest railway and road junctions in the country. Thus it enjoys greater locational advantage than any other city of the State. The locational advantage and the surrounding rich hinterland made the city an important commercial and transport centre.

The growth of Vijayawada city may be attributed mainly to in-migration consequent upon rapid development of transport and communications linking the city with other parts of the country and a spurt in commercial activity. In terms of economic activities it is functional specific i.e., it is predominantly a trade-transport city. The rate of population growth of the city has been more consistent than the other cities in the State and its population increased from 8,026 in 1871 to around 5 lakhs in 1981.

Since the 1940s the city has been growing enormously in various economic activities such as trade, transport, industry, construction and services. The growth potential of the city has attracted large streams of migrants since then. According to a survey of the city (Prakasa Rao and Ramachandran 1975 : 273) as much as 74 per cent of the heads of the total households (1075 in all) surveyed were migrants. The report points out that there has been a steady influx of migrants into the city since 1945 (Prakasa Rao and Ramachandran 1975 : 258). Out of the total migrants nearly three-fifths (58.9%) migrated from Krishna and Guntur districts, which is considered as the "city region" or city hinterland and 37.3 per cent migrated from other districts but within the State and only 3.8 per cent migrated from other States. A large number of the migrants from the 'city region' possessed technical and non-technical skills and some capital to invest.

The pattern and process of migration into slums is different from that of the pattern and process of migration into the other parts of the city as a whole. The upper and middle class migrants belonging to Brahmin, Kamma and Kapu castes and the Muslim community are mostly from Krishna and Guntur districts. The poor belonging to Reddi, Yadava, Nagara, Nagasipu, Turpu Kapu castes migrated from far-off districts such as Prakasam and Visakhapatnam. The scheduled caste migrants moved in both from the city region as well as other districts like Khammam, a border district, and Prakasam a district far away from the city.

The Job Structure of the City

The job structure of the city should be understood against its trade-transport background. The city is an important wholesale centre for cloth, bullion, machinery parts, automobile parts and agricultural produce. It is the headquarters for film distribution companies and has more than 30 cinema theatres. Most of the entrepreneurs and businessmen of the city belong to the Vysya, Kapu and Kamma castes. While the Vysyas are largely natives of the city many of the Kapu and Kamma businessmen are migrants from Krishna and Guntur districts. Vysyas control much of the business like cloth, gold, utensils, drugs, etc., in the old city. Many businessmen running hotels, film distribution, book, cloth, automobile and engineering trades in the new city are largely Kamma migrants; a few of them are Kapus. Most of the Brahmin migrants are working in the All India Radio, newspaper establishments, schools and colleges and in various government offices as officers or white-collar employees. The professionals such as doctors, lawyers, engineers, etc. are largely drawn from Brahmin and Kamma castes. These upper and intermediate caste groups—Brahmin, Vysya, Kamma and Kapu—live in non-slum localities. As for the Christians even though some are in Government services and teaching organizations, many of them live in slums.

Many Muslims are in skilled jobs in the automobile and transport industry and are traders in junk. In fact most of the junk traders in many cities in the State of Andhra Pradesh as well as other States are Muslims. The migrants from States like Kerala and Tamil Nadu are running small hotels in the city. Of course, a few persons from outside the State are in offices of the Central Government.

A higher proportion of lower and scheduled castes practice occupations which are at the bottom of the job hierarchy when compared to the intermediate castes among whom a few are engaged in different kinds of manual labour. A large majority of the rikshaw-pullers, for example, belong to scheduled and lower castes. All the sweepers in the city are scheduled castes, and most junk collectors are scheduled castes or Muslims. Vadderas, a lower caste, work as construction or sand labourers. The other lower castes like barbers, washermen, Medaris (mat weavers) are largely engaged in their respective caste occupations. Madigas, a scheduled caste, are found in sand labour and a few of them are leather workers. Malas, another scheduled caste are rikshaw-pullers and work as junk collectors and casual labourers.

Slums in the City

Most, if not all, poor migrants put up huts on any piece of land lying vacant and in course of time hutment colonies grow in number and in size. It is no different in Vijayawada city. Nine out of 43 census localities in the city are predominantly hutment colonies. There are small and large clusters of huts in many other census localities.

A comparative analysis of the nine slum localities in the city shows that the proportion of Christians, lower castes, scheduled castes and tribes is greater in slum localities and the proportion of Hindus in general and of the upper and intermediate castes in particular is greater in the city as a whole. The slum localities are characterized by lower educational levels, lower-status and income and occupational categories, poor housing conditions, absence of, or unsatisfactory civic services when compared to the city as a whole. The rates of employment of the slum populations in general, and that of females and children in particular, are higher. All these characteristics of the slums in Vijayawada are more or less similar to that of the slums in other cities in the country (D'Souza 1976; Desai and Pillai 1972; etc.).

Many migrants of upper and intermediate caste groups came to the city seeking, or on, employment in the organized sector. Some came to start or expand business or as self-employed professionals. Growth in various economic activities such as trade, transport helped the emergence of occupations like *mutha* labour, cart pulling and riksha-pulling, collection of old iron, brokerage and skilled and unskilled jobs in transport activity. The demand for labourers in such activities attracted thousands of migrants from near and far-off districts within the State. The role of kinship and caste linkages in information flows, motivation and migration, job getting and settlement in the city are crucial. A large majority of them, being poor at the time of migration, put up huts on vacant lands—wherever they are—on canal banks, hills slopes, near rail tracks.

Case Study

Krishna Puram is one of the nine slum localities in the city. It came up as a small colony of migrant construction labourers of lower and scheduled castes on vacant land by the side of the Krishna River in 1885 when the rail bridge was constructed across the Krishna River. It is now a large multi-caste and a multi-occupational settlement consequent upon changes in the city economy and resulting in migration of various caste groups into it. In 1971 Krishna Puram (or Puram) had a population of 7,887. Its population now consists of 20 castes belonging to upper (a microscopic minority), intermediate, lower and scheduled strata and a group of tribals and Muslims each. The single largest caste group is Vaddera with 263 households, Madiga caste occupies the second place with 200 households.

There are some striking dissimilarities between the caste composition of the city and Krishna Puram. The households of the three upper castes namely Brahmin, Kshatriya and Vysya together account for 20.7 per cent of the city sample (Depart ment of Human Geography 1975) whereas in Krishna Puram they account for just 0.6 per cent. The households belonging to intermediate castes, lower castes, scheduled castes and tribes to the total households of the sample in the city are 32.9 per cent, 9.6 per cent, 16.7 per cent as against 37.8 per cent, 23.6 per cent, and 29.8 per cent in Krishna Puram. Thus the representation of upper castes in the latter is almost negligible and the proportion of lower castes and scheduled castes and tribes is higher when compared to the city as a whole. On the basis of available data on caste composition of the slum and non-slum localities of other cities it can be surmised that the proportion of lower castes, scheduled castes and tribes would be much lower and the proportion of upper castes would be higher in the non-slum localities in the city. While some intermediate castes such as Telaga and Kamma are less represented and others like Reddi and Yadava are highly represented in the Krishna Puram slum when compared to the city as a whole. The relative preponderance of Reddis and Yadavas in Krishna Puram is due to in-migration of the poor belonging to these caste groups from agriculturally underdeveloped areas of Prakasam and Guntur districts.

Around 55 per cent of the sample population is in the working age group. While the literacy rates are lower in general, they are higher among the lower age groups—a pointer to the change due to urban residence. Almost all of the males who are in the working age group are earners. Female employment rates are lower compared to males. Intermediate castes have higher proportion of persons in the working age-group, less proportion of female and child workers when compared to the lower and scheduled castes. Child and female workers are the highest and the literacy rates are the lowest among the lower castes. Intermediate castes differ in several respects from the other groups of castes. Muslims however share most of the characteristics of the intermediate castes.

Process of Migration and Characteristics of Migrants

The demand for construction labourers was created by the construction of the first railway bridge across the River Krishna in the 1880s. Vadderas, whose traditional occupation is earth-work, and Malas and Madigas from Guntur and Prakasam districts responded to this demand. These migrants put up their huts on the vacant lands near the bridge site. Around the 1890s some more scheduled caste households moved into this area from other parts of the city as they were forced to vacate these areas by upper caste people. This is how Krishna Puram was born. Since then the process of in-migration into Puram has been continuing. The migrants in Puram belong to three generations and among them first generation migrants are predominant. Vaddera, Mala and Madiga castes have a large number of third generation migrants. Second generation migrants are found among intermediate, lower and scheduled castes but they are predominant among Vaddera and Madiga castes and Muslims. First generation migrants are predominantly found among intermediate castes and also among Malas—a scheduled caste. All but one intermediate caste migrants, a majority of lower and scheduled castes and Muslims migrated into the city after 1941. The large scale in-migration during this period was a response to the rapidly growing employment opportunities in the city in trade, transport, industry and other sectors of the economy. The rate of in-migration among the intermediate castes is more than the others due to continued availability of employment in *Mutha* labour in which these castes are engaged in larger numbers than the others and this job is more remunerative than other jobs. By and large, caste rank and economic position of the migrants are positively correlated to the distance covered during migration. A majority of the migrants have lower educational levels. Land ownership and indebtedness at the time of migration was greater among the intermediate castes. But after migration all of these were successful in clearing their debts. Following M.S.A. Rao's (1976) typology these migrants may be considered as "development migrants".

At the time of migration while all the lower caste migrants were following their caste occupations only a few of scheduled caste migrants were doing so. A majority of the intermediate castes were cultivators and some of them were agricultural labourers, whereas in the case of scheduled castes a majority were agricultural labourers and few were farmers. Among Muslim migrants small business and cultivation were the main occupational categories. Those who had landed property were greater among intermediate castes and Muslims, less among scheduled castes and lower castes.

Occupational Structure of Krishna Puram

The city is mainly a centre of trade, commerce and transport and the occupations followed by the inhabitants of Krishna Puram are related to these activities. Both road and rail transport require a large number of manual labourers to load and unload the goods and this demand is largely met by the migrant *mutha* labourers. Road transport also throws open opportunities to skilled persons in driving and ancillary services. White-collar-clerical and broker jobs are also created due to lorry transport. The goods are distributed to various localities in the city by cart-pullers. The city, as mentioned earlier, is one of the biggest railway and bus junctions in the country. The Railways and Andhra Pradesh Road Transport Corporation employ hundreds of skilled and educated persons. Some inhabitants of Puram are employees of these organizations. The floating population of the city creates a demand for cheap transport activity like man-driven three-wheeler cycle rickshas. Most of the ricksha-pullers in the city are slum dwellers. The construction activity, a consequence of rapid growth of the city, coupled with the availability of cheap and good sand on the bed of Krishna River provide employment largely to the Vadderas who work as sand labourers (loading and unloading the lorries) and earth workers. Another important occupation of the residents of Puram is junk collection. There are ten merchants in Puram who buy old iron and in turn sell it to the local iron foundries or export it to Visakhapatnam. The local iron foundries and small-scale industries employ some skilled and semi-skilled persons belonging to Puram.

There are several wholesale and large retail shops of cloth, medicines, utensils, paper and books, furniture, etc., in the city which are mostly located in the old city. Such shops employ a good number of clerks, sales assistants, etc. Some persons with middle and secondary levels of education, especially belonging to the intermediate castes of the slum are employed in these trade establishments.

The hotel industry in the city also employs a large number of workers like cooks, servers and cleaners. Very few inhabitants of Puram are employed by the hotels situated outside Puram. There are a few small tea shops in Puram which are run by the owners themselves. These are manned by single individuals. There are three coffee shops which employ 6 to 8 workers each in Puram. Besides the small tea shop owners there are others who are small grocery and *pan* shop owners, vegetable sellers, kerosine vendors, sweet and butter milk vendors.

There are a couple of tobacco grading companies in Gollapudi, a sub-urban village, which employs tobacco graders for 3 to 4 months a year. Women belonging to the scheduled castes only work as graders. It is a semi-skilled work and fetches around Rs. 5 a day. Women graders commute to Gollapudi.

The city, being a commercial centre, creates a lot of demand for packing materials like baskets. The Medaris are exclusively in this occupation. They also make bamboo ladders as well as wooden screens which are used in summer.

The important occupations, apart from exclusive caste occupations like basket making, leather work, cloth washing, hair cutting and earthwork, of the Puram inhabitants are sand labour, *mutha* labour, junk collection, riksha-pulling, cart pulling, petty trade and skilled jobs. Thus the bulk of the residents of Krishna Puram are in the lower levels of the job structure of the city. The migrants with higher educational levels or financial resources or both are in the higher levels of the job structure such as white-collar, professional jobs, business, etc. and live in the non-slum localities. The nature of some of the occupations followed by Puram inhabitants is given in the following pages.

Sand Labour

It involves the work of loading the lorries with the sand which is used for construction of buildings in the city. The nearby Krishna river bed is the perennial source of sand. Each group consists of 15 to 20 persons of above 12 years of age.

Each group loads a lorry with the sand and unload the same at the place of delivery. The rate of payment for loading and unloading a lorry was Rs. 5 in 1972 and Rs. 7 in 1977 and Rs. 14 in 1981. The daily income of sand labourers depends upon the number of trips they make and the income is shared equally by the elder labourers and the children under 16 years are paid half-wages. Since they are not sure of the exact date of birth, age of the persons is estimated on the basis of physical features as also from their acquaintances. The *maistry* (leader) of each group gets double the wages of an adult. On an average an adult earns Rs. 300 a month now. However, work in sand labour is available for 9 to 10 months in a year depending upon the duration of the monsoon.

During the last ten years the cost of the sand has gone up by four times but the increase in the rates of payment to the sand labourers is not commensurate with the increase in the cost of sand. And even this increase would have been denied them but for their unionization. However their unions are not as strong as that of the *mutha* labourers. A large majority of the sand labourers belong to Vaddera and Madiga castes. Though this work is not very remunerative, entry into this work is not easy. One can enter into a sand *mutha* only through kinship or caste linkages. The contractors generally give business to Vaddera and Madiga *muthas* because they are known to be hard-working.

Mutha Labour (*Contract Labour*)

The nature of the work of *mutha* labour is loading and unloading goods lorries, passenger buses, and goods wagons. There are about 5000 *mutha* labourers in the city. The membership of each of the *muthas* varies between 15 and 160. Every *mutha* has a '*Maistry*'. Goods lorry *muthas*, passenger bus *muthas* and goods wagon *muthas* are attached to the lorry owner and some are attached to a particular type of commercial shop (vegetable shops, table shops, cloth shops, iron shops, etc.) and undertake the work of loading and unloading of goods. The *muthas* attached to the transport companies function on different lines. The *mutha* labourers load and unload the transport lorries and are paid by the clients who book their goods with the transport companies. Passenger bus *mutha* labourers load and unload the luggage of the bus passengers and are paid by them. In the case of transport company and passenger bus *muthas* the charges are fixed through bargaining, though rates are fixed on the basis of the weight of the luggage.

Goods wagon *muthas* operate at the railway goods shed. They load and unload the railway goods wagons. There are separate *muthas* for different rail routes. For example one *mutha* exclusively deals with Vijayawada-Bombay goods wagons, another with Vijayawada-Delhi. It is an arrangement agreed to by the *mutha* labourers to avoid conflict of interests in operation. The rates of loading and unloading vary according to the goods. For example, Rs. 2.50 are paid per ton of iron angulars and Rs. 5.00 per a ton of heavy iron plates and Rs. 44 for a wagon of fertilizers. Each *mutha* is headed by a *Maistry* and a *Cheyyi Maistry* (sub-leader). While the former acts as the overall-supervisor, the latter obtains the work orders and confirms the job of loading and unloading. A representative of the concerned merchant also supervises the work and makes payments. He also receives one share of the payments made to the *mutha*. While the *mutha* leader is entitled to two shares and the sub-leader gets only one share along with the other labourers. The *Maistry* and *Cheyyi maistry* do not, however, undertake any manual work. Goods wagon *muthas* were the first to come into being (in late 1940s) followed by transport company *muthas*, lorry *muthas* and passenger bus *muthas* which are popularly called RTC (Road Transport Corporation of Andhra Pradesh) *muthas* in that order. Anyone seeking admission into a particular *mutha* has to pay some fixed amount (between 8 to 10 thousand rupees) which is like an admission fee and this amount is distributed among the existing members. Any member can nominate a new person in his place if he chooses to leave the *mutha*, provided the others do not have any specific objection, or else he can sell away his right. The membership also can be inherited by one's son or brother.

More often than not one nominates or sells his job to a person who belongs to his own kin group. This is how the new migrants enter into *muthas*, and secure a job soon after their arrival into the city. The entry into *muthas* is regulated by financial resources as well as caste and/or kinship membership.

The *mutha* workers in the city are members of trade unions which are controlled by political parties, namely C.P.I., C.P.I. (M) and Congress. In fact some political leaders in the city derive their strength largely from *mutha* labourers and riksha-pullers In turn the political leaders extend their support to the *muthas* in their agitational activities for higher rates of payment. During the 1970s the *muthas* attached to shops and railways independently went on strike demanding higher piece rates and on both such occasions they emerged victorious with the help of the political parties.

Though this occupation yields relatively higher income i.e., around Rs. 700 or more per month the job is quite strenuous and the working hours are long spanning between 9.00 A.M. to 12 P.M. Though they have to hang around the place of work during these hours, they need not work for all the 15 hours. The actual working hours are usually not more than eight per day.

Many *mutha* labourers belonging to Reddi, Yadava, Telaga and Kamma castes save a major part of their incomes by leading austere lives and lend the money at interest rates varying between 24% to 48% per annum or invest it in business of varying scales. Some of them gradually acquired skills like driving and became lorry or taxi drivers or owner-cum-drivers. Thus many of them have entrepreneurial skills and use them for further upward mobility.

Collection of Scrap Iron

This is an important source of livelihood to the scheduled castes in general and the Malas in particular. Prior to 1950, this occupation was followed predominantly by the Muslims in the city. One Mala who worked with a Muslim merchant broke off and started his own shop. He encouraged Malas to take up this occupation. Out of the ten shops in Puram seven are owned by Malas, two by Kammas and one by a Rajaka.

Usually a group of 10 persons form a batch and engage in the collection and purchasing of scrap iron. The *modus operandi* is as follows : A room is rented in each town for storing scrap iron purchased in town or in the villages around.

They go into villages with a hand-driven cart or with small gunny bags and carry the scrap iron to the store room in town. Once a lorry load of iron scrap is accumulated, it is carried to Vijayawada and sold to the merchant.

Usually the trip may take anything between 2 weeks to 3 months depending upon the number of persons of a batch, scrap availability, etc. The general practice is that each local merchant advances money to the group attached to it and the group sells the scrap iron to that merchant only and rarely to anyone else. The local merchants in turn sell the scrap to the wholesale merchants in the city.

Those who make their living by collection of scrap iron are generally exploited by the merchants in several ways. From every lorry load of old iron (i.e., about 8 to 9 tons) ¼ of a ton of scrap will have to be given to the merchant by the sellers free of cost. This is called '*pattu*'. The merchants claim '*pattu*' on the pretext that at least ¼ of a ton of scrap out of a lorry load is useless and will go waste. Secondly, the market is controlled by a few merchants and as a result the old iron is bought by the merchants at a lower price with a very good margin of profit for them. Thirdly, many merchants advance loans to those who collect scrap iron and this makes them indebted to the merchants. This indebtedness prevents them from selling the scrap iron to some other merchant for a higher price since the merchant who advances money will demand his money back in case the group doesn't sell the scrap to him at the price quoted by him. Hence the seller is forced to sell at a lower price even though other merchants offer more. Though those who are in this occupation have a union it is not effective as that of the *mutha* labourers. However, at one time they stopped selling scrap iron for a few weeks in order to stop this exploitation. They succeeded only in getting a somewhat higher price but could not see that the '*pattu*' system is scrapped or come out of the 'advance-trap'. Though it is easy to make an entry into this field it is difficult to get an advance from the merchant in the beginning which discourages new entrants.

Riksha-pulling

Most of the riksha-pullers rent their three-wheeler man-driven rikshas from their owners living in Puram as well as in other localities. The hiring charges are Rs. 1.50 paise per shift, each shift consisting of 12 hours i.e., 6 a.m. to 4 p.m. and 4 p.m. to 6 a.m. Minor repair charges costing less than a rupee are borne by the riksha-puller and any charges costing more than a rupee are borne by the owner. The monthly average income is around Rs. 300 a month. Out of 8,000 estimated riksha-pullers in the city 6,000 are members of different trade unions owing allegiance to AITUC, CITU, and INTUC.

Cart-pulling

Intra-city movement of goods is done through man-pulled carts. The carts are rented out by the owners at the rate of Rs. 2 per day. Mostly intermediate caste people are engaged in this occupation. The cart owners of Puram also belong to intermediate castes. They are unionized like the riksha-pullers. Though it is easy to enter into riksha and cart pulling work to hire a riksha or a cart, one needs to approach the owner through someone known to the latter. It is not difficult for the migrants who move in the same circles to find an acquaintance to provide them with an introduction. Other important occupations of the slum dwellers are : (1) Petty traders such as vegetable sellers, groceries and kerosine oil sellers and as cigarette and pan shopkeepers which is carried out in the slum, (2) self-employed skilled workers like tailors, blacksmiths, etc., and skilled workers like drivers, mechanics, painters, rod-benders, fitters, etc., in small and big enterprises, (3) clerks, typists and salesmen in large shops or government establishments, and (4) as peons and watchmen in government and private establishments.

Conclusion

From the foregoing analysis of various cccupational categories followed by the migrants living in non-slum and slum localities in Vijayawada, it is clear that the migrants with better economic resources and skills get into various kinds of business—wholesale, distribution as well as retail, contracts, transport, etc., or into supervisory and white-collar jobs either on their own or using kinship linkages. Whereas the migrants with lower economic resources get into the lower levels of job hierarchy such as petty trade, and different types of manual labour. However, some of those could achieve upward mobility and become businessmen. Those with some technical skills could enter into skilled jobs provided they had necessary contacts.

Some of the occupations followed by the slum dwellers do not quite fit into the 'informal sector'. For example, *muthas* have a strong informal organization not only with regard to the rules of entry and quitting but also with regard to nature and mode of payment, division of clientele, etc. The *mutha* workers are strongly unionized and enjoy the support of the political parties. Several other occupational groups also have unions though the degree of solidarity and effectiveness of the unions vary considerably. The unions of *mutha* labourers to a great extent and of sand labourers and cart-pullers to a lesser extent, could enhance their piece-rates through organizing strikes like industrial workers do.

The entry into many occupational categories is not easy as the conceptual scheme of the informal sector assumes. Entry into *mutha* labour depends on the ability of the aspirant to purchase work and the influence of his caste and kinship networks have with the existing members of the *mutha*. To hire a riksha or a pull-cart or to claim advance from a junk merchant one needs the recommendation of his relatives. The opportunities available in such occupations are not abundant and this scarcity of opportunities and competition will lead to some form of selectivity. The ease with which one enters into an occupation/enterprise depends upon certain traditional or modern skills, economic resources or kinship networks that one possesses.

The small enterprises or self-employed persons do have access to formal credit systems. Our data show that a sizeable number of riksha and autoriksha owners purchased the vehicles with the help of the nationalized banks in the form of loans. Thus it is wrong to assume, as some have done that all activities categorized under the informal sector do not have access to formal credit systems.

Different occupational groups which are normally categorized under the supposedly homogeneous category of the 'informal sector', in actual fact differ from each other in most of the characteristics such as ease or difficulty in gaining an entry, nature of ownership, scale of operations, levels of skills, mode of acquiring skills, regulation of land competition in the market, degree of unionization, etc. Such a diversity of lower level urban occupations make the concept of the informal sector more complex in relation to rural-urban migration and the labour markets (Sinclair 1978). It is also necessary to recognize that some occupational categories develop customs and practices (Joshi 1980) in course of time, which are as strong as the formal rules. They organize themselves into unions and seek the support of the political parties in their efforts to protect their interests. Hence disaggregate analysis of the labour markets is necessary for proper understanding of the urban labour markets.

REFERENCES

Bienefeld, M.A. and M. Godfrey, "Measuring Unemployment and the 'Informal Sector'," *Institute of Development Studies Bulletin*, Vol. 7, No. 3, October 1975.

Breman J., "A Dualistic Labour System? A Critique of the 'Informal Sector' Concept", *Economic and Political Weekly*, 27 November, 4 December, 11 December (3 parts), 1976.

Connel, J., Dasgupta, B., Caishley, R., Lipton, Michael, *Migration from Rural Areas : The Evidence from Village Studies*, Oxford University Press, Delhi, 1976.

Dandekar, V.M. and N. Rath, "Poverty in India", *Economic and Political Weekly*, Vol. VI, 2 Jan., 1971.

Desai, A.R. and S.D. Pillai, *A Profile of an Indian Slum*, University of Bombay, 1972.

Deshmukh, M.B., "A Study of Floating Migration", in R.B. Textor et al., *The Social Implications of Industrialization and Urbanisation*, UNESCO Research Centre, Calcutta, 1956.

De Souza, Alfred (ed.), *The Indian City*, Manohar, New Delhi, 1978.

Eames, E., "Some Aspects of Urban Migration from a Village in North Central India", *Eastern Anthropologist*, 8 : 13-26, 1954.

Elkan, W., "Concepts in the Description of African Economics". *Journal of Modern African Studies*, Vol. 14, No. 4, Dec. 1976.

Epstein, T.S., *South India : Yesterday, Today and Tomorrow*, Macmillan, London, 1973.

Gerry, C., *Petty Production and Capitalist Production*. (Paper presented to British Institute of Geographers London, 19th March), 1977.

Government of India : *Draft Five Year Plan—1978-83*, Government of India Publications, Delhi, 1978.

ILO, *Employment, Incomes and Equality : A Strategy for Increasing Productive Employment in Kenya*, ILO, Geneva, 1972.

ILO, *The Poor in Asian Development*. A ILO Programme, ILO, Geneva, 1975.

Jolly Richard., Emanuel De Kadt., Hans Singer, Fiona Wilson, (ed), *Third World Employment*, Penguin, Hammondsworth, 1973.

Joshi, Heather, "The Informal Urban Economy and its Boundaries", *Economic and Political Weekly*, Vol. XV, No. 13, 29 March, 1980.

Joshi, Heather and Vijay Joshi, *Surplus Labour and the City : A Study of Bombay*, Oxford University Press, New Delhi, 1976.

Lynch, Owen, M., *Potters, Plotters and Plodders in a Bombay Slum : Marx and Meaning or Meaning Vs. Marx*. A paper presented for Busy Wartenstein Symposium, No. 73, New York : Wenner-Green Foundation for Anthropological Research, 1977.

Prabhu, P.N., "A Study of the Social Effects of Urbanization", in R.B. Textor et al., *The Social Implications of Industrialization and Urbanization*, UNESCO Research Centre, Calcutta, 1956.

Papola, T.S., "Informal Sector : Concept and Policy", *Economic and Political Weekly*, Vol. XV, No. 18, 3 May, 1980.

Prakasa Rao, V.L.S. and R. Rama Chandran, *A Report on the Socio-economic Survey of Vijayawada*, Delhi School of Economics (Memeo), Delhi, 1975.

Radhakrishna, R. Bhanumati, K. Parikh, Naresh C. Whaw, *An Exploratory Study on Slums : Employment, Poverty and Liquor Consumption* (A Case study of Ahmedabad Slum), Sardar Patel Institute of Economic and Social Research (Memeo), Ahmedabad, 1977.

Rao, K. Ranga, K.S. Rani, K.R. Murthy, "Migration Experience of Japan Slum Dwellers", *The Indian Journal of Social Work*, Vol. XXXVIII(1).

Rao, M.S.A., "Migration and Urban Area Development", *Social Change*, Sept.-Dec., 1976.

Rowe, William, M., "Caste, Kinship and Association in Urban India", in *Urban Anthropology* (ed.) by Aidan Southall, Oxford University Press, New York, 1973.

Safa, Helen, N.I., Brian M. Du. Toit, *Migration and Development*, Mouton Publishers, The Hague.

Sethuraman, S.V., "The Informal Urban Sector in Developing Countries: Some Policy Implications", in *The Indian City*, (ed.) Alfred de Souza, Manohar, New Delhi, 1978.

Smclair, W., *Urbanization and Labour Markets in Developing Countries*, The English Language Book Society and Croom Helm, London, 1978

Weeks, John, "Politics for Expanding Employment in the Informal Urban Sector of Developing Economics", *International Labour Review*, January 1975.

Woodruff, G.M., "Family Migration into Bangalore", *Economic Weekly*, (12), 1960.

PART III

Peasant and Labour Migration in Rural Areas

7. *Peasant-Farmer Colonization, Development and Deprivation in Tribal Andhra*

M.S.A. RAO

The term colony is derived from the Latin term 'colonia' meaning possession in land, landed estate, a farm and a settlement. Historically three types of colonization, which are not mutually exclusive, are distinguished on the basis of method and purpose of acquisition (Morris 1900 : 8-9): those colonies acquired by military conquest; those that are settled for agricultural pursuits including plantation colonies; and those that are acquired for purposes of trade and commerce. In the present political conditions of nation states and anti-imperialist forces, colonization involves migration of certain streams of people whether overseas or internal, and establishment of their setttlements. There are two ways in which a new settlement gets established. First where the state takes the initiative in settling different types of groups and categories of people such as refugees, nomads, tribals, economically backward sections and ex-military men as part of rehabilitation programmes. This type of planned and sponsored colonization can occur either by claiming semi-forest land or by settling people in large irrigation project areas. Farmer (1957, 1974) has described such a process of agricultural colonization in Ceylon and India. Similar schemes of colonization can be found elsewhere too, for instance in Latin America (Dozier 1969) and Africa (Amin 1974 : 111-112). In such state sponsored colonization schemes, the exploitation of one group by another will be absent as many of these schemes will be for the welfare of the deprived sections of society.

Besides the situation of sponsored migration, however, there are situations of voluntary migration with different implications for the relationship between migrants and locals. In one situation, peasants and farmers may voluntarily migrate to flow-irrigated regions, buy land from the locals and establish their camps. Since the migrant farmers will have bought the land legally from the locals, the latter do not feel alienated from their land, although they may feel jealous of the success of the migrants who have the capital and the skills of organization. In another situation of agricultural colonization the peasant-farmers migrate voluntarily to areas reserved for the tribals and establish their camps and villages. Unlike the first situation, here the migrants are not legally allowed to buy or lease-in land from the tribals. Still they do it through various means resulting in land alienation and other forms of deprivation.

This paper deals with the last mentioned situation of migration and agricultural colonization by the farmers in the tribal area of West Godavari District in Andhra Pradesh, a State in South India. The aim of this paper is to describe the different phases of immigration streams of peasant-farmers, the process and nature of colonization, and the consequences of colonization in terms of agricultural development and deprivations for the tribal autochthons. The description of the whole process of colonization and its consequences is set in the Development-Deprivation framework rather than Wallerstein (1979) and Gunder-Frank's (1967) model of world capitalism or Development and Underdevelopment model, which will be discussed in the concluding part of the essay.

POLAVARAM TALUK OF WEST GODAVARI DISTRICT

Ecologically West Godavari district is divided into low and delta area and upland dry area. In 1960 the upland area in which the Polavaram taluk lies was found suitable for the cultivation of light soil flue-cured virginia tobacco which has a large and expanding export market. The taluk consist of 135 villages of which 102 are located in the Agency area, and 33 are situated in the plains. *Agency* is a Scheduled Tribal area governed by special laws relating to land, education, employment and other aspects. For instance, the Agent, equivalent to a Collector of a District, is in charge of collecting revenue and administering both civil and criminal laws. The total area of the taluk is 1,417.3 sq. kms. of which the Agency area forms 89.8 per cent. However, in terms of population only 39.7 per cent live in the Agency area.

Koyas are the dominant tribe in the *Agency*. In 1971, they formed 55.1 per cent of the Agency population. Out of the remaining 44.9 per cent of non-tribal population, scheduled castes constituted 32.0 per cent and the rest (12.9 per cent) were caste Hindus. The Christian missionaries were unable to convert the Koyas, but succeeded in converting about fifty per cent of the scheduled castes. The major non-tribal cultivating and land owning castes are the Kapu, Kamma, Raju, Komati (merchant), Distiller (Setty Balajiga) and Gollas or Yadavas (cowherds and goatherds).

Early History

Immediately before British occupation, the Godavari area as part of Northern Circars was under the Nizam of Hyderabad. During the early period of British occupation from 1765 to 1828, there was one lineage of Hill Reddi (tribe) which owned three estates—Polavaram and Gutala in Polavaram taluk and Kothapalli estate across the Godavari river in Chowdavaram taluk. British Administration made arrangements sometimes combining and at other times dividing the estates, that were expedient for collection of revenue. In this process they interfered with the legal ownership of estates which caused resentment. Thus the step-mother of Mangapati Devu, who was the legal guardian of her minor heir to Gutala estate rebelled against the Administration in 1970, which was no doubt quelled by superior military force.

Another cause of resentment of the tribal chiefs or zamindars was the increase in the revenue demanded by the Administration each year. Some of the British officers who visited the zamindari area saw the rich alluvial land on the banks of the Godavari and were convinced that the zamindars were collecting more revenue than what they gave to the East India Company. They also noticed the royal style of the zamindars which meant for them lavish and wasteful expenditure. When more revenue was demanded, the zamindars were reluctant to pay and many of them became defaulters and the estate revenue fell into arrears. The last resort for the Administration was to use military force, confining zamindars to their forts forcing them to pay the arrears. Under such circumstances of humiliation the tribal zamindars revolted against the Administration.

The usual pattern of revolt for the zamindars was to escape from the fort into the forests in the adjoining Nizam territory, build up an army and attack the police stations and engage in guerilla warfare in the forests, against the military. In 1799 Mangapati Devu, the zamindar of the three estates (Polavaram, Gutala and Kothapalli) who was considered to be a regular payer of revenue, fell into arrears and revolted against the Administration. He did not surrender while his two other brothers did, and he could not be captured either. The estate was confiscated and was given to a cousin of Mangapati Devu on a permanent settlement in 1802. However, the estate again fell into arrears and came into the auction market finally in 1827. This ended the political supremacy and economic dominance of the tribal zamindars in Polavaram taluk. It also marked the beginning of a steady increase in the migration of the non-tribal peasants into the tribal territory, exercising control over diverse productive resources which were hitherto in the hands of the Hill Reddis and Koyas. It was the second step in the deprivation process, the first step being the interference by the Administration.

The present administrative boundaries were fixed in 1934 when Polavaram formed part of West Godavari District. Earlier (from 1901) it was part of East Godavari Agency Division consisting of Bhadrachalam, Polavaram, Chandavaram are Ellavaram.

Between 1827 and 1947, one may identify four major forces which altered the socio-economic conditions of the tribals in Polavaram. These are : 1. The change in the nature of the zamindari system with the permanent settlement and the consequent immigration of the plainsmen, 2. The increasing inroads that the Administration made through forest, *abkari* (liquor) and civil and criminal laws, 3. The series of tribal revolts as response to the indiscriminate interference by the Administration, and 4. Ryotwari settlement of villages. All these forces encouraged, in different ways, the migration of the plainsmen into the tribal area.

First Phase of Immigration

The first phase of migration of peasants from the plains occurred around 1820 when a number of zamindaris either in whole or in parts came into the auction market and the highest bidder got the rights of ownership. Thus the Gutala zamindari passed into the hands of a rich Vaisya of Manyam lineage in 1827. Raja Manyam Venkataratnam was originally a resident of Yanam on the coast which was under the French occupation. He later moved to Kakinada before he finally settled in Rajahmundry. He encouraged the Kapus of Elur and Rajahmundry to migrate and settle the villages in his zamindari. He gave them semi-forest land and asked them to clear it and bring it under cultivation. The Koyas who were there already had to move to the interior regions. The Kapu peasants took along with them the agricultural labourers and service castes and in this process the existing villages grew in size and also new villages came into being. However, the Koyas did not come into violent conflict with the new migrants. They held the Administration responsible for their conditions of relative deprivation.

The Administration steadily increased its control of the productive resources of the tribals by passing forest laws in 1882 and *abkari* (liquor) laws in 1864. Large areas of forests were reserved making them inaccessible to the tribals in many ways. Their economy which was mainly based on forests, was upset. They had to pay a tax on slash-and-burn (*podu*) lands. There were restrictions on tapping toddy (country liquor) from any palm tree, and on collecting the forest produces for trade. The *abkari* laws encouraged the migration of distiller castes who had bought the licence to tap, distil and sell liquor. The distillers easily had the tribals indebted to them, as the latter loved toddy and developed a taste for other types of distilled liquor. They acquired the land of the Koya customers in lieu of petty debts. This was similar to the practice of the merchants and moneylenders, who had acquired tribal land. The tribals only lost more and more of their land in this process.

The tribals' response to rack-renting by the zamindars was violent. Two major revolts broke outside Polavaram but inside the Godavari Agency, one in 1879 and another in 1922. The Rampa rebellion of 1879 was the result of rack-renting and oppression by the Rampa zamindars, the general discontent of the tribals against the forest and *abkari* laws, and the civil and criminal laws which supported the merchants and zamindars who attached cattle, produce and land in adjustment of their debts. The 1922, Alluri Seetharama Raju's rebellion was also against the administration laws which alienated the tribals from productive resources. In particular, this rebellion was against the forced labour demanded by the British officers to construct a road in the tribal areas. The Administration was able to quell the revolts only after getting repeated military reinforcements.

The British did realise the severity of the tribal problem soon after the 1879 Rampa rebellion. The revised Rules of India (Act XXIV of 1839) were made applicable and Godavari Agency was set up in 1874 (Scheduled Area Act, *Madras Manual* 1885 : I, 69). The British also made certain concessions to the tribals in respect of forest and *abkari* laws, and established direct contacts with the zamindars (muthadars) and ryots. In 1917, the Agency Tract Interest and Land Transfer Act was introduced. Under this Act no tribal could sell his land to a non-tribal without permission.

With the failure of the Permanent Settlement Act of 1802-3, the old zamindaris were parcelled into small blocs and sold for arrears. In the absence of bidders, the government took these into its own possession, made a survey of land and settled them. Thus the first Ryotwari settlement was done in 1899 and a resettlement was made in 1933. The government villages were called *Izara* villages and the revenue was collected directly through the village head (*munsif*) who was assisted by the village accountant (*karnam*), peons (*taliaris*) and others. Thus in the Polavaram taluk different types of tenure villages co-existed: there were the zamindari villages, gift for service (*inam*) villages and lands, gift to Brahmins and temples (*agraharam*) villages, and government (*Izara*) villages. Cultivators, merchants and others who had influence with the Administration could move into the Agency area and buy land with permission. Rich zamindars from the delta area bought large chunks of land in the semi-forest area, in order to graze their cattle. Thus the *Izara* and zamindari villages received more migrants consisting of peasants and labourers from the plains.

Second Phase : Developmental Migration

The second phase of migration of farmers, who were part of the market economy, from the plains occurred during the post-independence period. In the *Agency* land came into the market in thousands of acres in the 1950s. The non-tribals owning land in large quantities began to sell in anticipation of the forthcoming land ceiling legislation. The beneficiaries here were primarily the Kammas, who migrated from the delta area of West Godavari district, and established colonies in different remote villages. The migrants also 'bought' land from the Koyas.

The stream of migration of Kamma farmers in the 1950s was of a different character from the earlier migration of peasants before 1947. While the latter was one of subsistence, the former was one of development. The Kamma migrants who moved from the delta area in the 1950s had the necessary capital and organizational and technical skills of development agriculture. They lost no time in exploiting the natural resources. The colonizers cleared the jungle, removed the boulders and brought the land under plough. They initially faced the horrors of malaria, the fear of wild animals and the fear of serpents, but soon overcame these horrors. They put up pumps, lifted water from the streams running below the field level, and irrigated their lands. It had not occurred to the Kapu and Raju peasants who were staying in the Agency Area for generations to use the water resources in this way. The Kamma colonizers thus brought about significant agricultural development in the region.

The buyers knew that they had to spend a lot on reclaiming land for cultivation. But the land, for that reason was very cheap—about Rs. 100.00 or less per acre. This was in contrast to the high price of land in the delta area, where the man-land ratio was very high. If the peasants could sell one acre in the delta area, they could buy ten acres in the upland semi-forest area where there were potentialities of improvement including irrigational facilities.

Third Phase : Tobacco Rush—Commercialization of Agriculture

The third phase of migration started when light soil flue-cured Virginia tobacco was introduced in Polavaram taluk in 1960 as both land and water were suitable. The Kamma migrants who were already there, were the first to take advantage of this opportunity. The FCV tobacco cultivation generated a further demand for land. But the 1959 legislation prevented the non-tribals from buying land from the tribals. Hence the former started leasing in land from the latter. The tribals were not interested in cultivating barn-tobacco as this season (December to April) overlapped with the toddy season. They preferred tapping and drinking toddy to growing tobacco. Secondly, they got cash income by leasing out their land. The lease rate varied from Rs. 300.00 to Rs. 600.00 per acre per season. The non-tribal farmers who leased land made an enormous profit (about Rs. 3,000.00 per acre).

The tobacco-rush resulted in both extension of commercialized agriculture by the farmers who had already migrated, and also a fresh wave of migration of non-tribal farmers either as transients (for the tobacco season) or as domiciles. However, for the tribals, it meant further loss of land and control over the exploitation of the vast benefits from commercialized agriculture. Although the non-tribal farmers were 'tenants' from the point of view of tenure position, they were the real exploiters in terms of production relations reaping vast profits. The tribals who were the landowners came to be exploited by the tenants as a major share of the benefits of the tobacco economy went to the latter.

Peseant-Farmer Colonization of a Tribal Village

In this section we shall discuss all the three phases of peasant-farmer migration in one tribal village—Kanakapalli (fictitious name) with a view to gaining insights into the conditions under which peasant-farmer migration has occurred, and the causes thereof.

Kanakapalli is situated on the road that connects Buttayagudem, the Development Block headquarters on the east and Jilugumilli which is on the border of Khammam District on the west. The village is located at a distance of seven miles from Buttayagudem. The village is situated in between two streams-Jalleru and Kalava. While these streams provide sources of lift irrigation, they make the village inaccessible for most of the time during the monsoon. The village has the reserved forest to its north and north west, Mulagampalli and Routhugudem to its west, Mysannagudem to its south, Jainavarigudem and Buttayagudem to its east.

Kanakapalli is an Izara village in the *Agency* area. It is a village which is directly under the control of the government. It lies in the administrative division of Jhilugumilli *fi·ka*, one of the five *firkas* (Polavaram, Gutala, Kannapuram, Jangareddigudem and Jhilugumilli) into which the Polavaram taluk is divided. It is one of the 102 *Agency* villages of the taluk. The head of the civil and criminal administration of the *Agency* is the Agent (equivalent to the Collector) who has his office in Polavaram. The village is under the jurisdiction of Buttayagudem Panchayati Samiti (Block Development). The village is served by the *Agency* Seva Sangha, an organization for tribal welfare affiliated to the All India Adimajati Seva Sangha with its office in New Delhi. There is also the Kanaka Durga Cooperative Society which organizes credit and fertilizer distribution for the farmers. The society has its Head Office located in Rajahmundry. The public buildings in the village are a panchayat office, a school and a temple located at the old village site.

Kanakapalli has two sites : old and new. The old site is half a mile to the south of the main road which passes through the new site. There are 45 households distributed over such castes as Raju (Kshatriya), Kapu, Gola, Carpenter, Potter, Washerman and Brahmin and the Koya. There is a temple devoted to Kanakadurga which was built by the Rajus.

The new site is divided into six sections. The oldest section is the hamlet of the Koyas. The others are those inhabited by Setti Balagigas, Malas and Madigas. The two new sections are the ones in which migrant Kammas live lying in the west and the new extended area of the Kammas which is in the east. The Panchayat office and the school are located in the latter area.

Kanakapalli is one of the six hamlets constituting the Village Panchayat. Out of the five hamlets three hamlets are of Koyas: Vilthruvarigudem located on the southern side, Bedadanolu on the north-west, and Palakonta on the north-east near the stream. The two other hamlets are located on the other side of the stream to the east: while Karadlivarigudem to the north of the road mainly consists of Kapus, Barbers, Washermen and Carpenter; Ramaravupeta consists of Malas and Madigas.

The geographical area of the Village Panchayat (including all the six settlements) is 6,457.86 acres, with a cultivable area of 2,910.48 acres, a cultivable waste of 2,000 acres and 1,547.36 acres of waste. The cropping pattern shows that paddy forms the main food crop and FVC tobacco the chief commercial crop. There are 62 irrigation wells, one tank and two streams. In addition there is a minor stream (Jummulu Vaghu) and five private tanks. There are thirty electrically operated and thirty-two diesel oil operated pumps to lift the water from streams and wells. This is in addition to six bore well fitted with motor pumps. Electricity was introduced in the village only in 1970.

The population as shown in Table 7.1 may be divided into four sections: the tribes, the Caste Hindus, the ex-untouchables, and the Muslims forming 73.4, 14.2, 6.4 and 1.0 per cent of the total households (708) respectively. The Caste Hindu category consists of two upper castes of Brahmins and Komatis, four farming castes—Rajus (Kshatriyas), Kammas, Kapus

TABLE 7.1

Social Composition of the Kanakapalli Village Panchayat

Serial Number	Name	Traditional Occupation	Number of House-holds	Per cent	Number of House-holds	Per cent
1	Koya	Tribe	480	67 8	1200	49.83
2.	Koya Nayaka	Tribe	40	5.6	200	8.31
3.	Kamma	Framing	34	4.8	261	10.84
4.	Madiga	Agricultural Labour	33	4.7	180	7.48
5.	Kshatriya (Raju)	Farming	25	3.5	130	5.40
6.	Setti-Balagiga or Idiga	Toddy-tapping and selling (distiller)	20	2.8	120	4.98
7.	Kapu	Farming	15	2.1	50	2 08
8.	Golla	Herding	14	2.0	100	4.15
9.	Mala	Agricultural Labour	12	1.7	30	1.25
10.	Sakali	Washerman	8	1.1	30	1 25
11.	Muslims	Agricultural Labour and Trade	7	1.0	15	0.62
12.	Komati	Merchant	6	0.8	20	0.83
13.	Kummaralu	Potter	4	0 6	10	0.41
14.	Upparalu	Salt Sellers and Earth Workers	4	0.6	20	0.83
15.	Brahmin	Priesthood and Village Accountant	2	0.3	16	0.66
16.	Mangali	Barber	2	0.3	12	0.50
17.	Vaddarangi	Carpenter	1	0.1	6	0.25
18.	Kamsali	Blacksmith	1	0.1	8	0.33
	Total		708	100.0	2,408	100 00

and Setti Balagigas, the artisan and servicing castes—Smith, Barber, Washerman, Potter, and the herding caste of Gollas, roughly in that order of caste hierarchy.

The social composition of the village shows that it is still

TABLE 7.2

Distribution of Land by Caste and Tribe in Kanakapalli

Serial Number	Caste	Number of Owner/ Cultivators	Land Owned and Cultivated	Share in total land (per cent)
1.	Kamma	34	1,143	39.3
2.	Koya and Koya Nayak	252	507	17.4
3.	Setti Balagiga	20	198	6.8
4.	Raju	25	80	2.7
5.	Other Castes (Kapu, Golla, Brahmin, Komati Washer-man, Smith)	38	103	3.5
6.	Castes residing in other Villages	191	879	30.2
	Total	430	2,910	100.0

TABLE 7.3

Distribution of Non-Resident Castes Owning and Cultivating Land in Kanakapalli

Serial Number	Caste	Villages	Number of Persons	Land Owned	Per cent to total land owned by Non-Residence
1.	Kapu	(Mysannagudem, Srinivasapuram, Pattennapalem, Mulagampalli, Koyyalagudem	40	454	51.6
2.	Kamma	(Mysannagudem)	10	170	19.3
3.	Brahmin	(Mysennagudem, Kovvur and Hyderabad)	4	95	10.8
4.	Komati	(Kamayapalem, Jangareddigudem)	13	50	5.7
5.	Golla	(Mulagampalli)	3	10	1.1
6.	Others	(Mysennagudem) Except Koyyalagudem, Kovvur and Hyderabad	21	100	11.4
	Total	the radius of 7 Villages is 8 miles	91	879	100.0

TABLE 7.4

A Statement of 34 Kama Households According to Year of Migration, Place of Origin, Place of Residence and the size of Land Owned and/or Cultivated in 1978 in Kanakapalli

Serial Number of Households with Family Names	Year of Migration	Village from which Migrated	Place of Residence		Land Owned and Cultivated (in acres) in 1978
1	2	3	4	5	6
AR 1	1949	Chityala	Kamma	Colony	87
AR 2	1958	,,	,,	,,	42
AR 3	1965	,,	,,	,,	37
GS 4	1950	,,	,,	,,	100
GV 5	1950	,,	,,	,,	90
GV 6	1950	,,	,,	,,	40
GV 7	1950	,,	,,	,,	20
GA 8	1949-50	,,	,,	,,	17
GA 9	1964	,,	,,	,,	16
GB 10	1950	,,	,,	,,	10
GC 11	1960	,,	,,	,,	25
GSA 12	1950	,,	,,	,,	70
GSA 13	1950	,,	New Extension		4
G 14	1950	,,	,,	,,	4
AC & ACG 15	1953	,,	Kamma	Colony	50
NV 16	1950 & 1973	,,	,,	,,	50
PB 17	1949	,,	,,	,,	60
PG 18	1949	,,	,,	,,	60
PVE 19	1950	,,	,,	,,	58
PR 20	1950	,,	,,	,,	50
PV 21	1962	Maddunu	,,	,,	9
PV 22	1962	,,	,,	,,	9
TS 23	1950	Chikkala	,,	,,	40
GAN 24	1962	Chityala Gajjaram	,,	,,	60
GAN 25	1962	,,	,,	,,	3
R 26	1962	Potavaram	,,	,,	50
M 27	1971	Potavaram Buthayagudem	,,	,,	15
M 28	1971	,,	New Extension		11

1	2	3	4	5	6
NAN 29	1953	Duddukuru Muppinavari-Gudem	"	"	11
NAN 30	1953	"	"	"	11
NAN 31	1953	"	"	"	11
NAN 32	Born in K. Palli	—	"	"	11
LS 33	977	Mallavaram	"	"	2
C 34	1950	Chityala	Kamma	Colony	6
					1,143

predominantly a tribal village. This is true only demographically but misleading in terms of ownership and control of productive resources. Thc position of respective caste group in regard to ownership and cultivation of arable land in the village is given in Tables 7.2 and 7.3. It is seen that Kammas average as the single largest caste owning 58.6 per cent followed only by Kapus, Koyas, Setti Balagigas, Brahmins, Raju and other castes. In the context of ownership and cultivation of land non-resident castes play a significant part. Except two Brahmins and one Kapu who reside in far-off places and hence may be considered absentee land owners, the other non-resident owners and cultivators come from villages which are located within a radius of eight miles.

It is a common phenomenon that residents of one village, lease in land or own land in the neighbouring villages and actively engage in cultivation. Similarly the farmers resident in Kanakapalli own and lease in land in the neighbouring villages. For instance, three Kammas have taken 40 acres on lease in the two neighbouring villages. Thus from the point of view of the latter, the social boundaries of a village do not coincide with the physical boundaries. The physical boundary itself is an arbitrary decision of the Settlement Officers mainly guided by consideration of size and revenue collection. The village is a revenue unit, it is neither a productive unit nor a social one.

How did the Kammas come to own and cultivate a little more than half of the arable land of the village? Where did they come from? Who were the residents of the village before they came? How did the former come? What was the position of the Koyas before the migrants came? What is their position now? What is the impact of peasant colonization on the Koyas? These are some of the questions that we might consider in the following pages starting with a history of migration patterns.

Kanakapalli was first settled for revenue in 1899 and it was resettled on January 12, 1933. The village establishment comprised of one village headman, one *Karnam* (record keeper), one *Talaiyari* (assistant) and two Vettis (watchmen) and two *Nirgantis* (water revenue collectors). In 1933, it was part of East Godavari District. There were only a few but big land owners, chief of them being the Rajus and the Kapus. It may be noted that the Kapus were dominant in Buttayagudem (7 miles east) area which was part of Gutala Zamindari and they bought lands in the village in the process of expansion. But the story of the Rajus owning land in the village is different.

One Kanta Raju, an influential wealthy Kshatriya Zamindar from China Nandra Kolanu in Tadepalli Gudem Taluk, a village on the Godavari delta, bought about 1,000 acres in Kanakapalli in 1920. It is said that he possessed 1,200 acres of wet land in his village area. He bought the land in Kanakapalli at the rate of ten rupees per acre and expanded the area of ownership in the late 1930s. The reason for buying land in the semi-forest area was to graze his cattle. He had a herd of more than 600 cattle consisting of cows, buffaloes, goats and sheep. As there was no grazing land in the delta area, he bought the semi-forest land forty miles away from his village. Every year, a team of fifteen to twenty herdsman (paleru) used to drive the cattle for nearly three days to cover the distance in July, stay there up to November and return to the delta village after the paddy harvest when the dry fodder (paddy hay) became available to the cattle.

Later in 1930, four Rajus bought the land from the son of Kanta Raju. According to Sita Ratnam Raju, one of the old Raju migrants (interviewed on 28.4.1978), these Rajus originally belonged to Chittur district and they migrated to Mulagampalli (3 miles from the village) where they had a relative. They migrated under conditions of famine in Chittur district, a district of Rayalaseema of Andhra Pradesh. From Mulagampalli, they moved to Kanakapalli and established themselves forming the nucleus of the old village settlement.

Around 1900, a few members of the Distiller castes migrated to Kanakapalli, having bought the rights, on contract, of tapping toddy and selling it. They also got a licence to distil liquor. They settled down on the outskirts, (the present new village site) of the old village with their *abkari* shops and stills nearer the Koya hamlet (now in the new village). The Koyas gradually got indebted to the Distillers, pawned their lands and eventually forfeited it.

A few Komatis came to own the land in the village. The merchants (Komatis) in Kamayapalam, a market place near the village advanced loans to the Koyas, who being unable to pay the exorbitant interests and being afraid of court cases, parted with their land to the merchants.

The Koyas were distributed in different hamlets, practising settled as well as *podu* cultivation. With the expansion of peasant colonization more and more semi-forest was cleared for their plough cultivation. Hence many Koyas receded into the forests to practise their *podu* (shifting) cultivation. But even here their movements were restricted due to strict forest laws. They were not allowed to cut down trees and collect and use the forest produces in the reserved forest area. The Koyas at that point of time, did not oppose the migration of the peasants from the plains to the village. This is corroborated by the view expressed by the leader of the Koyas, an ex-M.L.A. (interviewed on 27-4-1978).

This was the first phase of the colonization process which lasted up to the 1940s. According to 1871 Census, Kanakapalli was a part of Yarnagudem Taluk at that time. It was a small village of 572 persons, with 120 houses. The main castes were Kapus, Kshatriyas, Chettis and Brahmins. At the time of the first settlement in 1899, it consisted to ten hamlets (Bandarlagudem, Nimmalagudem, Ramavarupeta, Nagulagudem, Gavarampeta, Bedadanuru, Chimlavarigudem, Chinna, Palakunta, Pedda Palakunta, Mallayagudem) besides Kanakapalli. All of them were mainly inhabited by the Koyas and Koya Nayakas. It had an area of 5,506 acres, with only 48 cultivators most of whom were Kapus, Kshatriyas and Komatis.

Obviously this presents a contrast with the present profile of the village with 708 households and 2,408 persons (Table 7.1).

The increase in the size of the village and the heterogeneity of its social composition has to be explained in terms of two phases of migration. The first phase from 1899 up to 1940s has been discussed in the successive migration of Kapus, Idigas (or Setty Balagigas), Komatis and Kshatriyas. During this phase some of the service and artisan castes also migrated. However, the major colonization process occurred in 1949-50 with a sizeable group of the Kammas migrating to the village from Kovvur taluk. The circumstances under which they came to the village were quite different, which we shall describe below.

Second Phase of Migration

Initially thirteen households belonging to six different families but to one village, Chityala in Kovvur Taluk, migrated to Kanakapalli in 1949-50. All the thirteen heads of households together bought 900 acres of land from Kanta Rajudu's son who had 1,200 acres of semi-forest grazing land. While the land owned by each household varied, they cultivated the land jointly for a period of five years. Table 7.4 shows the size of land owned by each household. They migrated because they thought that the land which they had in Chityala would not be sufficient for their children and grand children. Chityala is on the main road from Koyalagudem to Annadevarapeta. It is a big village with an area of 11.97 square miles and a population of 3,220. Being in the delta region, 71.9 per cent of the area (5,636 out of 7,836 acres) is under irrigation. The land value Rs. was 1,000 per acre in 1949.

Although many of the Kammas owned thirty to sixty acres, they preferred to sell their land and migrate mainly because of the perception of long term advantages. Kammas are enterprising and highly foresighted, and they do not hesitate to sell off their ancestral land, house and everything in their native villages to migrate to areas for better prospects. As the saying goes, Kammas move where the water is, either potential or actual. They are not only hardworking but they take risks and succeed against odds. They have all the necessary skills for irrigated and unirrigated cultivation and are very sensitive to market conditions.

The preparedness of the Kammas to buy land and move to Kanakapalli was complementary to a set of conditions which was responsible for the land to come into the market. After Independence and especially the Police Action in Hyderabad the Andhra Pradesh Government promulgated the land reform measures. The major objectives of the land reforms were the abolition of the intermediaries, that is the Zamindari system, transfer of land titles to tenants and ceiling on the size of land holding. While the measures were being debated in the Assembly, the Zamindars, and big land-owners got the message and started selling land in large chunks.

Besides, just as Kanta Raju owned large areas of semi-forest land in the *Agency*, there were many other plainsmen—Komatis and others—who owned considerable amount of land in these or in the villages now located on the area covered by plains in the taluk. All of them were eager to sell land at a bargaining price to the buyers, rather than surrendering it to the government. There were also overnight transfers of land titles in the name of minor heirs and other relatives. The land that came into the market was the land that could not be transferred beyond limits to the heirs. This led to the creation of a buyers' market. The buyers knew that they had to spend a lot on reclaiming land for cultivation. But the land, for that reason was very cheap—about Rs. 100.00 or less per acre. This was in contrast to the high price of land in the delta area, where the man-land ratio was very high. If the peasants could sell one acre in the delta area, they could buy ten acres in the upland semi-forest area where there were potentialities of improvement including irrigational facilities. Thus in the fifties arable land came into the market both in the upland Polavaram taluk and the delta areas of West Godavari district. While the land market in the delta area was confined to the kith and kin and the caste circles, that in the upland *Agency* area was relatively an open one.

Under these circumstances the thirteen Kamma households decided to buy land in Kanakapalli. There were two leaders of this group : NV and PB. The first was the Panchayat President in Chityala and the second was leading the rich farmers, who knew Kanta Raju's son, and he took the initiative in negotiating the sale deed, after a couple of visits to the village. Eight families moved in 1949 and the other five came in a year later. All of them put up huts in the open space of the present Kamma Colony. They moved with their wives, children and cattle. The thirteen heads of household who moved first are shown in Table 7.4. They also brought ten Madiga families who erected their huts in the place nearer the Koya hamlet.

The pioneer settlers were young (in the age group of 20-40). They had to fight against odds. The first major problem was to clear the jungle full of boulders and stones, bushes and trees, and level the ground. This released the snakes who infested the area. The second problem was the fear of wild beasts—tigers, hyena and jackals. Tigers used to attack the bullocks at night, and in two cases the tigers had killed and dragged away the bullocks. The jackals used to take away the fowls and chicken. The third major problem was malaria. Without exception every one suffered from malaria and there was no medical help. The nearest hospital was eight miles away in Buttayagudem. A few of the migrants, who could not bear risking their lives returned to Chityala. But after the initial five years of hardship and three good crops, more Kamma families joined them. In 1955 Kammas brought a doctor and gave him a horse and money to buy medicines. They brought more labourers (thirty more families), a washerman, a barber, a carpenter and a smith from Chityala. The Brahmin priest came from a neighbouring village. Thus they had a near complete set of services. By 1965, the Kamma Colony had grown into a village. The Madiga and Mala labourers joined the earlier immigrants and set up new huts near the Koya hamlet.

Kinship played an important part in the colonization process. The initial settlers were not only from the same village but the lineages were linked by affinal ties. Later, many more families joined, and they came from different villages. Table 4 gives the statement of 34 Kamma households according to the year of migration and size of land owned and cultivated by them in 1978. In give at this stage two kinship diagrams by way of illustrating the agnatic and affinal relations and the developmental process of the migrant households. They show the household's number encircled with the year of migration. The age of the persons at the time of migration is given only in the case of first settlers. It can be seen in diagram 1 that one household of GB family consisting of husband, wife and three children, moved to Kanakapalli in 1949-50, but GB's eldest son (GC) moved only in 1960. Two households belonging to PR family moved to Kanakapalli in 1949-50. While one household of PR consisted of separated son (PVE) and his wife, the other one consisted of husband, wife and the second son (PV). The two families were related by marriage : GB was married to his sister's daughter, i.e. PR's daughter. The diagram also shows the developmental process of each of the households. It is seen that GB's daughter is married to his elder sister's son (PV) after migration. In simpler terms, her husband is both her mother's brother and father's sister's son. The diagram also shows that at the time of migration, PVE's household consisted of only husband and wife, but in 1978 it had grown into a compound household consisting of one married son, his wife and a daughter, three unmarried sons and one unmarried daughter. Two daughters having been married in different villages, have moved out of Kanakapalli. The PV household, in 1978, consisted of husband wife and four unmarried children. His father and mother died in 1970. Similarly the GB's household has expanded from husband, wife and three unmarried children at the time of migration to include two daughters-in-law and three children of each of the two sons. The eldest son and his household consisting of wife and three children moved in later. The married daughter of GB has crossed over to PV's household as wife of PV and is staying in Kanakapalli with four children. In terms of numbers, while the three households (GB, PR and PVE) together consisted of 10 members at the time of migration in 1949, they, in 1978, consisted of 27 members, excluding GC's household which was added in 1960 by migration spread over four generations—an increase of 17 members over a period of twenty-eight years. While break up of joint family and death reduce the number of persons in a household, marriage of sons and births increase the numbers. Marriage of daughters results in out-migration only when they are married out of the village. But death of a son-in-law might bring the widowed daughter with children back to the village. Under certain circumstances, when a person has no adult sons, he might invite his son-in-law to move to the village, instead of his daughter moving out, to help in cultivation. Such instances are not infrequent.

It is not necessary to describe in detail the pattern of movement of all the households listed in Table 7.4. But diagram 2 may be described as it shows the marriage links between four families : PB (17), AR (1), GS (4) and GAN (24) and (25). While the households belonging to first three families migrated in 1949, one of the households of the fourth family (GAN) migrated in 1960 and the other in 1965. The PB, AR and GS families were related by marriage before the migration. AR (3) was first married to PB's second son's daughter before migration. But after migration she died and he remarried GS's second daughter. The GAN family established marriage links with GS after migrating to Kanakapalli.

As can be seen from Table 7.4, out of 34 heads of households of Kammas 17 migrated in 1949-50, 6 between 1953 and 1960, 7 between 1961 and 1970, and 3 after 1970. The head of one household was born in Kanakapalli (Table 7.4). Twenty-three heads of household have migrated from Chityala and others from five other villages in Kovvur Taluk. Since migration is mostly associational, it would be of interest to note the contacts through which others migrated. PV and his brother were invited by their mother's sister's husband ACG. Similarly GAN (24) came from Gajjaram near Chityala in 1962 through his wife whose father migrated to the village through his sister's husband. In the case of NAN, he took the initiative to come to the village from Muppinavarigudem (near Buttavagudem), which is at a distance of ten miles, where his brother had already migrated from Duddukuru, near Chityala. He came to the village in 1953, bought some land but took more land on lease for cultivation. He quarrelled with other Kammas and shifted his residence to the extension.

Migration is ubiquitous and imminent depending on the situational context. For instance, the first son of GB (Diagram 2) left the village Kanakapalli in 1965 (that is three years after coming to the village from Gajjaram along with his elder brother), to Mekkinavarigudem in Chintalapudi taluk at a distance of about 20 kms. at the invitation of his mother's brother. Both centripetal and centrifugal movements are mediated through kin links, women acting as important contacts. Exchange of women also provides a potential link for migration, and the merging of several affinal relations such as MBD and D, increases the chances for changing places of residence. All the female links—mother mother's mother, mother's sister, wife, brother's wife, sister and daughter—all provide potential links for movement if an occasion should arise. Many of these links are actually used by Kamma migrants. LS (33) migrated to Kanakapalli through his married daughter. PV came to the village through his mother's sister.

There is an additional factor running through the female links and that is the land transactions in the form of dowry. Dowry among the cultivating Kammas is mainly paid in the form of land and gold. A certain number of acres of land (3 to 5 acres) is given to a sister or daughter at the time of marriage. Sister's husband or daughter's husband has an interest in it as the manager of this land and in cases where male heirs are absent or are still minors, he can move in to control and manage the property of his wife. When a Kamma says that he invited his son-in-law to migrate to the village, it is only a part of the story. A shrewd son-in-law will take advantage of the situation, as his rights in his share are secure and he can sell it any time.

While the women move after marriage, they cannot take with them the land that is given to them. But the wife-takers have an interest in the wife giver's land and cash on it if an occasion should arise. Similarly, when a married woman becomes a widow at a young age, she can come back to her father's place where her land lies. If she becomes a widow at an older age when she has grown up sons, she will not go back to her father's or brother's place. But her sons are free to move to mother's brother's place if there are better opportunities of cultivation of their mother's land. Thus changes in place of residence occur to a great extent through female links and the associated interests in land.

The opposition between alliance and agnatic relations, among other things, is expressed in the opposition between the mobile and stationary states. Agnatic relations tend to make men more stationary, binding them to relations of blood and land. It is generally not easy to transcend these to move out, although Kammas show a propensity to migrate, which means selling off ancestral land and house and leaving the place of origin. It is a custom with the Kammas to bury the deceased old parents and grand parents in the ancestral land. A *brindavan* (tomb) is built with a platform and occasionally a *tulsi* plant (ocimum sanctum) is grown on it. This is the process of deification of the ancestor. On the *Sankranti* day (January 14) food is offered to them at this place. Ancestor worship assures the family progress and prosperity, and the ancestors guard the land and crops. Selling ancestral land implies the breaking of physical symbolic relations with ancestors. Similarly the place of birth is considered to be a 'sacred' place, in the sense that the body first touched *ground* there. The growing-up experiences are rooted in the physical dimensions of home, playground, streets, trees, plants, flowers, thorns, rocks, tanks, brooks, wells, canals, paddy fields, schools, shops, tea-stalls, gossip corners, temples and gods, romances, fights, different kinds of good and bad smells, sound of the flour mill, birds and animals and music and tastes of food, fruits and vegetables, and water—all these form part of ones mental make-up and objects of common sharing of experiences with others of the village. The territoriality is thus part of their growing-up experience.

How do Kammas look upon them while leaving their ancestral lands, lineage homes and villages? They argue that they have to look to the future and not the past. "The past binds you but the future releases you, and there is joy in creating a bright future for yourself and for your children. We have to sacrifice our comforts for the sake of the children". There is no doubt much truth in it. But this is not without the acquisitive impulse and a spirit of adventure as well as an aspiration to improve status and comfort by hard work. What gives them confidence is their control, through technological skills, over different aspects of agriculture and irrigation and their ability to mobilize capital, capacity for hard work on the part of both men and women, and organizational abilities to deal with the bureaucracy, the market, native population and labourers. Equipped with these skills, qualities and attitudes, they are ready to migrate.

At the 'ideological' level Kammas emphasize spatial mobility as opposed to stationary state, future as opposed to past, alliance as against descent, semen bonds as opposed to blood bonds, acquisition of land and home as opposed to ancestral land and home, place of destination as opposed to place of origin. They consider one set of symbols (past, agnatic ties, blood bonds, ancestral land and home, place of origin) as imposing structural restrictions and promoting stationary state and consider another set of opposed symbols (future, alliance, semen bonds, acquired land and home, place of destination) as freeing them from the structural limitations, promoting expanding relations and spatial mobility. Thus migration, is a transformation from the stationary to the mobile state with the symbols that are associated with them. Kammas have achieved this transformation with considerable success.

It may be argued that over a period of years they will have recreated the same structural conditions as those that were there at their place of origin. This is no doubt true, but they can repeat the process of dispersal. Settlement and dispersal, stationary and mobile states alternate and are parts of a single dynamic process for the Kamma farmers' lives.

Agricultural Development and Tribal Deprivation

As a result of collective colonization and entrepreneurship, the Kamma farmer migrants were able to bring about a high degree of agricultural development in different areas of Polavaram taluk. For instance, in Kanakapalli, they brought about 1,400 acres of semi-forest land under cultivation. In the main they introduced the capitalistic mode of production but combined it with non-capitalistic modes in different ways. They have invested in oil pumps, now also electric pumps (tube-wells), tractors, fertilizers, pesticides and improved seeds, and in improving land and water resources and management. The village had two streams running well below the land level. They lifted water from the two streams by electric pumps,

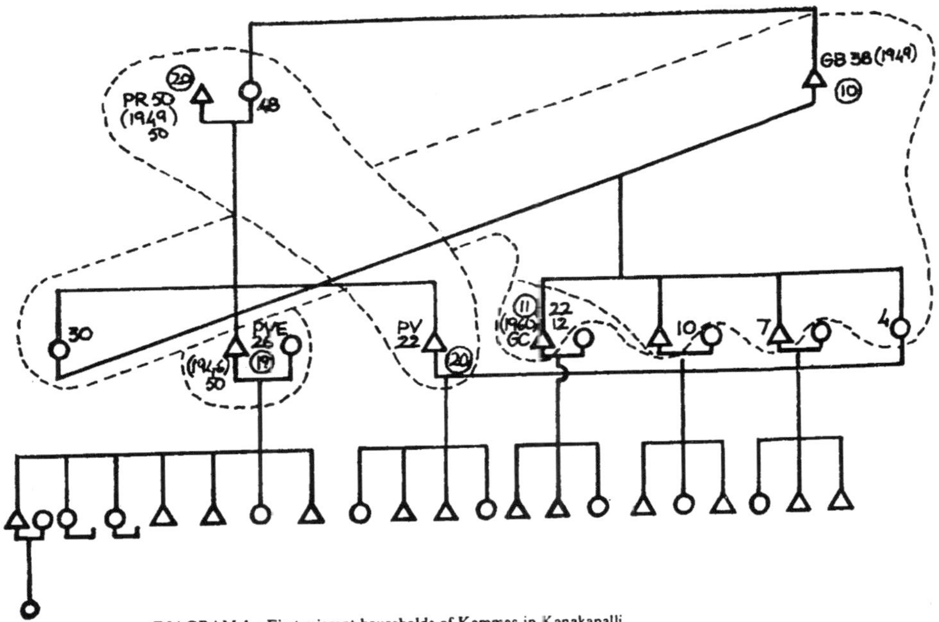

DIAGRAM 1 : First migrant households of Kammas in Kanakapalli. Number represents age of migrants at the time of migraticn. Number in circle represents the serial number of separated households listed in Table 4. Year of migration is shown in brackets. Dotted line demarcates households at the time migration.

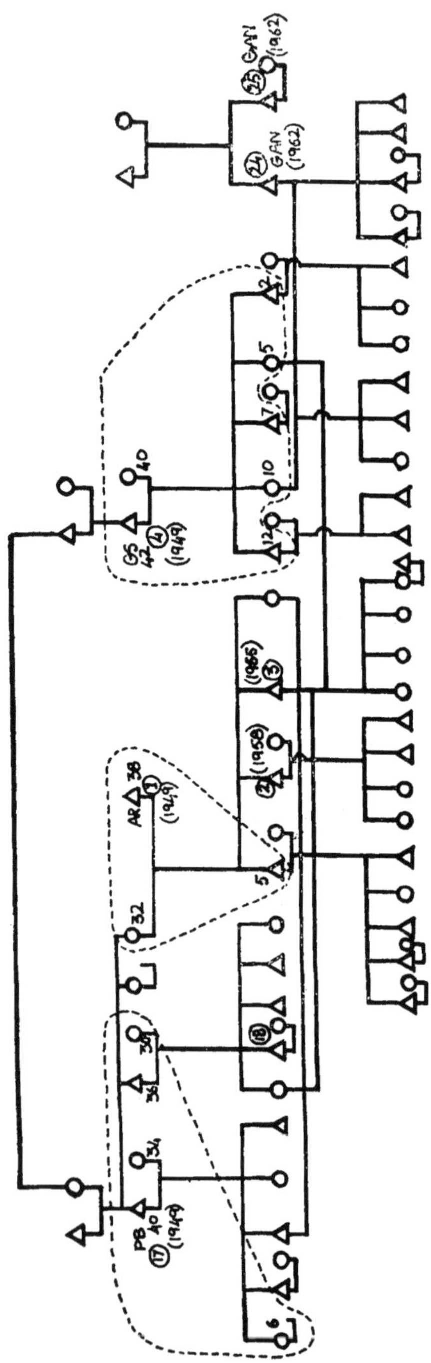

DIAGRAM 2: Cluster of related first migrant households of Kammas in Kanakapalli.

improved tanks, installed tube-wells. With such improvement in irrigational facilities, they started growing paddy but combining it with millet, pulses, jingilly, chilli and country tobacco. They established Kanaka Durga Service Cooperative Society in 1961 to obtain credit, fertilizers and other inputs. With all this infrastructure the agricultural production of the village increased ten-fold in three decades (1950—1980). It is necessary to note that the Raju peasants who had migrated before the Kamma farmers practised subsistence farming and their economic gains were not as conspicuous as those of the Kammas.

In 1960, the Indian Leaf Tobacco Development Company of the former Imperial Tobacco Company introduced a new variety of cigarette tobacco called light soil flue cured virginia (LSFCV). The Kammas of Kanakapalli were one of the first to grow LSFCV as they already had experience of growing FCV on black cotton soil in their place of origin in Kovvur taluk. In 1978, the Kamma farmers owned 47 out of 53 barns in Kanakapalli.

Cultivation of LSFCV drove the Kamma to look for suitable land with irrigational facilities all the time since barn tobacco cannot be grown on the same plot every year. There is a competitive demand for leasing-in land as buying land legally from the tribals is out of question. In 1978, twelve Kamma farmers had leased in 45 acres from the Koyas in Kanakapalli and another 40 acres from the Koyas of the two neighbouring villages. Thus they made huge profits from the tobacco cultivation.

Many Koyas lack both skills and interest in growing tobacco, although a few of them have started growing it since 1976. The tobacco season overlaps with the toddy season, and the Koyas prefer to realize a certain cash income by leasing out their land and at the same time have all the time for themselves to enjoy the toddy season and cock fights. The lease rate in Kanakapalli area for growing barn tobacco is Rs. 400 to 500 per acre per season. But some of the Koyas who have acquired skills and who are interested in growing barn tobacco resent the clever Kamma migrants who have become very affluent. The government gives the tribals easy credit and other inputs to grow tobacco. For instance, only the tribals are entitled to get a loan for installing a rig, which is a special tube-well which can go below the rockbed to reach the water level. The Koya Ex-Member of the Legislative Assembly in Kanakapalli resented the way the entrepreneurial Kammas have amassed wealth at the cost of the tribals, encroaching on their land and having many tribals as their farm servants. In 1978 there were 47 tribals out of 85 farm servants who were working on the migrant Kamma farms. About 60 tribals have migrated out of the village to other villages in the plains in search of jobs.

The foregoing account of the process of migration and colonization by the Kamma farmers in Kanakapalli shows that Kammas have been able to bring about significant agricultural development including commercialization of agriculture. However, along with development there is deprivation of the tribals in terms of land alienation, joining the ranks of farm servants and agricultural wage labourers, and out-migration in search of jobs. The conditions of relative deprivation of the tribals have been further worsened because of the stringent forest laws which prevent their access to forest and other resources such as hunting, fishing, food and non-food gathering and free extraction of toddy, but encourage the non-tribal contractors to exploit the forest resources.

Land Alienation

Of all the forms of tribal depivation as a result of peasant-farmer colonization in Polavaram taluk, land alienation is the main. Complete data, for all the 102 *Agency* villages, regarding the extent of land in the possession of the non-tribals are not available. In any case the land leased in by the non-tribals can not be known from land records, as the transactions are informal or *benami* (in some other name). On the basis of my investigations in nineteen villages, it may be estimated that about one-third of the cultivable land is in the possession and control of the non-tribals. However, the land owned and leased in by the non-tribals is of the best quality.

An all India study of land alienation among the tribals (Dubey and Murdia 1977) fails to give an all India estimate of land alienation, due to the paucity of data. But it indicates that the incidence is very high. According to Census figures, between 1961-1971, the percentage of cultivators in tribal population decreased from 68.15 to 57.16 per cent. But the percentage of agricultural labourers among them increased from 19.73 to 33 per cent.

Under such circumstances, the government has introduced several measures in order to alleviate the conditions of relative deprivation accompanying the agricultural development brought about mainly by the migrant farmers.

Administrative Measures to Alleviate Conditions of Deprivation

The State Government has taken several measures to alleviate the conditions of relative deprivation of the tribals. The *Agency* Land Transfer Regulation Act of 1970 prohibits any kind of land transaction between the tribals and the non-tribals and also holds all earlier transfers after 1917 as null and void. The Andhra Pradesh Scheduled Tribes Debt Relief Regulation of 1970 writes off the accumulated interest. Under the Andhra Pradesh Scheduled Area Ryotwari Settlement Regulation II of 1970 the last batch of the 29 ex-zamindari and other remote villages were surveyed and settled for the first time in 1975. The settlement officer in most cases has restored the land to the tribals. In 1977 a special Deputy Collector was appointed to restore land to the tribals in accordance with the 1970 Act. These legislations along with the intensive tribal development programmes in regard to agriculture, horticulture, sericulture, animal husbandry, employment and education have, to some extent, retrieved the Koyas from the position of land alienation and relative deprivation.

A trend in this direction is seen in the Buttayagudem Development Block, where 34 Koyas have started growing FCV since 1976. There are in all 41 out of about 900 barns in the block, owned by the tribals. If this trend continues, the feeling of alienation that they have been left out of the gains from the new commercial economy will be reduced to a considerable extent.

With the possibilities of irrigation facilities and commercialization of agriculture, there is an increasing demand for labour. Tribals are only beginning to acquire new skills of paddy and tobacco harvesting. About one-third of the Koyas work as farm servants and casual agricultural labourers. Many Koyas like to work as farm servants rather than casual labourers because the former provides a sense of security and gives them an advantage of a cash loan from the farmers whenever they want. As farm servants they are not required to learn the skills of harvesting and stringing of tobacco leaves, or harvesting tobacco.

The immigration of the plainsmen—cultivators, labourers and others—has to some extent resulted in the out-migration of the tribals from the *Agency*. In 1971, 42.52 per cent of the total number of tribals living in West Godavari District were found residing outside the *Agency* area i.e. on the plains. A majority of 85.18 per cent of the tribals living on the plains resided in rural areas. They are employed as agricultural labourers, farm servants, domestic servants and as unskilled workers in various construction and repair works. The out-migration of the tribals from the *Agency* area is due to several factors. There is a shrinkage of job opportunities for the tribals in the *Agency* area with increasing restrictions on using and selling of forest resources. They are dispossessed of *podu* and other lands. Generally they lack skills to engage in paddy and tobacco harvesting operations. Here the migrant cultivators prefer migrant labourers who are highly skilled, regular and more reliable than the tribals. For the same reason the forest contractors prefer migrant labourers from the plains to the local tribals in cutting bamboo, felling trees, cutting wood and for road construction. It should be noted here that out-migration of the tribals in itself is not undesirable as long as it is developmental in nature. But in this context they are forced out of their habitat as a result of the colonization of the non-tribals.

Migration Development and Deprivation

On the basis of the foregoing case study, we may discuss here the general theoretical problems concerning migration, development and deprivation, indicated in the introduction. First, there is the framework of a set of related concepts such as core-semi-periphery-periphery, metropolis-satellite dependency; economic development-underdevelopment; capitalist world-economy; colonialism and internal colonialism. Wallerstein

(1979 : 285-293) argues that capitalism is the only mode of production in which the maximization of surplus creation is rewarded *per se* through the market structure. It is the state system which encrusts, enforces, and exaggerates the patterns. Capitalism has regularly required the use of state machinery to revise the pattern of the worldwide division of labour. The core states become stronger than the peripheral states. In capitalism the surplus value of the proletariat is appropriated by the bourgeois. The proletariat is located in the periphery and semi-periphery and the bourgeois in the core. One of the mechanisms that has affected the process of surplus appropriation is the manipulation of controlling flows over state boundaries which results in uneven development. Core, semi-periphery and periphery are conceptual tools in analysing forms of class conflict in the capitalist world economy.

Gunder Frank (1967:8-21) has argued earlier that in this system of dependency of the periphery on the core, there was a step-wise linkage of national and international metropolises. At each step of the way up the economic ladder surplus from each of the minor and major satellites gravitated up or into the capitalist world's metropolitan centre. This initiated a process of the underdevelopment of the satellite on the one hand and the economic development of the metropolis on the other.

This framework of analysis claims that such a process of development of capitalist world economy is a global one and its pattern of development is the centre-periphery or metropolis-satellite dependency system. However, this is a very simplistic assumption, because it associates the exploitative and the exploited groups with different territorial units and secondly it points in only one direction of flow of labour from the periphery and pattern of dominance of the centre. In the light of the data presented above it is clear that the development-deprivation situation can develop within a single area with the immigration of entrepreneurial farmers and the deprivation of the autochthons who in Polavaram are tribals. But in other situations it would be different groups under the term "sons of the soil" : the Maharashtrians in Bombay, Assamese in Assam, Mulkis in Hyderabad and Kannadigas in Bangalore (see Weiner 1978).

While the centre-periphery argument is weak in respect of its universal applicability of migration trends and location of different groups involved in development, the political aspect as it is considered has also its limited validity. The part played by the entrepreneurial migrant farmers is no doubt closely related to the policies of administration. The state is intimately connected with the nature of economic development opportunities that open up in an area and the nature of migration of different groups. The part played by the state further is directly relevant in its forest and tribal policies. The manner in which these forces have operated in Polavaram taluk both in pre- and post-Independence periods has been illustrated. However, the centre-periphery, metropolis-satellite hypothesis ignores the intervention of the state in promoting developmental policies to rectify the imbalances in development. In this respect the land restoration policy of the government, preventive laws and the developmental schemes for the tribals are important.

Another related aspect of the Marxian analysis of development relates to the modes of production debate in the context of Indian agriculture. Recently Alice Thorner (1982) has meaningfully summarized the debate whether modes of production in India can be characterized as semi-feudalistic or capitalistic. In the light of data presented in this paper, there are not only multiple modes of production but different combinations. Still the slash-and-burn agriculture, hunting, fishing, food-gathering, non-food collecting of forest produce and selling, all, with ideas of shared work collective control and egalitarian redistribution rather than ownership, are prevalent among the Koyas. Although the migrant Kamma farmers show a spirit of entrepreneurship in their practice of development agriculture, their mode of production is far from being wholly capitalistic. There is greater dependence on family labour, farm servants, semi-attached labourers than on free floating market-determined wage labourers. Secondly, the farmers are not big land-owners but medium and small landholders. The first-generation big landholders in the fifties have become medium and small landholders in the seventies thanks to large size families and non-primogeniture or ultimogeniture system of property inheritance. This has resulted in fragmentation of holdings some of which become uneconomical. Such a process has given rise to a multi-tier agrarian system. Thirdly, the centre and state policies are clearly against buying or leasing-in land from the tribals in the region which prevent any expansion of capital accumulation in the form of land.

If by these facts, the mode of production is not capitalistic, has the consequence been one of class conflict? The course of migration and development is such that it has not led to class formation in the sense of class for itself. On the contrary, there is ethnic formation based on tribal and non-tribal identities. The non-tribals are the migrants and the tribals are the autochthons. The former are the exploiters and the latter the exploited. In fact, the Naxalite movement led by Marxist-Leninist Communist Party of India in Srikakulam tribal area of Andhra Pradesh thrived on ethnic conflict which transcended internal 'class' differences among the tribals. In Polavaram and other *Agency* tracts of Andhra Pradesh tribals form the mainstay of the Naxalite movement, although in Polavaram, the tribals are disillusioned with the Naxalite non-tribal leaders who organize them against the migrant landlords but later disappear from the scene because either they are rounded up by military police or go in the hiding. Such a situation forces the tribals once again to depend on the landlords for work, subsistence and cash loans for rituals. Without self-organization, they either become farm servants of the landowners or move out of the *Agency* in search of work. All this empirical evidence points to the fact that there is no class formation but increasing patron-client relationship on the one hand, and ethnic formation on the other, which is expressed in frequent tribal and non-tribal conflicts. The conflict is also a conflict between migrants and the autochthons. Thus both ethnic and territorial identities coincide.

The evidence for ethnic conflict instead of class conflict can be seen in other regions, under similar conditions of migration and development-deprivation. Myron Weiner (1978) has produced evidence from Assam, Chota Nagpur in Bihar and the Mulkis movement in Hyderabad. All these illustrate different forms of ethnic conflict based on diverse patterns of development-deprivation. At the root of the ethnic conflict is the opposition between the autochthons and the aliens. It is, however, necessary to stress that all situations of migration do not result in ethnic formations and conflicts, but only those where there is competition and where the migrant groups have become successful as a result of their having greater access to economic and political resources, and an attempt on their part to establish their cultural, economic and political dominance. Under conditions of such acute forms of deprivation, conflict gets articulated through sons of the soil movements based on defined ideologies of ethnicity.

In the tribal context, there have been messianic and millenarian movements, and cargo cults, all over the world in the developing countries (see Fuchs 1965; Raghaviah 1971; Roy 1970; Suresh Singh 1966; Bharadwaj 1977; Mahapatra 1968, 1972; Rao 1979, 1980, 1981). Such tribal movements are also to be found in developed countries like the U.S.A. and Canada. It is seen that various American Indians and Eskimos have organized themselves into movements resisting different forms of exploitative processes by the non-tribals. All these are different kinds of responses to acute conditions of relative deprivation.

To conclude, the analysis of development process in the tribal *Agency* tract of Andhra Pradesh in terms of the Marxist laws of motion of capitalist development is not borne out of empirical facts. Such a framework is more misleading rather than throwing any light on the process of development. On the contrary the framework that is evolved here, namely, development-deprivation is open and flexible to identify the trends, nature and direction of the process of development and the consequences in terms of deprivation based on ethnic, caste and migrant-non-migrant identities. The development-deprivation framework at the same time takes into account the sources of conflict changing patterns of dominance in the wider political economy context.

REFERENCES

Amin, Samir, *Modern Migrations in Western Africa*, Oxford University Press, London, 1974.

Bharadwaj, Gopal, "Socio-Political Movements among the Tribes in India" in S.C. Dube (ed.) *Tribal Heritage of India*, Vikas, New Delhi, 1977.

Dozier, C.L., *Land Development and Colonization in Latin America*, 1969.

Dubey, S.N. and Ratna Murdia, *Land Alienation and Restoration in Tribal Communities in India*, Himalaya Publishing House, Bombay, 1977.

Farmer, B.H., *Pioneer Peasant Colonization in Ceylon : A Study of Agrarian Problems*, Oxford University Press, Oxford, 1957.

Farmer, B.H., *Agricultural Colonization in India since Independence*, Oxford University Press, London, 1974.

Frank, Andre Gunder, *Capitalism and Underdevelopment in Latin America*, Monthly Review Press, New York, 1967.

Fuchs, Stephen, *Rebellious Prophets: A Study of Messianic Movements in Indian Religions*, Asia Publishing House, Bombay, 1965.

Mahapatra, L.K , "Social Movements among Tribes in Eastern India with Special Reference to Orissa", *Sociologus*, Vol. 18, 1, 1968.

Mahapatra, L.K., "Social Movements among the Tribes of India" in K. Suresh Singh (ed.) *Tribal Situation in India*, Indian Institute of Advanced Study, Simla, 1972.

Raghaviah, V., *Tribal Revolts*, Andhra Rashtra Adimajati Sevak Sangh, Nellore, 1971.

Rao, M.S.A., *Social Movements and Social Transformation : A Study of Two Backward Classes Movements in India*, Macmillan, New Delhi, 1979.

Rao, M.S.A. (ed.), *Social Movements in India*, Vol. II, Manohar, New Delhi, 1980.

Rao, M.S.A., "Prophecy and Heritage in Social and Cultural Movements", *Social Action*, Vol. 31, April-June, pp. 174-181, 1981.

Roy S.C., *The Mundas and Their Country*, Asia Publishing House, Bombay, (First edition published in 1912), 1970.

Singh, Suresh K., *Dust Storms and Hanging Mist : Story of Birsa Munda, and His Movement*, Firma K.L. Mukhopadyay, Calcutta, 1966.

Thorner, Alice, "Semi-Feudalism or Capitalism? Contemporary Debate on Classes and Modes of Production in India", *Economic and Political Weekly*, XVII, 49, pp. 1961-1968; XVII, 50, pp. 1993-1999; XVII, 51, pp. 2061-2066, 1982.

Wallerstein, Immanuel, *The Capitalist World Economy*, Cambridge University Press, Cambridge, 1979.

Wallerstein, Immanuel, *The Modern World System : Capitalist Agriculture and the Origins of European World Economy in the Sixteenth Century*, Academic Press, New York, 1974.

Weiner, Myron, *Sons of the Soil : Migration and Ethnic Conflict in India*, Oxford University Press, Delhi.

8. *Subsistence and Labour Mobility*

N.E.C. VIDYASAGAR

Understanding population redistribution, apart from promoting knowledge of socio-economic and demographic processes, has a direct bearing on planning and policy formulations. More so, since development is closely associated with migration both in developed and developing countries. But, migration studies have given a disproportionately large share of attention to rural-urban migration. Urbanization coupled with industrialization has generated and geared up rates of migration. But rural development and agricultural progress have also resulted in considerable migration. The Census of India monograph (1974), Kshirasagar (1973), NSS (1960) and Vidyasagar (1978) have pointed out that most of the migration in India is intra-district and rural to rural. Rural-to-urban migration becomes important not because of its magnitude (within different types of migration) but due to its linkage with industrialization, and associated problems of health and hygiene, under or unemployment, and formation of squatters' settlements and slums. At present, the information available is too scanty on rural-to-rural migration. Hence the need for studying it.

A related problem pertains to the existing theories of migration. They are developed in the context of rural-urban migration. Would they be equally relevant in the case of rural-rural migration? Further, using the theories of migration explaining the non-occurrence of migration is difficult at present. An examination of existing theories suggests that they do not so readily explain the non-occurrence of migration as they do explain its occurrence. This results from an *ex-post-facto* analysis of migration and a strong bias in collection of data regarding reasons for migration mainly from places of destination.

This paper reports the patterns of rural-rural migration occurring as a result of agricultural colonization which, in turn, was a consequence of irrigation and development of agriculture. It focuses on one village, place of origin of migrants, and attempts to identify the factors associated with emigration and seeks to answer some of the questions arising about the theory of migration. There is, in the argument, an inherent plea that aggregation of migrants into one type and offering a single frame of explanation may not be satisfactory.

Rural-Rural Migration and Agricultural Colonization

The study was conducted in Bellary district in the State of Karnataka. Construction of the Tungabhadra dam, a large scale hydro electrical irrigation project, in the district has brought surface water irrigation to the region (See Map 1).

The tapping of surface water through tanks and canals has a long history in Bellary district. It started during the days of the Vijayanagar empire (1336-1565) and channels that were constructed during those days are being used even today. However, the Tungabhadra dam construction commenced in 1945 by the then Governments of Madras and Hyderabad and was completed by 1953. The dam is estimated to irrigate 1,244,786 acres, of which 69.2 per cent is in the State of Karnataka and the rest in Andhra Pradesh. The dam has right bank low level (LLC) and high level (HLC) canals, and a left bank canal irrigating 0.93, 1.82 and 6.02 lakhs of acres respectively.

As a result of irrigation the region has been transformed from an uncertain monsoon dependent economy to a multi-crop economy. The people in this, and neighbouring districts, whose lands are irrigated by this project were not used to flow irrigation and Government had to take special interest in diffusing the necessary knowledge, constructing an infrastructure to provide finance and other material inputs to develop the land. If 1950 is taken as the base, the irrigation has brought about a fourfold increase in production of cereals, pulses and cotton (mimeographed report on Tungabhadra project issued by the dam project command areas authority 1976).

Migration and Formation of New Settlements

Irrigation coupled with development has led to considerable migration into the region covered by the Tungabhadra dam. The initial stream of migrants consisted of entrepreneurial farmers who bought lands from the natives original inhabitants before they were irrigated, and developed them. Such new arrivals were mostly from the neighbouring state of Andhra Pradesh. Natives of the region were unfamiliar with techniques of flow cultivation and were also sceptical about the benefits. They were keen to dispose the lands even before the region was irrigated, in order to avert what, according to them was a disaster, in the form of salination of lands and loss of fertility. The migrant farmers bought the lands from the local farmers, levelled and brought them under flow cultivation. This process led to the establishment of new settlements, locally called *camps* (Map 1).

The size of a camp varies from 10-15 houses to 100-150 houses. Where the immigrants were too few in number, they lived in the main village itself. A *camp*, typically, consists of groups of landholders who have migrated from a cluster of villages, and, more often than not, are related to each other, although distantly. Migration into the irrigated region occurred between 1950-1975, and is evidently a consequence of irrigation and agricultural transformation.

The agricultural colonization resulting thus is a specific type of rural-rural migration. Agricultural colonization the world over, had been taking place generally in regions which were sparsely populated and those with waste lands. Such colonizations were sponsored by the State in Ceylon (Farmer 1974), India (Farmer 1974), Asiatic tropics (Pelzer 1948), and Malaysia (Scott 1983). Agricultural colonization in regions irrigated by the Tungabhadra was non-sponsored and spontaneous.[1]

The intensification of farming and the consequent growing

BELLARY DISTRICT

DISTRIBUTION OF CAMPS AND LOCATION OF MAHAKADAKU

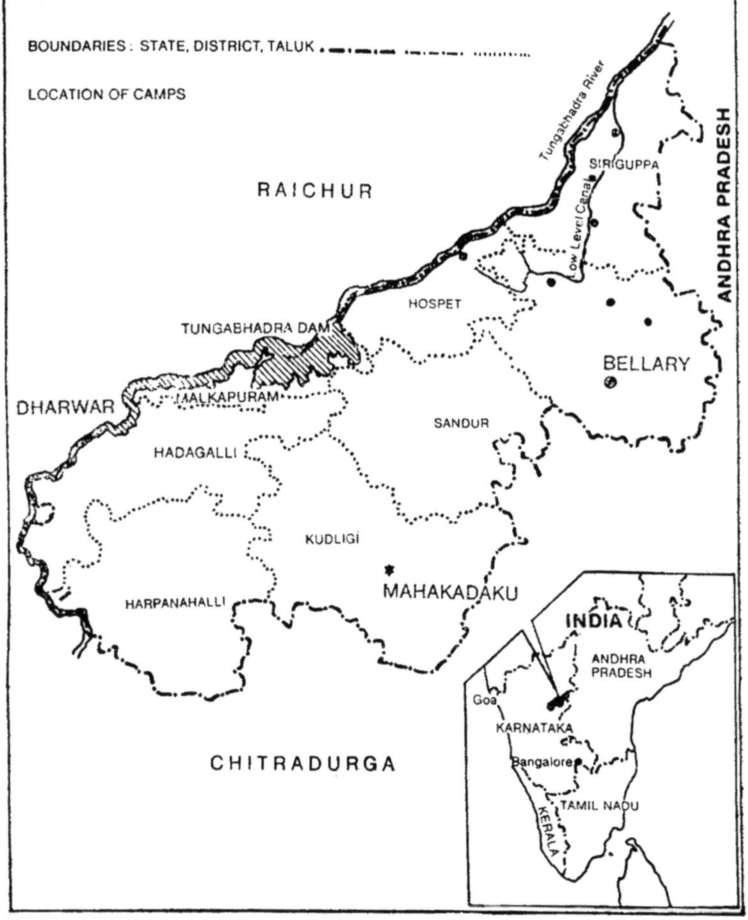

demand for labourers, especially during peak periods of cultivation, namely, sowing or harvesting/transplanting, has developed a stream of landless labourers migrating from within and from neighbouring districts. In the initial stages, immigration of labourers was temporary and seasonal in nature. But many of them have become permanent settlers in later years.

Majority of the labourers have travelled small distances. The distribution of the villages of origin of these immigrant labourers is non-random. There is a clustering of villages in a close geographic area. The villages slightly far from the cluster are the ones with close relatives of the migrants from these clusters. One factor common to all these villages is, that they all depend on the monsoons for agriculture and the region may generally be termed semi-arid. Failure of the monsoon and consequent non-availability of work forces a person to migrate. This paper enquires into the pattern of labour out-migration from a subsistence farming village to intensive cultivating areas.

Earlier Studies

The push-pull theory of migration, in its earlier stages, assumed that places of origin exert pushes and places of destination exert pulls.[2] Within this framework, ideally, migration should occur from regions and groups where the number of push factors is more. For instance, from economically less developed regions and strata. But most urban parts of rural areas show more migrations (Bradfield 1973) and the rate of migration increases with decreasing isolation (Tschopichs 1947). Migration also occurs disproportionately from upper and middle strata of villages (Simmons and Cordona 1972), upper castes (Valunjkar 1966; Eames 1954), but not from Scheduled Castes (D'Souza 1975) or from landless, poor labourers (Das Gupta and Laishley 1975). These findings cast grave doubts on the predictability of the framework. In a modified push-pull theory both the places of origin and destination were conceived of as exerting push and pull simultaneously.[3]

This modified analysis, which implies advantages and disadvantages operating simultaneously in both places of origin and destination, lead to the cost and benefit approach. Relatively more restricted studies, restricted in theoretical outlook and geographic coverage undertaken by Sociologists and Anthropologists, have been pointing to the importance of non-economic costs and the social and psychological benefits. They also brought to the forefront the importance of kinship ties which not only are active in the post-migration context (contrary to the belief it would not be so in developed countries at least)[4] but also in generating migration through information flows and sponsorship. The role of information has received particular attention.[5] Together with kinship ties, information flows partly accounted for the discrepancies observed in expected and actual migration flows. Approaches like Human Capital Investment (which takes into account the present benefits and costs of the move as well as 'discount rates' taking future benefits of both migration and non-migration) and subjective perception (which considers differences in perception (Graves 1966), personal values (Dutoit 1975), and biographical and personal differences (Bradfield 1973) attempt to answer further anomalies in the cost benefit approach to migration.

But despite all this, some differences remain unexplained. Benefits and costs being almost similar, why does every one in same social level not migrate? (Cf. Simmons and Cordona 1972). Bradfield (1973 : 352) wrote : "Many factors normally used to explain why some migrate and others do not are general conditions which affect many more than those who respond to these pressures . . . not all respond in the same manner. . . . It is hard to find out communities where all people with a given set of characteristics have left for the city".

Two questions which suggest themselves are : (1) Cost-benefit approach in an overall sense fails to account for lower migration rates among landless labourers. Undoubtedly for them both monetary and non-monetary costs are lesser than the benefits of those of the landholders. (2) There is no sound basis for presupposing that everybody in a village would be calculating the costs and benefits of migration. It would be tantamount to maintaining that migration is most natural and everybody should migrate. If only some people calculate, what are the characteristics of these peoples? When do they calculate?

Restatement of Objectives of Study

To explore the above and related questions it was decided to undertake the current study. It has the following specific objectives:

(1) To assess the importance of theoretically suggested and empirically identified, migration influencing variables and their role in explaining non-occurrence of migration.
(2) To find out in what respects migrants and non-migrants in place of origin (in this case a village in Karnataka) differ, and thereby to isolate the critical variables in the occurrence of migration.
(3) To see if in different strata different factors operate in generating migration, the assumption being that social strata in villages show syndromes of socio-cultural characteristics which result in different patterns of migration.

Methodology

Data were collected from one village namely Mahakadaku (pseudonym) located in Bellary district in Karnataka State. The village depends on the monsoons for agriculture. A failure of monsoons, an imminent crop failure, and non-availability of work prompts a person to migrate. Failure of monsoons is cyclical occurring once in every 3-4 years (Cf. Morris 1974 : 1856), and therefore migration is recurrent through the years. The migrants have moved out of the village for reasons of subsistence as labourers to areas which were irrigated and where there was a demand for extra labour. No upward mobility either in economic or prestige spheres was observed among them.

Two interview schedules were used in collecting data:

(i) *Village Level*: Seeking information about farming, agricultural cycle, work and division of labour, wages, social-cultural life. This does not show inter-respondent variation. So key informant technique was used.
(ii) *Household Level*: Seeking demographic, economic and familial information covering migration history, occupation, income and expenditure, marriage and family formation and

landholding. A 24 per cent random sample of households was drawn from the village for this purpose.

In the analysis which follows in this paper, a household is taken as the unit of analysis, not the individual person.

The Village Studied: Mahakadaku

Mahakadaku is located in Kudligi taluk in Bellary district in the State of Karnataka (See Map). It consists of four nucleated hamlets each functioning as a separate unit in its cultural and social life. The soil is red, gravelly and relief undulated with gentle slopes. The region in which Mahakadaku is located can be described as semi arid.

Technically an arid area is defined on the basis of evapo-transpiration. This is calculated in the form of moisture index. In arid-zones cultivation is not possible unless irrigation is available. In semi-arid zones rain-fed crops can be grown. The agricultural problems of semi-arid zones are : low amount and annual variability of ram fall and its tendency to cluster in a few months in a year. As a result of these climatic features, choice of crops becomes very limited. Growing cash crops is impossible under these conditions and even among cereals millets are the only possibility (Grigg 1970). The yield fluctuates from year to year and in a below average rainfall year, crops may fail completely.

The cost of tapping the underground water source is prohibitive for many households in the village. The limited rain-fall, and underground water which is not easily accessible leave little choice for the villagers in crop selection. Jowar (Andro-pogen Sorghum) is extensively grown with a few acres of paddy and vegetables where the ground water has been tapped through well irrigation. Jowar is grown in this region because of its resistance to dry and hot weather, and a capacity to withstand an especially unfavourable rainy season with no marked effect on output.

Ten castes are represented in Mahakadaku. The Valmikis are numerically the most dominant followed by Scheduled Castes. Among other castes, Lingayats have a sizeable number of households (Table 8.1).

TABLE 8.1

Distribution of Households by Castes

Caste	Traditional Occupation	Present Occupation	Households	
			Numbers	Per cent
1. Barika (Walikara)	Limestone preparation, palanquin bearing	Agriculture and wage labour	1	0.15
2. Brahmin	Priesthood, education, landowning	Landowning, teacher	1	0.15
3. Idiga	Toddy tapping	Toddy tapping and agriculture	20	3.09
4. Korcha	Mat/basket weaving	Mat/basket weaving	3	0.46
5. Lingayat	Varies widely	Agriculture	78	12.04
6. Madavala (Agasa)	Washing	Agriculture	1	0.15
7. Scheduled Caste	Leather-work & wage labour	Wage labour, some landowning	146	22.53
8. Valmiki (Naiker)	Hunting	Agriculture	390	60.19
9. Wodda	Earth-work & construction	Earth-work, wage labour	8	1.23
Total :			648	100.00

All castes have deviated from their traditional occupations except the Korchas.

Landholding : Distribution of landholding in the village is not skewed. Households are more or less evenly distributed in all the categories of size of landholding (Table 8.2) with highest in 1-4 and lowest in 10-14 categories respectively. Compared to all India averages (Patnaik 1976) the sample village has lesser number of households in the landless category and slightly more in the category owning 15 and more acres. Although it would be difficult to draw any generalisation, Farmer's (1974) comparative data on landholding sizes in dry and wet cultivating villages also confirms non-concentration of land at the top in the given agrarian ecology and technology.

TABLE 8.2

Distribution of Households in Mahakadaku by Size of Landholding

Acreage	Number	Per cent
Landless	30	18.99
1—4	41	25.95
5—9	37	23.42
10—14	24	15.19
15 and more	26	16.45
Total base for percentage	158	100.00

Caste and Land : Valmikis show the widest distribution, of all the castes, in different landholding sizes (Table 8.3) and Idigas the most even. Larger landholders are in the Lingayat caste and the Scheduled Castes do hold some lands though not many fall in the categories of more than 5 acres.

A Case Study of Migration in the Village (Mahakadaku)

One can observe both emigration and immigration in Mahakadaku village.

Immigration : There are 12 immigrant households and 5

TABLE 8.3

Distribution of Castes in Different Sizes of Landholdings

Caste		Landholding Categories (acres)					Total
		Landless	1-4	5-9	10-14	15 & more	
Brahmin	Numbers	—	—	—	—	1	1
	Per cent	—	—	—	—	100.00	100.00
Valmiki	Numbers	15	28	25	15	12	95
	Per cent	15.79	29.47	26.32	15.78	12.63	100.00
Idiga	Numbers	1	1	1	1	1	5
	Per cent	20.00	20.00	20.00	20.00	20.00	100.00
Lingayat	Numbers	1	2	2	4	10	19
	Per cent	5.26	10.53	10.53	21.05	52.63	100.00
Scheduled	Numbers	9	9	9	3	2	32
Castes	Per cent	28.13	28.13	28.13	9.37	6.27	100.00
Others	Numbers	3	1	—	1	1	6
	Per cent	50.00	16.67	—	26.67	16.67	100.00

immigrant individuals in the village. Caste-wise distribution of these households is as follows:

Lingayat : 5; Valmiki : 3; Idiga : 1; Madavali : 1; Mala : 1; Korcha : 1.

Lingayats are the most numerous among immigrants. Proportionately, their number in the indigenous population is less than among immiggrants which shows that Lingayats are over-represented among immigrants. There is a teacher among the Lingayats who immigrated for professional reasons and is staying in a rented house. Others have migrated for management of property. Usually a father-in-law who has a single daughter and no male issues brings his son-in-law to look after agriculture and family. The custom is known as *manethena.* A variation of the same pattern of migration is where a person has more than one daughter, but no male children. In such cases only one of the sons-in-law is brought in for *manethena.* The choice of son-in-law is based on subjective valuation and bias has a major role. Then again, if a person is very old and cannot look after agriculture himself, he requests husband of the eldest daughter to immigrate, because, even though he has sons, they are too young to work in the fields. In the last type of immigration the son-in-law gets a share at the time of property division. Only one case of the third type occurred, where a washerman brought his son-in-law, while for the second type there were two cases, one in Lingayat and another in Valmiki. In the first type there were 5 cases, 3 of them in Lingayat, 1 in Valmiki, one in Mala and one in Korcha caste.

Sometimes a villager brings his sister's children when the children's parents die and there is no one to look after them. A Korcha family in the village is an example of this type of migration.

In the rest of the cases, as immigration has occurred even though the father-in-law had male issues in working age. The immigrants had their own reasons for migrating, such as, an insecure position in the native village, or too many brothers in the family. One Lingayat migrated because his father-in-law offered him capital to start a petty shop and a tea-stall in the village.

In two cases, persons migrated to their daughter's house in the village, because the sons concerned left their fathers to themselves. In one case, a widow brought her elder sister's daughter (informally adopting her) and her family since she had no children at all. Two cases of women immigrating through uxorial extension (i.e., through wife's lineal ties) are noticed, and in both the cases the women had none to look up to for support in their old age. Crisis migration of this sort totals to five. This plus the above-mentioned immigrations add to 12 immigrant households and 5 individuals.

Emigration: In the analysis that follows out-migration from the village is considered, and the term migration refers to emigration.

Emigration occurs for two reasons. Firstly, it is for purposes of taking up service in the Government or in private undertakings. From Mahakadaku 4 persons have out-migrated as teachers, 2 as drivers and 9 as toddy contractors or are employed by such contractors as toddy-tappers. A toddy-tapper gets Rs. 120 per month. All the toddy-tappers who migrated from the village belong to Idiga caste. Tapping requires some skills, wrong tapping can kill a tree. It is learnt, rather informally, by working under experienced hands. Thus, in all 15 persons have emigrated out of the village with their families for non-agricultural work.

Secondly, emigration occurs for the purposes of agricultural work which is seasonal in nature. Major part of such migration occurs during harvests. There are 48 (30.4 per cent) such households out of the 158 households in the sample. The places of destination in the case of all these emigrants are the villages in the districts of Raichur and Bellary which are irrigated by the low level canal, high level canal and the left bank canal of the Tungabhadra dam. A large proportion of them have migrated to villages within Bellary. The map shows the administrative division of Bellary district into eight taluks namely, Bellary, Hadagalli, Haranahalli, Hospet, Kudligi, Malkapuram, Sandur and Siriguppa. Out of eight taluks three taluks namely, Bellary, Siriguppa and Hospet are irrigated by the Tungabhadra dam. Migration occurs to the camps in these three taluks (location of some of the camps is shown in the map). A tendency among the migrants to migrate every year not only to the same village but also to work on the lands of the same farmer is noticed. Conversation with the migrants suggested that over a period of years personal and economic interaction between the landholder and migrant labour has led to such patterns.

As for the pattern of emigration, it was observed that in some cases the entire family consisting of husband, wife and children, if any, moves out and in other cases single members migrate from a household. Usually when a household emigrates, the older members like parents are left behind in Mahakadaku. During their intermittent visits the migrants bring with them grains and cash to provide for the older members in their absence. The single member emigrants are mostly unmarried.

Increase in Wages : Needless to say, as a result of migration there had been an increase in the wages of migrants. The magnitude of the increase can be stated only approximately. Because in irrigated areas wages differ according to nature of work. Heavier works like earth-work, ploughing, spade work are paid more. Lighter works like weeding are paid relatively less. Added to this, the payment is also done on contractual basis rather than on per diem payment. In the contractual arrangement the agricultural work is divided into operational tasks like preparation of the field, transplantation, harvesting and are given on contract separately. The rates are as follows:

		Rupees
Earth-work (per cubic yard)	:	150
Spade work	:	30 to 40 per acre
Plantation	:	50 to 60 per acre
Harvest	:	30 per acre

The institution of contract is totally absent in Mahakadaku. Also in this arrangement the actual monetary gains are decided by the number of persons involved and the speed with which it is carried out.

The daily wage rates in Mahakadaku and at the places of destination are as follows :

		Male	Female
Wages in Mahakadaku	Heavier work	2.50	2.00
	Lighter work	2.00	1.50
Wages at places of destination		3.50	2.50

The increases are 28 per cent for males and 20 per cent for females when heavier work is considered. When lighter work is taken into consideration the increase is 43 per cent among males and 40 per cent among females. What is to be noted in this context is that apart from these increases in wages, which are not significant, places of destination offer continuous work throughout the year to the migrant. Whereas Mahakadaku offers them work only during a part of the year and even in this period only intermittently.

Factors Affecting Migration : Among several factors influencing emigration from Mahakadaku socio-economic valuables related to landholding and household are taken into consideration. In the analysis, however, the two kinds of emigrants namely agricultural and non-agricultural are treated together in the initial stages. This is done to demonstrate how disaggregation of migrants into agricultural and non-agricultural promotes better understanding of identifying and separating the factors influencing migration.

Landholding and Migration : The percentage of migrants gradually decreases with an increase in the landholding size, with a slight upward and contradictory trend in the size groups 5-9 and 10-14 (Table 8.4). But the rise is only 2.2 percentage points. (The difference between the observed and expected frequencies in the chi-square values is lowest in 10-14 and 5-9 groups) which indicates that these two size groups are not really heterogeneous. Nearly one quarter of population in the 15 and more group migrate. This and a moderate value of contingency coefficient shows the not very explanatory character of landholding size.

Production Relationship and Migration : Since the size of land holdings, as such, is not a reliable indicator of economic classification in the village, the relationship between land and man in the production sphere is considered as well as its relationship with migration. The village population is divided into 5 categories for this purpose using hiring of labour as the criterion.

1. Landowners cultivating with hired labour
2. Cultivators hiring labour
3. Cultivators using mainly family labour

TABLE 8.4

Landholding and Migration

		Landholding size (in acres)					
		Landless	0—4	5—9	10—14	15 and more	Total
Migrant households	Numbers	19	20	12	8	6	65
	Per cent Rowise	29.23	30.77	18.46	12.31	9.23	41.14
	Per cent Column-wise	63.33	48.78	32.43	33.33	28.08	
Non-Migrant households	Numbers	11	21	25	16	20	93
	Per cent Rowise	11.83	22.58	26.88	17.20	21.51	58.86
	Per cent Column-wise	36.67	51.22	67.57	66.67	76.92	
Total base for percentage		100.00 (30) (18.99)	100.00 (41) (25.95)	100.00 (37) (23.42)	100.00 (24) (15.19)	100.00 (26) (16.46)	100.00 (158)

$X^2=12.40$; d.f.$=5$; $0.02>P>0.01$; $n=158$.

Mean Square Contingency : 0.2697.

Means, Standard Deviations, Standard Errors and t-value

	Mean	*S.D.*	*S.E.*	*t-value*
Migrant Households	5.61	±5.94	±0.74	1.75*
Non-Migrant Households	9.91	±13.32	±1.38	
Total	8.18	±10.16	±0.81	

*Significant at 5% level.

$0.05 > P > 0.025$ (one tailed test).

4. Cultivating labourers
5. Wage labourers

Difference between the first and second categories is whether the landowner himself is involved in cultivation. Between 3rd and 4th, however, the hiring of labour is used in a relative sense. Cultivating families does not mean they do not hire labour nor does it mean they do not go for wage labour at all. And in the same way differences between cultivating labourers and labourers also is relative. The devising of two categories is based on the fact that in an agricultural year that would be the predominant kind of production relationship, predominance being a term denoting the majority of man days in an agrarian year.

Table 8.5 shows that the maximum deviation from the expected norm occurs in category II and the minimum in the third. As will be shown later, migration in categories I and II is not for subsistence reason. Many have migrated for jobs like teachers in these categories. In almost all the categories from III through V migrants and non-migrants are more or less equally distributed, the difference never exceeding 10 percentage points. It is a high value of contingency coefficient which points to a search for a better predictor, the implication of which is that in understanding migration, its occurrence or non-occurrence one needs further details about the people in these categories.

Household Size, Type and Migration : The percentage of migrants is the least in complete nuclear households (Table 8.6). All other types of households differ only marginally in sending out migrants. The chi-square value also is not significant.

There is an overall increase in percentages of migrants as the household size increases (Table 8.7). But the increase is not large (5. percentage points) except in the last category. A very small number of cases in the last category leaves a large margin of doubt to draw any conclusions.

Family Phase and Migration : Maximum migration is seen in the families in fission phase (Table 8.8). These are the joint households in the process of becoming nuclear. Families in the formative stage are midway between the two in sending out migrants.

TABLE 8.5

Production Relationship and Migration (Percentages)

		Category of Production Relationship*					
		I	II	III	IV	V	Total
Migrant households	Number	2	9	9	28	17	65
	Per cent	28.57	21.95	40.91	48.28	56.7	41.14
Non-Migrant households	Number	5	32	12	30	13	93
	Per cent	71.43	78.05	59.09	51.72	43.33	58.86
Total base for percentage		100.00	100.00	100.00	100.00	100.00	100.00
		(7)	(41)	(22)	(58)	(30)	(158)
		(4.43)	(25.95)	(13.92)	(36.71)	(18.99)	

$X^2=10.99$; d.f. 4; $0.05>P>0.02$; $n=158$.

Mean Square Contingency ; 0.2550.

**Note* : The explanation of categories of production relationship is given in the text.

TABLE 8.6

Household Type and Migration (Percentages)

		Household Type*				
		Nuclear		Joint		
		Complete	Incomplete	Lineal	Lineal and Collateral	Total
Migrant households	Number	15	14	23	13	65
	Per cent	28.30	48.28	48.94	44.83	41.14
Non-Migrant households	Number	38	15	24	16	93
	Per cent	71.70	51.72	51.06	55.17	58.86
Total base for percentage		100.00 (53) (33.54)	100.00 (29) (18.35)	100.00 (47) (29.75)	100.00 (29) (18.35)	100.00 (158)

*Complete nuclear household is one with husband, wife and their unmarried children, and it is incomplete in the absence of any one of the above-mentioned persons. Lineal Joint household is one extending along descent lines; and lineal collateral is one extending both on descent and sibling lines.

X^2 : 5.60; d.f.=3; 0.20>P>0.10; n=158.
Mean Square Contingency : 0.1850.

TABLE 8.7

Size of the Household and Migration (Percentages)

		Household Size				Total
		<4	4 –6	9—13	14—18	
Migrant households	Number	16	36	10	3	65
	Per cent	36.26	42.86	40.00	60.00	41.14
Non-Migrant households	Number	28	48	15	2	93
	Per cent	63.64	57.14	60.00	40.00	58.86
Total base for percentage		100.00 (44) (27.85)	100.00 (84) (53.16)	100.00 (25) (15.82)	100.00 (5) (3.16)	100.00 (158)

$X^2=1.19$; d.f.$=3$, $0.80>P>0.70$; $n=158$.

Mean Square Contingency=0.0865.

Means, Standard Deviations, Standard Errors and t-value

	Mean	*S.D.*	*S.E.*	*t-value*
Migrant households	6.39	±3.05	±0.37	
				0.91*
Non-Migrant households	5.86	±2.64	±0.27	
Total population	6.12	+2.76	±0.22	

*Not Significant.
$P>0.10$.

TABLE 8.8

Family Phase and Migration (Percentages)

		Family Phase			
		Formation	Expansion	Fission	Total
Migrant households	Number	11	17	37	65
	Per cent	42.21	26.56	54.41	41.14
Non-Migrant households	Number	15	47	31	93
	Per cent	57.69	73.44	45.59	58.86
Total base for percentage		100.00	100.00	100.00	100.00
		(26)	(64)	(68)	(158)
		(16.46)	(40.5)	(43.04)	

X^2=11.10; 0.01>P>0.001; n=158.

Mean Square Contingency : 0.2562.

Number of Children and Migration: In each group of the number of children, there are more non-migrants than migrants (Table 8.9). Migrants have a slightly larger mean than the non-migrants. But the difference between means is less than 1. Migrants tend to decrease as the number of children increases.

Relationship between migration, household type and size, and number of children is more complex than it apparently looks. Higher propensities for migration among unmarried, and a lowering of the same after marriage and child birth (Nolan 1975) contradicts Wiests' (1973) finding on relationship between the number of children and migration. In the present data migration shows an inverse relation to number of children and direct relation with size of household, which on the face of it looks contradictory. However, household size is related not only to number of children but to type of household as well. Table 8 7 shows the presence of larger proportions of migrants in extended households. This also is corroborated by the maximum occurrence of migration from families in the fission phase (Table 8 8). Overall, migrants have a higher mean number of children than non-migrants.

Dependency Ratio and Migration: The proportion of migrants increases as the number of dependents in the household increases up to 1.4 non-workers per one worker category and after that it dwindles (Table 8 10). The mean number of dependents is less among migrants.

Number of dependents and the size of land owned are positively related. Women withdraw from agricultural work in favour of domestic work or housekeeping as the landed property increases, and the children become economically productive at later ages in these households. Generally, the more the land under possession the lesser will be the propensity to migrate. When the dependency ratio is dichotomised at 1.4 in to high and low, and landholding at 10 acres, in the above 10 category there is a drop in the percentage of migrants both in high and low dependency categories. But the decrease is steeper in the high category (Table 8.11-a) When land is controlled an increase in dependency ratio results in lessening of propensities to migrate (Table 11-b). But the effect is negligible in less than 10 acre categories (difference of

TABLE 8.9

Number of Children and Migration (Percentages)

		Number of Children			
		Less than 3	4—6	7—9	Total
Migrant households	Number	39	24	2	65
	Per cent	44.82	39.34	20.00	41.14
Non-Migrant households	Number	48	37	8	93
	Per cent	55.17	60.66	80.00	58.86
Total base for percentage		100.00	100.00	100.00	100.00
		(87)	(61)	(10)	(158)
		(55.06)	(38.61)	(6.33)	

$X^2 = 2.42$; d.f. $= 2$; $0.95 > P > 0.90$; $n = 158$.
Mean Square Contingency : 0.1228.

Mean, Standard Deviations, Standard Errors and t-value

	Mean	*S.D.*	*S.E.*	*t-value*
Migrant households	3.36	±3.40	±0.42	1.43*
Non-Migrant households	2.69	±2.15	±0.22	
Total population	3.08	±2.11	±0.17	

*Not Significant
$P > 0.05$

TABLE 8.10

Dependency Ratio and Migration (Percentages)

		Dependency Ratio					
		0.-0.4	0.5-0.9	1-1.4	1.5-9	2 or more	Total
Migrnt households	Number	10	15	22	4	14	65
	Per cent	35.71	46.87	55.00	33.33	30.43	41.14
Non-Migrant households	Number	18	17	18	8	32	93
	Per cent	64.29	53.13	45.00	66.67	69.57	58.86
Total base for percentage		100.00 (28) (17.72)	100.00 (32) (20.25)	100.00 (40) (25.32)	100.00 (12) (7.59)	100.00 (46) (29.11)	100.00 (158)

$X^2=6.63$; d.f.$=4$; $0.20>P>0.10$; $n=158$.
Mean Square Contingency : 0.1977.

Means, Standard Deviations, Standard Errors and t-value

	Mean	*S.D.*	*S.E.*	*t-value*
Migrant households	1.25	±0.98	±0.12	
Non-Migrant households	1.94	±1.23	±0.13	3.9*
Total Population	1.36	±1.14	±0.09	

*Very Significant.
$P \leq 0.001$.

TABLE 8.11 (a)

Dependency Ratio, Landholding and Migration (Dependency Ratio Controlled Percentages)

		Landholding				
		Below 10 Acres		Above 10 Acres		
		Dependency Ratio		Dependency Ratio		
		Less than 1.4	More than 1.4	Less than 1.4	More than 1.4	Total
Migrant households	Number	36	14	11	4	65
	Per cent	47.37	43.75	45.83	15.4	41.14
Non-Migrant housebolds	Number	40	18	13	22	93
	Per cent	52.63	56.25	54.16	84.6	58.86
Total base for percentage		100.00	100.00	100.00	100.00	100.00
		(76)	(32)	(24)	(26)	(158)
		(48.1)	(20.3)	(15.2)	(16.5)	

TABLE 8.11 (b)

Dependeney Ratio, Landholding and Migration (Landholding Controlled Percentages)

		Dependency Ratio				
		Below 1.4 Landholding		Above 1.4 Landholding		
		<10 acres	>10 acres	<10 acres	>10 acres	Total
Migrant households	Number	36	11	14	4	65
	Per cent	47.37	45.83	43.75	15.38	41.14
Non-Migrant households	Number	40	13	18	22	93
	Per cent	52.63	54.16	56.25	84.62	58.86
Total base for percentage		100.00	100.00	100.00	100.00	100.00
		(76)	(24)	(32)	(26)	(158)
		(48.1)	(15.2)	(20.3)	(16.5)	

7 percentage points) and considerable (23 percentage points) in more than 10 category.

Land-Man Ratio (*LMR*) *and Migration* : The landholding size holds a moderate relationship with migration. Household size and type hold weaker relationship. One of the possibilities may be that the variables landholding size and household size do hold an influence but their significance is lost when they are considered separately. Also household size may have an effect on migration in smaller holdings and no effect in larger holdings. A more accurate index to measure the pressures generated on subsistence need would be a combination of landholding size and household size. Land-man ratio is used for this purpose.

As in the case of landholding, the proportion of migrants consistently decreases as the land per head in a household increases (Table 8.12). The decrease is not pronounced in less than 1 and 1-2 categories. (The deviations from the expected chi-square calculations are maximum in the group where land per head exceeds 2 acres and next in landless categories). This means the two groups are transitional zones below and above which the land man ratio has a clear effect on migration In these two groups some other variables are also acting apart from land per head. Few cases of non-occurrence of migration in the landless category and its occurrence in the group with LMR exceeding 2 acres call for explanation using other variables.

The different castes in the village show different patterns of migration. The higher castes like Brahmins and Lingayats migrate to take up jobs in other places. There are two Brahmins who migrated as teachers to other villages. One Lingayat also has moved out for the same reason. The Idiga caste men in the village have migrated as toddy-tappers, or arrack vendors or as arrack contractors all of which are related to their traditional occupation, and their migration is in no way connected with agriculture. With the lifting of prohibition these castemen have found new vistas, the opening up of which resulted in the exodus.

In order to understand the pressures generated from the agrarian and population spheres the migrants and non-migrants from these groups are dropped. The persons in the caste groups

TABLE 8.12

Land-Man Ratio and Migration (Percentages)

		Land per Head in a Family				
		Landless	<1	1-2	>2	Total
Migrant households	Number	19	19	22	5	65
	Per cent	67.86	48.72	44.90	11.9	41.14
Non-Migrant households	Number	9	20	27	37	93
	Per cent	32.14	51.28	55.10	88.1	58.86
Total base for percentage		100.00	100.00	100.00	100.00	100.00
		(28)	(39)	(49)	(42)	(158)
		(17.7)	(24.7)	(31.0)	(26.6)	

$X^2=29.62$; d.f.$=3$; $P<0.001$; $n=158$.
Mean Square Contingency : 0.3973.

Means, Standard and Deviation, Standard Errors and t-value

	Mean	*S.D.*	*S.E.*	*t-value*
Migrant households	0.92	±0.89	±0.11	
Non-Migrant households	1.76	±2.05	±0.21	3.50*
Total population	1.42	±1.74	±0.14	

*Very Significant.
$P<0.001$.

directly involved in agricultural production are analysed. They belong to 3 caste groups : Valmiki, Mala and Madiga. The latter two are grouped as Scheduled Castes. Any fluctuations in agriculture has an immediate effect in these groups in this village. Among the Valmikis the general trend in village population en masse is repeated with higher percentage in each category including the last group (Table 8.13) with 2 or more LMR. What is of interest is, that in the Scheduled Castes the percentage of migrants decrease initially but suddenly goes up (Table 8.14) only to come down steeply in the next group. In fact the percentage is highest in the group where LMR ranges between 1-2. Although the small number of Scheduled Caste persons places a heavy limitation on discussing these fluctuations, one of the indications is that the two groups, Valmiki and Scheduled Castes, do behave differently and different explanations are called for.

Generally for both the groups 2 or more acres per head removes the subsistence need of the family and places it above poverty line. A consequent need to leave the village to tide over a bad year or two is removed as well. Among Valmikis, there are two migrants in this category with more than two acres, and they did migrate because, in one case it was for developmental reasons to take up a teaching job and in another a domestic quarrel caused their leaving and not subsistence.

In the case of Scheduled Castes, the percentage of migrants comes down slightly as the land per head increases and then rises and falls steeply. Mostly, the land held by Scheduled Castes is an average of 5 acres, which is not sufficient in a bad year. Among the landless, non-migrants are working as *Jeetha* servants (a yearly contractual labour-landlord relationship), which reduces the subsistence pressures on them considerably. Others have not migrated for lack of capital to move. The largest landholders need not migrate. But the next largest are the ones who migrate most because they can extend the capital and also because they are the ones free with no *Jeetha* bonds. They also have relatives to help them in providing information and to sponsor them.

In other categories of LMR, migration is indicated. What accounts for its non-occurrence? Among Valmikis, 2 households in the landless category had supplementary income in the

TABLE 8.13

Land-Man Ratio and Migration (Percentages)
(Among Valmikis only)

		Land-Man Ratio				Total
		Landless	1	1-2	2	
Migrant households	Number	11	13	11	2	37
	Per cent	73.33	54.17	31.43	9.52	38.95
Non-Migrant households	Number	4	11	24	19	58
	Per cent	26.67	45.83	68.57	90.48	61.1
Total base for percentage		100.00 (15) (15.8)	100.00 (24) (25.3)	100.00 (35) (36.8)	100.00 (21) (22.1)	100.00 (95)

$X^2 = 18.44$; d.f. : 3; $P < 0.001$; $n = 95$.

TABLE 8.14

Land-Man Ratio and Migrant (Percentages)
(Among Scheduled Castes only)

		Land-Man Ratio				
		Landless	1	1—2	2	Total
Migrant households	Number	4	3	8	—	15
	Percent	44.44	27.27	80.00	—	46.88
Non-Migrant households	Number	5	8	2	2	17
	Percent	55.56	72.73	20.00	100.0	53.12
Total base for percentage		100.00	100.00	100.00	100.00	100.00
		(9)	(11)	(10)	(2)	(32)
		(28.1)	(34.4)	(31.3)	(6.3)	

Mean Square Contingency : 0.4474; n=32.

village apart from wage labour. The other two have not migrated for certain other reasons. They have small children, and in another case the head of household had a daughter who is married and he is too old to migrate with his wife. In the next category of holdings less than one acre per head in a family, the ownership of some wet lands as a part of their total holdings, or having a supplementary occupation in the village, like owning a petty shop or hotel negates the subsistence pressure.

In other cases, the position of responsibility as head of household, age of head of the household or phase in family cycle play an important role in this respect. Generally :

(1) complete nuclear households show lesser propensities to migrate.
(2) Migration increases with size of household.
(3) Migration is maximum in households in fission phase.

In extended households the occurrence of migration depends upon the availability of sons in the migrating age group and absence of very small children (below two years) who need a continuous and prolonged attention from mothers. In nuclear households the age of head of the household which has a direct bearing upon family phase plays an important role. Members in families in an incipient growth stage do not migrate because there are no elders to look after the children during their work period. Families in an advanced stage of expansion and moderately away from fission, have older children to look after the young. Here again, if the last child is less than 2 years old, the probability of members of that particular family migrating shrinks considerably.

Consequences of Migration

Migration occurs mainly to tide over a bad monsoon year and this goal is fulfilled. There is substantial increase in wages. Even during a year with normal crop 50 to 60 per cent wage increase is brought about by migration. None of them had to wait long in order to get work after migrating. A day or two's delay was due to bad weather like rains, which forced the agricultural work to be discontinued. Everybody in a household gets employed. In the words of a labourer in the village—"Those who migrate can employ all children in the different types of work. Whereas any work in one's native place does not and cannot employ all people in the household". The wages also are paid regularly and promptly at the place of destination. But majority of the income elasticities are for demand for food and the second important item is clothing (see also Clark and Haswell 1969).

Cultivation at Place of Origin : Migration has little effect on cultivation in Mahakadaku. Only when a family is absent throughout an agricultural season, does the necessity for the lands to be looked after arise. The absenteeism is directly related to the behaviour of the monsoon. When the monsoon is good and the landowner has not come back it means either the landholding is too small and the person prefers usufructuary arrangements; or he is staying off to multiply the family resource utilization, in which case his siblings look after the lands. Overall, the subsistence seasonal migration has no noticeable and sustained adverse effect on the agrarian system of the village.

Connections with Native Place : In the initial stage, a migrant is expected to maintain strong ties with his native place in the form of visits and monetary remittances. Levine (1973) on the strength of his Turkish data observed that the ties weaken with length of residence, and only a possibility of returning to the village makes them not to sever contact completely.

Migrants from Mahakadaku who have gone for longer periods come to their native place twice or thrice in a year for important festivals like *ugadi*, their new year day, and village level *jataras* (communal festivals). This serves the purpose of meeting relatives and renewing friendships.

A migrant who has lands and has leased them out, ideally, comes to his native place at the time of leasing, and visits a second time when the crop is ready and a third time at the time of harvest. Since many migrants in Mahakadaku have meagre amounts of land, with very low yield potential, the majority visit only once during harvest and leasing out is done by some relatives in the village.

No cash remittances were reported by the migrants. In fact they seem to be having hardly any savings to send home. For the older members of the family who are left behind, the migrants bring foodgrains, mostly Jowar, in large quantities (1 or 2 quintals). The strength of these ties had not been weakening with passage of time.

Feedback Effects: In the case of subsistence migration described above, availability of work during the drought year, steady employment in any year, and higher wages constitute important information. The already migrated spread this information selectively to friends and relatives in Mahakadaku and other villages. Though initially this constituted a very important resource, as time passed and more people migrated there had been an even spread of information and at present it could be treated as something with equal access to all potential migrants, and therefore a constant.

But being well off during famine years and richer in their life-style the migrants and their families in Mahakadaku do formulate a model to be emulated, particularly by the families below the poverty line. The constraints like family phase, indebtedness, absence of males in migrating age act as barriers for the expected response.

CONCLUSION

The foregoing discussion suggests that, except in cases where migration is for extra income or personal reasons, occurrence of migration is decided by the poverty line. The best index to mark this line is land-man ratio. But LMR in itself does not explain occurrence and non-occurrence of migration. Only when LMR is seen in conjunction with other variables does it emerge as an explanatory variable. In the village, the poverty line below which subsistence becomes a problem, is flexible and shifts according to the land available to a family, number of workers in a household, family phase and size, days of employment and extent of indebtedness. Households with 2 acres of land per head (42 in number in the sample) are above the poverty line in Mahakadaku. In households with less than 2 acres per head (116 in number in the sample), the flexibility of poverty line becomes important. Not infrequently, the variables act simultaneously and together in generating and not generating migration.

Absence of males of migrating age, yearly contractual labour, presence of poorly irrigated lands, supplementary income source explain the non-occurrence of migration in groups where the land-man ratio would indicate its occurrence. In other cases, the family phase, age of head of household account for variability. Further statistical analysis of these variables within land-man ratio categories would be unreliable with too low frequencies in cells. So individual cases were analysed and gross differences have been reported.

Data suggest that migration has some impact on the village of origin, though it is not very significant. Monetary transfer from destination to origin is almost non-existent and there is hardly any investment ploughed back into the lands of the migrants. Most of the earnings are used for necessities like food and clothing. There is, however, a sustained contact maintained with relatives, and it is somewhat stronger in the case of migrants with lands who lease them out.

One of the questions raised in the beginning was who does the calculation related to costs and benefits of migration? For migrants of Mahakadaku subsistence is a problem and its fulfilment, the need. The resource to fulfil this need exists in the form of available work and higher wages. This resource lies outside the village in the wet areas that are too far-off. In fact the mentioned resource is spread over a region. Calculation is set in motion by the failure of the monsoon, at least in the initial decision to migrate.

NOTES

1. This could be contrasted with the introduction of new paddy varieties as a factor in facilitating rural-to-rural migration, suggested in the work of Kikuchi and Hayami (1983).
2. Most commonly mentioned factors pushing people out of a village are (1) population increase; (2) inadequate usable land; (3) imbalanced distribution of landholding (Mar 1961; Texter 1956); (4) unprofitable farming; (5) ambitions of youth; and (6) an already established custom of migration. Urban oriented education in rural schools is

yet another cause (Mar (1961). Pull factors of migration expressed by urban respondents are : (1) economic livelihood, higher wages; (2) social and educational facilities; (3) military aud compulsory services and transfers; (4) wars and political events; (5) search for specific employment (Rao and Rao 1975); (6) social discrimination against scheduled castes (Deshmukh 1956); (7) dependent migration of children and wives. In the Indian context skilled castes migrate because they are unwanted in village and social discrimination prompts untouchables to migrate (Deshmukh 1956). Pursuit of enhanced prestige, adventurous spirit, need for change have also been mentioned by respondents in the city, at least as secondary causes behind process of migration (Gugler 1969). Putting them together with migration of barren women divorcees, and disputes Gulliver (1965) coined a term "last straw causes".

3. Differently put, people do not migrate from villages because of certain advantages or pull factors. Security gains in family and kinship relations, investments in labour and patron-client relations (Siegel 1971), possession of land and house, respect in village (Karve and Damle 1963), pleasure in traditional economy, financial benefits of no taxes and bills (Graves 1966) are few factors mentioned which discourage migration. The push factors or disadvantage in urban areas are: possibility of unemployment (Todaro 1969), higher costs of living and low wages, traffic and transport problems (Graves and Arsdale 1966), and psychological factors such as absence of close relatives.
4. Either by being reference group to the potential migrant, because of their enhanced prestige, or through conveying information about city and/or jobs, friends and relatives play an important part in the process of migration. They also give initial security when a migrant arrives in new environment. Tendency of migrants from the same region to concentrate in a locality in city is often observed in South America (Germani 1961; Mar 1961), Middle East (Abu-Lughod 1961), Africa and South Asia (Little 1957, Mythili 1974). Sub-group formation in certain localities in cincinatti (Killian 1953) and the fact that more than 50 per cent migrants were sponsored by relatives in Chicago (Choldin 1973) imply that industrial development is not disruptive of kin ties and its utilisation. In India, factors such as particular castes coming from more or less the same region (Rao and Rao 1975), extension of this tendency to sub-caste level (Deshmuk 1956), and the manner in which linguistic groups take the place of caste in interstate migration (Mythili 1974), suggest that region, language and caste together might influence residential distribution of recent migrants. However, migration under informal sponsorship appears to decline with rising ranks of persons (Tilly and Brown 1967) and is more frequent among blue-collar workers than white-collar workers (Parish 1973).
5. Inconsistencies and disturbances have been noticed in the models of migration which assume perfect information flow (Ritchey 1976).

Apart from the role of informal ties in this regard, which is duly acknowledged, the information lag is used to explain unexpected fluctuations from predicted rates of migration (Lianos 1970, Ranke 1972). Lianos (1970) 'Stock' (of potential migrants) and 'flow' (of actual migrants) approach takes explicit account of such a lag.

REFERENCES

Abulughod, Janet, "Migrant Adjustment of City Life ; The Egyptian Case", *The American Journal of Sociology*, 67(1) : 22-32, 1961.

Bradfield, Stillman, "Selectivity in Rural Urban Migration : The Case of Huaylas, Peru", in Aidan Southal (ed.), *Urban Anthropology*, Oxford University Press, New York, 1973.

Census of India, *Birth Place Migration in India*, Special Monograph No. 1, Office of the Registrar General : India, 1974.

Choldin, Harvey M., "Kinship Networks in the Migration Process", *International Migration Review*, 7(2) : 163-175, 1973.

Clark, Colin and Margaret Haswell, *The Economics of Subsistence Agri-culture*, MacMillan, London, 1969.

Connel, J. *et al.*, *Migration from Rural Areas: The Evidence from Village Studies*, Institute of Development Studies, University of Sussex, Brighton, 1976.

Dasgupta, B. and R. Laishley, "Migration from Villages", *Economic and Political Weekly*, 10(42) : 1651-1662, 1975.

Deshmukh, M., "The Study of Floating Migration", in *The Social Implications of Industrialization and Urbanization*, UNESCO, Calcutta, 1956.

D'Souza, Victor S., "Social nequalities and Development in India", *Economic and Political Weekly*, 10(19) : 770-773, 1975.

Eames, Edward, "Some Aspects of Urban Migration from a Village in North Central India", *Eastern Anthropologist*, 8(1) : 443-46, 1954.

Farmer, B.H., *Agricultural Colonization in India Since Independence*, Oxford University Press, Delhi, 1974.

Germani, Gino, "Inquiry into the Social Effects of Urbanization in a Working Class Section of Greater Buenos Aires", in Philip M. Hauser (ed.), *Urbanization in Latin America*, UNESCO, 1961.

Graves, Thedore B., "Alternative Models for the Study of Urban Migra-tion", *Human Organization*, 25 (4) : 295-299, 1966.

Graves T.B. and M.V. Arsdale, "Values, Expectations and Relocation : The Novaho Migrant in Denver", *Human Organization*, 25(4): 300-307, 1966.

Grigg, David, *The Harsh Lands: A Study in Agricultural Development*, McMillan, London, 1970.

Gugler, Joseph, "On the Theory of Rural Urban Migration The : Case of Sub Saharan Africa", in J.A. Jackson (ed.), *Migration*. University Press, Cambridge, 1969.

Gulliver, P.H., *Labour Migration in a Rural Economy : A Study of the Naomi and Ndendeuli of Southern Tanganyika*, East African Institute of Social Research, Kampala, 1955.

Karve, I. and Y.B. Damle, *Group Relations in Village Community*, Deccan College, Poona, 1963.

Kikuchi, M. and Yujiro Hayami, "Rice, Migration and Institutional Innovation in the Philippines", *Population and Development Review*, Vol. 9, No. 2, pp. 247-257, 1983.

Killian, Lewis M., "The Adjustment of Southern White Migrants to Northern Urban Norms", *Social Forces*, 32: 66-69, 1953.

Kshirasagar, S., "Patterns of Internal Migration of Males in India: Inter-State and Intra-State Flows", *Artha Vijnana*, 15(2): 161-179, 1973.

Levine, Ned, "Value Orientation among Migrants in Ankara Turkey: A Case Study", *Journal of Asian and African Studies*, 8(1-2): 50-68, 1973.

Little, Kenneth, "The Role of Voluntary Associations in West African Urbanization", *American Anthropologist*, 59(4): 579-596, 1957.

Mar, Matos J., "Migration and Urbanization—The Barriados of Lima : An Example of Integration into Urban Life" in Philip M. Hauser (ed.) *Urbanization in Latin America*, UNESCO, 1961.

Morris, Morris D., "What is Famine", *Economic and Political Weekly*, 9 (4): 1855-1865, 1974.

Mythili, K.L., "Little Madras in Bombay", in M.S.A. Rao (ed.), *Urban Sociology in India*, Orient Longman, New Delhi, 1974.

National Sample Survey, *No. 56 Tables and Notes on Internal Migration*, Indian Statistical Institute, Calcutta, 1960.

Nolan, Riall W., "Labour Migration and the Bassari: A Case of Retrograde Development", *Man*, 10(4): 571-588, 1975.

Parish Jr., William L., "Internal Migration and Modernization: The European Case", *Economic Development and Cultural Change*, 21(4): 591-609, 1973.

Patnaik, V., "Class Differentiation within the Peasantry: An Approach to Analysis of Indian Agriculture", *Economic and Political Weekly*, XI (39): A-82-101, 1976.

Pelzer, Karl J., *Pioneer Settlement in the Asiatic Tropics*, American Geographic Society, 1948.

Ranke, Desmondo, "A Stocks and Flows Approach to a Theory of Human Migration with Examples from Past Instances of Migration", *Demography*, 9(2): 263-274, 1972.

Rao, R.K. and M.S.A. Rao, *Cities and Slums: A Study of Squatters Settlements in the City of Vijayawda*, Concept, New Delhi, 1984.

Ritchey, Neal P., "Explanations of Migration", Alex Inkeless (ed.) *Annual Review of Sociology*, Annual Reviews Inc. California, 1976.

Siegel, Bernard J., "Migration Dynamics in the Interior of Ceara, Brazil", *South Western Journal of Anthropology*, 27(3): 234-257, 1971.

Simmons, A.B. and R.A. Gardona, "Rural-Urban Migration: Who

Comes, Who Stays, Who Returns? The Case of Bogota Columbia, 1928-1968", *International Migration Review*, 6(2): 166-181, 1972.

Texter, R.B., "From Peasant to Pedicab Driver", *South East Asia Studies Cultural Report Series, No. 9*, Yale University Press, New Haven, 1956.

Thomas, D.S., *Research Memorandum on Migration Differentials*, Social Science Research Council Bulletin, 43, New York, 1938.

Tilly, Charles and Brown, Harold C., "On Uprooting, Kinship and the Auspices of Migration", *International Journal of Comparative Sociology*, 8(2): 139-164, 1967.

Todaro, M., "A Model of Labour Migration and Urban Unemployment in LDC's", *American Economic Research*, 59 : 138-148, 1969.

Tschopichs, Harry, *Highland Communities of Central Peru: A Regional Survey*, Smithsonian Institute of Social Anthropology, Publication No. 5, Washington D.C, 1947.

Valunjkar,, T.N. *Social Organization, Migration and Change in a Village Community*, Deccan College, Poona, 1960.

Vidyasagar, N.E.C., "Agrarian Structure, Development and Migration with Special Reference to Andhra Pradesh", *Society and Culture*, 9(2) : 77-90, 1978.

Wiest, Raymond, "Wage Labour Migration and the Household in a Mexican Town", *Journal of Anthropological Research*, 29(3) ; 180-209, 1973.

Zachariah, K.C., "Bombay Migration Study : A Pilot Analysis of Migration to an Asian Metropolis", *Demography*, 3(2): 378-392, 1966.

PART IV

Tribal Migration

9. *19th Century in Chota Nagpur and Santal Parganas—Political Economy of Migration*

S.D. BADGAIYAN

The nineteenth century in Chota Nagpur and Santal Parganas can appropriately be called the century of rebellions. Almost all the tribal groups inhabitating this tribal tract of Bihar, the Santals, Mundas, Hos, Bhumij and Cheros, rose in revolt against the State, not only once but many times during this period. The accounts of these rebellions given by Roy (1970), Datta (1940), Jha (1964, 1967) and Singh (1983) bring out the fact that these rebellions can be traced, among others, to the large scale expropriation of land suffered by the tribal groups.

Chota Nagpur and Santal Parganas were also characterized by large scale migration in the nineteenth century. The decennial censuses, beginning with 1872, give a clear idea of the magnitude of the migration into as well as migration out of the Chota Nagpur and Santal Parganas. Weiner (1978: 161), on the basis of the analysis of place of birth data in the decennial censuses, reports that the out-migrants from Chota Nagpur and Santal Parganas numbered 3,33,000 in 1891. This number continued to increase in the early decades of the twentieth century and by 1921, nearly one million tribals has migrated out of this tribal tract. He estimates that by 1921 nearly one-third of the tribal population of Chota Nagpur and Santal Parganas had left the tribal territory.

Chota Nagpur and Santal Parganas were thus characterized by land alienation insurrection and migration. That insurrection was caused, among others, by land alienation has been established in a number of studies. What has not been examined is the question whether this large-scale out-migration was also caused by, among others, land alienation and insurrection.

Perspectives

In this paper I wish to examine whether it is possible to establish any link between the three important features that characterized Chota Nagpur and Santal Parganas in the nineteenth century.

An effort has thus been made in this paper to see the large scale out-migration of tribals in the context of the widespread economic and political forces sweeping the tribal territory for well over a century. Instead of locating the causes of migration in individual minds, an effort has been made to see whether the causes can be located in the changing economic and political processes operating in the entire tribal belt of Chota Nagpur and Santal Parganas.

Studies of human migration are more than a century old and a wide variety of factors have been examined to explain human migration. Ravenstein, in two classic papers (1885 and 1889), stressed the role of distance, technology and communication in influencing the volume and direction of migration. But he felt that economic causes were the most significant causes of migration. He says, "Bad or oppressive laws, heavy taxation, an unattractive climate, uncongenial social surroundings and even compulsion (slave trade, transportation), all have produced and are still producing currents of migration, but none of these causes can compare in volume with that which arises from the desire inherent in most men to 'better' themselves in material respects" (1889: 286). Supporting Ravenstein, Todaro (1976) speaks of the role of rural-urban differential in expected income in causing rural to urban migration.

Ravenstein's emphasis on the role of distance finds an echo in Ziph's (1946) 'principle of least effort' but Stouffer (1940) questions this assumption and says distance as such is not the determining factor. Instead he stresses the influence of the intervening opportunities between the origin and destination of migration. Reformulating his earlier proposition, in 1960 Stouffer considered migration as a direct function of the opportunities at the destination and an inverse function of intervening opportunities and the number of competing migrants. In contrast to the concept of intervening opportunities developed by Stouffer (1940), Lee (1969) stresses the role of intervening obstacles. The decision to migrate, according to him, is influenced by the nature and magnitude of intervening obstacles between the origin and destination of migration.

Despite the difference in the phraseology and the conceptual apparatus utilized, the perspectives developed by Ravenstein and Todaro, Stouffer and Lee, represent one neat bundle of ideas wrapped around by strings of economic 'rationality'. The view of migration determined purely by economic 'rationality' is only another expression of the assumption of 'homo-economicus'.

The fact that factors other than purely economic calculation are involved in migration has been brought out by a large number of studies of tribal migrations in Africa. Anthropologists studying tribal societies in Africa have stressed the role of non-economic factors in inducing migration. Winter (1955) writing about the Amba of Western Uganda stresses the role of disputes and witchcraft in forcing people to move out. Southall (1954) and Skinner (1965) speaking respectively of the Alure and Mossi draw attention to the social prestige enjoyed by the tribal migrants. Schapera (1947) brings out the fact that in Botswana migration to the urban centre has nearly taken the role of initiation rite to manhood. Analysing the situation among the Red Xhosa, Mayer (1961) highlights the tendency among the Red Xhosa youth to move out to the urban centres immediately before or after the initiation rites.

But it would be wrong to assume that economic factors do not enter into the calculations at all in African migration. The youth of Freetown told Banton (1957) very clearly that in moving to the urban centres they were motivated by chances of earning more money as well as the desire to run away from the control of the chiefs. The assertion of the Freetown youth may find an echo in a number of other African towns and indeed in a number of non-African towns as well. But it does not very much advance our understanding of the causes of migration. There is need to structure the role of economic and non-economic factors in causing migration.

It is interesting to find that some efforts have indeed been made to structure the differential roles of the economic and non-economic factors in inducing migration. Gulliver (1955), in his analysis of the situation among the Ngoni and Ndendeuli of southern Tanzania both develops and demolishes the 'bright lights theory' of attraction to the urban centres. He concedes the fact that non-economic factors do enter into the decision to migrate but he treats them as 'the last straw'. For him the 'real' causes are economic. Mitchell (1959) takes the argument further and speaks in terms of the necessary and sufficient causes of migration. According to Mitchell, for any migration economic causes are necessary but economic causes themselves may not cause migration. He (1959: 32) says, ". . . if the economic drives to labour migration are not present it is unlikely that it will occur, but if the economic conditions are present, the actual migration may not occur until some event in personal life of the individual precipitates events and triggers off his decision to go". Thus Mitchell brings out very clearly the relationships between the economic and non-economic factors. Whether or not to go is determined by the economic factors but when to go is decided by the non-economic factors.

The analysis of the differential role of the economic and non-economic factors is carried further by Mitchell, when he, making use of the Durkheimian distinction (1897) between the rate and incidence of a phenomenon, says that the economic factors influence the rate of migration but the non-economic factors influence the incidence of migration. Gugler (1969) disagrees with Mitchell and Gulliver with regard to the differential role of the economic and non-economic factors in causing migration. He gives primacy to economic factors and says that economic forces determine the rate of migration, but they may also determine the incidence of migration. He goes further and stresses that even the time of migration may be decided by economic factors.

Thus a wide diversity of perspectives have been utilized in the study of migration, but together they succeeded in telling us only a part of the story. This is because of the basic assumption underlying all these perspectives, namely that a man decides on the basis of his own free will whether or not to migrate; that he weighs rationally the pros and cons of migration before he actually embarks on an outward journey. It is no doubt true that lots of people do calculate before migrating out and do so in the exercise of their free will. But, unfortunately, it is also true that lots of other people are forced to migrate and the force varies from indirect economic coercion to direct physical force.

The history of colonial Africa bears testimony to the fact that large masses were forced in one way or another to migrate to work in the mines and factories. The natives in many parts of Africa were dispossessed of their rights on land and forest. In addition they were forced to pay tax per head in cash and kind. Where these methods failed to meet the labour demands of the European plantations, mines and factories, physical force was resorted to to recruit labour force. The following passage from Cohen (1979: 66) describes the recruitment of labour and treatment meted out to them during the colonial period in Africa.

> Every method has been used to make Africans sign these contracts—taxes, low prices for their products and straightforward coercion. Clearly such a contract does not constitute the free hire and sale of labour. Africans so recruited are despatched in batches of 50 to 250 on a journey, by stages, to the place of work. Current legislation fixes the daily travelling distance at 30 kms. with one rest day every six days. Considering that some of the Africans recruited live one to two thousand kms. away from their place of work, it follows that they spend approximately two months in travelling time alone. The length of work is usually stipulated as nine months by the contract but since festival days, rest days and illness are not included in this period, work usually lasts 12 to 14 months. If one adds the journey by stages in both directions, it turns out that the worker is away from home for almost two years. Breach of contract or leaving work before expiry of the contract, are regarded as criminal offences and are punishable by two to four months' imprisonment. After serving his sentence during which the African also performs work for the state or for a private individual, he is returned to his hirer to work off the remainder of his contract. Despite these draconian

measures 20 to 30% of all workers recruited desert from work.

The labour migration in colonial Africa in the first phase of colonial capitalism, had a strong political dimension, the might of the colonial powers. The planters and the colonial state joined together to develop a captive labour force which could be moved, by direct and indirect force, from the place of native residence to the place of industrial work. The armed might of the colonial powers forced the tribes to suffer in angered silence this colonial coercion and exploitation but in some parts the tribes rose in violent revolt. The Gussii in Kenya rose in revolt in 1905, 1908 and 1914 (Maxon 1972). The Giriama (Kenya) also revolted against the colonial state in 1913-14 (Stichter 1982). In the early 1930s, the Watch Tower movement, which was clearly anti-imperialistic, spread in Rhodesia (Cohen 1979). In Belgian Congo uprisings broke out in Kikwit region and Kwango province in 1932 (Cohen 1979). Needless to say all these uprisings were brutally crushed. Many of these tribal uprisings were supported by millenarian dreams. For instance among the Kamba of Kenya millenarian movement was quite strong during 1896 and 1911 (Stichter 1982).

Labour migration in Africa is then a product of colonialism. With the imposition of colonial rule, plantations, mines and factories, all owned by Europeans, came into being. To provide labour force to these establishments, a wide range of measures, including expropriation of rights over land and forests, coercive taxation policy and forced recruitment, were used. The story of labour migration in Africa is thus very different from the picture that emerges from the writings of Ravenstein (1885, 1889 and Todaro 1976; Stouffer 1940 and Lee 1969). The writings of British anthropologists discussed above, also fail to bring out adequately the repressive character of labour recruitment in Africa. The tribal rebellions against the colonial state have not been able to become the central focus of anthropological investigations.

In India too, in the nineteenth century, Chota Nagpur and Santal Parganas represent a colonial situation. Plantations and mines had just been opened up. The British owners of these plantations and mines were frantically looking for labour to work in these establishments. We shall see to what extent the British colonial policy pertaining to agriculture and industry is related to the large scale labour migration from the tribal tract of Bihar. But before we come to these policies, let us have a look at the ethnographic profile of Chota Nagpur and Santal Parganas.

The Ethnographic Profile

Chota Nagpur forms the southern part of Bihar and consists of the districts of Palamau, Hazaribagh, Dhanbad, Ranchi and Singhbhum. The Santal Parganas is contiguous to Chota Nagpur and forms its north eastern extension. Before the seventeenth century, both Chota Nagpur and Santal Parganas were populated entirely by the tribals but during the last three centuries there has been a large scale in-migration of non-tribals. As a consequence, in many parts of Chota Nagpur, the tribals have been reduced numerically to nearly one-tenth of the district population. Table 9.1 gives the percentage of tribal population in the different districts of Chota Nagpur and Santal Parganas in 1971.

We find that in Chota Nagpur less than one-third are tribals. In Dhanbad and Hazaribagh districts only about one-tenth are tribals. But in Ranchi and Singhbhum, we still find tribals in large proportions. The tribals in Chota Nagpur and Santal Parganas are concentrated in the rural areas, the urban areas being dominated by the non-tribals. In urban Chota Nagpur, the tribals form less than one-tenth of the urban population. In Singhbhum, the tribals form only 1 per cent of the urban population. Again in Ranchi district we find the tribals forming a little less than one-fifth of the urban population.

The tribal population in Bihar (nearly 50 lakhs in 1971), forms 8.8 per cent of the State population. About 30 different tribal groups live in Bihar (1971); but the following four tribes—Santals, Oraons, Mundas and Hos—form nearly 80 per cent of the tribal population. Though these 30 tribes are concentrated in Chota Nagpur and Santal Parganas, within this tribal tract they are not evenly distributed. Each tribe has its own area of heavy concentration within Chota Nagpur and Santal

TABLE 9.1

Percentage of Tribal Population in Chota Nagpur and Santal Parganas, 1971

Serial Number	Area		Per cent of Tribal Population
1.	Santal Parganas	Total	36.2
		Rural	38.2
		Urban	3.4
2.	Chota Nagpur	Total	31.0
		Rural	36.0
		Urban	9.0
i)	Palamau	Total	19.0
		Rural	19.7
		Urban	4.3
ii)	Hazaribagh	Total	11.0
		Rural	11.8
		Urban	5.2
iii)	Dhanbad	Total	10.6
		Rural	15.3
		Urban	4.4
iv)	Ranchi	Total	58.0
		Rural	64.4
		Urban	18.2
v)	Singhbhum	Total	46.0
		Rural	58.6
		Urban	1.1

Source: Census of India, 1971.

Parganas. Table 9.2 gives the distribution of different tribal groups in Chota Nagpur and Santal Parganas.

Table 9.2 shows that different tribes are numerically dominant in different districts of Chota Nagpur and Santal Parganas. Of the entire tribal population Santal Parganas, 87 per cent are Santals. The Santals are numerically dominant also in Hazaribagh and Dhanbad but they are nearly absent in Palamau and Ranchi. Of the four tribes, only Oraons live in any significant numbers in Palamau. They form more than one-third of the tribal population in this district. In Ranchi both Munda and Oraon are in significant strength. In Singhbhum, a little less than half of the tribal population consists of Hos. The Santals form nearly one-fourth of the tribal population in this district. Thus we find that out of the six districts, three (Santals Parganas, Hazaribagh and Dhanbad) are numerically dominated by the Santals, one (Ranchi) by Oraons and Mundas, and the remaining two (Singhbhum and Palamau) respectively by Hos and Oraons.

TABLE 9.2

Distribution of Selected Tribal Groups in Chota Nagpur and Santal Parganas, 1971

Serial Number	Area	Total Tribal Population	Santal	Munda	Oraon	Ho
			(percentage)			
1.	Santal Parganas	11,48,030	87 0	0.1	0.6	0.0
2.	Chota Nagpur	32,24,492	17.5	21.1	23.5	14.9
i)	Palamau	2,83,904	0.0	4.2	37.0	0.0
ii)	Hazaribagh	3,11,031	64.4	9.6	6 5	0.0
iii)	Dhanbad	1,27,105	86.7	1.7	1.7	0.2
iv)	Ranchi	14,51,597	0.1	34.9	42.1	0.0
v)	Singhbhum	10,50,855	24.1	12.2	1.8	45.5

Source: Census of India, 1971, Series: 4: Bihar, Part V-A: Special Tables for Scheduled Castes and Scheduled Tribes.

But the above discussion does not give much idea as to how each of the four tribes is distributed in each of the six districts. To bring this out, the following Table has been drawn.

Taking together Tables 9.2 and 9.3, we find that though Santals form 87 per cent of the entire tribal population in Santal Parganas, they represent only about 64 per cent of the Santal population in this tribal tract. Similarly 12.8 per cent and 7.0 per cent of the Santals live in Hazaribagh and Dhanbad but in

TABLE 9.3

Percentage Distribution of Selected Tribals in Chota Nagpur and Santal Parganas

Serial Number	Area	Santal	Munda	Oraon	Ho
1.	Santal Parganas	63.9	0.2	0.9	0.0
2.	Chota Nagpur	36.1	99.8	99.1	100.0
i)	Palamau	0.0	1.8	13.8	0.0
ii)	Hazaribagh	12.8	4.4	2.6	0.0
iii)	Dhanbad	7.0	0.3	0.3	0.0
iv)	Ranchi	0.1	74.4	79.9	0.1
v)	Singhbhum	16.2	18.9	2.5	99.9
	Total	100.0	100.0	100 0	100.0
	Total Tribal Population	15,63,178	6,80,213	6,64,067	4,79,183

these two districts they form respectively 64.4 per cent and 86.7 per cent of the tribal population. On the other hand, much larger percentage (16.00) of the Santals live in Singhbhum but there they form only 24 per cent of the tribal population. We thus find that relatively smaller proportions of Santals have been able to contribute relatively larger proportions of the district tribal populations in Hazaribagh and Dhanbad. This is because of the fact that in these districts other tribal groups also do not have large concentrations.

The relatively smaller proportions of tribals in what were essentially tribal areas only a couple of centuries back, speaks of the magnitude of the non-tribal in-migration into these areas. In the seventeenth century, the Raja of Chota Nagpur took to Hinduism and invited Hindus from north Bihar and Orissa to perform a wide variety of functions, social, political and religious, necessary for a Hindu King in a tribal environment. In course of time Hindu, Muslim and Sikh traders also streamed in to take advantage of the new opportunities of trade and barter. All these led to a large scale influx of non-tribals.

By 1872, when the first census was taken, the ethnic composition of Chota Nagpur and Santal Parganas had already become greatly diversified. To give just one example, the ethnic composition of Hazaribagh in 1872 (Hunter 1876, Vol. XVI) included 133 communities, of which only 14 were recorded as aboriginal tribes. Table 9.4 gives the ethnic composition of Chota Nagpur and Santal Parganas in 1872.

Table 9.4 shows that by 1872, the tribal population in Chota Nagpur and Santal Parganas was reduced to a little more than one-third of the total population. The tribals formed the majority of population only in the district of Singhbhum. The Hindus were in a majority in Hazaribagh, where the tribal population formed only 7.4 per cent of the total population. In Santal Parganas, the tribals outnumbered the Hindus and formed 44.3 per cent of the total population. The Mohamedans were present in some strength in all the areas except Singhbhum.

The demographic composition of Chota Nagpur and Santal Parganas in the nineteenth century was a product not only of the in-migration of non-tribals but also of the out-migration of tribals. Though the total population kept on increasing over the centuries, the tribal proportion kept on declining as a consequence also of large scale out-migration. In fact, it was the in-migration of the non-tribals which resulted in the out-migration of the tribals. How precisely did this happen is taken up for discussion in the following sections.

Land Alienation

The history of land alienation in Chota Nagpur and Santal Parganas is a well documented and well established fact. All the historical writings on Chota Nagpur and Santal Parganas (Roy 1912, 1970; Datta 1940; Jha 1964, 1967; Singh 1983) have

TABLE 9.4

Ethnic Composition of Chota Nagpur and Santal Parganas in 1872

Serial Number	Area	Total Population	% of Tribal Population	% of Non-Tribal Population		
				Hindus	Mohamedans	Others
1.	Santal Parganas	12,59,287	44.3	31.0	6.3	18.4
2.	Chota Nagpur	24,24,021	34.3	39.5	5.5	20.7
i)	Hazaribagh	7,71,875	7.4	54.6	9.4	28.6
ii)	Lohardaga	12,37,123	41.9	33.4	4.7	20.0
iii)	Singhbhum	4,15,023	61.7	39.9	0.6	7.8
	Total	36,83,308	37.7	36.6	5.8	19.9

Source: Hunter (1876): A Statistical Account of Bengal, Vols. XIV, XVI and XVII (computed on the basis of the figures given for different ethnic groups).

drawn attention to this phenomenon. We shall only briefly give an outline of this process.

After moving around for centuries in the plains of north India, the tribes of this region finally settled down in Chota Nagpur and Santal Parganas. They cleared the forest, established their villages and took to cultivation on the basis of what among the Munda is called the *Khuntkatti* system. Each village was led by a *Munda* and *Pahan* and groups of such villages were led by a *Manki*. Initially they had no kings and the political and religious functions were performed by the *Munda*, *Pahan* and *Manki*. Mundas of non-Khuntkatti clans, non-Mundas and even non-tribals, like the weaver, blacksmith and the cowherd, came to settle among them to meet the various needs of the village communities.

In course of time, kingship developed among the Mundas and this king soon came to be recognized as king not only of the Mundas but also of the other tribal communities in the region. But like the '*Munda*' and '*Manki*' he was only a leader of men and not owner of the tribal territory. It was in the seventeenth century that this traditional political order underwent a radical change. King Durjan Sal of Chota Nagpur was captured by the Mughals and was kept in prison in Gwalior for twelve years along with other Hindu rulers. During his imprisonment, he came to learn of the glamour and glory of other Hindu kings. On his release in 1628, he took to Hinduism and styled himself on the pattern of other Hindu rulers. He encouraged Hindus from north Bihar and Orissa to become his courtiers and to join his militia. Hindu priests of various denominations came in to perform Hindu rites and rituals which had now become necessary for the newly converted Raja as well as for the Hindu nobility. Hindu jagirdars came in to help the king rule over the tribals.

All these non-tribals were rewarded with land and in order to reward them with land, the tribal owners were dispossessed of the land they had owned for generations. These non-tribal jagirdars followed in their turn the life-style of the Raja and brought in fresh groups of non-tribals to help them subjugate the tribals. These new in-migrants were given land by the jagirdars. This process of subinfeudation spread throughout the tribal tract of Chota Nagpur.

The non-tribals were not just priests and intermediaries between the cultivators and the Raja. A wide variety of merchants and traders trooped in with their merchandise to meet the newly acquired demands for non-tribal goods. These merchants in many cases were paid in land for their goods for want of ready cash. Whenever land was given to a non-tribal, a priest, an intermediary or a merchant, it always meant dispossession of some tribal. Many Hindu intermediaries even settled Hindu tenants on their land, driving away the recalcitrant tribal tenants.

All this had already happened before the British arrived on the scene in 1765 with the grant of Dewani of Bengal, of which Chota Nagpur then formed a part. Before the imposition of external colonialism, Chota Nagpur was already under some kind of internal colonialism. Chota Nagpur which, up to the seventeenth century, was predominantly an egalitarian society, now got sharply divided along class lines into producers of surplus and the appropriators of surplus. The tribals remained the producers of surplus; but now had to accept the superimposition of the non-tribal appropriators of surplus, on them.

With the imposition of British colonialism, the class cleavage became more deep and wide. The Permanent Settlement recognized the intermediaries as owners. The new administrative edifice that was erected only brought new waves of non-tribals into the tribal areas in the form of police, revenue and forest officials. The tribals found all these forces arrayed against them and in league with the non-tribal jagirdars. Emboldened by the new order the petty Rajas and the jagirdars accelerated the process of dispossession and ejectment of the native owners of land.

Writing about Ranchi district, Singh (1969: 551) mentions that in 1856 there were as many as 600 jagirdars, some of them owning more than hundred villages. He further says that by 1874 all the Munda and Oraon chiefs had almost been entirely eliminated by Hindu farmers introduced by their landlords or by numerous holders of religious and maintenance grants. Thus the land which up to the seventeenth century was owned entirely by the tribals, came to be owned, just in two centuries, mostly by the non-tribals.

Khuntkatti lands were converted into *Rajhas, Manjhihas*

and *Bhuinhari* tenures. Owners became tenants. Many were ejected even from their tenancies. They were deprived of their ownership as well as tenurial rights over the land which their forefathers had cleared and which they had cultivated for generations. Those still enjoying tenurial rights were subjected to frequent rack-renting and a number of praedial exactions.

The tenants were required to perform 14 days *Begar* duties. Thapar and Siddiqui (1979:52) list them to be the following: (i) three days ploughing; (ii) three days digging; (iii) three days sowing or planting paddy: (iv) three days cutting paddy; (v) one day threshing corn; (vi) one day in assisting in making the granary; (vii) carrying the lord of the domain to the places he went to.

These were only customary dues, the jagirdars in fact extracted much more than what was customary. In addition to *Begar*, the tenants were also required to pay a large number of other dues. Even in the beginning of the twentieth, century, in 1902, Reid listed (Singh 1969: 553-554) twenty-one such praedial payments in cash and kind. The purpose behind all these exactions had been to extract from the tenants whatever little was left with them after paying the rent.

The plight of the tenant in Chota Nagpur is graphically described in an article in *Calcutta Review* of 1869 (cited in Roy 1970: 127-128):

> When the oppressor wants a horse, the Kol must pay; when he desires a *palki*, the Kols have to pay and afterwards bear him therein. They must pay for his musicians, for his milch cows, for his *pan*. Does some one die in his house? He taxes them, is a child born? again a tax; is there marriage or a *puja*? a tax. Is the *thekedar* found guilty at *cutchary* and sentenced to be punished? The Kol must pay the fine. Or does a death occur in the house of a Kol? The poor man must pay a fine. Is a child born? Is a son or daughter married? The poor Kol is still taxed.

In spite of the tall claims made by the British to have abolished all such praedial obligations and dues, these continued to be extracted with impunity by the jagirdars in Chota Nagpur throughout the nineteenth century. In fact, they continued to be added on depending on the capacity and the avarice of the jagirdars. The situation in Chota Nagpur was replicated in various forms in Santal Parganas also The expropriation of native owners, rack-renting and ejectment of tenants, the imposition of praedial obligations were all present in the Santal Parganas as they were in Chota Nagpur.

Like the tribes in Africa, many in Chota Nagpur were forced to suffer the dispossession and indignities in angered silence but many others rose in violent insurrection.

Insurrection

Beginning with the last decade of the eighteenth century till the end of the nineteenth century, Chota Nagpur and Santal Parganas were in a state of turbulence and turmoil. Roy (1970), Datta (1940), Jha (1964, 1967), Singh (1983) and Guha (1983) have discussed at length the rebellions and insurrections that rocked this tribal tract during this period. We shall give here only a brief outline of the events based on these sources. Almost all the tribals of Chota Nagpur and Santal Parganas rose in armed revolt against the non-tribal jagirdars, money-lenders and the state functionaries.

The Mundas had been in the forefront during this whole period of insurrection. They rose in revolt in the last decade of the eighteenth century and in the first decade of the nineteenth century. They joined other tribes in 1820 and 1831. Throughout the latter half of the nineteenth century, they carried on a litigational war which has been called *Sardar Larai* and finally, under the leadership of Birsa Munda, they had a violent struggle in 1899. The Hos and Cheros joined other tribes in armed insurrection in 1831, which is better known as 'Kol insurrection'. The Santals rose in revolt in 1855-57. The Bhumij took to armed uprising in 1832, soon after the suppression of the Kol insurrection.

In these armed uprisings the tribes were led by their traditional leaders and the decisions to launch violent attacks were taken in large tribal gatherings. Bindrai, a leader during Kol insurrection says, "We returned home, invited all the Kols our brethren and caste to assemble at the village Lankah in Tamor, where we had a consultation. . . Our lives we considered of no value and we being of one caste and brethren it was agreed upon that we should commence upon to cut, plunder, murder and loot" (cited in Jha 1964: 157-158). The news of tribal gatherings and the decisions taken therein were communicated through traditional and ritual means of communication, for instance, through *sal* leaves among the Santals. The leaders and their followers claimed that they were fighting a religious war against the *Dikus* and hence sought the support and blessings from their traditional spirits and deities. Among the Mundas, particularly under the leadership of Birsa Munda, the *Olgulan* of 1899 took the form of a millenarian movement (Singh 1983).

These uprisings were not confined to small groups of violent tribals but were mass phenomena where thousands of tribals participated. A notable feature was the participation of tribal women in these uprisings. Large groups of tribals armed with their traditional weapons used to march from village to village and indulged in destruction, arson and murder of their enemies. But behind all this destruction, arson and murder there was a pattern. They attacked only the *Dikus*, the non-tribal exploiters of the tribals.

In the native consciousness, *Diku* does not refer to all non-tribals (Sinha *et al.* 1969). As said earlier, among the tribals of Chota Nagpur lived a number of Hindu artisans, the blacksmith, the weaver and the cowherd. These are not included in the category *Diku*, despite the fact that these are also non-tribals. The non-tribal jagirdars and moneylenders are invariably in the category of *Diku* and were the targets of most violent attacks. But the tribal jagirdars and Rajas were, by and large, spared, even in the most violent phase of the uprisings.

Many of the uprisings initially sparked off in areas of large scale dispossession of traditional leaders. the *Munda* and the *Manki*. Even the tribal Zamindars and Rajas harboured sentiments of social, economic and political injustice done to them by the British. In the tribal consciousness the non-tribal zamindars and jagirdars, moneylenders and the *amlas* were identified with the British and they were all blamed for their misery and indignities. There had also been instances of abduction and criminal assault on tribal women.

The tribals reacted to all this with all the fury and rage

they were capable of. Hence many attacks were barbarous. Writing about the Kol insurrection of 1831, Jha (1964: 159) refers to the seven cuts made on the victims by the tribals, one for each of the following seven levies: *batta* (Commission on Exchange of Coins), excise tax, postal tax, tax on opium, fines for crimes, village salamies, and forced labour on roads. O'Malley (1917: 193-194), discussing the Santal rebellion of 1855-57 speaks of the mass frenzy indulged in by the tribals when they used to catch hold of a moneylender during the rebellion. "They would cut off his fingers and yell 'here you get four annas in a rupee', cut off his feet and yell, 'here you get eight annas in a rupee' cut up his body into two and yell, 'here you get twelve annas in a rupee' and finally would cut off the head with a maddening yell, 'here you get sixteen annas in a rupee'."

All these violent uprisings were short-lived. The tribals on each occasion gained initial success but were soon crushed with all the might of the colonial power. Their dream of driving away the *Dikus* remained unrealized; their faith in their traditional spirits and deities also failed them. The crushing defeat must have left them dejected and demoralized. They came to be treated as outlaws in their own territory by outsiders who came and dispossessed them of their traditional rights on land and forest.

Thus in the latter half of the nineteenth century, the tribals in Chota Nagpur and Santal Parganas stood alienated and ejected from the ownership of their land. Many might have even lost the right to stand on the land their ancestors had cleared and which they had nourished with their sweat and blood for generations. They had fought with all their might, with all their ferocity, to restore to themselves their own land. At the end of all these efforts, they stood alienated and defeated, despised and demoralized. It is not surprising that faced with such a situation, many of them would have looked for a new home outside the territory for themselves. The painful decision to leave their ancestral land and resettle themselves in new lands for some might have appeared to be the only alternative. Those who did so were not doing this for the first time, they were only following the precedents they had learnt in their tradition of migrations.

MIGRATION

Roy (1970) discusses at length the tribal traditions of migration among the tribes of Chota Nagpur and Santal Parganas. Many of these tribes moved together for the greater part of their journey. Speaking about the Mundas, Roy (1970: 33-34) says "From Azimgarh, so runs the Munda tradition, the Mundas migrated successively to Kalanjar, Garh Chitra, Garh Nagarwar, Garh Daharwar, Garh Pali, Garh Pipra, Mandar Pahar, Bijnagarh, Hardinagar, Laknourgarh, Nandangarh, Rijgarh and Ruidasgarh and then across Burmughal to Omedanada in Jharkhand Chota Nagpur". Thus before settling down in Chota Nagpur, the Mundas according to their own traditions, had already lived at fourteen other places.

Taking help of archaeological, epigraphical, linguistic and literary pieces of evidence, Roy has been able to identify these places and reconstruct the path adopted by the Mundas in their migrations. He says "if we follow the order indicated in this tradition, the Mundas would appear to have migrated from northern India southwards to modern Bundelkhand and central India, then across eastern Rajputana, back again to north-western India and thence through modern Rohilkhand and Oudh to Behar and finally to Chota Nagpur" (1970 : 34).

It is quite likely that from many of these places they were pushed away by stronger forces. We know of the struggles between the Aryans and the tribal chiefs in the plains of north India. Munda traditions speak of the conflict with the Kharwars before they left Rohtasgarh (Roy 1970 : 59). Thus the tradition-conscious Mundas knew of the course their ancestors has taken when defeated in struggles with more powerful adversaries.

In the middle of the nineteenth century the colonial capitalists were busy developing tea plantations in Assam. They had already tried and failed to recruit local labour to work on the plantations. They toyed with the idea of recruiting Chinese labour but failed in this effort also (Weiner 1978 : 89). The planters then turned to tribal labour from Chota Nagpur. Initially, the recruitment was through the *arkattis* who were professional recruiters and maintained no contact with the labour after recruitment. The abuses of this system brought in the *sardari* system of recruitment. A *sardar* is a plantation labourer who is sent back to his own area to help recruit additional labour for the plantations. The *sardar* is in a position to win the confidence of the native labour because of his social contacts. He maintains contact with the labour recruited by him even in the plantation. He performs two functions simultaneously, one for the newly recruited labour and the other for the tea plantation. Because of the continued contact with a *sardar* from their area, the tribal recruits join the plantation with a greater sense of security. The new recruits also get a variety of help and hints in settling down to a new way of life, new work rhythm and a new industrial discipline. On occasions of illness and personal distress the *sardar* is looked up to for help and solace.

The plantation also stands to gain by the *sardari* system. This system helps the man who has the confidence of the plantation manager, the *sardar*, to gain the confidence of the labour force also. Through the *sardars*, the plantation helps develop new work habits and new work culture among the recruits. The labour recruited by the *sardar* is also likely to be more stable. The *sardar* also gains in the process in the form of commission per worker recruited. In addition the *sardars* gain in status in their interaction with the labour force as well as with the plantation management.

For the alienated tribals of Chota Nagpur, this possibility of outside employment must have come as a good opportunity. Centuries of economic, political and social dispossession, exploitation and repression might have already prepared them psychologically to leave. It is no wonder that the tribals of Chota Nagpur and Santal Parganas responded to these opportunities in vast numbers. Whether '*arkatti*' or *sardari*, in both systems, the recruiters came to enlist them and this must have facilitated large scale recruitment.

Three other factors must have helped them in deciding in favour of large scale exploitation of the new opportunities of employment. First, the plantation was recruiting not individuals but whole families. Tea plantation needs the services of both men and women. In fact the women have the reputation of being better tea leaf pluckers. Even grown up children were employed for a variety of light work on the plantation. This family recruitment made it possible for every member of the family to earn, besides making it possible for the entire family to live together.

Secondly, this would allow and help them live as communities on the plantations. Hence it was possible not only for the whole families to live together but whole lineages, clans and tribal groups could live together. And indeed in the labour lines of the tea plantations one does find many tribal groups living as communities rather than as individual tribal workers. Living as communities has made it possible not only to enjoy a greater sense of solidarity and security but has also helped them recreate their society and culture in an alien environment, hundreds of miles away from their native area.

Finally, in addition to industrial employment, there was also the possibility of getting land for cultivation, not only after their contract had expired but, in many cases, even before that. For the agricultural tribal community deprived of its ancestral land, the attraction of this opportunity can well be imagined. Both the Government of Assam and the tea plantations were interested in settling the time-expired labour in the cultivable waste land close to the plantations. The state was interested in additional land revenue and the planters wanted to have a labour reserve to draw from in times of peak labour demand during plucking season (Phukan 1984).

Given these features of labour recruitment and the large scale response to these opportunities, one is tempted to think that the decision to move out might not have been taken individually but collectively. The tribals have structures of collective decision making for their collective activities. They used these structures during their years of rebellion and they might well have used them in arriving at the collective decision to move out. For want of direct evidence on such a collective decision to move out, one cannot emphasize this process too strongly but the likelihood of this process cannot be ruled out.

Needless to say, all those people who left Chota Nagpur and Santal Parganas did not all go to the tea gardens in Assam and Bengal. But it is also true that a great majority did. Table 9.5 gives the number of people born in the different districts of Chota Nagpur and Santal Parganas but enumerated elsewhere in 1891.

TABLE 9.5

Out-Migrants from the Districts of Chota Nagpur and Santal Parganas, 1891

Serial Number	Area	Actual Population	Enumerated outside the District of Birth	Percentage of Out-Migrants to Actual Population
1.	Santal Parganas	17,53,775	1,17,142	6.7
2.	Palamau	5,96,770	29,043	4.9
3.	Hazaribagh	11,64,321	1,13,622	9.8
4.	Manbhum	11,93,328	1,18,893	10.0
5.	Ranchi	11,28,885	2,46,022	21.8
6.	Singhbhum	5,45,488	43,531	8.0
	Total	63,82,567	6,68,253	10.5

Source: Data collected from relevant tables in Census of India, 1901, Vol. VI: Lower Provinces of Bengal and their feudatories, Part I: Report.

The above Table shows that in Santal Parganas and Chota Nagpur more than six lakh people, equivalent to more than one-tenth of the actual population were enumerated in 1891 in districts other than the districts of their birth. It should be noted that all those who were enumerated outside the districts of their birth were not all enumerated outside Chota Nagpur and Santal Parganas. It is natural that some of them might have been born in one district of the tribal tract of Chota Nagpur and enumerated in another district within this tribal tract. Weiner (1978 : 161) reports that more than three lakhs of those born in Chota Nagpur and Santal Parganas were enumerated outside this tribal tract in 1891, nearly two lakhs of these only in Assam.

Within this tribal tract, Ranchi had the highest percentage of out-migrants, equivalent to more than one-fifth of the actual population. It is interesting to remember that the Ranchi district is the home district of the Mundas, who had been the most turbulent of the tribes, right from the last decade of the eighteenth century to the end of the nineteenth century. Hazaribagh, Manbhum and Singhbhum are other districts from where people equivalent to nearly one-tenth of the actual population were enumerated outside the districts of birth. Table 9.6 compares the situation in 1891 with that obtaining in 1901 and 1911.

When we compare Table 9.5 with Table 9.6, we find that Ranchi district continued to register the highest percentage of out-migrants, with a population equivalent to more than one-fifth of the actual population having being enumerated outside the district. In 1901 and 1911 Santal Parganas also joined Hazaribagh, Manbhum and Singhbhum in having out-migrants equivalent to more than one-tenth of the actual population. In Chota Nagpur and Santal Parganas as a whole in 1901 and 1911 relatively higher percentages of people were enumerated in districts other than the districts of their birth than we had in 1891. In 1911, more than 10 lakhs in Chota Nagpur and Santal Parganas were enumerated outside the districts of their birth. Weiner (1978 : 161) reports that more than seven lakhs were enumerated outside this tribal tract.

Weiner's (1978 : 161) analysis makes it clear that majority of the out-migrants moved over to Assam. It would be interesting to know as to where in Assam did they settle down. Did they settle down in a few contiguous districts or did they spread themselves widely in Assam. Table 9.7 gives us the distribution in Assam in 1901 and 1911 of the people born in Chota Nagpur and Santal Parganas. The Table also gives the number of tea gardens in the different districts in 1881.

We find that of the people born in the Santal Parganas and enumerated in Assam in 1891, a little more than one-third were in Surma Valley and about two-third in Brahmaputra Valley. Only five persons out of more than eighteen thousand were in the hill districts. In the Brahmaputra Valley, Lakhimpur had the largest concentration with one-fourth of all in-migrants from Santal Parganas living in this district. Sibsagar and Lakhimpur districts together had more than two-fifth of the in-migrants. Thus only four districts, out of eight plain districts, accounted for more than three-fourth of the

TABLE 9.6

Out-Migrants from the Districts of Chota Nagpur and Santal Parganas, 1901 and 1911

Serial Number	Area	1901			1911		
		Actual Population	Out-Migrants	Percentage of Col. 4 to 3	Actual Population	Out-Migrants	Percentage of Column 7 to 6
1	2	3	4	5	6	7	8
2.	Santal Parganas	18,09,737	2,26,008	12.5	18,82,973	3,21,283	17.1
3.	Palamau	6,19,600	32,210	5.2	6,87,267	37,481	5.5
4.	Hazaribagh	11,77,961	1,50,356	12.8	12,88,609	1,44,541	11.2
5.	Manbhum	13,01,364	1,35,972	10.4	15,47,576	1,15,492	7.5
5.	Ranchi	11,87,925	2,75,251	23.2	13,87,516	3,05,309	22.0
6.	Singhbhum	6,13,579	63,820	10.4	6,94,394	1,05,634	15.2
	Total	67,10,166	8,83,617	13.2	74,88,335	10,29,740	13.8

Source: Data collected from the relevant tables of Census of India, 1911, Vol. V: Bengal, Bihar and Orissa and Sikkim, Part I, Report.

TABLE 9.7

Persons Born in Chota Nagpur and Santal Parganas Enumerated in Assam, 1891 and 1901

Serial Number	Area	Number of tea gardens (1881)	1891 Born in Santal Prganas Per cent	1891 Born in Chota Nagpur Per cent	1901 Born in Santal Parganas Per cent	1901 Born in Chota Nagpur Per cent
1	2	3	4	5	6	7
1)	Surma Valley	276	35.1	25.6	19.3	20.2
i)	Cachar Plains	184	16.6	15.2	8.6	10.4
ii)	Sylhet	92	18.5	10.4	10.6	9.8
2)	Brahmaputta Valley	557	64.8	74.4	79.7	79.2
i)	Goalpara	7	4.5	0.5	4.7	0.2
ii)	Kamrup	30	4.7	0.5	2.9	0.8
iii)	Darrang	115	8.4	13.9	11.1	15.9
iv)	**Nowgong**	64	4.1	5.1	3.6	4.2

TABLE 9.7 (*Contd.*)

1	2	3	4	5	6	7
v)	Sibsagar	210	18.1	28.1	27.9	30.0
vi)	Lakhimpur	131	25.0	25.9	29.5	28.0
3)	Total Plains	833	100.0	100.0	98.9	99.4
4)	Total Hills	6	0.0	0.0	1.1	0.6
5)	Total Assam	839	100.00	100.0	100.0	100.0
No. of Persons enumerated in Assam			18,294	1,90,774	1,237	2,49,997

Source: Computed from data in IO Census of India, 1891: Assam Vol. II Fables (for 1891).
ii) Census of India, 1901, Vol iv, Assam Part II Tables (for 1901).

in-migrants These four districts had more than two-thirds of the tea gardens in Assam. Of the remaining districts Goalpara, Kamrup and Nowgong had relatively much smaller number of tea gardens and they also had relatively much smaller number of in-migrants.

In 1901 also, these four districts with heavy concentration accounted for two-thirds of the non-migrants but the internal distributions among these had changed. The two Brahmputra districts (Sibsagar and Lakhimpur) accounted for more than half of the in-migrants from Santal Parganas, the Surma Valley districts having only a little less than one-fifth of the in-migrants.

Looking at the distribution of people from Chota Nagpur we find the pattern to be similar. In 1891, more than half of the in-migrants from Chota Nagpur were in the two contiguous districts of Sibsagar and Lakhimpur. The Surma Valley received only one-fourth of the in-migrants. In 1901 the pattern continues. The concentration becomes a little more heightened, with the two districts of high concentration (Sibsagar and Lakhimpur) having about 60 per cent of all the tribal in-migrants in Assam. Darrang is another district which received significant in-migrants from Chota Nagpur both in 1891 and 1901.

This pattern of distribution of in-migrants makes it clear that there is a strong tendency among people coming from particular districts to keep together in Assam. This has been demonstrated in the case of Santal Parganas. Let us see as to what is the situation with regard to the five districts of Chota Nagpur. The following Table gives the distribution of in-migrants in Assam coming from Chota Nagpur districts.

Table 9.8 makes it clear that even in the districts of Chota Nagpur, the tendency we found in Santal Parganas is strongly present. More than two-thirds of those who came from Palamau went to Darrang district. Similarly, nearly two-thirds of those who came from two contiguous districts of Ranchi and Singhbhum were enumerated in two contiguous districts of Assam, Sibsagar and Lakhimpur. More than half of those who came from Manbhum also settled down in these two districts, Sibsagar and Lakhimpur. These two districts had in 1901 nearly 60 per cent of those who came from

TABLE 9.8

Distribution of In-Migrants in Assam Coming from Chota Nagpur, 1901

Serial Number	Area	Total in-migrants	Surma Valley			Brahmaputra Valley								
			Ca-char	Syl-het	Total	Goal-para	Kam-rup	Dar-rang	Now-gong	Sib-sagar	La-khim-pur	To-tal	To-tal Hills	Grand Total
1	2	3	4	5	6	7	8	9	10	11	12	13	14	15
1.	Palamau	6,776	1.2	1.1	2.3	0.1	0.1	68.7	0.9	17.7	10.2	97.7	0.0	100.0
2.	Hazaribagh	68,772	12.1	13.6	25.7	0.1	0.7	10.7	3.1	42.4	16.9	73.8	0.5	100.0
3.	Ranchi	91,794	8.2	8.2	16.4	0.3	1.3	14.5	5.7	23.1	37.9	82.8	0.7	99.9
4.	Manbhum	69,728	13.9	9.3	23.2	0.2	0.6	17.5	3.6	29.4	25.0	76.3	0.4	99.9
5.	Singhbhum	12,927	3.1	8.0	11.1	0.2	0.6	17.0	4.7	22.4	42.9	87.8	1.0	99.9
	Total	2,49,997	10.4	9.8	20.0	0.2	0.8	15.9	4.2	30.0	28.0	79.2	0.6	100.0

Source: Census of India, 1901, Vol. IV, Assam, Part II Tables.

Hazaribagh. From among those who came from Singhbhum, more than two-fifth settled down only in one district of Lakhimpur.

That fact that people originating from particular districts have decided to stay together in the place of resettlement gives support to the view that the decision to leave was not an individual one but a collective decision. And similarly, the decision as to where to resettle seems to be not an individual but a collective decision.

A majority of those who migrated to Assam went to work in the tea plantations. Hence among the tea plantation workers also we should expect similar concentration of labour on the basis of their districts of origin.

Table 9.9 gives the distribution in Assam of the labour coming from Chota Nagpur and Santal Parganas.

Table 9.9 giving the distribution of tea plantation labour supports the findings of Tables 9.7 and 9.8 In-migrants from all the districts in Chota Nagpur and Santal Parganas have shown a strong tendency to keep together. Between 50 to 60 per cent of labour coming from the various districts of Chota Nagpur and Santal Parganas have settled down only in two districts of Assam, Sibsagar and Lakhimpur. The only exception is provided by the labour coming from Palamau district. Only one-fourth of the labour coming from this district settled down in these two districts. But this does not mean that the labourers from Palamau evenly distributed themselves throughout Assam. In fact, they were the ones with the largest concentration. A little less than three-fourth of these settled down only in one district, the district of Darrang.

These large concentrations of tribals originating from a common place have no doubt helped them recreate their life and culture. This has also resulted in their being numerically dominant in the labour force of the districts of resettlement. In most districts they form nearly 70 per cent of the tea garden labour. Table 9.10 brings out this fact clearly.

This shows that the Surma Valley in 1891 had only one-third of the plantation labour coming from Chota Nagpur and Santal Parganas. But in the Brahmaputra Valley, a little less than three-fourths had come from Chota Nagpur and Santal

TABLE 9.9

Percentage Distribution of Tea Garden Labour in Assam In-Migrated from Chota Nagpur and Santal Parganas, 1901

Serial Number	Area	Total enumerated in Assam	Surma Valley			Brahmaputra Valley							
			Cachar	Sylhet	Total	Goalpara	Kamrup	Darrang	Nowgong	Sibsagar	Lakhimpur	Total	Grand Total
1	2	3	4	5	6	7	8	9	10	11	12	13	14
1.	Santal Parganas	23,457	9.7	12.3	22.0	—	2.4	11.3	3.4	30.5	30.5	78.0	100.0
2.	Chota Nagpur	1,90,721	11.2	11.9	23.1	—	0.5	16.0	3.1	30.3	27.0	76.9	100.0
i)	Palamau	5,977	0.6	1.1	1.7	—	—	71.9	0.4	16.9	9.1	98.2	1(0.0
ii)	Hazaribagh	54,351	13 2	15.9	29.0	—	0.1	10.1	2.2	43.0	15.6	71.0	99.9
iii)	Ranchi	60,020	9.1	10.6	19.7	—	1.1	14.2	3.8	24.0	37.1	80.3	100.0
iv)	Manbhum	53,569	14.6	11.4	26.0	—	0.4	17.2	3.2	28.3	25.0	74.0	100.0
v)	Singhbhum	10,804	3.1	8.8	11.9	—	0.2	19.0	4.1	21.5	43.3	88.1	100.0

Source: Computed from data presented in Census of India, 1901, Vol. IV: Assam, Part II: Tables.

TABLE 9.10

Percentage of Labour Coming from Chota Nagpur and Santal Parganas in the Total Plantation Labour Force in Assam Districts, 1891

Serial Number	Area	Total In-migrant Labour	Per cent born in		Total of Chota Nagpur and Santal Parganas
			Chota Nagpur	Santal Parganas	
1	2	3	4	5	6
1.	Surma Valley	1,50,253	29.4	4.0	33.2
	i) Cachar Plain	76,846	32.6	3.6	36.2
	ii) Sylhet	73,407	25.6	4.3	29.9
2.	Brahmaputra Valley	1,74,109	66.7	5.2	71.9
	i) Goalpara	458	23.8	69.2	93.0
	ii) Kamrup	3,128	39.4	24.5	63.9
	iii) Darrang	31,715	68.6	3.8	72.4
	iv) Nowgong	11,111	68.5	6.2	74.7

TABLE 9.10 (*Contd.*)

1	2	3	4	5	6
	v) Sibsagar	71,618	63.0	4.0	67.0
	vi) Lakhimpur	56,079	71.8	5.9	77.7
3.	Total Plains	3,24,362	49.3	4.7	54.0
4.	Total Hills	1	—	—	—
5.	Total Assam	3,24,363	49.3	4.7	54.0

Source: Computed from the data presented in Census of India, 1891: Assam; Vol III, Provincial Tables.

Parganas. In Goalpara 93 per cent of the labour force had come from Chota Nagpur and Santal Parganas. There is, however, some difference in the numerical dominance of Chota Nagpur and Santal Parganas labour force in Assam districts. The labour force from Chota Nagpur was numerically dominant in 1891 in Darrang, Nowgong, Sibsagar and Lakhimpur districts. But the Santal Parganas labour was numerically dominant in only one district, Goalpara, which had a small labour force of only 458 workers. Even when we combine Assam plains together we find that in 1891 more than half of the labour force came from Chota Nagpur and Santal Parganas.

Discussion

Chota Nagpur and Santal Parganas were thus characterized by large scale out-migration in the nineteenth century. A great majority of the out-migrants went over to Assam. Here they did not spread themselves evenly but concentrated themselves in some selected areas. People with common place of origin showed a strong tendency to stay together. The scale of migration as well as the pattern of resettlement are suggestive of a collective desire and decision to first to move out and then to re-establish themselves in some distant land. Their successful effort in recreating their society and culture in the plantations lends further support to the view that the decision to leave was collective.

This pattern of migration, it seems to me, cannot be adequately explained by any view which locates the decision to move in individual consciousness, "the desire inherent in most men to better themselves in material respects" (Ravenstein 1889 : 286) would not be able to move the relatively less mobile tribals in such magnitudes to a common destination during such a short period. Something more than 'the desire inherent in most men to better themselves' is necessary. Other tribal groups in adjoining territories of Madhya Pradesh, the Murias and Marias of Batar, the Korwas and Kawars of Raigarh and Bilaspur and the Baigas of Mandla, did not move out in perceptive numbers. When 'the desire inherent in most men' could not move these tribals, then why did only the tribals of Chota Nagpur and Santal Parganas move? Obviously, there were other forces.

Zipti's (1946) theory of 'least effort', Stouffer's (1940) view of intervening opportunities and Lee's (1969) stress on the role of intervening obstacles seem to have been clearly scaled over by the tribals in their move from Chota Nagpur and Santal Parganas to Assam. They covered the largest distance available to them in the country east of their territory, without 'bothering about intervening opportunities and intervening obstacles. They went to a place where the largest number among them could be accommodated simultaneously.

The differential role of economic and non-economic factors in providing the necessary or sufficient conditions or in determining the rate, incidence and time of migration seem to undermine greatly the political forces behind migrations. Inadequate recognition of the political factor in the anthropological writings analysing migration in colonial Africa seems to miss, possibly, the most dominant factor behind migration in Africa during European colonialism. Large scale tribal migration took place in Africa to meet the needs of colonial industry. Not just economic but political force as well was used to get the required level of migration. Even the incidence of migration was politically determined. The tribal chiefs made use of the opportunity to get rid of their troublesome subjects.

In Chota Nagpur and Santal Parganas also political factors seem to dominate. With the tribal chief becoming a Hindu in the seventeenth century the whole character of the state changed. The tribal groups that were in the past sources of strength now become targets of repression. They were economically exploited so that they may become politically weak. And measures of economic exploitation could be pushed through because of the might of political institutions. The advent of the British only strengthened these instruments of economic and political exploitation. The British developed a whole range of new economic, political and judicial institutions which, to the utter dismay of tribes, came to be manipulated by their enemies for further exploitation. With the imposition of the colonial rule, came in the missionaries. Initially, they helped the tribals in fighting for their rights, but soon large sections of the tribals got disillusioned with them.

For the tribals colonialism did not start in the eighteenth century, it was already a century old in the form of internal colonialism. The colonizers in the first case were non-tribal Hindus, in the second case they were non-tribal British. The tribals viewed, in the nineteenth century, the two groups of colonizers in league with each other in their common aim, the exploitation of the tribes.

Colonialism, both internal and external, for the tribals in Chota Nagpur and Santal Parganas, resulted in large scale political and economic alienation. For more than a century, the tribals fought with all their strength, with all the rage and fire they had within them, but the might of the colonial power crushed them every time they raised their head. Painfully it must have dawned on them that their territory was no more theirs. They came to be deprived of their land, their political power and their status. Gradually they must have prepared themselves psychologically to leave this territory. The opportunity of large scale employment in tea plantations must have readily appealed to them and as a consequence we find large groups of tribals moving over to Assam.

It is interesting to note that the colonial system which helped deprive them of their land and traditional employment was also the one that provided them with alternate employment. On examining the functioning of colonial systems one finds that there is nothing paradoxical about the two opposite roles of 'depriver' and 'provider' played by the colonial system of India. Indeed it is the essence of the colonial system.

Colonialism brings along with it new instruments of exploitation of the natural and human resources. Plantations, mines and factories are opened. Since labour has to be provided from within the colony, the traditional occupational distribution of work force has to be destroyed to the extent necessary.

Since agriculture was the mainstay of most of the colonies, intervention in the agrarian system assumed high priority. The owners of land were expropriated from their ties with the land; in a way they were rendered 'surplus', free from obligations to work on the land they had nourished with their sweat and labour for generations. This labour force was then transported on to the plantations and other industrial establishments and forced to work under repressive conditions. This happened in Latin America; this happened in Africa. This was naturally also bounds to happen in India. This is not to say that there are no differences in the colonial systems in Latin America, Africa and India. Indeed there are vital differences but the dominant aim of colonizers the world over is the same. In India, with the help of their agrarian policies, the British helped develop a labour force alienated from land and with the help of their plantation policies they provided for employment. In the tea plantations these workers were forced to work in bondage and servility (Badgaiyan 1983).

These colonial policies operated in Chota Nagpur and Santal Parganas as they did in other parts of the country. But in this tribal tract the consequences became much more severe because of the structures of internal colonialism which had already expropriated a significant section of the tribal community before the British came. During the eighteenth and the nineteenth centuries expropriation of owners and ejectment of tenants continued. The tribal chiefs suffered economic loss and political humiliation at the hands of the British. The tribals hence rose against the system and suffered repression. The large scale migration is, to my mind, a consequence of the whole sequence of economic and political events.

The point that I have tried to stress in this paper is that there is need to go beyond individual psyche and the immediate social and economic environment of the migrant to get at the real causes of migration, particularly when we analyse large scale migrations. Often, individual migrants fail to appreciate the impact of the wider environment on their psyche and their actions. It is the business of the social scientists to examine the impact of the wider social, economic and political environment on what people think, say and do. Only such an analysis is likely to explain human thought and actions.

REFERENCES

Badgaiyan, S.D., "Tribal Worker in Colonial Industry", in S.N. Mishra and Bhupinder Singh (ed.), *Tribal Area Development*, Society for the Study of Regional Disparities, New Delhi, 1983.

Banton, M., *West African City: A Study of Tribal Life in Freetown*, Oxford University Press, London, 1957.

Census of India, (1891): Assam Vol. II and Vol. III.

———, (1901): Vol. IV: Assam Part II Tables.

———, (1901): Vol. VI: Lower Provinces of Bengal and the Feudatories, Part I, Report.

———, (1911): Vol. V: Bengal, Bihar and Orissa and Sikkim, Part I, Report.

———, (1971): Series 4: Bihar, Part V-A: Special Tables for Scheduled Castes and Scheduled Tribes.

Cohen, R., (ed.) *Forced Labour in Colonial Africa* (A.T. Nzula, I.I. Polekhin and A.Z. Zusmanovich), Zed Press, London, 1979.

Datta, K.K., (1940), *The Santal Insurrection of 1855-57*, Calcutta University, Calcutta, 1940.

Durkheim, E., *The Suicide*, Routledge and Kegan Paul Ltd,, London, 1952.

Gugler, J., "The Theory of Rural-Urban Migration" in J.A. Jackson (ed.) *Migration*, Cambridge University Press, Cambridge, 1969.

Guha, R., *Elementary Aspects of Peasant Insurgency in Colonial Ind a*, Oxford University Press, Delhi, 1983.

Gulliver, P.H., "Labour Migration in a Rural Economy", East African Institute of Social Research, Kampala, 1955.

Hunter, W.W., *A Statistical Account of Bengal*, Vol. XIV, XVI, XVII, (London, 1877) Concept Publishing Company, Delhi, 1976.

Jha, J.C., *The Kol Insurrection of Chota Nagpur*, Thacker, Spink and Co., Calcutta, 1964.

———, *The Bhumij Revolt*, Munshiram Manohar Lal, Delhi, 1967.

Lee, E., "A Theory of Migration" in J.A. Jackson (ed.) *Migration*, Cambridge University Press, Cambridge, 1969.

Maxon, R., "Early Gusil Resistance to British Rule, 1905-14" in B.A. Ogot (ed.) *War and Society in Africa*, Frank Cass, London, 1972.

Mayer, P., *Townsmen or Tribesmen: Conservatism and the Process of Urbanization in a South African City*, Oxford, 1961.

Mitchell, C., "The Causes of Labour Migration", *Bulletin of the Inter-African Labour Institute*, 6, pp. 12-47, 1959.

O'Malley, L.S.A., *Bengal, Bihar and Orissa and Sikkim*, Ess Ess Publications, New Delhi, 1979.

Natrajan, L., "The Santal Insurrection: 1855-56", in A.R. Desai (ed.) *Peasant Struggles in India*, Oxford University Press, Delhi, 1979.

Phukan, U., *The Ex-Tea Garden Labour Population in Assam*, B.R. Publishing Corporation, Delhi, 1984.

Ravenstein, E.G. "The Laws of Migration", in *Journal of the Royal Statistical Society*, June, pp. 167-227, 1885.

———, "The Laws of Migration", in *Journal of the Royal Statistical Society*, June, pp. 241-301, 1889.

Roy, S.C., *The Mundas and Their Country*, (Calcutta 1912), Asia Publishing House, Calcutta, 1970.

Schapera, I., *Migrant Labour and Tribal Life: A Study of Conditions in the Bechuanaland Profectorate*, Oxford University Press, London, 1947.

Singh, K.S., "Tribal Land Organization in Chota Nagpur" in *Trends of Socio-Economic Change in India*, Indian Institute of Advanced Study, Simla, 1969.

———, *Birsa Munda*, Oxford University Press, Delhi 1983.

Sinha, S., Sen, J. and Sudhir, P., "The Concept of Diku among the Tribals of Chota Nagpur", *Man in India*, 49: 2 (April-June), pp. 121-138, 1969.

Skinner, E.P., "Labour Migration among the Mossi of Upper Volta" in Hilda Kuper (ed.) *Urbanization and Migration in West Africa*, University of California Press, Berkeley, 1965.

Southall, A.W., "Alur Migrants" in A. Richards (ed.) *Economic Development and Tribal Change: A Study of Immigrant Labour in Buganda*, W. Heffer and Sons Ltd., Cambridge, 1954.

Stichter, S., *Migrant Labour in Kenya*, Longman Group, London, 1982.

Stouffer, S.A., "Intervening Opportunities: A Theory Relating Mobility and Distance", *American Sociological Review*, 11, (December), pp. 845-67, 1940.

———, "Intervening Opportunities and Competing Migrants", *Journal of Regional Science*, 2, 1960 Reproduced in Stouffer, Social Research to Test Ideas, The Free Press of Glencoe, 1960.

Thapar, R. and Siddiqui, M.H., Chota Nagpur: The Precolonial and Colonial Situation in Unesco. Trends in Ethnic Group Relations in Asia and Oceania, Paris, 1979.

Todaro, M.P., *Internal Migration in Developing Countries*, Geneva, International Labour Office, 1976.

Weiner, M., *Sons of the Soil*, Oxford University Press, Delhi, 1978.

Winter, E.W., *Bwamba Economy: The Development of a Primitive Subsistence Economy in Uganda*, Kampala, 1955.

Ziph, G.K., "The P_1 P_2/D Hypothesis: On the Intercity Movement of Persons", *American Sociological Review*, 11 (December), pp. 677-86, 1946.

10. *Migration of Chota Nagpur Tribals to West Bengal*

NIREN C. CHOUDHURY AND SHARIT K. BHOWMIK

Migration has been defined broadly as a permanent or semi-permanent change of residence (Lee 1969 : 285). It has several dimensions, among which, the demographic and economic have received more attention than the others. But, above all, migration is a sociological phenomenon. It is not merely a shift of population from one place to another. Migration creates conditions for deep-rooted changes in the social and cultural life of both the migrant community as well as the host community. Not only does the internal structure of the migrant community undergo transformation, as the present paper attempts to illustrate, it may also structurally modify the pattern of inter-community relations at the destination.

For over a hundred years, the tribals of Chota Nagpur and Santal Parganas region of Bihar, have been steadily migrating out of their homeland in search of new places of residence. A large section of them have poured into West Bengal. In this paper, we have tried to investigate the socio-economic and demographic aspects of this migration. We have also tried to show how the different socio-economic conditions at destination may lead to different patterns of socio-cultural integration and adaptation of migrant communities to a new environment.

Historical Context of Migration

During the last hundred and fifty years or so, a situation

was created in Chota Nagpur and the Santal Parganas which caused a tremendous upheaval of the local Adivasi (tribal) population, forcing them to move out of the region and spread out to the adjoining States of West Bengal, Assam, Orissa and Madhya Pradesh. In order to understand the nature of this phenomenon, one must understand the nature of agrarian relations which emerged out of some specific historical situation.

Tribal society in Bihar in the nineteenth century was in a state of turmoil. This is evident from the series of revolts and the general unrest prevailing in the area. Decay in their traditional society had started earlier, in the seventeenth century, when Hinduism crept into the ruling family. The tribal *raja* of Chota Nagpur, who belonged to the Munda tribe, sought to elevate his status through the process of Hinduising himself and his family. The princely family no longer considered itself Munda but traced its lineage to the *Nag devata*, the serpent god, and called itself *Nagvanshi* (descendants of *Nag devata*) hence the name of their princedom became Chota Nagpur.

Land Alienation

Hinduisation, firstly, alienated the tribal *raja* and his kinsfolk from the rest of the people. Secondly, it brought in an infiltration of non-tribals into the region. These people were known as *dikus* (aliens) by the local tribal population. They were encouraged to settle in Chota Nagpur by the members of the princely family. As most of these people (the *dikus*) had some rudimentary education, the ruling family encouraged them to take up administrative posts. Soon most of the key posts in the administration came under their control. Davidson, the Governor General's agent, noted that "it became a great object with them (the Nagvanshi rulers) to induce other Hindus to settle down in Nagpore." The royal administration came to be staffed, not by local tribals, but by Kayasthas from outside (Jha 1964 : 31).

The Nagvanshi rulers introduced the system of granting large portions of land (jagirs) which were already being cultivated by the local tribals, to these aliens, in lieu of payment. In addition, huge jagirs were also granted to Brahmin priests, "whose influence over the new converts was very strong" (Ibid: 32). They encouraged traders, who were Hindus, Muslims and Sikhs, dealing in horses, shawls, brocades and other luxury goods which "fetched enormous offers. . . from the Nagvanshi chief and obtained farms of villages instead of cash" (Haldar 1880).

The practice of granting jagirs dealt a severe blow to the traditional agrarian structure. It increasingly alienated the tribals from their lands and a class of jagirdars became firmly entrenched, prospering and multiplying at their expense. Within a hundred years or so, i.e., during the seventeenth and eighteenth centuries, these petty landlords not only usurped most of the *Khunt-Khatti* villages (original tribal villages based on common ownership of land) but also encouraged other Hindu and Muslim aliens to settle down. In most cases, the Adivasi was reduced to a rent paying tenant, having no rights on his traditional property. The word *diku*, which at first meant a non-tribal or Hindu landlord, came to be used as a word of abuse (Hoffman 1964: 1062).

While the tribals were struggling with the unhappy effects of Hinduisation, came the British penetration into the area. Chota Nagpur, as a part of Bihar, was leased to the British East India Company in 1765. The district of Ranchi was set up in 1768. Both events, that of Hinduisation and British rule, thrust alien people and alien ideas on the tribals. They caused an influx which led eventually to the economic ruin of the people (Jha 1964: 1).

Introduction of British rule resulted in a change of masters. The judicial powers of the local raja were initially curtailed and finally forfeited (Saha 1972 : 231). Moneylenders and traders poured into the area with renewed vigour and cornered lands through various means. Land was available in plenty, but those virgin, hilly tracts were difficult to level and cultivate, so the next best bet was to grab the tribal's land which was already under the plough (Hunter 1877: 116).

The British administrators made no attempts to understand the traditional rights on land, which were unwritten, and treated documents as sole proof of ownership. The simple minded, illiterate tribal, on the other hand, was innocent of the complicated deeds and documents relating to ownership, which were completely in contrast with his traditional right to proprietorship. The *dikus* could cleverly manipulate documents relating to their advantage and, before the Adivasi realized it, he was relieved of his right to cultivation.

The village headman (known as Mahato) who had the final say in matters regarding land was powerless as his authority had been superseded firstly, by the ritish administrators and then by the economic power of the *dikus* who were steadily dispossessing the Adivasis. E.T. Dalton notes that the Adivasi found no solace with the civil authorities. Their offices were usually far away and he could rarely meet the expenses of the journey there. Even if someone was bold enough to reach the "far-off station," he would find that the other party was well armed with a host of witnesses "who would swear that he had not only no rights in the land, but was a turbulent rebel besides" (Dalton 1872 : 170). Dalton summed up the situation thus: "The unfortunate simple tribal races were neglected by their new masters, oppressed by the aliens and deprived of the means they had formerly possessed of obtaining redress through their own chiefs" (Ibid: 170). In many villages the tribals had lost all their lands to aliens and had been reduced to the status of agricultural labourers (Saha 1972 : 38).

The notorious Permanent Settlement Act of 1773, which gave legal sanction to the class of zamindars (landlords), was not applicable to Chota Nagpur initially, as the authorities feared adverse consequences. They could sense the hostility among the tribals and felt that the revenue collectors (the zamindar's men) would meet with resistance. A resolution to this effect was passed by the Governor-General's Council on 18 September 1789 (Jha 1964 : 41). However, as if to rub salt into their wounds, this decision was revoked in 1823 and the Act came into force. Along with it came all its disastrous effects—rack-renting, resumption, sub-letting. The ancient tillage rights of the tribal peasantry were now legally merged with the power of the zamindar's permanent property in the soil.

The adivasis, who were now powered to the status of tenants to the respective zamindar, were burdened with a series of taxes imposed by the landlord and the East India Company.

The zamindars would collect tolls from their tenants for almost every occasion—births, deaths, social functions, festivals, religious gatherings. Taxes were imposed on almost everything—possession of cattle, construction of new houses, even the Mahua tree which was regarded by the tribals as nature's gift, was taxed. Individually, each tax or toll might seem light, but when added up they were crushing (Jha 1964: 42; Saha 1972: 38; Singh 1965: 3-4).

While the *diku* jagirdars and later, zamindars, were usurping land, the British rulers managed to corner whatever remained through its legislations on forests. Six forest legislations were passed between 1857 and 1877 curbing Adivasis from the free use of forest resources. The seventh legislation, the Indian Forest Act of 1878 (Act VII), deemed in addition, that all waste lands in villages be constituted as 'protected forest'. These lands were used till then as common grazing grounds for cattle.

Tribal Unrest

Unable to bear these tyrannies, Adivasis frequently rose in revolt. The entire nineteenth century is dotted with tribal uprisings—1795-1800, 1811, 1820, 1831, 1885 and 1899. These reflected the unhappy state of affairs. The unrest of 1831 was the first major revolt against the *dikus* and the British. All cultivating tribes—Munda, Kharia, Oraon, Ho, etc.—joined hands to fight their enemies. It was "the bursting forth of a fire that had long been smouldering" (Dalton 1872: 171).

The other two insurrections after this were of the same magnitude. In 1885, the Santals revolted against the British rulers and the *dikus*. This revolt was fairly widespread and the British army suffered heavy casualties while quelling it (Dutta Mazumdar 1956).

In 1899, the Chota Nagpur tribals rose in revolt under the leadership of Birsa, a young Munda in his early twenties. This movement was known as the 'Ulgulan' in Mundari. It was a social movement, which was violent. The *ulgulan* (meaning, uprising) was directed against all outsiders—landlords, money-lenders, traders, the British rulers, and also the foreign Christian missionaries—as these people were identified for having destroyed tribal culture. In this sense, it was a reformist.

or rather, a revivalistic movement which aimed at returning Mundas their lost glory (Singh 1965 : 8).

The British rulers did provide some marginal relief to the tribals as a result of the insurrections; but alongside, they unleashed a reign of terror and repression every time there was a revolt. This resulted in a large number of people being forced to move out of their homeland to avoid the wrath of the rulers. Dutta Mazumdar (1956 : 30) observed that "as a result of the (Santal) rebellion, the Santal people experienced economic hardships, and again large scale migration took place, especially in the districts of Northern Bengal across the river Ganga."

Natural Calamities

In addition to the turmoil which alienated the tribals from their lands and their traditional rights, the forces of nature also played havoc with their lives. Famines and floods plagued the area. Prior to 1859, there was no information on famines. The first recorded famine occurred in 1868-69, followed by famines in 1873-74, 1893-94 and 1918. The severest was in 1897 when the death rate rose to 36 40 per mille (Singh 1975 : 30-33). Major Archer, one of the members of the Enquiry Committee on Coolie Emigration from Bengal Presidency (1836), while commenting on the conditions of existence of the tribals, noted that they were "necessitated to subsist upon the products of the chase (wild animals), reptiles and insects . . . to satisfy the cravings of nature and avert famine" (Saha 1972 : 41).

Out-Migration and In-Migration

As a result of the above factors, there was a steady exodus of tribals to other places in search of land or work. During the same period, thousands of outsiders poured into this area. The 1891 census shows that out-migration from Chota Nagpur totalled 421,000 while in-migration was 95,400. The 1901 census shows the respective figures as 282,000 and 121,300 and in 1911 they were 386,000 and 189,740. The bulk of the outflow was obviously the tribal population while those who moved in were non-tribals.

The Chota Nagpur division of Bihar (consisting of Palamau, Hazaribagh, Dhanbad, Ranchi and Singhbum districts) and Santal Parganas have remained the focal area of tribal migration to the adjoining states during the last two centuries. The rate probably accelerated with the opening of tea plantations in north Bengal and Assam since the last hundred years, up to 1950s. There is reason to assume that the process of out-migration goes on unabated. The following Table shows the declining growth of the tribal population in the region.

TABLE 10.1

Tribal Population as Percentage of Total Population

District/Division	1961	1971	Per cent Variation
Palamau	19.25	19.09	—0.06
Hazaribagh	11.25	10.99	—0.26
Ranchi	66.61	58.08	—8.53
Dhanbad	11.08	10.61	—0.47
Singhbhum	47.31	46.12	—0.12
Chota Nagpur Division	32.05	30.93	—1.12
Santal Parganas	38.20	33.08	—4.12

Source: Roy Burman 1979.

All the districts have shown a declining growth rate of tribal population in the 1961-71 decade. At the national level the growth of tribal population in the same decade has been 27.23 per cent as against the growth rate of 24.85 per cent among the general population. There is no reason to believe that the fall in the growth rate of tribal population has been due to natural causes. It is probably due to migration of tribals and in-migration of outsiders. According to the 1951 Census, while the tribal population in Chota Nagpur declined (as shown in Table 10.1), the in-migration figure was 787,500. Obviously, these in-migrants were non-tribals, and not tribal return migrants, or else the growth rate of tribal population would not have declined.

Munda, Oraon and Santal constitute the bulk of the tribal population of Chota Nagpur. But their rate of growth, and consequently their out-migration, has shown variations, as Table 10.2, which covers the period 1951 to 1971, will illustrate.

There is a wide variation in the growth rate of the population among the three large tribes during the two decades 1951-61 and 1961-71, in the various stages. Bihar and Orissa show a low growth rate for all the tribes in the decade 1961-71 (data for the decade 1951-61 are not available) except the Oraons who seem to have maintained the average growth rate. In West Bengal, however, the growth rate for all the tribes in the 1951-61 decade has been strikingly high, particularly among the Mundas. But in the next decade, except the Mundas, the Oraons and Santals show a declining or low rate of growth. The only reasonable explanation for this phenomenon can be that in the 1951-61 decade, a large number of these people had migrated to West Bengal, but in the next decade a number of Oraons and Santals had moved out of the state. The substantial increase in the Munda and Oraon population in Madhya Pradesh in 1961-71 decade can also be attributed to in-migration of these people from the adjoining areas of Bihar.

This fluctuating feature of the growth of population can been seen in Table 10.3, in the case of West Bengal. Migration is again the main factor causing the fluctuating growth.

The 1951-61 decade witnessed a phenomenal increase in the population of tribes of Chota Nagpur origin in West Bengal. Obviously, this large increase, ranging from 41.94 per cent to 226.32 per cent can only be explained by the inflow of population from the adjoining areas of Chota Nagpur and Santal Parganas. In the next decade, however, the pace of migration has been considerably limited except for the Bhumij, Malpaharia and Mahali. Some larger tribes such as Santal and Oraon show a decline in their numbers in this decade. There may be two explanations for this fluctuation. Assuming that the natural growth rate of population of these tribes have remained

TABLE 10.2

Growth of Population of Three Tribes during 1951-71

Srate	Munda			Oraon			Santal		
	Census Year	Population	Percentage of Variation	Census Year	Population	Percentage of Variation	Census Year	Population	Percentage of Variation
Bihar	1951	n.a.		1951	n.a.		1951	n.a.	
	1961	628,931		1961	735,025		1961	1,541,345	
	1971	723,166	+15	1971	876,218	+19.2	1971	1,801,304	+16.8
Orissa	1951	n.a.		1951	n.a.		1951	n.a.	
	1961	221,399		1961	129,061		1961	411,181	
	1971	222,447	+0.5	1971	164,619	+27.5	1971	452,953	+10.1
West Bengal	1951	83,005		1951	206,566		1951	845,422	
	1961	160,245	+93.05	1961	297,394	+43.97	1961	1,200,019	+41.94
	1971	198,701	+24	1971	291,173	—2.1	1971	1,316,980	+14.7
Tripura	1951	n.a.		1951	n.a.		1951	n.a.	
	1961	4,409	+21	1961	2,875		1961	1,562	
	1971	5,347		1971	3,428	+19.2	1971	2,222	+42.3
Madhya Pradesh	1951	n.a.		1951	n.a.		1951	n.a.	
	1961	4,114		1961	283,073		1961	n.a.	
	1971	14,007	+240	1971	370,652	+30 9	1971	n.a.	

TABLE 10.3

Growth of Population of Selected Scheduled Tribes in West Bengal in the Decades 1951, 1961 and 1971

Scheduled Tribe	1951	1961	1971	Percentage of Variation	
				1951-61	1961-71
Santal	845,422	1,200,019	1,376,980	+ 1.94	— 14.7
Oraon	260,556	297,394	291,173	+ 43.97	+ 2.1
Munda	83,005	160,245	198,701	+ 93.05	+ 24.0
Bhumij	84,476	91,289	169,426	+ 8.06	+ 48.5
Malpaharia	4,813	15,706	31,016	+226.32	+ 100.0
Mahali	26,338	28,233	47,247	+ 7.19	+ 31.9

constant, either a flow-back of the tribal population has taken place, or, a large number of them have migrated outside the State. In view of the decline in the proportion of tribal population in all areas of Chota Nagpur and Santal Parganas (Table 10.1), the second reason seems more plausible.

PATTERN OF MIGRATION

After having discussed the reasons for migration and the changes in population, we can now turn to the nature of migration, i.e., the type of economic activity the tribals were engaged in. The period covers the early stages of migration till the present.

At the time when the tribals were being steadly uprooted from their ancestral lands, new ventures requiring labour were beginning to spring up in Bengal and Assam. 1840 marked the beginning of indigo plantations in Bengal, the loop railway line project was started in 1854, tea plantations opened up areas in Assam from 1839 and in north Bengal (Dooars) from 1874 and finally large tracts of forest and marshy lands belonging to zamindars of the southern part of Bengal required clearing up. The common factor in these ventures was that they all required cheap labour. Naturally, the most tempting target was the hapless Adivasi who, due to alienation from land and natural calamities, had become a sturdy, hardworking (and submissive) person and who was able to live at a sub-human level of existence.

Indigo Plantations

According to W.W. Hunter, the first record of migration of tribals is found in 1835 (Hunter 168 : 225). Around that time there was a great demand for cheap labour in indigo plantations. The bulk of such labour was provided by the Santals. Hunter (Ibid. 226) observes,

> in every part of Nuddea (i.e., Nadia district) little communities of Santals, Dhangars, or other hill-men, may be found living apart from the Hindus, and preserving their national customs in the middle of the lowland population. Many indigo factories in the eastern districts have villages of these eastern highlanders. A family of them makes its appearance whenever manual labour is wanted, builds its leaf huts in a few days, and before the end of the month feels as much at home as if it were still among the mountains.

Risley notes that in 1872 they numbered 58,312 (Risley 1891:).

Eastern India Loop Line

This loop line, stretching over 200 miles (320 kms.), was being built in 1854. The line stretched along the outskirts of the Santal Parganas through Birbhum district and Rajmahal hills. This work created a demand for labour and here again, the Santals seem to have joined the labour gangs in large numbers (Dutta Mazumdar 1956: 26; Hunter 1868: 255).

Tea Plantations

In West Bengal, the Chota Nagpur tribals were mainly recruited to the tea gardens in Jalpaiguri district. This area is known as Dooars. The tea industry was started here in 1874. The methods of recruitment of labour to the tea gardens in Dooars differed from those adopted by planters in Assam, even though labour in both places was from Chota Nagpur and nearby areas. The tea industry started in Assam in 1839, while in Dooars it started thirty-five years later. The planters in Dooars had the advantage of learning from the mistakes committed by the planters in Assam.

Recruitment to tea gardens in Assam was mainly done by local recruiters who were called *arkatis*. These people used all sorts of dubious means to entrap unsuspecting tribals and send them off on a hazardous journey to Assam. These emissaries of the labour agent would stoop to any level to lure people away from their homes to the unhealthy tea districts. Young people and unhappy wives were given false promises of better marriage prospects. Through lying and trickery, they would get some people ex-communicated, leaving them no alternative but to go to Assam. Wives were kidnapped from their husbands and husbands from their families, leaving their members destitute. "Heart-rending tragedies which can rack everyone of the most sacred feelings of a human family, were enacted so to say, constantly in all villages" (Hoffman 1964 : 154-64).

The *arkatis*, with their notorious reputation, were not trusted by the tribals. The planters in Dooars entrusted their recruitment to *sardars*. These people were tea garden labourers. They were sent to the recruiting grounds between the months of October and February. Once they returned to the tea garden they resumed their work (DPA 1920 : 292). It was easier for these people to induce new recruits, by showing all the advantages of work and the prospects of ultimately settling down on independent holdings. The *sardar*, being an employee of a tea garden, was readily believed when he extolled the good points of tea garden work. Investigating the causes of migration to tea gardens, several older and retired workers, who were first generation migrants were interviewed. Quite a few of them had been lured to the tea gardens by the prospects of good wages and cultivable land—both of which proved false (Bhowmik 1981).

The tea industry in Jalpaiguri developed rapidly from 1885 onwards. Demand for labour increased and consequently, there was an increase in migration to the district. The following Table, based on 1951 *District Gazetteer*, shows the migration to the district from outside West Bengal.

TABLE 10.4

Immigration to Jalpaiguri District from outside West Bengal 1891-1941

Year	Actual Population	Immigrants
1891	433,334	44,329
1901	544,906	95,899
1911	661,282	152,174
1921	694,054	163,024
1931	739,160	158,757
1941	845,702	156,765

Source: Mitra 1951: lii or Census 1951: 264.

The above figures for immigrants include all immigrants to Jalpaiguri district from outside West Bengal. Separate figures for immigrants from different districts are not available in the Gazetteer or in the Census of 1951. The Gazetteer, however, notes that the bulk of immigrants from outside West Bengal were from Chota Nagpur and Santal Pargana (Mitra 1951: liii).

The censuses prior to 1951 give the break-up of immigrants from different districts, but the total number of immigrants shown in those censuses are not comparable with the figures given for the same period in the 1951 census. Prior to 1947, Jalpaiguri was a larger district containing sixteen police stations. Five of these were transferred to East Pakistan (now Bangladesh). The total immigration figures are therefore larger than those shown in the 1951 census. All the same, the earlier census figures will give us an indication of the volume of migration.

According to the 1901 census, there were 188,223 immigrants to Jalpaiguri district as compared to 143,922 in 1891. Most of them were enumerated in the Dooars region and "half of the immigrants (were) tea garden coolies from Chota Nagpur and Santal Pargana" (Census 1901: 66). The statements on migration in the census report show that in 1901, 80,436 immigrants were from Ranchi district and 10,562 from Santal Pargana (Ibid , Appendix I: iii). The 1921 census report notes that "the number of persons born in Ranchi and enumerated in Jalpaiguri district in the last census (i.e., 1911) was no less than 126,214" (Census 1921: 145). The report further states that "the most numerous people among the labour force (were) Oraons and Mundas" who had migrated from Chota Nagpur. In 1921, "90,348 coolies were born in Chota Nagpur and 20,018 in the district (i.e., Jalpaiguri) and these were also children of imported coolies" (Ibid. 389).

Migration to the tea estates was mainly 'family migration' and not of individuals. The tribals were encouraged to migrate with their families. The nature of production in the tea industry requires the participation of male and female labour. Moreover, since the planters wanted cheap labour, they had to have workers who would be permanently settled in the industry and who would be more or less cut off from their place of origin. Coercion and lack of alternative employment were two ways of keeping down the wage rate.

Rural Areas

The process of slow but steady infiltration of various tribal communities into rural areas of West Bengal from the adjoining areas of Chota Nagpur and Santal Parganas had begun in the nineteenth century. This migration followed two different streams. One followed the northerly course, across the river Ganga and spread over the rural areas of Malda, West Dinajpur, Cooch Behar and Jalpaiguri districts. The other followed a southerly course, through the district of Midnapur, entering from there, the lower regions of 24-Pargana district, which is known as Sunderban. Both streams avoided industrial and urban areas.

Though no actual yearly figure of migration is available, it seems the Santals preferred the northerly route and the Oraons and Mundas followed the southerly route (note—this is only in case of migration to rural areas and not to plantations). The *Birbhum District Gazetteer*, (1910 : 30), records that

> Many of the Santals, particularly from the northern portion, have, owing to the greater pressure on the soil, or to the dispossession by mahajans or Zamindars, either emigrated to *Barind*, a quasi-laterite tract of country in Dinajpur, Rajshahi and Bogra (now Bangladesh), or else to Murshidabad, there to break fresh country, to clear the jungles, and to make terraces of rice land, for doing which they possess singular aptitude, even in the most unpromising country.

Some years ago, one of the authors made a study of migration of Mundas to lower Bengal rural areas. It was pointed out that these immigrants, along with other tribals, had come to the Sunderban area to clear the forest and settle down there. The whole area had been divided into large tracts by the colonial rulers and was leased out to the highest bidder as his estate for collecting revenue (known as the Zamindari). The group of eighteen villages studied, were leased out in 1870 and 1898. Shortly after this period the Mundas immigrated to this area.

At the time of the study, the Mundas were mostly second or third generation immigrants. After leaving their homelands, their forefathers had lived in other places before settling down to their present abode. Almost all the one hundred and seventeen families, whose migration history was studied, had lived in more than two places before coming to their present site. Hence, migration had taken place in several stages and at each stage the tribals settled for a few years, before moving to the next place.

At each of their former sites of residence, the tribals had reclaimed land, which was either marshy or forest, for cultivation. After the land was made cultivable, the landlords and mahajans, manoeuvred to evict them from these lands. On being forced to leave their lands, the tribals had to move out in search of more unreclaimed land, and the process started again. The migrants moved southwards, keeping in line with the receding forest line. In other words, they kept reclaiming forests as cultivable land. In a few cases, however, they moved in order to be closer to their kinsmen.

When the tribals were evicted from their reclaimed land, they moved to the next place along with their families. Migration, in this case, was in driblets and not in great numbers. A few related families would move from one place to another. This form of migration caused a dispersal of the tribal community over a large area. This was unlike migration of tea plantations, which firstly, involved great numbers and secondly, brought about a concentration of tribal population in one area, namely, the tea gardens (Choudhury 1963: 26-32).

Types of Migration

From the data presented above, two distinct types of tribal migration emerge. These are firstly, migration to rural areas and secondly, migration to tea plantations. In both cases similar economic circumstances pushed the people out of their homeland. However, the difference between the first type of migration and migration to tea plantations is that, with the former their destination was diffused and uncertain. The tribals settled wherever opportunities arose. This type of migration could be termed as drifting or hopping migration. Tribals migrating to the tea districts had a clear, pre-set destination and they were recruited in a systematic manner by the planters' agents. We can call this type, destination-orientation migration.

On analysis the phenomenon of migration to the tea districts in terms of push and pull factors, we find that the push factor did operate. The tribals were forced to leave their homeland because of the reasons mentioned earlier. However, the pull factor, which presumes that they willingly went to the tea districts in search of a better life, was not present. The people had hardly any idea about the tea industry. They only knew that they were going to 'Bhutan', as Dooars was earlier referred to, where they would get regular employment. Moreover, the tribals went directly to their destination and were more or less permanently removed from their place of origin.

In the other type, migration to rural areas, people in small numbers settled on waste land and forests. They worked on the land, converted it to cultivable land and after a few years they were pushed out of the reclaimed area by the landlords or moneylenders. Instead of going back to their homeland, the tribals moved further away, in search of land and work. In course of time this movement in stages, caused a wide dispersal of tribal population among the dominant Hindu peasantry. Perhaps the factor of 'intervening opportunities' has primarily determined the character of this type of migration. Here also, removal of people from their place of origin has been more or less final.

Another variant of drifting population has been noticed in the rural areas of West Bengal. At the time of jute harvesting and paddy transplantation (between July and September) and paddy harvesting (between December and January) when the demand for labour is high and wages are better, a large number of tribals move out of their villages to seek temporary employment in other villages. We do not know the average distance travelled by such migrant labourers nor do we know what percentage of them go back home after their period of employment is over. Sociological factors associated with such seasonal migration appear to be different from that of permanent migration. Perhaps a closer study of this type of migration will give us an insight on rural to rural migration.

Sociological Consequences

The two types of migration have resulted in different types of socio-cultural adaptation of the tribals to their new environment. These can be dealt at two levels. Firstly, adaptation to their new type of work (such as in the case of tea garden workers) and the impact this has had on their social life. Secondly, adaptation to the environment and their commitment to their present homeland.

In the case of Dooars, by joining the ranks of plantation

labour, the Adivasis are engaged in an economic activity which is different from their traditional mode of livelihood. There is a hierarchy among the Adivasi workers which is based on the traditional occupations of the tribes. The Adivasis can be placed into two categories—cultivating tribes and non-cultivating or artisan tribes. The former claim themselves superior to the latter. Cultivating tribes are Oraon, Munda and Kharia. The rest fall into the latter category. In order to assert its superiority the former group observed certain taboos and concepts of pollution and purity, relating mainly to marriage and food. These tribal barriers have, however, been eroded to a large extent now, mainly as a result of their homogeneous economic activity. The tribals have, however, sought to retain their identity as a separate group, distinct from the local population.

The Adivasis have adapted themselves successfully to plantation work. The trade union movement, which is well developed among them, has helped fight for better wages and living conditions. Though, even today, wages of tea garden labour are lower than those in other industries in the State such as jute, cotton textiles, light engineering, the economic condition of the plantation worker is better than that of agricultural workers and most cultivators in the district. This is in contrast to the earlier state of affairs when wages of tea garden labour were lower than those of agricultural labour. Development of a strong trade union consciousness and their willingness to fight for better conditions of work show a greater commitment of these people to their industry. Politically too, the workers are active participants in influencing the affairs of the State.

There is a large spill-over of Adivasi population which has settled down as cultivators and agricultural workers. These people are descendants of former plantation workers. There are some differences between tea garden workers and those engaged in agriculture apart from the fact that the former are better off than the latter. Adivasi peasants interact more frequently with other communities, especially the dominant Hindu community. Many of them are share-croppers or labourers to Hindu landowners. This section has become more Hinduised than their brethren in plantations. They speak the local Bengali dialect more fluently than the plantation workers.

Adivasis in plantations have been more successful in maintaining their separate identity, mainly because of their numerical strength and because they live in close proximity to each other and hence, interact with each other more frequently. Changes in the social structure of the Adivasi communit , (i.e., erosion of status divisions), has also resulted in its awareness of being a distinct group. At the same time, though the Adivasis strive to retain their separate identity as a group, they are not necessarily antagonistic to the local population. Separatist movements, which are so predominant in Chota Nagpur, are almost non-existent among the Adivasis here. Attempts have been made in the past to form regional parties, such as the Jharkhand Party and Hul Jharkhand Party, but these have never been successful. The trade union movement is mainly responsible for this. Development of a strong political consciousness, as manifested in the growth of trade unionism, has on the one hand, helped them maintain their tribal identity and, on the other hand, helped them assimilate with their new homeland.

The picture is substantially different in other parts of the State where tribes from the same stock have migrated. Because of the dispersal and subsequent land alienation, they have been pauperised and have been reduced to being landless agricultural labourers. In a study on the Mundas in Sunderban conducted by Choudhury in 1956-57, it was found that their per capita landholding was about 0.33 acres, slightly more than that of scheduled castes and 'untouchables' (Choudhury 1961). In the regional caste hierarchy also, they were considered as low castes occupying a position with other Scheduled Castes, namely, Namasudra, Bagdi, Bhumij, etc. Very little of their tribal customs were retained. Culturally too, they had become more akin to the Hindus. Except for a few old persons, none could speak their original dialect.

This process of socio-cultural assimilation of tribals is continuing in all rural areas of West Bengal, though the rate of assimilation may vary depending on the number of people and local conditions. The recent Jharkhand movement in West Bengal, mainly in the south-western district of Midnapur, bordering Chota Nagpur, has been possible because of large concentration of migrant tribals in the area. It also reflects their desire for separation, possibly due to their extreme backwardness. Along with their political movements, attempts are now being made by the tribal leaders to revive some of their tribal customs and redefine their tribal boundaries.

CONCLUSION

Tribal migration to West Bengal from the Chota Nagpur and adjoining regions, which began in the second half of the nineteenth century was inspired by certain economic and political factors. The demographic factor by itself does not seem to have acted as the decisive force to motivate the people to migrate to unknown destinations. The type of migration and the number of migrants have, by and large, determined the nature of the resulting adaptive processes. In one instance, that is, in the destination-oriented migration, the tribals could maintain their language and identity; whereas in the other situation, they have become more Hinduised and assimilated into the regional socio-cultural matrix. In the political process also, tribals in plantations have gone in for trade unionism, whereas the tribals in the rural areas have given support to some contemporary peasant movements. In both cases, migrants have avoided urban industrial areas.

The question now arises, why did the tribals not migrate to growing urban centres, where new economic opportunities were available? The answer, we feel, lies in the fact that in voluntary and natural migration, though inspired by the 'push' factor (Bose 1973: 147-49), the direction of the migration stream depends not only on the value placed on the opportunities at the destination, but also on the nature of ecological compatibility that may exist between the places of origin and destination of migration. If the environment remains similar, as has been the case in rural areas of West Bengal, migration in drifts takes place. Even the destination oriented migration, to the tea gardens, the lure of a forest environment, with which the migrants were familiar, and the possibility of owning cultivable land after retirement, must have added strength to their decision to migrate to an otherwise unknown region.

Lastly, from another feature of tribal migration, namely,

absence of sex selectivity, we may generalize that when migration takes place with the family as the unit of migration, it tends to become permanent or, at least the duration of stay in one place tends to become longer provided, of course, conducive economic opportunities are available. In other words, ecological consideration and economic opportunities decide the volume and direction of migration; the family being the unit of migration, together with economic opportunities, decide the permanency of migration.

REFERENCES

Bhowmik, S.K., *Class Formation in the Plantation System*, Publishing House, Delhi, 1981.

Birbhum District Gazetteer, Calcutta, 1910.

Bose, Ashish, *Studies in Indian Urbanization*, Bombay, 1973.

Census (of India), *Bengal Report, Part I*, Calcutta, 1901.

Census, *Volume V, Bengal, Part I*, Calcutta, 1921.

Census, *Volume VI, Part IA (West Bengal, Sikkim and Chandernagore) Report*, Calcutta, 1951.

Choudhury, N.C., *Acculturation Among the Munda: A Study in Differential Change and Caste Formation*, Ph.D thesis (unpublished), Northwest University, 1961.

Choudhury, N.C., "Munda Settlement in Lower Bengal: A Study in Tribal Migration", *Bulletin of the Cultural Research Institute*, Calcutta, 1963.

DPA (Dooars Planters' Association), *Detailed Report of the General Committee*, Jalpaiguri, 1920.

Dalton, E.T., *Descriptive Ethnology of Bengal*, Calcutta, 1872.

Dutta, Mazumdar N., *The Santhals : A Study in Cultural Change*, Calcutta, 1956.

Haldar, R.D., *Supplement to Calcutta (Government) Gazette*, December, 1880.

Hoffman, Reverend, *Encyclopaedia Mundarica*, Patna (Reprint, Bihar Government) 1864.

Hunter, W.W., *Statistical Account of Bengal, Santhal Pargana District*, Calcutta, 1868.

Hunter, W.W., *Statistical Account of Bengal, Hazaribagh and Lohardaga Districts*, Calcutta, 1877.

Jha, G.C., *The Kol Insurrection of Chota Nagpur*, Thacker, Spink & Co., Calcutta, 1964.

Lee, Everett, "Towards a Theory of Migration", *Migration*, J.J. Jackson (ed), Cambridge University Press, 1969.

Mitra, Asok, *Jalpaiguri District Gazetteer*, Calcutta, 1951.

Risley, H.H., *Tribes and Castes of Bengal, Volume II*, Calcutta, 1891.

Roy Burman, B.K., Experts' Committee on Race Relations, UNESCO (in press), 1979.

Roy Burman, B.K., "The Post-Primitives of Chota Nagpur—Identity Dilemmas and Ethnic Relations", *Trends in Ethnic Group Relations in Asia and Oceania*, UNESCO, Paris, 1979.

Saha, Panchanan, *Emigration of Indian Labour, 1834-1900*, Peoples' Publishing House, Delhi, 1972.

Singh, K. Suresh, *Dust Storm and Hanging Mist : A Study of Birsa Munda and His Movement*, Firma K.L. Mukherji & Co., Calcutta, 1965.

Singh, K. Suresh, *Indian Famine 1967: A Study in Crisis and Change*, Peoples' Publishing House, Delhi, 1975.

PART FIVE

International Migration

11. *Indian Migration to South Africa*

THOMAS R. METCALF

Everyone knows that Mahatma Gandhi began his political career fighting for the rights of the Indian residents of South Africa. Gandhi's campaigns on their behalf were, however, but one chapter in the 120 year saga of the South African Indians. Gandhi's campaigns, too, halted only temporarily the deterioration in the status of the Indians, which resumed, and even intensified, in subsequent years of Afrikaner rule and apartheid legislation. Today the Indian community—now three-quarters of a million strong—is wooed both by the government, which seeks to strengthen its position by giving the Indians at least the appearance of inclusion in a new constitutional order, and by the black opposition, anxious to bury the explosive ethnic rivalries of the past in a united front against white rule. Yet the Indians still regard their position as profoundly unsatisfactory.

This turbulent history has made the South African Indians the subject of substantial scholarly attention (Palmer 1957; Huttenback 1971). Yet in all of this, surprisingly few writers have asked how there came to be an Indian community in South Africa in the first place, nor have they examined closely why they ended up sandwiched between white and black. I should like to take a closer look here at the Indians in South Africa during the formative years of the community, from the arrival of the first Indians in 1860 to the end of colonial rule, and of immigration, in 1911. In so doing we will have to examine two separate, but related, questions. First, why did certain Indians and not others migrate; and how did they choose South Africa? Gandhi, it must be remembered, came to South Africa, not to tone his political weapons, but to make money. Did his compatriots travel to South Africa for the same reason? Secondly, what was the character of the Indian's integration in South Africa's socio-economic order? Was it fixed at an early date, or did it change as South Africa developed? How well did the Indians as an immigrant community prosper in their new home?

The bulk of South Africa's immigrants came under the indentured labour scheme. The system operated in the same way for South Africa as for other colonies needing unskilled labour—most notably Mauritius, Fiji, and the Caribbean islands. In each case the Colonial Government, under the supervision of the Government of India, set up an emigrant depot, at a major port, and then employed agents to scour the interior districts for recruits. Once signed up the recruit was despatched overseas, bound to serve usually for five years as an unskilled labourer on a white-owned plantation at normal pay. On the expiry of his indenture, the labourer was free either to return to India, usually with a free passage guaranteed, or to remain where he was as a free man (Tinker 1974). In addition to these indentured (and ex-indentured) labourers the South African Indian community contained also a sizeable number (perhaps ten per cent in all) of voluntary migrants, drawn by the opportunities of trade and commerce (See Meer 1969, 15-21).

Let us look first at the indentured labourers. Where did these migrants come from, and why did they leave India? At the outset it is important to bear in mind that the various regions of India did not contribute equally to the emigrant stream. Except for brief occasions (such as the building of the Uganda Railway) Bombay presidency remained closed to indentured recruitment. Nor was this only a matter of legislative prohibition. Initially, in 1855, Natal had sought labourers from Bombay. The Indian Government, in denying this request, had pointed out that in Bombay there existed a steady demand for labour, that employers there were prepared to pay higher wages than South African plantation owners, and that in consequence it would be pointless to attempt to recruit indentured labourers in western India.[1] Even within the rest of India, however, all of which was open to recruitment, only certain districts supplied substantial numbers of overseas migrants. To some degree this was a result of informal agreement between overseas and inland recruiters, for the latter drew labour for the Assam tea plantations and Calcutta factories from Bengal and the tribal belt of southern Bihar.

By and large, overseas migrants were drawn from northern Bihar, eastern U.P., and the central and southern coastal districts of Madras. Why did these areas contribute almost all recruits? The answer at one level is obvious. These were areas, especially eastern U.P. and Bihar, of intense poverty and dense population, so that the poor and underprivileged were driven into the arms of colonial recruiters. Clearly poverty—the "classic" push factor in migration—lay behind this migration stream. But one cannot find a simple correlation between poverty, or overpopulation, and overseas migration. Even within the Gangetic plain, for instance, similarly situated districts often contributed unequally to the migrant stream. Basti and Gonda, but not Gorakhpur; Shahabad more than Saran. At the same time, some districts sent migrants to certain colonies and not to others. This phenomenon was most marked in the South. Ganjam supplied recruits for Burma, and Tinnevelly for Ceylon, while South Africa secured a vastly disproportionate number of its emigrants from North Arcot. Geographical propinquity, of course, explains some of this, e.g., the Tinnevelly-Ceylon flow. But there is no obvious reason why North Arcot should have supplied nearly one-third of Natal's inflow of south Indian migrants in the decade from 1901 to 1910.[2] Then too, over time, recruitment became increasingly narrowly focused. In the 1860s and 70s, Bihar contributed twenty per cent of North India's emigrants; by 1900 only five per cent or less came from Bihar and Bengal together. Indeed by 1910 the two districts of Basti and Gonda alone supplied almost one-quarter of the total emigrant flow from northern India.[3] These patterns of recruitment are not susceptible to easy explanation. Though, it was clear that it had much to do with the establishment of networks of recruitment: recruiters would tend to concentrate on those areas which were (so to speak) the most remunerative, while villagers who had friends and relatives already overseas might well be more tempted themselves to undertake the long and hazardous voyage.

As the pattern of emigration varied across the face of India, so too did the flow of migrants vary over time. During the last quarter of the 19th century, for instance, the annual emigration through Calcutta fluctuated wildly from about 10,000 to 30,000. These variations in flow seem, by and large, to have been determined by the interaction of two variables: the Indian harvest, and the colonial economy. At home, bad years reduced employment opportunities in the countryside, and so increased migration. Indeed the emigration reports, in almost macabre fashion, dwell fondly on years of drought and famine. But the critical determinant was colonial demand; and this in turn was set, as most Indian labourers worked in the canefields, by the world demand for sugar. When sugar prices were depressed, plantation owners required less labour. Precisely how these two factors—of the demand for labour, and its supply—fitted together to determine each year's migrant flow, however, is not a simple matter. Colonial quotas sometimes went unfilled for want of recruits, low caste agricultural labourers were not the only migrants, and recruitment did not invariably rise in the immediate post-harvest months. Indeed some observers have detected a subtle wave pattern *within* the cycle of the agricultural year.[4]

South Africa's voluntary (so-called "passenger") migrants differed dramatically from those of the identured labourers. Drawn to South Africa by the opportunities of trade and commerce, these men were largely Gujaratis of the established trading castes. For many in fact, South Africa was only a part of a wider network of kinship, and of trade, which radiated out of Kathiawar and Kutch to Bombay, Karachi, Mombasa and other ports on the rim of the Indian Ocean. Indeed some even moved beyond. The first Indian traders in Fiji, for instance, were two jewellers, originally from Kathiawar, who in 1906 went from Natal to that far-off South Pacific isle, which they had first heard of from Indians who had been there as indentured labourers (Gillion 1962: 133). Other Gujarati migrants to South Africa were agriculturalists, from areas such as Surat district. Particularly in the famine years of the later 1890s, lower caste Kolis and more substantial

Kunbis alike sought employment as labourers and traders in Africa. Nor was this migration wholly a product of destitution. As the Collector of Surat wrote in 1903, "The profits obtained in South and East Africa induced a large number of persons to go out after the [Boer] war. The number of persons from this district was about 1000 altogether; of no one caste in particular." The following year one taluqa alone was estimated to have sent 1350 migrants to South Africa. That these emigrants prospered can be judged from the volume of postal remittances. Estimated at four lakhs annually in Surat, these funds were used to liquidate debts, build houses, and buy land.[5]

Any assessment of indentured emigration must begin by asking whose interests it served. From the outset the Government of India had justified their participation in the recruitment of such labourers in terms of the benefits it brought India. These benefits were of two sorts: those that accrued to the individual emigrant, and those secured to India as a whole. It was accepted as a matter of course by all concerned with emigration that those who went overseas would be, as the Bengal Lieutenant-Governor noted, "happier and better off than they had ever been in their native land." The annual reports on emigration emphasized the amounts of remittances sent back by emigrants, and the cash and valuables brought back by those who returned.[6]

About the benefits of emigration for India opinion was mixed. For many the "main object" of emigration was to secure "the relief of overcrowded tracts" by drawing off their excess population. Committing the Government to a more systematic encouragement of emigration, Salisbury as Secretary of State in 1875 argued:

> Having regard to the greatness of our Indian population, and to the probability that, under the protection which the British Government affords from depopulation by war, and, as far as possible, from famine and other evils, that population must continue very greatly to increase, especially in the healthier and more densely peopled parts of the country where the numbers already press on the means of subsistence, and the lowest classes are at all times

> little removed from want, it appears to me that, from an Indian point of view, it is desirable to afford an outlet from these redundant regions into the tropical and sub-tropical dominions of Her Majesty, where people, who hardly earn a decent subsistence in their own country, may obtain more lucrative employment and better homes.[7]

Others were less sanguine. "The benefit to British India," the Bengal Lieutenant-Governor cautioned, "is of very limited character. . . . Let it be imagined that the number of some few tens of thousands (of annual emigrants) were doubled or quadrupled, were raised from 25,000, the present maximum, to 50,000 or 100,000. What effect would that have on a prolific people inhabiting the North-Western Provinces, Oudh and Behar, the total population of which may be set down at 65 million?" Still, he argued, the number of emigrants ought to be increased, for "such a result would manifestly conduce to the advancement of the British Colonial Empire, and must therefore command the earnest sympathy of every British officer." India in sum must labour so that the colonial empire might prosper.[8]

But why, one must ask, were Indians ever brought as indentured labourers to South Africa? That country, after all, unlike Mauritius or the sugar islands of the Caribbean, contained a substantial black African population. One might have expected that these reservoirs of manpower, which from the beginning provided the massive unskilled labour force required by South Africa's gold and diamond mines, could have met its plantation needs as well. Yet such was not to be the case. Geography and political economy together dictated a different outcome. The only area of South Africa suitable for plantation agriculture is the warm well-watered coast of Natal, facing the Indian Ocean. In the 1850s, the Colony of Natal, annexed to the British Empire only a decade earlier after the expulsion of the Boer trekkers, contained a straggling white population, mostly British, of under 10,000. Within the colony there lived in addition from 120 to 150 thousand Africans. Outside it, in the as yet unsubjugated areas of Zululand, resided perhaps a quarter of a million more Africans.

Surely these seemed to be labour in plenty. In fact there was almost none.

When first the Boers, and then the British, moved into Natal, its African population had been much reduced by the devastating wars of Shaka's Zulu state. Vast tracts of land were therefore unoccupied, and at once laid claim to by the earliest white settlers. By 1849, nearly two million acres of land had been divided among 360 claimants. A decade later fifteen men controlled 700,000 acres. For such landholders direct capitalist farming was out of the question. Indeed most were speculators, whose limited capital was wholly tied up in the purchase of land, and who sought a return in a later appreciation of its value. In the meantime these men—joined after 1860 by the Natal Land and Colonisation Company, with its mammoth holdings of half a million acres—found in the extraction of rent from African tenants the most attractive way of securing some return on their investment. They had no interest in measures designed to force Africans off the land and into labour relationships (Slater 1975).

While the spéculators were purchasing their broad acres, the colonial government was developing a policy of paternalist protection for the Africans flooding back with the end of the wars into the colony. Under Theophilus Shepstone the government set aside native reserves in Natal totalling two million acres, in which the authority of the traditional chiefs was reaffirmed and white settlement prohibited. Though inadequate to maintain twentieth century populations, these reserves were expressly made large enough at the time to avoid, in Shepstone's words, "so crowding the Kaffirs as to compel them to leave their location and seek work." Hence those Africans—by no means all of course—who settled on the reserves were able to resume their traditional subsistence agriculture. Their hut taxes, and other obligations, they could meet by the cultivation of commercial crops on part of their land. Indeed, with only a small and largely urban white population in Natal, many African cultivators found in the towns a ready market for their produce, and so prospered (Bundy, 1978: 166-82).

Between the reserves, with their bulwarking of the traditional economy, and the tenancies available on crown and speculators' land, the African had little incentive to labour for a wage for a white farmer. Yet plantation agriculture, above all such demanding crops as sugarcane, where the cane had to be cut as soon as it ripened, could not subsist with an erratic and uncertain labour supply. From the beginning, therefore, the white farmers had railed against the system of reserves. One Natal newspaper listed what was required: "the breaking up of the locations; a readjustment of native taxation; the cautious, but firm discouragement of the heathen customs that bind the Kaffir to an indolent and licentious life; a more comprehensive and stringent magisterial surveillance; . . ." and so on. But none of this was practical politics. So, encouraged by the example of Mauritius, where Indian labour had reversed the decline of its sugar industry since 1843, Natal's farmers turned in 1860 to the importation of indentured labourers from India (Thompson 1952).

The Natal sugar industry had its origins in the 1850s as one among a number of experiments designed to find a profitable export crop for the fledgling colony. In this competition sugar faced several disadvantages. Natal's mild subtropical climate, first of all, enforced longer growing seasons and lower yields than were found in the hotter, moister lands of the tropics. Nearby Mauritius, with its flourishing sugar industry, provided not only a model and a source of talent—for many of Natal's planters and their technical staff came from that island. It also provided its upstart rival, in an era of free trade, with stiff competition both in export markets and in South Africa itself. Nor was the local market, before the development of the Rand gold mines in the 1880s, at all expansive. Hence indentured labour was indispensable to a successful sugar industry. Growth in output went hand in hand with the increase in the number of Indian labourers. In 1859, the industry produced about 1,100 tons of sugar. A decade later, with 4,000 Indian labourers, total output had reached nearly 10,000 tons. By the mid-1880s, with a resident indentured population of some 10,000 Indians, sugar production had doubled, to 20,000 tons. The industry had of course its ups and downs. A severe depression in the mid-1860s led to a six year halt in the importation of Indian labour, while a sharp fall in the world price of sugar in 1884 precipitated declines in acreage and in Indian migration which were not made good till the early 90s. Sugar nevertheless always remained a mainstay of the Natal economy, and its major export crop (Hurwitz 1957; Osborn 1964). At the same time a steady flow of Indian migrants was transforming the colony's society. By the turn of the century the Indian community equalled in numbers that of the Europeans themselves.

As their contracts of indenture expired, most Indian labourers, foregoing their return passage home, took up employment as free residents of Natal. Many continued for some time to work in the cane fields. In 1888, free, or ex-indentured, Indians comprised some thirty per cent of the planters' labour force. J.R. Saunders, one of the largest planters, employed only free Indians (Watson 1960 : 105). Others worked for such public enterprises as the railways, or took up market gardening in villages near the plantations, or on the outskirts of Durban city. Such cultivation, wrote the Protector of Immigrants in 1895, was "the principal object in view" for Indians whose term of indenture had expired. During the 1890s, the acreage of land cultivated by Indians expanded dramatically—to 38,300 acres, or six per cent of the cultivated area; and they came to control the commercial cultivation of certain crops, above all tobacco, beans, and (in the coastal districts) maize. They also supplied almost the entire fruit, vegetable, and fish requirements of the Durban market, and were successful rice growers as well. Outside agriculture, free Indians gained employment as hawkers and domestic servants. The demand for Indian house servants is always constant, wrote the harassed Protector of Immigrants in 1887, and "hotel-keepers frequently apply to me for cooks, waiters, dhobies, etc."[9]

How far Indians prospered in South Africa is of course hard to judge. Certainly the figures for the wealth held in Indian hands show substantial increases during the later nineteenth century. Indian deposits in the Natal Government Savings Bank rose from £ 2,800 in 1885 to £ 23,300 in 1900; remittances to India over the same years rose from £ 580 annually to £ 1,854; while Indian owned property in the city of Durban increased in value from £ 14,000 to £ 50,000. Even taking into account the doubling of the Indian population over those fifteen years, it is clear that some Indians at least had amassed a financial stake in their new home. Of those who left the colony on the expiry of their indentures, from two to three times as many in the 1890s sought their fortune in the Transvaal gold fields, thereby renouncing their right to free passage, as took up that passage and returned to India. These emigrants to the mines, mostly cooks and domestic servants, obtained there, so the Protector of Immigrants reported, substantially "higher wages than they could possibly get in Natal."

As the South African Indian community prospered, they reaped the jealous hostility of the European settler. The Indian of course posed no threat to the livelihood of the sugar planter or rich exporter. But, unlike other areas of substantial Indian migration, East Africa, say, or the Caribbean, Natal possessed a white population large enough and poor enough to see in the Indian, once emancipated from plantation labour, a rival as trader and as agriculturalist. While little evidence exists that many Europeans were ever driven out of business by Indians, still the spectre of Indian competition helped precipitate the spate of discriminatory legislation that marked the mid-1890s in Natal, and drew Gandhi, the newly-arrived lawyer, into political activity. This legislation was directed explicitly at those who were the most prosperous, and hence most threatening. An Engligh literacy test put an end to free immigration; a residential tax of £ 3 per year was imposed on ex-indenture labourers to force them to return to India; while harassing restrictions were placed on the renewal of commercial licences to drive traders out of business. In short, Natal wanted indenture labourers from India, but none other. Behind this legislation lay the award of responsible government to Natal in 1893, and the consequent restriction of the franchise to whites. Natal was, like the Cape, Australia, and Canada, freed thenceforward from the tutelage of the Colonial Office in London.

This restrictive legislation placed the Indian Government in a most awkward and unpleasant dilemma. As Calcutta wrote to the presidency governments in February 1894:

> The Government of India would prefer the continuance of the existing system . . . and they have no sympathy with the

> views which would prevent any subject of the Crown from settling in any Colony under the British Crown. Nevertheless the facts have to be dealt with that such views exist; that they are likely to assume tangible form whether emigration is continued or not; that they have already gone far to exclude British Indian subjects from the Australian Colonies and from the Cape; and that they will probably end in keeping British Indian subjects altogether out of Natal, unless, while the party favourable to the maintenance of emigration is still in power in the Colony, a compromise can be arranged on . . . reasonable terms.[10]

In a word, in order to preserve the opportunity for indentured labourers to go to South Africa, the Indian Government agreed to condone the imposition of harsh restrictions on all classes of South African Indians. They insisted only that no ex-indentured labourer be compulsorily repatriated to India under penal sanction. Indeed they themselves suggested the alternative of a residence tax as a way of encouraging freed Indians to return to their homeland.

Yet politics are but part of the picture, for the years at the turn of the century witnessed a far-reaching transformation of Natal's economy, which was to catch up Indian and African alike. The growth of the mining industry, the spread of railways, and the quickening pace of urbanization in South Africa brought in their wake new markets, and a steady demand, for Natal's agricultural produce. This drove up the price of land, and at the same time made commercial farming profitable for white landowners, who had previously been content simply to rent land to Africans. As a result white absenteeism and block share-cropping fast gave way to a vast expansion of commercialized white agriculture. By 1909, the amount of land cultivated by Europeans, 85,000 acres twenty years before, had risen to 45 ,000 acres. Squeezed out of the market, and increasingly denied access to land, the African had no option but to take up employment, where his labour was needed, on the burgeoning white farms. The Land Act of 1913 drove home the principle that the African was to labour for the European, not to farm himself (Slater 1975: 275-81; Bundy 1978: 183-92).

For the Indian the effects of this vast upheaval were hardly less momentous. With local African labour now available, there was no longer any need to import indentured Indian labour. The ending of indenture is usually portrayed as a response to the agitation mounted by Gandhi in South Africa and Gokhale in India against the treatment meted out to the South African Indians. This ceratinly played a major part, for the Government could not ignore its increasingly vocal and well organized nationalist constituency. At the same time the Government of India itself became increasingly exasperated at the stiff and unyielding attitude of Natal, which refused to do anything to ameliorate the condition of its Indian residents. Lord Curzon was by far the most outspoken. As early as 1902, he had written:

> What Natal wants is our labour, but not our competition. They are willing to cringe for the one, but they are. . . adamant when it is a question of the other. I do not say that, in their own interests, they are wrong. . . . They are a self-governing Colony: and we cannot expect from them altruistic emotions. On the other hand we are equally the guardians of the interests of our own people; and I have not the slightest desire to increase the dimensions of what is already a "raw sore" on the surface of the Imperial body politic, for no other return than that a few more thousands of Indians shall be able to make their livelihood outside of India.[11]

Slowly, over the subsequent five years, the Government of India screwed up its courage, so that by 1908 it was willing to consider playing its one trump card: the ending of indentured recruitment unless the treatment of the Indians in South Africa improved. But by then it was too late. The threat was empty; for Natal's economy no longer required a steady flow of labourers from India. Indeed, before Calcutta could act, a Bill calling for an end to indentured immigration was introduced into the Natal Legislature. Planter opposition caused that Bill to be withdrawn. But the writing was on the wall. As the Natal Governor wrote:

TABLE 11.1

Indian Immigration to Natal

Year	Number	Year	Number
1860	1,226	1886-87	496
1861	368	1887-88	897
1862	—	1888-89	1,585
1863	1,021	1889-90	4,124
1864	1,979	1890-91	4,330
1865	1,320	1891-92	3,349
1866	534	1892-93	3,119
		1893-94	3,612
1867	—	1894-95	3,592
1868	—	1895-96	3,337
1869	—	1896-97	4,038
1870	—	1897-98	6,036
1871-72	—	1898-99	4,958
1872-73	—	1899-1900	4,590
1873-74	—	1900-01	6,312
1874-75	6,025	1901-02	7,763
1875-76	393	1902-03	6,140
1876-77	761	1903-04	4,601
1877-78	3,510	1904-05	9,436
1978-79	4,452	1905-06	8,108
1979-80	743	1906-07	10,049
1880-81	2,378	1907-08	6,664
1881-82	2,229	1908-09	1,722
1882-83	1,647	1909-10	2,935
1883-84	2,775	1910-11	6,257
1884-85	3,548	1911-12	3,401
1885-86	—		

TABLE 11.2

Indian Population of Natal

Year	Number	Year	Number
1862	1,184	1897	53,370
1866	5,041	1900	70,369
1870	4,858	1901	74,385
1874	6,787	1902	79,777
1877	12,823	1903	79,857
1880	18,877	1904	100,918
1883	26,978	1905	108,409
1885	29,357	1906	112,126
1888	35,270	1907	115,807
1891	35,411	1908	116,679
1894	41,142	1909	118,714

Source: Colony of Natal, *Statistical Yearbook for the Year 1909* (Pietermaritzburg, 1910), p. 3.

> The planters appear to anticipate that greater use may gradually be made of native labour, and also that by more and more Indians reindenturing the necessity for fresh importations will gradually decline so that eventually, if the matter is treated cautiously, it will be possible to stop the importation without the industries which have hitherto depended on it being ruined.[12]

Hence the Government of India—with domestic industry booming and wages at record levels no longer so concerned about the need of its own labourers for overseas employment—took the decisive step. Indentured migration to South Africa came to an end on June 30, 1911.

As the Governor of Natal had already predicted, this act did little more than hasten the inevitable. Initially, free Indians and those reindenturing to avoid the residential tax made good the shortfall. But as time went by even free Indian

TABLE 11.3

Value of Sugar Exported from Natal by Sea: 1854-1898

Year	£	Year	£
1854	2	1876	135,201
1855	16	1877	184,788
1856	483	1878	141,077
1857	2,008	1879	56,958
1858	3,067	1880	215,191
1859	8,368	1881	172,237
1860	32,005	1882	84,668
1861	19,415	1883	122,084
1862	21,178	1884	185,131
1863	26,153	1885	144,064
1864	94,372	1886	100,500
1865	76,519	1887	114,079
1866	66,191	1888	71,912
1867	70,563	1889	93,990
1868	90,387	1890	18,491
1869	145,982	1891	23,156
1870	111,068	1892	119,461
1871	180,686	1893	95,943
1872	153,987	1894	99,093
1873	161,854	1895	—
1874	159,115	1896	22,376
1875	169,815	1897	—
		1898	17,801

labour was gradually displaced by black in the cane fields. Ironically, the last great Gandhian strike, that of 1913, which spread from the mines to the sugar plantations, only hastened the process, for the planters found Indians no longer the docile

TABLE 11.4

Comparative Population Figures for Indians and Europeans in Natal

Year	European	Per cent of total	Indian	Per cent of total
1861	12,538	8.2	c. 1,100	1.0
1871	17,380	6.0	5,000	1.8
1881	28,480	7.6	20,200	5.3
1891	46,790	8.2	41,140	7.2
1904	97,100	8.8	100,900	9.1
1921	136,830	9.6	141,650	10.0
1936	190,550	9.9	183,660	9.5

labour force they had originally hired. By the 1930s, Indian farm labourers, had dropped from fifty per cent to a mere eleven per cent of the farm labour force. A decade later only two per cent of the labourers in the cane fields were Indian (Watson 1960: 133-57; Hurwitz 1957: 30-31, 44).

Where did the Indians go? Despite repatriation schemes and the repeated urging of the South African Government, they did not return to India. Some remained on the land as small scale farmers and market gardeners, or as supervisory staff on European farms. But by and large, despite the intense continuing white dislike of the Indian as trader and city-dweller, the Indians moved to the urban areas. By 1950, three-fourths of the community was urban, and spread through the professional, commercial and industrial sectors of the economy.

Hence, within less than a century of his arrival, the Indian's position in South Africa had been utterly transformed. Labourers, brought to Natal to make possible a prosperous white agriculture, the Indians found themselves first displaced from the plantation, and then from the countryside altogether. At the same time, with immigration from India stopped, they lost touch with their homeland. But the Indian nevertheless remained a member of an encapsulated community. To be sure it was increasingly prosperous, but it was still one which was walled off by apartheid from black and white alike. Whether this precarious isolation will come to an end in a multi-racial South Africa, or whether the Indian will simply exchange one hostile master for another, time alone will tell.

NOTES

1. Secretary to Government of India to Colonial Secretary Cape Colony, 2 January 1857, NAI Legislative Dept., Papers Relating to Act XXXIII of 1860.
2. For the figures for each district see the Annual Reports on Emigration from Madras in NAI Emigration proceedings.
3. Figures for all of northern India are given in the Annual Reports on Emigration from Calcutta in the NAI Emigration proceedings.
4. See, e.g., G.A. Grierson's report on the recruitment of emigrants in Bengal, NAI Emigration Proceedings August 1883, No. 9-15; and Major Pitcher's report on the North-Western Provinces and Oudh, February 1883, No. 1-12.
5. Collector Surat to Commissioner Northern Division, 22 September 1903, Assistant Collector Chorashi to Collector Surat, 28 July 1904, and Collector Surat to Commissioner N. Division, 14 September 1905, Bombay Revenue Department.
6. Minute of Lieutenant-Governor of Bengal, 11 September 1875, Bengal Emigration Progs. November 1875, No. 9-19.
7. Despatch No. 39 of 24 March, 1875, India Office Records L/PJ/1052, p. 133.
8. Minute of Lt. Governor of Bengal, 11 September 1875, *op. cit.*
9. The information in this and the following paragraph is taken from the Annual Reports of the Protector of Indian Immigrants, Natal, between 1886 and 1900.
10. Secretary to Government of India to Secretaries to Govt. of Bengal and Madras, 28 February 1894, NAI Emigration Programmes, March 1894, No. 11.
11. Note by Curzon of 24 May, 1902, NAI Emigration Programmes, June 1902, No. 21-22.
12. Governor Natal to Secretary of State for Colonies, 8 May 1908, NAI Emigration Programmes, September 1908, No. 21.

REFERENCES

Bundy, C., *The Rise and Fall of the South African Peasantry*, University of California Press, Berkeley, 1978.

Gillion, K.L., *Fiji's Indian Migrants*, Oxford University Press, New York, 1962.

Hurwitz, N., *Agriculture in Natal 1869-1950*, (Natal Regional Survey, Vol. 12), Cape Town, Oxford University Press, 1957.

Huttenback, R.A., *Gandhi in South Africa*, Cornell University Press, Ithaca, 1971.

Meer, F., *Portrait of Indian South Africans*, Durban, 1969.

Osborn, R.F., *Valiant Harvest*, Durban, South African Sugar Association, 1964.

Palmer, M., *History of the Indians in Natal*, Oxford University Press, Cape Town, 1957.

Slater, H., "Land, Labour and Capital in Natal : the Natal Land and Colonisation Company, 1860-1948," *Journal of African History*, Vol. XVI, 1975.

Thompson, L.M., "Indian Immigration to Natal (1860-1872)," *Archives Yearbook for South African History*, Vol. II, 1952.

Tinker, H., *A New System of Slavery*, London, 1974.

Watson, R.G. T., *Tongaati*, Hutchinson, London, 1960.

12. *Indians in England: A Study of the Interactional Relationships of Sending, Receiving and Migrant Societies*

ARTHUR W. HELWEG

An examination of the situation and behaviour of Indian immigrants in Britain with the existing literature on international migration (Bryce-Laporte 1980; Helweg 1979; Kritz, Keely and Tomasi 1981 and McNeil and Adams 1978) reveals that some new models are needed to understand the actions of international migrants of the post-World War Two era. Rapid transport, telegraph, telephone and postal services have facilitated communication with the community of origin. People can travel from one side of the globe to the other within two days and, a phone call or telegram can reach many remote areas within hours. An expatriate can now remain closely involved with his home community while residing thousands of miles away—he can continue to be an active participant in local affairs in spite of the vast distance separating him from his place of origin.

Migrants have generally wanted to maintain their native culture and interest in their home area. The communications revolution has helped facilitate the on-going transactional relationships between a sending society and their members residing elsewhere. Researchers are increasingly aware of the importance the cultural homeland exerts on the expatriate community (Porter 1975).

International migration of the previous century was perceived by scholars in the United States as a one-way movement with people leaving Europe and Asia for North America and not returning (Gmelch 1980: 135-137). Undoubtedly there was return migration, but it was generally ignored since it was sporadic. However, the resettling in or visiting their community of origin has increased significantly in the past thirty years. The East Indians of America and England, probably average one, visit home every four years; and, these frequent returns coupled with the recently devised rapid and efficient banking methods, (allowing huge sums of capital to be transmitted with ease across political boundaries) have had a phenomenal effect on certain areas of emigration. In fact, one aspect alluded to in this article which needs to be examined further, concerns the effect of emigration on a sending area; or more specifically, how Punjabis abroad contribute to the phenomenal economic progress of their home region in India. These expatriots have transmitted vast amounts of money, technology, and different cultural perceptions to their alluvial homeland. Yet, the emigrant factor is not mentioned in the literature on economic development concerning Punjabis in particular or Indians in general.

Development of Migration Studies

Traditionally, migration studies have concentrated on four broad categories which are still being considerably researched: 1) causes of population shifts, 2) social-psychological concerns of immigrant adaptation, 3) social problems caused by immigration, and 4) the nature and dynamics of migrant groups and individual social networks (Bryce-Laporte 1980; Jackson 1969; Jansen 1970; Kasdan 1970 and Shaw 1975). These topics are beginning to be dealt with on three levels of analysis: 1) the macro-level, which views migration in a world-wide context, 2) the mid-range level, with its focus on the adaptability or assimilation of the immigrant community to the host society, and 3) the micro-level with its emphasis on the individual. Yet, the vast majority of migrant studies and theory focus on just the interaction between the migrant and host communities on the mid-range level, especially in models concerning ethnicity (Glazer and Moynihan 1975 and Barth 1969).

The factors influencing a migrant individual or group to

adopt certain behavioural patterns can be the global economic situation (macro factor) the perceptions of the sending or host community (mid-range aspect) or an idiosyncratic perception (micro component); or, any number of combinations within this continuum). Although this study does not illustrate all of the possible interrelationships and factors involved in evaluating migrant behaviour, it does, among other things, show that the relationships and weight of different aspects influencing migrant actions vary over time and according to the situation of each society. The dynamic aspect must be considered.

Although lip service is sometimes given to the effect emigration has on the sending society, there is a dearth of knowledge concerning the ramifications of population out-flow on the place of origin (Connell, Dasgupta; Laishley and Lipton 1976: 3) which includes the effects and processes of return migration. It is only in the last fifteen years that the field of migration studies has begun to even consider both ends of population movements (Gmelch 1980: 135-137). More recently, the works of Hendricks (1974), Jeffrcy (1976) and Helweg (1978, 1979) have begun to show how the home society can have an on-going influence on their emigrants and indirectly influence the host community. And this effect may last for generations.

Nancy and Theadore Graves (1974) have laid a theoretical base for understanding the three-way interactional relationship between the host, sending and migrant groups. They argue that to comprehend the behaviour of expatriates the interaction of the three social arenas must consider: 1) the sending community, 2) the migrant group, and 3) the receiving society, for, a three-way diachronic process is taking place.

> The adaptive responses displayed by each of these three groups affects the problems confronting the others and the options open for their solutions. Thus the more holistic our view of the adaptive process, the more realistically we can understand and assess what is happening within each (Graves and Graves 1974: 118).

By examining migration from the holistic view, many of the issues that were formerly treated separately will be understood in a more systemic framework where they can be analyzed in their interrelationships. In other words, when one takes the broader approach, it is realized that the sending society, also has an on-going influence on the migrant and host groups.

The following data and conclusions will build on the framework of Graves and Graves and apply it to the behaviour of the Punjabi Sikhs in England, for the home, host and migrant groups of the England Sikhs have continually influenced each other directly or indirectly over the past thirty years. However, the degree and nature of this interactional impact has varied over time.

It must be kept in mind that the analysis presented here focuses only on three communities at the macro and mid-range level. However, in some cases, a proper understanding of migrant actions may involve more. For example, some Indians who lived in East Africa, moved to Britain, then shifted to Canada and finally settled in the United States, have many more influences than just one sending, receiving or migrant group. Also, the global political and economic situation influences their actions. The understanding of migrant behaviour is very complicated.

The People Studied

There are about one and a quarter million people of South Asian, origin in Britain. This category includes those from India, Pakistan, Bangladesh, Ceylon and East Africans of Asian heritage; and, they form about 2.2 per cent of Great Britain's population (Hiro 1979: 217). About 600,000 of these are Sikhs from India's Punjab (Helweg 1978 : 14). Sikhs and other colonials from the subcontinent started appearing in English universities around 1870, soon after Queen Victoria declared herself Empress of India (Hiro 1979 : 217-219) These numbers slowly increased although large numbers also returned home.

The period between the two World Wars was a time of economic austerity in the United Kingdom and although some

Sikhs were peddlars in the Hyde Park and East London areas, there were other Indians in the professions, such as medicine, who had a favourable reputation (Mehta 1972).

It was the post-Second World War era which brought Sikhs from rural Punjab and other South Asians to England in significant numbers. Their migration to England in the early 1950s consisted primarily of males with varied motivations as to why they shifted residence; but, considering Britain a place of financial opportunity was certainly a major criteria for many (Helweg 1979: 20-35). Like other Asian and West Indian immigrants, they aided United Kingdom's industry in the post-war recovery period by supplying cheap and needed unskilled labour. Of course, having such inexpensive manpower available may have hurt England in the long run for she did not feel the urgency to modernize her factories and make them efficient—she is presently paying a price for that mistake.

By 1960, when it was realized that immigration prohibitions in the U.K. would be implemented, relatives, friends, wives and children of those South Asians in England were sponsored to the United Kingdom. They wanted their friends and relatives to enter before the immigration option was closed. Thus, the Indian community of Gravesend, the focus of this study, and the Asian population in Britain expanded. The expulsion of Asians from Uganda in 1972 caused many more Indians to settle in the U.K.; swelling their ranks to the present count.

Gravesend, Kent, is located on the outskirts of London's industrial sector. Like other port cities in England, it has had a few Indian living there intermittently. Gravesend, with its paper mills, cable, rubber, printing, cement, engineering, ship building and ancillary industries, makes for a highly industrial region and attractive for immigrants to settle.

By 1978, Indians in Gravesend comprised about 7,000 or 13 per cent of the community of 55,160. In 1971, a breakdown of Gravesend's South Asians, termed by me "Gravesindians" was as follows: 20 per cent Ramgardiahs (some of whom came from Kenya), 220 Pakistanis, 20 West Indians, a couple of families from Malta, and the rest were Sikh Jats from the rural Doaba region of Punjab. These Jats knew each other directly or indirectly before leaving India. Due to the 1972 expulsion of

Asians from Uganda, the East African Indians segment increased. Around 1977, some Chinese arrived and opened about four family restaurants.

By the end of the decade, Gravesindia was fast losing its categorization as an immigrant community for forty-five per cent of its members were born in England. The Asian cultural emphasis on education and obtaining skilled technical capabilities by the Indians was being manifest, in that, eleven Asian doctors and one-third of the hospital staff were of Asian origin. Also, there were two accountants, twelve engineers, two bank clerks, seven school teachers, two clerks, one in the Bureau council and the other in the post office, one Indian social worker and one Asian occupational therapist.

Commercially, the Indians made their impact: owning six of sixteen chemist shops, four pubs, one automobile repair garage, a number of green grocers, two laundromats, a bicycle shop, an electric goods shop, four grocery stores, five driver training schools, three market stalls, one children's boutique, one clothing factory, two construction companies and even a tobacco and sweet shop.

The people of Punjab, from where most of the Gravesindians originated, have a history of mobility and flexibility. Located on the invasion route into India, they have often had to leave their homes or adopt new methods to survive. They have continually been exposed to new concepts originating from outside their groups; and, emigration has been one tactic traditionally practised in coping with or enhancing family circumstances. Under British rule, the Sikhs were favoured and used extensively in the armed forces. Also a great deal of investment was made in the Punjab under the Raj. Consequently, there was often a closer relationship between the British and Punjabis—a situation which periodically deteriorated. But, the basis was laid for the Sikhs to look to England for enhancement by migrating to their former colonial ruler.

Presently Punjab is the most prosperous region in India, boasting the highest per capita income (Rs. 1482), percentage of irrigated areas (79 per cent), agricultural production (82 per cent of its total area is under cultivation), number of tractors (60,000), milk yield and per capita milk consumption (production averages 2.45 kg. and 4.31 kg. per day from cows and buffaloes respectively and average per capita consumption is 443 grams per day), life expectancy (66.8 years for males and 61.9 years for females) and wages paid for agricultural labourers (Rs. 1450 annually); also, the first to launch an integrated rural development programme. One question that comes to mind is why did emigration to England centre on India's most prosperous region? Perhaps, that is the wrong question for probably it was emigration that made Punjab lucrative.

The village of Jandiali, Punjab, from which many Gravesindians and other Sikhs emigrated to Britain is located about halfway between the cities of Jullundur and Ludhiana. This village has sent over two-thirds of its 1,608 members to England. Other emigrants are scattered around in the north Indian States of Rajasthan and Uttar Pradesh with some in New Zealand, Australia, Canada and the Philippines. Since 1972, labour opportunities have developed in Dubai, Iran and other Middle Eastern countries. While most Jats went to England, the bulk of Chamar males and specialist castes grabbed the chance for economic enhancement in the oil rich countries.

The effect of emigrant remittances is certainly present in Jandiali. Of its 646 acres of land, 555 are irrigated primarily by tube-wells (almost all of which were financed by emigrant money). Jandialians also control approximately 215 acres of land in neighbouring villages and over 1,000 acres in the adjoining States of Rajasthan and Uttar Pradesh (most of this land was also purchased by emigrant capital). The casual visitor sees about 20 new multi-storey farm houses outside of the village that are estimated to be worth about Rs. 100,000 each. The dates inscribed on most of these elaborate structures range from 1961-1965, indicating that they were built with money from England after the 1950 emigration boom. A few England returnees, on holiday, are visible around the village in their gaudy attire and they frequently interject English words into the stream of Punjabi conversation. Compared to surrounding villages, Jandiali has better houses, (eight or more with flush toilets), more paved roads, newer school buildings and a huge Gurdwara, which cost Rs. 1.3 lakhs (it, however, was vacuous of people); and they have invested over Rs. 8 lakhs in other industries. Emigrant remittances have certainly helped enhance the prosperity of the village; but the community is much smaller, of the 400 left, there are few men under 40, the population is primarily women, children and old men.

Gravesindia, Gravesend and Jandiali Interact

The interaction of the receiving, sending and migrant groups of this study can be demarcated into four periods: 'Premigration', 'Freedom', 'Conflict' and 'Settlement'. Although the exact point where one period ends and another begins may not be precise, the important factor to consider is the changing nature and influence of the three-way interactional process. And, when applying this model to other communities, it must be realized that every immigrant group's process of development may or may not follow the pattern set forth here—a period may be skipped, or the process may not follow through completion. But, a classification scheme is being set forth which needs to be considered in light of other experiences.

Premigration is the period before the migration process develops. It is when minimal or no population movement has occurred. The information transmitted between the sending and receiving groups is frequently inaccurate, stereotypical and/or exaggerated. In the case of both the Punjabis and the Britons, there had been direct and indirect influence before the post-World War Two movement of manpower. Britain had ruled India for several hundred years and the English considered South Asians as their subjects who needed white rule—a common attitude among dominating groups. Writers like E.M. Forster and Rudyard Kipling, along with English civil servants reinforced the concept of the 'white man's burden'' where colonization was interpreted paternalistically—it was claimed that those subjugated were being helped by British control and should be obliged. The Indians were seen by the British as inferior. However, the exceptions were the princes who were esteemed in England; and the Indian students and professionals, such as doctors, who were frequently given favourable recognition. But paternalism and superiority continued to dominate the British attitude towards South Asians.

Punjabi villagers, had a mixed perception of the British. The Punjabis admired the abilities and strength of the English in their rule of India. They respected the stable political and economic situation brought on by the Raj. The colonizers had invested heavily in Punjab as opposed to other areas, making it a prosperous area; but there were times of dissatisfaction which resulted in movements like that of the Ghadr party,[1] in which a few Jandialians had participated. The villagers felt a sense of independence and maintained that the English may have controlled the Central Government but Jandiali was sufficiently insulated from domination: therefore they proudly claimed that "they had never been ruled by a foreign power"; There were, however, certain aspects of British behaviour which the villagers considered polluting and unhygienic, such as the English using both tubs and toilet tissue—both of which in Indian culture were considered unclean. Even at the turn of the century many Indians who ventured abroad were placed in the polluted category whether they went for higher education or economic enhancement. At the same time associating with the colonial rulers, going to England, or being able to manipulate the British, afforded an individual tremendous advantage in economic and political spheres. There may have been a dichotomy of a respect-contempt perception of the English; but, associating with these rulers gave a prestige that acted as a positive factor for choosing Britain when the option of emigration was being considered. There was a "colonial mentality" present where subjects regarded their administrators as prestigious—even though they claimed superiority and sought independence from them.

Immediately before the stream of emigration started in 1950, the situation in both the United Kingdom and Punjab influenced the decision for Jandialians to leave. In the case of the village, resources were severely taxed due to a massive influx of refugees from the western sector of Punjab. In 1947, the Muslim state of Pakistan had been created, resulting in one of the largest mass migrations in history. Muslims went to their new nation while Hindus and Sikhs were forced to start life anew in independent India. The region around Jandiali was crowded with refugees who desired help from more fortunate relatives and friends already residing there. Thus, emigration, which was historically an established behavioural pattern for Punjabis, was a consideration.

In England, World War II had left a shortage of manpower and labour was needed to build and maintain its industry. Britain's need for workers was only part of the incentive for Jandialians to emigrate. The information received by the villagers portrayed the United Kingdom glowingly, a country where wealth could be achieved with minimal effort.

Newspaper reports printed in Hindi, Gurmukhi, Urdu and English exaggerated the prosperity and opportunities abroad without considering deficiencies. The villagers were impressed by the few Indians who had been in England. In Punjab, the emigrants visiting home, would show off and spend lavishly, giving the impression of having limitless assets. They wore new clothes, bought just prior to leaving the U.K. for India, and spent money on relatives and friends in Jandiali as if the assets were nexhaustable. Those emigrants returning, especially in the 1950s, were reported in the press and their 'successes' abroad were greatly inflated. A clerk in the post office was referred to as a 'postal official', a sweeper in Bowater Scott Paper Company was an 'employee at Bowater's', a typist for the local burrough council was a 'member of the burrough civil service'. Later on, the myth of England as a paradise was further supported by the tales of travel agents and smugglers who wanted client fees.

The migrant's position in England may have been lowly, but in Jandiali, he was a *bara sahīb*, an important person whose emigration not only increased his esteem but also of his kin group. The tales of wealth and success in Britain were compatible with the experiences of the villagers. They had seen the power of the Raj and recalled lavish parades as well as the grand life-style of British in India who had lived in opulent houses, belonged to exclusive clubs, had numerous servants and travelled in magnificent entourages.

The result was that emigration automatically afforded males (initially females remained behind) and their family *Mann* or honour, a valued cultural goal of the Punjabis. Even if the migrant occupied a lowly position in England, he had prestige in Punjab for the myth developed that no one in

England ever failed. Escaping from a bad marriage, stigma of a low family, or just gaining wealth motivated people to leave, but Great Britain was the prestigious place to go and ranked over United States, Canada, or Australia. Besides, British immigration laws were more lenient and it was easier for many Indians to enter Britain than any other country.

Emigration was helped by the head man of Jandiali. He shrewdly saw a way to give individuals and groups pride while at the same time alleviating the pressure on local resources. Wisely, he opened the village's cooperative bank for loans to send Jandialians to England because he was sure the debt would be repayed to uphold *Mann* in the village. Some families pooled resources to send a capable member out, others used bank loans, but land was seldom sold or mortgaged for the purpose. Thus, the movement of males to Britain started. Britain was chosen because its immigration laws made it accessible and the colonial experience had helped to afford it a prestigious place to go. An ideology developed that made the traditional option of emigration desirable. Besides England needed unskilled labourers. One the other hand, the partition of India had taxed local resources so that emigration was considered and the knowledge of Britain made it a place to consider strongly. In England the Punjabi was merely a low unskilled labourer. But, to the people of his home village, he was someone to be respected, an important individual who by emigrating had raised his family's esteem, therefore, other villages wanted to follow his example.

The Freedom Period is that stage where the men emigrate and children remain behind. Thus, the immigrant community is composed primarily of males and as a result lacks the social and cultural constraints, goals and norms of a balanced group. During this stage, the migrants perceive themselves as sojourners and plan to return to their homeland when their fortune is secure. Because their stay is meant to be temporary, the migrants work insatiably hard, live frugally and remain apart from their host community. The past literature is not clear as to the degree of influence and involvement migrants have on their community of origin; but, this study reveals it is extensive and on-going.

In the past if the freedom period lasted for a long period,

it resulted in a deculturalized community that lacked a sense of permanence, responsibility and goals. Sexual abnormality and anomie had abounded—as the results of the indentured labour system of the 19th and 20th century illustrate (Tinker 1974 and 1977). The rapid and efficient transportation and communications with the home society has changed the behaviour during this phase. The situation of emigrants in the Middle East will be an illustrative drama to watch.

During this period, the host society does not consider the immigrants as part of their community and local issues are considered without consulting the migrant population. This is a time, however, when the chain migration process starts, that is emigrants prefer places where their relatives, friends or villagemates can guide them.

Since the migrant plans to return to his place of origin, he invests his surplus earnings in his home society increasing the economic resources in the region. Initially it may be to help needy family members improve their standard of living but later is to acquire economic assets, especially land. Furthermore the emigrant invests in conspicuous consumption, such as bigger house for his family, and public works for the benefit of the village, such as building a school or hospital. Lastly, there are investments in industry and or business activity. All these inputs may not take place during the freedom period, but may carry over into later stages.

Emigration, during this stage and subsequent periods, may challenge and alter the existing social order. Emigrants and those associating with them generally have the economic and political resources to force their will on the ruling group. There develops in the home community an ideology of emigration being a social goal as it automatically enhances the individual and his kin group. All these help to challenge the existing cultural and social order of the sending community—a situation that remains as the emigration process continues.

In the case of the Jandiali-Gravesend migration process, the Freedom phase was from 1950 through 1960 when India-England migration was free of governmental policies restricting population movements between these two countries; and, the periodical obstacles that arose were easily circumvented by the Sikhs. Males left their wives and children in Jandiali with the idea of entering Britain temporarily, acquiring a fortune, and returning to India with sufficient assets for them and their kin to live a life of wealth and ease.

Indians during this time relied heavily on the subjective advice of friends and relatives. The starting of Gravesindia came about when the enterprising Sikh, Bhuta Singh, hearing of the need for labourers to build an oil refinery on the Isle of Grain, which is near Gravesend, recruited Indian labourers. Responding to available economic opportunities, many Punjabis heeded his offer to be their employment agent and followed him to Gravesend to work; and, he, (for a fee) provided jobs, housing, and took care of bureaucratic requirements. One of these early labourers, Bhajan Singh of Jandiali, began encouraging his friends and villagemates to come to Gravesend and take advantage of the opportunities available there. Being a sponsor would give him prestige at home in England.

Indian men arriving in England in those early years were aided by other Sikhs, already present. South Asians relied heavily on each other rather than English institutions. For example, the Shepherd's Bush Gurdwara helped new arrivals find jobs and lodging. Other established villagers often took in wandering South Asians from the streets. They protected each other's reputation and did not write back to India concerning the detrimental behaviour of a friend or acquaintance unless two men were hositle enemies. Bhajan Singh gained respect among people in Jandiali, as well as in Gravesend for the way he aided fellow Sikhs to settle in Gravesend. Jandialians were grateful for his help to their sons or relatives: thus, when Bhajan Singh took a stand on a village affair, whether it be the location of a school or Gurdwara, his wishes were usually followed, even though he lived in England. The people in Jandiali were indebted to him. Jandialians in Gravesend felt so much gratitude toward Bhajan that whenever he solicited contributions for a village project, they generously contributed and furthered Bhajan Singh's esteem. Thus, large amounts of money came from Britain for projects that benefited the village as a whole.

Since England was considered a temporary abode, men worked insatiably hard, logging 90 hours a week. They wanted to earn money fast, and when they learned that the white English did not like to work on weekends, the concern was not with how much money they earned per hour, but how much was acquired totally. It there was a job that paid £ 1-50 per hour without overtime and another that paid only £ 1-00 with overtime options on weekends, the latter would always be taken. As a result, some chose difficult piece work over steady employment. Although construction work did not have the security of a factory job, it would pay more money, which would enable their return to Punjab sooner with prestige and assets.

The men lived in crowded conditions—thirty or more men to a three bed-room house, often men slept in shifts, when one left for work another took his cot. Their social centre was the Pub, where they quenched their thirst with a glass of beer or ale. The arrangements were meagre, but it was temporary and there was promise of greater prosperity and power upon returning to Punjab.

Men were so busy making their fortune that caste rules were often overlooked, and proud high caste men performed demeaning jobs which involved cleaning latrines and sweeping cigarette butts—work they would never do in Punjab. If they had to work beside a low caste individual, it was tolerated as they only wanted money and enhancement of social position in their home society not in England. For expediency many Sikhs discarded their turbans and shaved their beards because employers hesitated to hire a man with long hair, which was hazardous if caught in machinery. In sum, for these Punjabi males in England, their primary goal was making money, which would lead to enhancing prestige in India. Caste family and other issues were important only as perceived in their home villages.

It was also a time when sexual norms were absent and there was a lack of legal control. Some individuals were exploited, and violence and illegal means were the only way to restitute grievances. The Sikhs did not know how to use the British legal system and that of Punjab was not available to them. In the United States, such a period resulted in the development of organized crime which exists to the present day. Although that was not the case among the Punjabis in

England, factional behaviour, with allegiance to one particular individual, became a precondition for survival.

The British or host community in Gravesend did not view the Punjabi Sikhs as part of their community. And the Sikhs, being small numerically and living in poor ghettos, were no threat to the English. The Gravesindians were temporary labourers who resided in an isolated section of town, minding their own business; and, as long as they stayed in their place, there was no problem. In other parts of England things were not as calm. This was manifested by the 1958 race riots, and the increasing annual influx of ex-colonials from the New Commonwealth which reached 34,410 in 1959; causing race relations to become an issue and a public concern.

English employers liked these hard working Asians, who, according to English standards, worked under difficult conditions without complaint. Thus, when a Punjabi asked his boss to hire a friend, the foreman generally complied. The manager could put the immigrants in harder and more taxing jobs than the English locals would take. In addition, with Indian labourers, firms did not have to provide good working conditions. The unions did not object to the Asians because of the shortage of labour—there were enough jobs to go around, and these brown-skinned individuals were obedient and seldom questioned the dictates of their union bosses.

These early years of emigration brought some changes to the home villages; both socially and economically. For example Bhajan Singh and his family now acquired social esteem and political power in Jandiali. Prior to emigration, they had been considered a lowly family in spite of their being Jats. The village youth aspired and dreamed of going to England, becoming rich, and eventually returning to the village a *bara sahib* like Bhajan Singh. Although it may not have been a reality, they heard glowing stories of those who had emigrated, and when expatriates returned on a holiday, it seemed to the youngsters that the wealth and esteem these emigrants had obtained in such a short time was vast, so they too aimed for England.

At this time, a man's success abroad was evaluated by Jandialians according to the wealth he sent back or showed in the village. If a male earned in England and sent money back to his family and relatives, that kin group was proud. Dahya (1973) reports over 50 per cent of a Pakistani emigrant's earnings were transmitted to his village via official channels and additional amounts via black market. For Jandiali, less than that came back via official channels but much more than 50 per cent of a Gravesindian's earnings were invested in India. If the male, on the other hand, went to England and forgot about those in India, the family was shamed for not raising a proper son. There was more at stake for the relatives in the village than just getting money. They wanted to make sure that family honour was maintained or enhanced and this could only be obtained if the male member in England continued to show a loyalty and concern for his family in village India.

Not only did Bhajan Singh and his family gain political power but others who were associated with the emigrant faction gained esteem. Sajan Singh was one such Jandialian. His family was poor, but his father and brother emigrated to England and left Sajan behind to maintain the family farm. Along with that joint property, Sajan Singh managed the land of other villagemates who had gone to England and entrusted their small holdings to him. In all, he farmed forty acres (although only seven belonged to him), owned a tractor and tube-wells.

Sajan Singh also helped many families migrate to England. He became the spokesman for his less affluent villagemates and the lower castes, like the Ramgarhias, Jheers, Chamars and poor Jats. By helping these people he unanimously became their *Sarpanch* (head of the ruling village council) although the actual title belonged to the wealthiest man in the district.

Whenever any villager or emigré need help to look after a relative, to handle money in Punjab, care for land, or promote a village project, they approached Sajan Singh; being certain that it would be satisfactorily and expeditiously accomplished.

Sajan Singh's situation illustrates that one did not necessarily have to leave to reap the benefits of emigration. By helping those abroad with their assets in the village, he gained the necessary resources to become a man of power in Jandiali. Sajan Singh and Bhajan Singh later joined forces to present a challenge to the existing leadership in Jandiali.

Although assets were pooled and loans easily obtained for

emigration, land continued to be a surety. Men did not sell or mortgage their land to venture abroad since land was their security for the future and once it was lost, according to peasant mentality, their future was in jeopardy.

It was in these early years that the migrant community in Gravesend was relatively free of the dictates of either English or Punjabi culture. The English hosts were not threatened by their presence and employers liked their work. The village awarded their emigrants the automatic high esteem of an England-returned, and as long as money and aid flowed to Jandiali, the behaviour of their members in England was seldom questioned. True, wives worried about the loyalty of their husbands and there was the fear that he would leave her for a white girl. But, as long as he remained faithful to his charge, the evaluation of him by the villagers was always favourable, and few questioned or challenged his actual behaviour in England. If it was challenged, it was interpreted as idle gossip of individuals.

The Conflict Phase is when the situation changes so that both the host and migrant group must deal with one another—they cannot continue to live in mutual ignorance. The host society has to consider the immigrants as a possible permanent part of their community. But they react to that in various ways—hostility, exclusion, acceptance, tolerance, socialization, or some combination of the above. The immigrant community, on the other hand can no longer live a goalless, temporary existence. It is also a time when wives and children have joined the man. Therefore, freedom and lack of constrictive social norms are replaced by the cultural values and social organization of their sending community. But this has problems for the home culture and society has diametrically opposed some of the traits of the host society. Hence a set of compromises or a new system needs to be developed.

It is a time of rapid change but the immigrants continue to be involved in both their sending community and their immigrant society. They can be a part of their home village, if they choose; but there are some who will start making a life for themselves in their new surroundings, realizing that returning is not the viability it once was. Others will return to their homeland, only to realize they do not belong and shift back to the migrant society, where they do not necessarily feel at ease.

Involvement in the sending community continues as before. The results are the same, influx of capital, inflated prices, more resources, social tensions; but there is increased prosperity for many. Support from outside is imperative for some to survive or maintain their social position in the village. Those, especially the low caste or class poor, suffer while those with emigrant connections obtain a higher standard of living. A situation termed an 'External Economy' develops. In some cases, the survival of a village community is dependent on outside remittances. Jandiali did not reach that extreme, but money from abroad certainly enabled the village and the surrounding area to be more prosperous, not only through the influx of capital but also from new ideas learned by her members in England and the United States.

Having members abroad makes it possible for those in the home area to be more innovative and take risks. This gives them the chance to increase their profits while knowing that if they fail money from abroad will keep them solvent until they become successful. In the sending community, however, a new attitude develops towards the emigrants. Communications improve and villagers learn that emigration does not automatically bring success and some of the misinformation is replaced by reality and the aura of prestige held by the receiving society gradually diminishes.

In 1960, the Gravesend-Jandiali migrant group became aware of restrictions to be imposed on immigration by Parliament by 1962. This knowledge altered the population flow and also led to a period of conflict for the communities involved. The migrants had to cope with two conflicting cultural frameworks, British and Indian. Racial tensions had started developing in British society causing the imposition of immigration restrictions. Fearing that accessibility to this land of prosperity may be closed forever, Gravesindians, like other South Asians in Britain, sponsored kinsmen, villagemates, wives, children and friends to England. People who had not planned to leave India left reasoning, "Why not go to Britain. I may never have this opportunity again. If I am unhappy, I can always return to India." It was not just the opportunities in UK that motivated migration but the fear of being deprived of the option to emigrate. The economic conditions of the village had vastly improved by 1960 and Punjab in general was classed as moderately prosperous (Ballard and Ballard 1977). Thus, it was the fear of losing the option to migrate that caused the massive influx into Britain rather than the push of scarcity in the home region. The legislation produced the opposite effect that the British parliamentarians had expected—immigration increased with restrictions rather than decreased.

With the threat of controls, men brought their wives, children and friends. And although their plan was still to return to Punjab, it was the arrival of family members which began to impose village norms on a population that had previously lived in cultural freedom. It was described by one Gravesindian who stated, "We have one foot in England and one foot in India, and it hurts in the middle."

The "hurt in the middle" became a reality with the arrival of wives, children and villagemates for the Gravesindian males could no longer behave as they pleased, they came under closer scrutiny of their home village. Punjabi women abroad wrote home and portrayed a true representation of life in Britain. And since it was their responsibility to guard family honour for both their husband and their natal family, they pressured their spouses to adhere to village norms. Parents wanted to set a good example for their children. The increased communications with India had made all doubly careful and conscious of their behaviour for their goal was to be highly respected in Jandiali, where they planned to eventually resettle.

Gravesindians were caught in conflicting cultural demands. For example, Sikhs had learned that trimming their hair and beards increased their marketability in jobs while in England. But, such action often broke the heart of their parents in Punjab for religious dictates maintained that unshorn hair was crucial to spirituality and masculinity. Thus, cutting hair displeased Sikh elders in India. The Gravesindian male was torn between his desire for a good job in England and compromising Sikh beliefs and causing parental anguish.

For those who returned to India, life was difficult. They neither had knowledge nor business experience in Punjab and quickly lost their fortunes. Others were generally unhappy without English amenities. It may not have been any one thing in particular, but life in the village, especially for women, was difficult after having savoured privacy in Gravesend. Women preferred England where they were mistresses of their homes without having to yield to a mother-in-law. Teenagers returning to the village had their share of hard times. The young boys found their Punjabi language abilities in school were inadequate and jobs in Punjab were limited and, in addition, were frowned upon by elders, thus causing boredom. Girls, because of their chaperoned and restricted life in England, did not face the same problems as the boys. Youngsters were unhappy and wanted to return to their British ways of life despite discrimination and insecurity.

Although they would not admit it openly, by 1970, many Gravesindians began to realize that their stay in England was permanent. Some did not even admit it to themselves but their actions displayed this realization for they started modernizing their dwellings and installing amenities like central heating, carpets, new furniture and other trappings of prosperity. Returning to India was a myth—England was to be home. Now one of their main concerns was the fear that their children would become anglicized. As a result, their focus shifted towards methods to be used to instill their cultural heritage and pride into the second generation to keep children from absorbing the host culture and becoming "Brown British". Therefore, the migrants continued their interest in their place of origin; reacting to elections and politics in India as if it directly affected them. Immigrant vernacular newspapers described home riots, elections, and political figures in detail. For many, their major concerns shifted from their position in the village to their life in England, especially with regard to children and means to resist Christianity and English co-educational influences. There was a dichotomy. On the one hand Gravesindians did not want their children to become British, yet they were unwilling to give up the good life and wealth of England. But the longer they stayed the more they wondered whether they had made a wise decision. They could see their second generation already resisting their Asian culture and emulating some British norms.

The second generation Gravesindians changed their focus.

Boys with academic abilities preferred not to work in factories and opted for professions that were marketable on a world-wide basis. Thus, accounting, engineering and medical related areas were given priority over subjects like History, Sociology, Art and others that were not economically profitable. Even if the child was artistically inclined, he usually succumbed to parental pressure and went into the more profitable field.

These youngsters were highly motivated and studied very hard. They had seen their elders slave on assembly lines and did not want that kind of life for themselves. Their parents, being from the village, viewed careers like medicine as being important monetary, and prestigious professions. It was the income that gave the prestige.

Elders were often strict with their children and this caused many psychological conflicts. Indian boys attended school with English girls but were forbidden to even talk with a female on the street. An Indian youngster conversing with white girls was always reported to his parents. Yet they saw their English friends at school behaving freely. Gravesindian girls were required to come home directly from school without interaction with other friends like the English girls could.

These youngsters who were raised on 'English Telly' and taught by English teachers were confused as to which values to follow. At home they respected elders, lived for the family, and had their marriage arranged. In school, they were ridiculed by their teachers and friends, who told them that such practices were inhumane and archaic. Contemporary British culture dictated a high emphasis on individualism and not submitting to family control. Unlike the Punjabis, the British stressed doing what was satisfying to the individual and choosing one's own life partner. All these were in direct opposition to what the Indian children were taught in the home.

The Gravesindians countered western influence by strictness, holding language classes in the Gurdwara and conducting instruction on Punjabi and Sikh culture. The elders also downgraded English norms and tried to stop their offspring from interacting with the whites. This resulted in the second generation Punjabis becoming more confused as to what life rules, morals and goals they should follow.

The influence from India continued to be strong. Gravesindians preferred spouses of their children from India. They desired arranging marriages with those of rural background because of the high regard villagers were supposed to have for the elderly in-laws. There was some truth in the fact that a boy from the village was loyal and beholden to his wife's family for sponsoring him. Also since these boys seldom had kin support in England, they were at the mercy of the family that sponsored them; which shifted the balance of power in favour of the female and her family.

Although parental logic was valid, the marriage of a village-raised man to an English-bred Punjabi was seldom if ever compatible. These village raised husbands expected their wives to cook at any time convenient to them, thus necessitating round the clock service by their wives, to wait on. They expected them to walk behind their men, keep their head covered and behave modestly like the village women. The Gravesindian girls raised in England resisted these practices although they knew their mothers had obeyed them. Here again, there was confusion because English schools had made these girls aware of certain rights, especially if they brought in a pay cheque. This further clashed with expected behaviour and led to friction between husbands and wives, in-laws and daughters.

Second generation children were taught a glorified version of Indian village life by their elders causing them to long for India. However, a visit to rural Punjab was usually enough to convince them that the village was not a viable alternative, and since they were ignorant about the opportunities and luxuries of urban India, they considered all South Asia to be like their parents' village, which was undesirable in comparison to life in Gravesend.

In response to the increased racial animosity in Britain, many second generation Indians felt that they deserved the benefits they received in Britain. Unlike their parents who felt they were guests in England and should be grateful, the youngsters argued that the British had exploited their country for several hundred years and thus had no reason to resent the Indian immigrants. Many were also following Marxist or militant philosophies concerning racism after peaceful means had failed and the situation had deteriorated. In response to parties like the National Front and other forms of racism, they adopted a "fight fire with fire" doctrine.

The explosive influx of Indians after 1960 created fears among the host community. The British feared being taken over by a people they had once ruled, had not understood, a people who remained aloof, and did not want to emulate British ways. White Gravesend inhabitants did not like immigrants taking over. The racial clashes and friction in east London were exaggerated by politicians and reported daily in the British press. Discrimination became a major issue and although a Gravesindian may not have actually experienced unfavourable treatment, he read about it in the papers or heard reports on television, realizing that he was not wanted or accepted.

The common Englishman felt a hopelessness because in spite of the legal strictures, immigration of Indians did not abate. The arranged marriage system allowed those in England to bring brides or grooms, and after they were in England, these brides sponsored their siblings and parents, who in turn brought their spouses, and the cycle became endless.[2] When immigration officials tried to limit the influx, they were chastised for their unfair practices.

Their fear was accentuated by the 1972 influx of Asians who were expelled from Uganda. Although many of these African Asians were well qualified doctors and educated individuals who made a valuable contribution to British society, they were not accepted.

The Gravesindians were blamed for taking jobs which "rightfully" belonged to the English. In certain cases the Punjabis had seniority over English whites. However, it was the immigrants' willingness to work overtime, on weekends and night shifts that kept unemployment low among their ranks. The National Front[3] marched through Gravesend and caused a great deal of fear among the Indians, communicating that Asians were not wanted. There was further resentment against the immigrant group because Indian children worked insatiably hard and often scored better marks than many English children for academic positions of honour.

The average Englishman failed to understand these Asian immigrants who did not emulate British ways. Statistics showed that there was a decline in the West Indian population in England during the 70s due to emigration while the South Asians rapidly increased in spite of restrictive legislation. Thus, the English feared that the Punjabis would take over their country especially since the West Indians were returning to their homeland.

The casual visitor to Jandiali around 1970 saw new multi-storey farm houses outside the village. A few England returned people on holiday were visible around the village. But more specifically, sending members to England had affected social relations, village economy, and attitudes towards the British.

Social changes occurred because large numbers had emigrated. Being an England returnee began to lose its former charm and prestige. It was no longer enough just to be an English migrant or have a son or relative in Britain. Now the emigrant had to have a decent job and display proper behaviour in England. If a man was a janitor, villagers in Jandiali lost respect for that individual, although, on the face, they were cordial towards the visiting family. The emigrant was, however, unaware of comments like, "he is a mere slave or a lowly sweeper in England; he is nothing", made behind his back. Generally, the emigrants did not realize the true feelings the villagers had towards them. In spite of the demeaned status of the English emigrant, almost anyone who was not wealthy openly sought opportunities to migrate. Gravesindians had no difficulty marrying their boys to educated Indian girls and demanding excessively high dowries. The uneducated girls from Gravesend were much sought after in Punjab for this provided access to England.

The political situation of the village also underwent change. Sajan Singh, with the support of Bhajan Singh, had the capital, and with the support of poor Jat families, Ramgarhias and other castes, was able to challenge but not overpower the existing ruling family. However, this power faction gained considerable influence in village affairs and because of available foreign money, they often acted in ways they felt conducive, even going against the headman and his family.

Inflation in Jandiali as hard as other parts of Punjab, thus making it almost a necessity for a family to have relatives in England in order to maintain a decent standard of living.

Jandiali began to develop an external economy: meaning that the influx of outside capital enabled it to maintain its prosperity. In the case of Jandiali, there were over Rs. 1 million of visible assets acquired by money earned in England. These were in the form of houses, tractors, tube-wells, land and public amenities. Six of the eight tractors were paid for with emigrant money; most of the tube-wells were financed by emigrants, as were practically all the houses built after 1960. In addition, Jandiali's cooperative bank alone boasted a sizeable surplus which exceeded Rs. 3 million assets. This was in Jandiali and did not include capital invested by Jandialians in businesses in England and areas outside Jandiali.

The inflation results can be gauged by the rising land prices. An acre of land in Jandiali cost around Rs. 4,000 in 1954, but in 1968 it rose to Rs. 12,000; in 1971 it costed Rs. 25,000 per acre and by 1978 the cost was around Rs. 30,000. Not only had the price risen drastically, but in 1970, it was difficult to buy land at any price. Landholders, whether in Jandiali or England, were not willing to sell the land which was their security.

Emigration not only brought capital to Jandiali, but it also brought innovative ideas and modern agricultural technology. Relatives and friends abroad continually sent different varieties of seeds and information concerning innovative farm techniques. Jats tried these new methods and if successful, they implemented them.

Those individuals who had money and security from abroad could afford the risk of trying new techniques, thus becoming the opinion leaders of their village and surrounding areas. Although Jandiali farmers keenly listened to farm programmes on the radio and closely watched experiments conducted at Punjab Agricultural University, Ludhiana, they were often ahead of those sources because of information and shipments of new varieties of seeds from relatives in England, California, or British Columbia.

Without emigration, Jandiali and Punjab might have been the scene of starvation and poverty instead of being one of the most prosperous areas of India.

During this period, the Indian Government allowed Punjabis abroad to send gifts to their relatives in the homeland. The

Massey Ferguson Tractor Company, between October 24, 1968 and August 31, 1970, delivered 1,038 tractors, to Punjab, paid for in sterling by Indians in England.

It was with the mass emigration to Britain that villagers began watching the racial situation in Britain closely. The esteem they had held for the Crown dropped considerably. Newspapers reported discriminatory acts against their countrymen and the Jandialians, along with other Punjabis, changed their view towards the country that had once ruled them.

1978 saw visible increase in the external economy situation of Jandiali. They had a new Gurdwara at the cost of Rs. 1.3 lakhs and had invested Rs. 8 lakhs—primarily from pounds donated by migrant villagers in England—in a bus business and a loan company. The latter two enterprises were headed by Sajan Singh. Jandialians claimed that money continued to come back, but was not to the same extent as it was in the sixties. The newspaper, *Indian Abroad,* reports that in 1978 approximately 22,187 billion rupees (2,773 million dollars) came into India—a 16% increase over the previous year. In 1979, overseas Indians averaged sending approximately Rs. 1500 million (200 million dollars) per month, in the first quarter except during March when the figure rose to a fantastic Rs. 3,030 million (404 million dollars). This enabled India to maintain a Rs. 6,852.5 million (915 million dollars) surplus in her international balance of payments.

A 1978 sample survey in Gujarat indicated that the average household in the Bombay area with one or more members abroad received Rs. 12,615 ($ 1,682) per year from their expatriates and 80% received lemuneration ranging from Rs. 4,687.7 ($ 625) to Rs. 19,750 ($ 2, 500) annually. If Gujarat is representative of what happens in Punjab, and it most likely is, money certainly filters back to the local community and provides substance for local investments.

Most Jandiali emigrants continually held onto their land, which was cared for by a friend or relative who oversaw the fields. It was very important for the Gravesindian to keep his land in Punjab in spite of the shortage of labour caused by emigration. Interestingly most of the work was either done by mechanization or migrant workers from U.P. who came to Punjab because of the higher wages.

Jandiali emigrants continued to play an active role in village affairs, even though they resided in England. A group of emigrants donated money to build a new village place of worship to fulfil Bhuta Singh's dream of having a Gurdwara in Jandiali with a tower so high that one could see Phagwara from its top. The zaildar's group resisted the new construction but the emigrant faction, which was strongly supported by non-Jats and poorer Jat families, pushed for and constructed the new building. The poorer Jat element had initially emigrated to England from Jandiali to make money but an additional consequence was that they had power to influence village affairs. By 1970 most members of the emigrant group were abroad and their in-village representative leader was about to leave to join his son in Canada. This left the faction without guidance. The few inhabitants, however, complained of Jandiali being a lonely place with everyone going abroad.

In the case of immigrant villages like Jandiali, Jats had gone abroad mostly to England and some to Canada; but in the late seventies, large segments of Chamars and other specialized castes such as Tarkhans and Lohars in particular have ventured to the Middle East—sending money back to increase their family's wealth in the village. They too had been encouraged and exploited by agents just like the early Jats who went to England.

In the village, either rich Jat landowners or those with external support from their emigrant kin could afford to pay high wages to the itinerant workers and afford farm machinery. For those who neither had strong outside contacts from emigrants nor a rich background village life became miserable. The inflation rate in the village increased more rapidly than they had means to increase their income. In fact, with the mass emigration from Jandiali, it almost seemed like emigrating or having close contacts with emigrants was the only way for survival, especially for the middle income and poor.

It must be kept in mind that the Indian Government and political leaders were concerned with the emigrant plight because these sojourners in England were a good source of capital for the political parties in India. Newspapers followed their situation in England and censured the British for their racism.

Settlement is when the immigrant and host group realize that they are a permanent part of their new abode and returning is not a viable option. Their homeland may have an emotional appeal as being a place of their forefathers, but they will not return there to live. They no longer have a foot in both societies. However, the immigrant may not be an accepted element of his new community and the development of a suitable cultural and social system may take time.

The Gravesindian community has not reached the settlement phase yet. In some cases, like Gujarati community in East Africa, several generations may elapse before this phase is instituted, and may not come into effect for other areas. Much depends on the reaction of the host society, the communication ties with the home society, and the culture of the groups involved. With the advent of rapid communications system, settlement may take longer than in the past. The Indian community in Britain has not entered this aspect of the adaptation process yet although the vocal element of the second generation is reacting as if the UK is their permanent abode. How they will adapt in the future needs to be studied to complete the model as set forth here.

CONCLUSIONS

The above description of the Gravesend-Jandiali migrants shows that there has been a three-way interaction relationship between the emigrant, receiving and sending communities. And, the nature and strength of the transactional relationship between these three communities has changed as the migration process developed over time. During the *Premigration Period*, the communication link between the receiving and potentially sending community transmits inaccurate and stereotypical information.

The *Freedom Phase* is the period where males leave, with wives and children remaining behind. Money is remitted to help dependents in the sending community, but the migrant community is composed primarily of males who lack the controls and direction of a normal society. Thus abnormality and anomie are present. It is a time when the receiving and immigrant societies ignore each other. However the emigrants, while abroad, can have an effect on the economy and social ranking of those in their home area. The *Conflict Phase* is a time of social tension and rapid change Often, wives, children and other family members come and assert adherence to norms of the home society. In the meantime, they have to also live within the dictates of the receiving culture, which imposes on the migrants conflicting sets of rules to follow. The trauma becomes more acute as the second generation comes into prominence. During this time, the home village continues to be influenced by her emigrants, and it is likely that emigration continues to be popularized to make it a goal for many to achieve. The receiving society, however, can no longer ignore the new people settling in their midst and have to deal with the new population which is a matter of concern.

Settlement is when the immigrant community becomes a permanent fixture of their new abode. This does not mean that they lose interest in their homeland, but direct involvement with their natal community may be absent or decrease considerably. There may be an emotional appeal from time to time from the place of their cultural origins. More work needs to be done on this last area since the Punjabis in England have not fully reached this phase.

The question is now asked as to the degree of applicability this model has to other migrant societies. Much of the work has isufficient information. In comparing this work with that of Hendrick's (1974) study of Dominican Republicans in New York, the conclusions of Graves' survey on migration literature (1974), and the work of Dinnerstein and Reimers (1977), certain generalities seem to be forming. First, like in the premigration phase of this study, glorification of the receiving or potentially receiving society commonly occurs. Emigrants, even in a bad situation do not want to admit fully that they made a mistake or reveal anything that might reflect negatively on their choice, thus the exemplary myth of the receiving society in both the premigration and freedom phases is a common occurrence.

The Freedom Period, however, would seem to be only where the wives and children are not present. Thus, temporary internal migrants, like in rural-urban movements where the family remains in the rural sector, might be where the freedom phase dominates. However, once the wives and children follow, concern with the perception of the second generation necessitates the advent of the Conflict Phase, where opposing demands are made on the migrants. Of course, the degree of that conflict varies according to the culture but even migrants from England settling in the US have cultural conflict problems. For emigrants, there is always a strong identification with their land of origin. The new abode is for expediency and wealth, but allegiance does not readily change. Few however, admit the Settlement Phase. Even the Latvians, Polish, Dutch, Hungarian and other groups in the United States privately admit they will not return to their homeland under any conditions, but behave, demonstrate and organize to pressure the United States Legislature to take a favourable stance towards their motherland. They also set up institutions to instill their language, religion and culture into their second and third generation and want their offspring to marry within their own community. Planning to return is a myth that is carried on to the second generation, even though they are aware of its unlikelihood.

Although further study is an absolute necessity, this work illustrates that there is a strong on-going interaction between the sending, receiving and migrant communities, and each of the three communities must be considered at every stage of development.

When one examines the literature concerning the effects of emigration on a society (Papademetriou 1980 and Swanson 1979), they generally conclude that the net effects are detrimental. They argue that money is wasted on conspicuous consumption, repatriated people are unproductive and emigrant ideas and innovations are generally irrelevant. But, as this study indicates, emigrant capital and ideas have certainly helped make Jandiali in particular, and Punjab and India in general, more prosperous. It was not just the capital, but the new technology and the financial security to try out the new innovations that were beneficial for the economic development of Punjab. In fact, allowing emigration may be of much more help to certain Asian countries by the Western sovereignties than bilateral aid.

Further work needs to be done on understanding the

effects of emigration and the interactional relationship between host, home and migrant societies. But it is this holistic approach that is currently needed to fully understand migrant behaviour.

NOTES

1. The Ghadr Party was a revolutionary movement that functioned from around 1902 to 1915 although the communists appealed to its leadership as late as 1925. It was primarily a Sikh movement.
2. This law has changed in nature several times over the past thirty years.
3. The National Front is a political movement following the principles and symbols of the Nazis of Germany. It came into prominence in the mid-seventies and it first marched through Gravesend in 1978.

REFERENCES

Ballard, Roger and Catherine Ballard, "The Sikhs: The Development of South Asian Settlements in Britain", In *Between Two Cultures: Migrants and Minorities in Britain*, James L. Watson (ed). Basil Blackwell, Oxford, 1977.

Barth, Fredrik, *Ethnic Groups and Boundaries: The Social Organization of Cultural Difference*, George Allen & Unwin, London, 1969.

Bryce-Laporte, Roy Simon, (ed.), *Sourcebook on the New Immigration: Implication for the United States and the International Community*. Transaction Books, New Brunswick, New Jersey, 1980.

Connell John, Biplab Dasgupta, Roy Laishley and Michael Lipton, *Migration from Rural Areas: The Evidence from Village Studies*, Oxford University Press, Delhi, 1976.

Dahya, B., "Pakistanis in Britain, Transient or Settlers?" In *Race* 14(3), 1973.

Dinnerstein, Leonard and David M. Reimers, *Ethnic Americans: A History of Immigration and Assimilation*, New York University Press, New York, 1977.

Glazer, Nathan and Daniel P. Moynihan, *Ethnicity: Theory and Experience*, Cambridge, Mass., Harvard University Press, 1975.

Gmelch, George. "Return Migration". In *Annual Review of Anthropology*, Vol. 9, Palo Alto, California, Annual Reviews Inc., 1980.

Graves, Nancy B. and Theodore Graves, "Adoptive Strategies in Urban Migration". In *Annual Review of Anthropology*, Vol. 3. Palo Alto, CA, Annual Reviews, Inc, 1974.

Helweg, Arthur "Punjabi Farmers: Twenty Years in England", In *India International Centre Quarterly* V. 1, 1978.

——*Sikhs in England: The Development of a Migrant Community*, Oxford University Press, New Delhi, 1979.

Hendricks, Glenn *The Dominican Diaspora*, Teachers College Press, New York, 1974.

Hero, Dilip, "Indians in Britain", In *India International Centre Quarterly* VI (3), 1979.

Jackson, J.A. (ed.), *Migration*, Cambridge University Press, Cambridge, 1969.

Jansen, Clifford (ed.), *Readings in the Sociology of Migration*. Pergamon Press, London, 1970.

Jeffery, Patricia, *Migrants and Refugees: Muslim and Christian Families in Bristol*, Cambridge, Cambridge University Press, 1976.

Kasdan, Leonard, Introduction, In *Migration and Anthropology*. Robert F. Spencer, (ed.) American Ethnological Society, University of Washington Press, Seattle, 1970.

Kritz, Mary M., Charles B., Keely and Silvano M. (eds.), *Global Trends in Migration*, Center for Migration Studies, New York, 1981.

McNeil, Willian H., Ruth S. Adams, *Human Migration: Patterns and Policies*. Indiana University Press, Bloomington, 1978.

Mehta, Ved, *Daddyji*, Farrar, Straus and Giroux, New York: 1972.

Papademetrious, Demetros G., Effects of Emigration on the Sending Countries: Some Thoughts and Parallels Between the American and Recent European Experiences with "Labor Emigration." In *Sourcebook on the New Immigration*, Roy Simon Bryce-Laporte (ed.), Transaction Books, New Brunswick, New Jersey, 1980.

Porter, John, "Ethnic Pluralism in Canadian Perspective", In *Ethnicity: Theory and Experience*, Glazer, Nathan and Daniel P. Moynihan (ed.), Harvard University Press, Cambridge, Mass., 1975.

Shaw, R. Paul, *Migration Theory and Fact*, Regional Science Research Institute, Philadelphia, 1979.

Swanson, Jon, "The Consequences of Emigration for Economic Development: A Review of the Literature", in *Papers in Antropology* XX: 1, 1979.

Tinker, Hugh, *A New System of Slavery: The Export of Indian Labour Overseas 1830-1920*, Oxford University Press, Bombay, 1974.

———*The Banyan Tree: Overseas Emigrants from India, Pakistan and Bangladesh*, Oxford University Press, New York, Delhi, Karachi, 1977.

Index